The Medieval City

The Medieval City

EDITED BY

Harry A. Miskimin

David Herlihy

A. L. Udovitch

New Haven and London Yale University Press 1977

Published with assistance from the foundation established in memory of Philip Hamilton McMillan of the Class of 1894, Yale College.

Designed by John O. C. McCrillis
and set in Monophoto Baskerville type by
Asco Trade Typesetting Limited, Hong Kong
Printed in the United States of America by
The Murray Printing Co., Westford, Massachusetts.

Published in Great Britain, Europe, Africa, and Asia (except Japan) by Yale University Press, Ltd., London. Distributed in Latin America by Kaiman & Polon, Inc., New York City; in Australia and New Zealand by Book & Film Services, Artarmon, N.S.W., Australia; and in Japan by Harper & Row, Publishers, Tokyo Office.

Library of Congress Cataloging in Publication Data

Main entry under title:

The Medieval city.

Essays written in honor of Robert S. Lopez.
"Publications of Robert S. Lopez": p.
Includes index.
CONTENTS: The Italian city: Herlihy, D. Family and property in Renaissance Florence. Krekić, B. Four Florentine commercial companies in Dubrovnik (Ragusa) in the first half of the fourteenth century. Lane, F. C. The first infidelities of the Venetian lire. Cipolla, C. M. A plague doctor. Kedar, B. Z. The Genoese notaries of 1382. Hughes, D. O. Kinsmen and neighbors in Medieval Genoa. Peters, E. Pars, parte: Dante and an urban contribution to political thought—The Eastern city: Udovitch, A. L. A tale of two cities. Goitein, S. D. A mansion in Fustat. Prawer, J. Crusader cities. Teall, J. Byzantine urbanism in the military handbooks.—The Northern city: Miskimin, H. A. The legacies of London Munro, J. Industrial protectionism in Medieval Flanders. Strayer, J. R. The costs and profits of war. Hoffmann, R. C. Wrocław citizens as rural landholders. Cohen, S. The earliest Scandinavian towns.
1. Cities and towns, Medieval—Addresses, essays, lectures. 2. Lopez, Robert Sabatino, 1910–
I. Miskimin, Harry A. II. Herlihy, David.
III. Udovitch, Abraham L. IV. Lopez, Robert Sabatino, 1910–
HT115.M38 301.36'3'094 77-76302
ISBN 0-300-02081-3

In honor of
Robert S. Lopez

Contents

Foreword

The essays contained in this volume have been written in honor of Robert S. Lopez. But for what occasion? That must remain ambiguous, since it might be taken either as belated recognition of his sixty-fifth birthday or as premature acknowledgment of his retirement as Sterling Professor of History at Yale University. The nature of the literary enterprise accounts for the delay with regard to the first proffered occasion, while the nature of the man provides a more active and forceful excuse in the second instance. Such a vital and inquiring mind will never retire, so any endeavor to commemorate such an event must inevitably and happily fail in its purpose.

In planning the present volume, the editors met in New Haven some years ago and sought to structure a group of essays around Lopez's own interests. Three principal themes—commerce, urban history, particularly that of his native Genoa, and monetary history—emerged as major subdivisions of his writings. Yet even these broad categories could not circumscribe the work of a man who ranges easily from the art of Renaissance Italy to the career of Franklin D. Roosevelt and from the origins of the Merino sheep to questions of the authenticity of the Vinland Map and to the history of China. Faced with the impossibility of reflecting such diversity and scope within the confines of a single volume, the editors resolved to focus on but one facet of the Lopezian canon and arbitrarily to restrict the essays to the subject of urban history during the Middle Ages and in the Mediterranean Basin and Europe. By the same token, the editors resolved to limit the number of essays so as to permit each to offer substantial treatment of its subject and to draw the authors in roughly equal proportions from Robert's former students and from among those senior colleagues who had shared in the rapid expansion and rising popularity of economic history marked by the four decades of his career.

As a result of these constraints, only a small portion of the potential number of contributors have had the opportunity to participate in an enterprise that many would gladly have joined. The editors, therefore, speaking on behalf of the many scholars whose work is not included herein, express their collective desire to recognize and pay tribute to a remarkable man and a vital and ongoing career. We regret that there could not have been sufficient volumes to contain the offerings of all those who wish to honor Robert with us.

Finally, the editors, writing both as former students and as present colleagues, wish to express both professional and personal gratitude for the warmth and encouragement that Robert has so generously extended to so many and to pay homage to a man who has uncompromisingly defended the highest standards, directly, sometimes sharply, but never without humanity, humor, and justice, and always in the cause of truth.

THE EDITORS

The Italian City

1

Family and Property in Renaissance Florence

David Herlihy

During the epoch of the Renaissance in Italy, how was wealth distributed —between city and countryside; among great towns and small; and up and down the social hierarchy? What factors influenced the control and allocation of resources? And how did wealthy families seek to manage their patrimonies, and to preserve them, undiminished, from one generation to the next? In examining the material aspects of Renaissance social life, we continue a line of inquiry that is as old as the Renaissance itself. For contemporary social commentators were well aware that every form of social activity consumed resources. "Those whose talents are obstructed by poverty at home," Giovanni Boccaccio once complained, "do not easily make their mark."[1] Inevitably, methods of managing and channeling wealth influenced the shape of Renaissance society, the character of its government, and the level of its cultural achievement.

This is, in essence, the argument of the most original contemporary tract devoted to wealth and its role in society—Poggio Bracciolini's dialogue "On Avarice."[2] Poggio attributes the comments on wealth to the papal secretary Antonio Loschi, but we can hardly doubt that the sentiments expressed are Poggio's own. According to Antonio—or Poggio—without the spur of avarice, which is to say, without a sense of self-interest, men would remain tillers of the soil, content with the meanest subsistence; society would lack cities and all the amenities of urban life. "For no one," Antonio declares, "would [then] plant more than he needed to feed himself and his family."[3] Moreover, civilization depended not only upon the

1. "Haud facile emergunt, quorum virtutibus obstat / Res angusta domi," attributed to Boccaccio in the biography by Giannozzo Manetti. See *Philippi Villani Liber de civitatis Florentiae famosis civibus . . . et de Florentinorum litteratura principes fere synchroni scriptores*, ed. G. C. Galletti (Florence, 1847), p. 92. The biography was written in 1459.

2. "De avaritia," in Poggius Bracciolini, *Opera omnia*, with a preface by Riccardo Fubini (Basil, 1538; reprinted, Turin, 1964), I, 1–31.

3. Ibid., p. 13. "Nullus enim aret, nisi quantum sibi et familiae suae fuerit satis futurum."

acquisitive urge, motivating all, but upon great accumulations of wealth —upon the manifest triumphs of the avaricious spirit. Destroy the great fortunes, Antonio warns, and "you will destroy all the magnificence of cities, all ceremony and embellishment; no churches or buildings will be constructed; all the arts will cease."[4] Just as the well-ordered commonwealth maintained public deposits of grain, which fed the populace in years of famine, so also the great fortunes provided the state with barns of money, which supported it in times of monetary hunger.[5] Without the service of the rich, our governments, our very lives, would be a shambles.[6]

Like Poggio, historians too must recognize the importance of these "barns of wealth"; they should note their location in society, and peer into their contents. Here, we shall look at accumulated wealth within the city, countryside, and district of Florence in the year 1427. Florence then ruled nearly all of the province of Tuscany; among the major Tuscan cities, only Lucca and Siena retained their independence. In 1427 Florence undertook a vast survey of all its subject population—then numbering approximately 260,000—and of all their possessions.[7] This great survey, finished in 1430, is called the Catasto, and it allows us to discern, with unique precision, how both property and population were distributed across the Florentine state.

How did the redactors of this great survey define wealth, and what fiscal strategy did they adopt in taxing it? By 1427, the government was desperate for funds; since 1422, it had been locked in a costly struggle with Milan. While famished for money, the government still feared that indiscriminate taxation would harm the Republic as much as Milanese victories. While new taxes had to be imposed, they ought not to injure the economy nor to interfere with the productive activities upon which Florentine prosperity —and, ultimately, Florentine victories—depended. The goose ought not to be killed, as the government gathered its golden eggs. The "law of the Catasto," adopted in 1427, establishing the new system of assessment, therefore distinguished between two types of property: possessions considered essential for the maintenance of the individual household and the

4. Ibid. "Auferetur magnificentia omnis civitatum, tolletur cultus atque ornatus, nulla aedificabuntur templa, nulli porticus, artes omnes cessabunt . . ."

5. Ibid., p. 15. "Quam ob causam sicut in bene moratis populis ac civitatibus constituuntur horrea publica, ad subministrandum frumentum in caritate annonae, ita per commodum foret plures in eo collocari avaros, qui essent veluti privatum horreum pecuniarum, quod suppeditaret nobis."

6. Ibid., p. 13. ". . . perturbatio vitae nostrae et rerum publicarum sequetur . . ."

7. The fiscal character of the Catasto will be examined at length in a forthcoming work by David Herlihy and Christiane Klapisch, *Les Toscans et leurs familles*.

productive labors of its members; and surplus, disposable possessions, "d'avanzo alla vita," as one source calls them—"not essential for survival."[8] The life of the family required a dwelling, owned or rented; furnishings within it; the tools used in artisan crafts; and, in the countryside, one team of oxen to work the family farm, and one ass or donkey to allow the family to maintain contact with the outside world.[9] These possessions, while sometimes mentioned in the Catasto survey, were usually not assessed and never taxed; the Tuscan family was thus assured immunity in its life and work from crippling exactions.

In sum, each family could live in a tax-exempt, furnished house that was appropriate for its station in life. This policy seems to have had one notable effect in Florentine cultural history. The rich, ever searching for protection against ravenous assessors, could find a shelter in their own homes, in the furnishings and art with which they embellished them. Here as always, it is difficult to test the effects of general policy upon behavior, and the "law of the Catasto" was not consistently applied throughout the fifteenth century. Still, the regulations of 1427 encouraged the rich to live richly, to invest in palaces and furnishings, to manifest their social estate in domestic splendor. Perhaps inadvertently, the Florentine government was subsidizing the art which decorated domestic life. The community lost in current revenue, but it also enriched its artistic heritage.

Because the government exempted property needed "for life," the Catasto does not reveal the distribution of all forms of properties, but only of those considered surplus, disposable, taxable. Our picture of who owned what in Tuscany is therefore incomplete. Still, the distribution of surplus and disposable wealth—possessions not committed to the maintenance of the taxpayer in his station in life—has its own interest. This was the wealth which supported everything beyond subsistence living: private and public enterprises; activities of church, state, and all social groups; charity, learning, and entertainment; prayer and war. This was the wealth which, in large part, upheld Florence's role in contemporary Italian politics and made possible its cultural achievement.

All assessed possessions owned by Tuscans in 1427 were valued at

8. See Giovanni Cavalcanti, *Istorie fiorentine*, ed. F. Polidori (2 vols.; Florence, 1838–39), I, 197. "Fecesi il Catasto; del quale la natura e il modo fu questo: che chi avesse cento fiorini di valsente, d'avanzo alla vita, pagasse mezzo fiorino . . . "

9. The regulations of 1427 have been published by O. Karmin, *La legge del catasto fiorentino del 1427* (Florence, 1906). See also Elio Conti, *I catasti agrari della Repubblica fiorentina e il catasto particellare toscano secoli XIV–XIX* (Rome: Istituto Storico Italiano per il Medio Evo, 1966).

Table 1.1

The Distribution of Wealth in Tuscany, 1427

	Florence	*Six Cities*	*Fifteen Towns*	*Countryside*	*Total*
Hhlds	9946	6724	5994	37226	59890
Persons	37245	26315	24809	175840	264210
Percentage	14.10	9.96	9.39	66.55	100.00
		A. Real Property			
Value	4128024	1137466	614446	2178253	8058189
Percentage	51.23	14.12	7.63	27.03	100.00
		B. Movables			
Value	3467707	585357	170245	223792	4447101
Percentage	77.98	13.16	3.83	5.03	100.00
		C. Public Debt			
Value	2573378	3438	1888	1337	2580041
Percentage	99.74	0.13	0.07	0.05	100.00
		D. Total Wealth			
Value	10169109	1726261	786579	2403382	15085331
Percentage	67.41	11.44	5.21	15.93	100.00
		E. Deductions			
Value	2504041	332763	135341	321205	3293350
Percentage	76.03	10.10	4.11	9.75	100.00
		F. Taxable Wealth			
Value	7665068	1393498	651238	2082177	11791981
Percentage	65.00	11.82	5.52	17.66	100.00

NOTE: Totals can vary slightly depending on the types of households included in the count and the inclusion or exclusion of later additions to the survey.

approximately 15 million florins, before allowable deductions (see table 1.1).[10] A little more than one-half this sum—about 8 million florins—consisted of holdings in real property. The worth of movable wealth and business investments was 4.5 million florins, and shares in the Florentine public debt, known as the Monte, amounted to a substantial 2.5 million. With nearly one-half its social capital in movables, in liquid investments,

10. Because animals were frequently assessed together with the farms on which they were found, their value is not represented within the category of movables, but in that of real property.

or in the public debt, this community was critically dependent upon the success of its business ventures; and wars too, in affecting the commune's solvency, could have a powerful impact on private fortunes.

The distribution of this disposable wealth across geographical areas greatly favored the city of Florence. The Tuscan metropolis, which included only 14 percent of the region's population, claimed some 67 percent of its disposable wealth. Within Florence, the average household possessed more than 1,000 florins in taxable assets; in rural areas (that is, excluding inhabitants of cities and towns), the comparable average was only 61 florins.[11] Average wealth per person in the Florentine metropolis was 273 florins; it was only 13 florins among the Tuscan peasants. On the scale of wealth, the burgesses of Florence outweighed the peasants by a factor of 20 to 1. Even in the small cities of Tuscany, such as Pisa and Pistoia, households and individuals appear impoverished in comparison to the substantial Florentines.[12]

The Florentine domination of Tuscan resources was particularly overwhelming in the areas of business investments and shares in the public debt. Florentines owned a comparatively modest 51 percent of the taxable real estate in Tuscany. In contrast, they controlled 78 percent of movable property and business investments, and they owned virtually the entire public debt.

By these comparisons, Florence was a blazing sun of affluence surrounded by the dim planets of the small Tuscan cities—all of them set in the dark space of the nearly destitute rural areas. Still, it would be wrong to imply that this affluent metropolis contained only, or even chiefly, affluent people. On the contrary, some 15 percent of the households of Florence possessed nothing at all. The richest 1 percent of the Florentine households, numbering only one hundred, owned more than a quarter of the city's enormous wealth—a larger share of wealth than that which fell to the poorest 87 percent of urban households (see table 1.2).[13] This same small circle of the hugely rich, one hundred households, owned more than the 37,000 rural households. The richest 3,000 households within Florence were more wealthy than the remaining 57,000 Tuscan households, both inside and outside the city of Florence.

11. The six cities referred to in table 1.1 are Pisa, Pistoia, Arezzo, Prato, Volterra, and Cortona; their average population was 4,383 in 1427. The table also treats as a special category fifteen small towns with an average population of 1,654 persons. Tuscans living outside these communities are considered residents of rural areas.

12. The average wealth per household in the six cities was 257 florins.

13. The total worth of the hundred richest Florentine households (including additions of 1428 and 1429) was 2,883,447 florins.

Table 1.2

The Distribution of Wealth in the City of Florence, 1427

Poorest __ percent of households owns __ percent of wealth

Percent of Population	*Real Property*	*Movables*	*Public Debt*	*Total Wealth*
100	100.00	100.00	100.00	100.00
99	85.98	70.64	56.97	73.18
98	79.40	58.98	42.91	62.92
97	74.19	50.95	35.34	56.13
96	68.86	45.91	30.22	50.95
95	64.40	42.30	25.42	46.70
90	47.31	28.61	13.85	32.21
80	26.95	15.61	5.71	17.55
70	15.20	9.37	2.18	9.82
60	8.09	5.50	0.91	5.34
50	3.97	3.00	0.30	2.68
40	1.56	1.52	0.07	1.16
30	0.39	0.61	0.01	0.37
20	0.03	0.09	0.00	0.04
10	0.00	0.00	0.00	0.00
Gini Index of Concentration	70.48	80.06	89.67	78.75

NOTE: The range of the Index is 1 to 100. A score of 1 would indicate that each centile of the population owned 1 percent of the wealth; 100, that only 1 centile owned all the wealth. Households are ranked on the basis of their total wealth. Households added in 1428 and 1429 are included in the calculations.

Of all forms of wealth, shares in the public debt were most concentrated in the hands of the rich. At Florence, 78 percent of the households held no shares at all, and a mere 2 percent—approximately 200 households—held nearly 60 percent of the outstanding debt. Business investments were less concentrated, but only in comparative terms. Among the Florentine households, 36 percent had no assets in movable property, and the richest 300 households possessed about one-half the movable wealth.

Who then controlled the socially disposable wealth of Tuscany in 1427? The pattern is one of concentric circles, with wealth increasing exponentially as one approaches the center. The largest circle could be seen as the city of Florence which, in spite of its many destitute households, still owned more than two-thirds of all Tuscan assets. Within the city the richest 3,000 households owned the entire public debt, and in their total assets they surpassed all the other 57,000 Tuscan families. Still, even within this group, the distribution of wealth was highly skewed in favor of very few families. The richest one hundred Florentine households alone controlled nearly 20 percent of all the social capital of Tuscany.

How was it possible to maintain such enormous concentrations of affluence, in the face of need and greed on the part of both the government and the large masses of the people? Here, fiscal policy played a crucial role. Except for rare intervals, the Florentine government since the early fourteenth century had refrained from imposing direct taxes within the city; moneys collected from urban residents were considered interest-bearing, public obligations, eventually to be repaid. Why were the urban wealthy so favored? Leonardo Bruni, chancellor of Florence when the Catasto was redacted, has left us a succinct but illuminating analysis of Florentine fiscal policies since the thirteenth century. Specifically, he compares Florence under the commune of the Popolo or "people," first established in 1252, with the fifteenth-century regime that he was serving.

> In olden times [he notes] the Popolo was accustomed to go in arms to war, and since the city was densely settled, it conquered almost all its neighbors. Therefore, in those days, the city's power depended principally upon the masses, and for this reason the Popolo held supremacy, so as virtually to exclude the nobles from government. As time passed, however, wars came to be conducted rather by the mercenary soldier. Then the city's power was seen to depend not upon the masses, but upon the magnates and the wealthy, who supplied the government with money and utilized counsel rather than arms. The power of the Popolo gradually waned, and the regime took on the form it now possesses.[14]

In other words, money had become the sinew of war, and the rich owned the muscle of the republic. Fiscal policy not only protected the great fortunes, but it also contributed to their growth. The vitriolic chronicler Giovanni Cavalcanti, who lived during the period of the Catasto, alleges that the government was wont to pay interest only to the largest share-

14. Leonardi Arretini De Florentinorum republica, translated from the Greek by Benedetto Moneta, in *Principes scriptores*, ed. Galletti, p. 96. "Antiquitus siquidem populus cum armis in bellum exire, et res bellicas per se ipsum gerere solebat, et quod urbs maxime populosa esset, finitimos fere omnes debellavit. Tunc igitur Civitatis potentia maxime in multitudine erat, eamque ob caussam populus primas obtinebat, adeo ut nobiles fere omnes e Republica submoveret. Procedente vero tempore bellicae res, conducto milite, magis geri coeperunt. Tunc vero urbis potentia, non in multitudine, sed in optimatibus, et divitibus consistere visa est, quo [*sic*] pecuniam in Rempublicam conferrent, et consilio magis, quam armis uterentur. Hoc pacto attrita sensim populi potentia in hanc, quam obtinet formam, Respublica deducta est."

holders in the Monte, ignoring the claims of its humble creditors.[15] Furthermore, the rich speculated in Monte shares, buying up the holdings of humble citizens and of churches at a fourth or a fifth of their fair market value,[16] and reaping windfall profits when they sold them. Giovanni says that he could name many felonious speculators, but he identifies only two, Giovanni Pucci and Giovanni Corsini, who allegedly rose from small means to affluence almost overnight. "Just as no stream swells large from clear water," he observes, "so no one ever becomes rich from licit and honest profits."[17] "And so," he continues, "the wealth of Florence passes from powerless to powerful citizens, under the name of taxes, with the favor of war."[18]

That fiscal policies protected the great Florentine fortunes, and aided in the growth of some, seems unquestionable. But to conclude that the great fortunes were primarily founded upon fraud and speculation would be an exaggeration. Contemporaries unanimously state that the commercial successes of Florentine merchants abroad principally accounted for the wealth of the great families and of the city. Even Giovanni Cavalcanti comments: "just as the wet nurse nourishes babies, so the merchants feed the people, and keep the commonwealth fat."[19]

The fiscal system of Renaissance Florence thus rested upon a kind of symbiosis between the public treasury and the private fortunes. In time of war, the government tapped the wealth, which the great families had

15. "Seconda storia (dal 1441 al 1447)," *Istorie fiorentine*, II, 202. "Però e' fecero che la università de' cittadini non avessero le loro paghe, ma i maggiorenti fussero interamente pagati . . . " The identity of the "malvagi uomini" whom Giovanni condemns is not entirely clear, nor is the epoch to which he is referring. A supporter of the Catasto, he was, however, bitterly opposed to those who had abandoned the "way of the Catasto" after 1433.

16. Ibid., p. 203. ". . . e comperavano chi il quarto e chi il quinto della valuta di quello credito che aveva in polizza il cittadino. E questi comperatori erano tutti uomini che con meno tempo li traevano la intera quantità dal Monte: e per così fellonesco modo, molte povertà diventarono abbondantissime ricchezze."

17. Ibid., p. 189. ". . . come niuno fiume ingrossò mai d'acqua chiara, e così niuno arricchì mai di guadagno lecito nè onesto." On the career of Giovanni Pucci, a *merciaio* or dry-goods merchant, see ibid., p. 189. Pucci "trovò avere il credito di molti uomini piccolissimo pregio comperato. In sette anni si trovò per così sagacissima via avere avuto dal Comune cinquantaquattro migliaja di fiorini: e così molti altri cittadini dimestichi essere prestamente venuti abbondantissimi nelle ricchezze." On Giovanni di Stefano Corsini, see ibid., p. 195. ". . . il quale io vidi già poverissimo; e se io dicessi mendico, sarebbe più vero vocabolo . . . "

18. *Istorie fiorentine*, I, 24. ". . . conciossia cosa che le sustanze de' cittadini si mutano, perchè non hanno nulla di stabilità; anzi, come il vento tramuta la rena d'un luogo in un altro, così le sustanze di Firenze dagl'impotenti ai potenti cittadini si promutano, sotto il nome delle gravezze, col favore delle guerre."

19. Ibid., p. 276. "Come la balia nutrica i fanciulli, così i mercatanti pascono il popolo, e tengono grassa la repubblica . . . " See also the lengthy discussion of the importance of merchants in bringing money to Florence by Goro Dati, *L'istoria di Firenze dal 1380 al 1405*, ed. L. Pratesi (Norcia, 1904), book IX.

conveniently assembled. In time of peace, these "barns of money" had to be replenished, and the government helped in the harvest. Flagrantly regressive by any modern standard, the Florentine fiscal system nonetheless manifests an inner logic.

Still, the concentration of so much in the hands of so few created acute problems for the Tuscan economy. The most critical of all problems was the recycling of wealth, from the enormously rich to the destitute, from the city to the countryside. Public taxes and private rents constantly drew money from the humble to the mighty, and from countryside to city, most notably to Florence. In spite of the usury prohibition, interest payments doubtless moved in similar channels, adding to the abundance of those already wealthy. A "carestia di danari," a "money famine" as it is called in contemporary texts, settled upon the lower orders of society and threatened to paralyze whole sectors of the economy.[20] To find money, the humble could for a time sell their lands and possessions, and join the ranks of the totally destitute, with whom Tuscany abounded in 1427. But proletarianization offered no permanent solution to the cash famine; it aggravated the problem by immobilizing capital in the coffers of the wealthy and paralyzing effort in the ranks of the poor.

Their own great wealth could work against the interests of the wealthy. The peasant cultivator needed, for example, a constant flow of capital, for stock, seed, fertilizer, repairs, and a promise of security against the ever-present possibility of a poor harvest. The eventual result of stripping the countryside of capital would be urban starvation. Worse, the mounting debts and unpaid taxes in rural areas were forcing peasants to flee the Florentine domains, leaving their creditors with increased possessions and reduced returns.[21] The fiscal policy, which favored great concentrations of wealth, visited Florence with the curse of Midas; the city risked deprivation despite its accumulated gold.

How could the wealth be recycled? The simplest solution was to spend it for the purpose for which it had been collected—for war. According to

20. See, for example, the letter written by Matteo Strozzi to his brother Filippo, dated February 20, 1449, in Alessandra Macinghi negli Strozzi, *Lettere di una gentildonna fiorentina del secolo XV ai figliuoli esuli*, ed. Cesare Guasti (Florence, 1877), p. 40. ". . . io t'avviso che ci è sì grande la carestia di danari a Firenze, secondo ch'io sento dire, che ci è assai uomini che per carestia di danari tolgono delle mercatanzie . . . e a fatica che truovono la metà de' danari di quel che vale la mercatanzia che vendono."

21. According to Giovanni Cavalcanti, Maso degli Albizzi in 1417 alleviated taxes on the peasants in order to prevent their flight, *Istorie fiorentine*, II, 465, "Ancora ebbe riguardo al bisogno de' contadini, i quali per le incomportabili gravezze del Comune, s'erano partiti e andati a lavorare nelle terre strane alla nostra Repubblica; dicendo, che non era licita cosa, che a' contadini fusse necessario l'andare a lavorare le possessioni piuttosto dei nimici che de' vicini, partendosi dal lavorare le nostre."

the cynical but discerning Giovanni Cavalcanti, who attributes the thought to the great patrician citizen Rinaldo degli Albizzi, the poor artisans, the shopkeepers, the recent immigrants to the city—the *popolani*, in sum—consistently favored war. Although they paid taxes continually, their scarcity of possessions gave them immunity from single large imposts; in time of war, the magnates primarily had to disgorge their accumulated wealth. "When there are wars," the popolani allegedly reasoned, "the city is always filled by a multitude of soldiers [who] must buy all their needs; artisans grow prosperous and well rewarded . . ."[22] "War," claimed Rinaldo, "is their profit and their wealth, and thus through your deprivation [he was addressing the Florentine magnates] comes their abundance . . . your ruin is their glory and exaltation. War among the wolves has always been and is today peace among the lambs; [the popolani] say that they are the lambs, and you the wolves."[23]

In sum, the lambs of Florence liked to see the wolves at war, because such conflict brought about forced circulation of wealth. Paradoxically, if the fiscal system, largely designed in preparation for war, fleeced the lambs of the city, the waging of war fed them.

But war was a necessarily violent way of recycling wealth, and it did little to help the hard-pressed peasants. The need of the countryside for capital (and the fact that this need potentially threatened the landlords' own interests) promoted the diffusion in Tuscany of a distinctive type of agrarian contract—the famous sharecropping arrangement known as the *mezzadria*. Under the terms of this contract, in return for one-half the harvest, the landlord provided to his tenant not only a family farm, but also most or all of the stock and capital he needed to work it—seeds, fertilizer, and above all, oxen.[24] The landlords, in sum, assumed chief responsibility for providing the capital needed in agricultural production.

The classical mezzadria did not, however, create a recognizably modern economic relationship, based on cold calculation and the cash nexus. The

22. Ibid., I, 79. "Quando c'è le guerre, la Città è sempre abitata da moltitudine di soldati a piede e a cavallo: chi viene per acconciarsi, e chi si è acconcio; chi per le sue paghe, e chi per fare la mostra; e così tutta la terra sta sempre piena di gente bellicosa, la quale conviene che ogni sua necessità compri, là ove gli artefici ne stanno grassi e bene indanajati." Goro Dati makes the same point; see above, n. 19.

23. Ibid. "Così, in ogni modo, la guerra è la loro grandigia, ed è la loro ricchezza; e così per la vostra indigligenza [*sic*] risulta la loro dovizia. Savii cittadini, e voi signori Militi, dovete considerare che la vostra rovina è la gloria e l'esaltazione di loro. La guerra de' lupi sempre fu ed è pace degli agnelli: e' dicono essere gli agnelli, e voi i lupi . . ."

24. On the mezzadria, see I. Imberciadori, *Mezzadria classica toscana con documentazione inedita dal IX al XIV secolo* (Florence, 1951). For a typical example of a mezzadria contract in the fifteenth century, see Bernardo Machiavelli, *Libro di ricordi*, ed. Cesare Olschki (Florence, 1954), pp. 11–12.

landlord, the "host" as he is called in contemporary texts, expected to receive gifts—acts of reverence, really—from the *lavoratore* or "worker," as the sharecropper was known; and the host did favors in return.[25] He counseled his worker and aided him in times of need, and thus earned his respect and love. He was protector and patron as much as landlord.

Perhaps the favor most visible in the documents is the monetary loan, which the host almost always extended to his sharecropper when the latter assumed possession of the farm. These rural loans could amount to substantial sums. Palla di Nofri Strozzi, Florence's richest citizen in 1427, lists in his declaration 122 such loans to lavoratori, amounting to 3,200 florins. At the end of the list he notes that he had many other claims on other peasants, now dead or "gone with God."[26] He does not bother to record names and amounts, lest he bore the tax assessors; the loans, he assures them, are worth so little. As a general policy, the Catasto officials refused to consider loans of this sort authentic obligations on the part of tenants, or taxable assets on the part of landlords. Loans contracted among members of the same household were similarly excluded from consideration, which suggests that the ties between host and worker were regarded by the tax officials as intimate, almost familial.

These largely uncollectable agrarian loans evidently partook of the nature of gifts or favors. Within the Florentine bastion of early capitalism, we mark the existence, perhaps the survival, of what anthropologists might identify as a primitive "gift economy," in which payments are made not exclusively in return for goods and services, but in accordance with social roles, in recognition of status, in response to need.

The highly skewed distribution of wealth, the juxtaposition in the same

25. Giovanni di Pagolo Morelli, *Ricordi*, ed. Vittore Branca (Florence, 1956), p. 236. urges his descendents not to cultivate close relations with their lavoratori, but his words imply that most "hosts" expected gifts from their workers: "Non andare caendo [cercando] loro presenti e non gli volere; e se pure te ne danno, non ne fare loro di meglio nulla." And even Morelli tells his readers to help and counsel the sharecroppers, and so to earn their respect: "Servigli della ragione e aiutagli e consigliagli quando fusse loro fatto torto o villania . . . ; va presto e fa loro questi servigi. . . . E facendo questo . . . sarai amato più che gli altri e sarannoti riverenti, secondo loro, e arai quello bene di loro ch'è possibile avere." Lavoratori occasionally appear as sponsors at the baptism of the landlord's children, which implies a close relationship. See David Herlihy, *Medieval and Renaissance Pistoia: The Social History of an Italian Town, 1200–1430* (New Haven and London, 1967), p. 196.

26. Archivio di Stato di Firenze, Archivio del Catasto, reg. 76, 195. "Truovomi dovere avere da piu lavoratori morti e che sono andati con dio . . . di che non ve gli do per non tenere a tedio le vostre menti e sonne piccholosima stima . . . " Bernardo Machiavelli extended a loan in order to attract a worker from the farm of another landlord, *Libro di ricordi*, p. 11. "Io debbo loro prestare lire venti per rendere all' oste loro vechio . . . nel cui podere al presente stanno . . . " For complaints against sharecroppers who allegedly wanted the loan but not the land, see Herlihy, *Pistoia*, p. 137, n. 19.

small community of the numerous destitute and the few hugely rich, invited, we would argue, the formation of patron-client relationships, and, beyond that, of factions and factional alignments which cut across the entire society.[27] Within these associations, the exchange of favors and gifts between rich and poor helped to recycle wealth, however irregularly, and to relieve among the destitute the money famine that might otherwise have paralyzed society.

That the rich should dispense resources, often without thought of compensation, was an expression of the moral sense of the age. The Neapolitan humanist Giovanni Pontano, in five tracts written between 1493 and 1498, has left probably the most extended statement on the ethics of affluence, as viewed in the Renaissance.[28] The rich must cultivate liberality, beneficence, magnificence, splendor (by which he meant the maintenance of a large and elegant home), and hospitality. They should favor with their gifts the destitute and the sick; poor women, especially girls in need of dowries; and the young, particularly those possessing talent.[29] They should not, however, excessively endow the "gods," Pontano's name for the clergy, lest the gods be made to appear avaricious and unjust.[30] In their private lives, the rich should not only live in splendid surroundings, but they should also be prepared to entertain throngs. In particular they were obligated to stage magnificent weddings and funerals. Pontano singles out a Florentine, Cosimo de' Medici, as the very model of the ethical uses of wealth. "In our age," he relates, "Cosimo the Florentine imitated the ancient magnificence both in building churches and villas, and in founding libraries; not only did he imitate, but, I would say, he was the first to revive the custom of changing private wealth into public benefit and into an ornament of the fatherland. Not a few men, although less advantaged than he, now seek to follow this custom."[31]

The kernel of Pontano's teaching is that the rich should dispense their resources generously, expecting nothing in return beyond a satisfied conscience.[32] Superficially considered, his essays may appear ridiculously

27. For illustration of the remarkable size of factions at Pistoia, see Herlihy, *Pistoia*, pp. 198–212.

28. Pontano, *I trattati delle virtù sociali. De liberalitate, De beneficentia, De magnificentia, De splendore, De conviventia*, ed. Francesco Tateo (Testi di letteratura italiana, Rome, 1965).

29. Ibid., p. 37.

30. Ibid., p. 36. "Hoc quid est aliud, quam deos ipsos avaros et iniustos existimare."

31. Pontano, De magnificentia, p. 101. "Aetate nostra Cosimus Florentinus imitatus est priscam magnificentiam tum in condendis templis ac villis, tum in bybliothecis faciendis; nec solum imitatus, sed, ut mihi videtur, is primus revocavit morem convertendi privatas divitias ad publicum bonum atque ad patriae ornamentum, quem non pauci, quanquam minore in re constituti, imitari student."

32. Pontano, De beneficentia, p. 77. "Itaque non semel, sed iterum ac saepius dicendum, finem ipsum beneficentiae gratuitum esse debere, quippe qui propter se tantum quaerendus sit, neque aliud inde praemium quam rectae conscientiae expectandum."

pedantic. But in the light of what we know concerning the economic realities and needs of Renaissance society, his counsel to the wealthy appears profoundly ethical and pragmatic.

The great concentrations of wealth also affected the directions of productive effort in the Renaissance economy, perhaps unfortunately. The purchasing power of the hugely rich dominated the market, and this turned the productive energies of society away from articles of mass consumption to luxury items, which supported the splendor and magnificence of the affluent life. The Italians of the Renaissance period would seem to have had the ingenuity, the business acumen, and the capital to progress in the industrialization of production, and thus to lead their society, and perhaps all Europe, towards industrialism. But the character of the market would not readily support efforts at mechanization and mass production. The rich were well served in the Renaissance, but their domination of the market tended to discourage efforts to supply abundantly wider segments of society.

We have so far examined some relationships, evident from the Catasto, between the great family fortunes and the total disposable wealth present in Tuscany in 1427. Now we wish to consider some few aspects of another, related topic: how did the affluent families seek to manage their properties, and particularly to preserve them undiminished for their heirs. The task was not easy. "The wealth of citizens fluctuates," Giovanni Cavalcanti observes, "and has no stability."[33] Even as the wind moves sand from one place to another, so does property shift among the people. Many factors could threaten a family's patrimony and status—business downturns, taxes, political disfavor, exile. But ironically, a major threat emerged out of the family's own efforts to survive, its need to rear and support children, and divide the patrimony among them. Cavalcanti again recognizes this. Dowries given to daughters were, he informs us, "reasons for inducing poverty and misery among men."[34] "Death similarly," Giovanni continues, "reduces riches, as it scatters them among many heirs."[35]

Thus the conveyance of property to offspring threatened to shift wealth away from even the greatest households. The patrician family faced a dilemma. If it sought to rear many sons and daughters, it invited financial ruin; if it tried to limit its offspring, it risked, in this age of high mortality, total extinction.

33. Quoted in n. 18. For a history of several Florentine families based largely on their account books, see Richard Goldthwaite, *Private Wealth in Renaissance Florence* (Princeton, 1968).

34. *Istorie fiorentine*, I, 24. "Ancora, queste permutazioni sono in oltre aumentate dalle dote che si danno, e non meno da quelle che si rendono; che sono le cagioni d'indurre la povertà e miseria negli uomini."

35. Ibid. "Simile per la morte si minuzzano le ricchezze, seminate in più posseditori."

The response of the Florentine patriciate, at least in the fourteenth and fifteenth centuries, was forthright: although the marriages of the young were carefully regulated, still the households of the wealthy abounded in children—perhaps it is more accurate to say surviving children. If not the most prolific, the patrician Florentines were the city's most successful parents, managing to bring numerous progeny through the dangerous years of childhood.[36] Some sons or daughters would enter the religious life, which usually cost their families less than a lay career, but even so the young generation could not be brought into exact balance with the old. If the patrician children gained no more than a share in the family patrimony, they would usually have to accept a status considerably lower than what their parents had known.

Constantly threatened by social slippage, the patrician families responded with a remarkable strategy. They gambled on their offspring; they counted upon the skill, energy, and success of the young to repair the family fortune in each new generation. They therefore equipped their children with a rigorous and superb education, and encouraged their sons, from an early age, to seek out opportunity and accept risks, lest they miss the main chance of their lives. The parents provided them with the initial capital and expected from them discipline, loyalty, and courage—usually including a willingness to wander through the world, sometimes for decades, in search of fortune. The patrician family threw forth many seeds in its struggle to survive. Some fell on barren ground and some among nettles; the family memoirs often contain complaints about young men who preferred to chase girls rather than florins and so "lost time."[37] The Catasto itself lists many household heads who bear prominent names but have no fortune. These are the failures. But some seeds would find fertile soil, prosper, and assure the continuing fortune, status, and honor of the lineage. The Florentine patriciate was not a comfortable plutocracy, resting upon its achievements and its laurels. Its position was maintained by a distinctive set of generational relationships: the willingness of the aged to invest in its young; the willingness of the young to accept the heavy charge laid upon them.

The numerous family memoirs and the biographies of Florentines give

36. The wealthiest 1,000 urban households—approximately 10 percent of all urban households—contain nearly 25 percent of all children under age eighteen.

37. See, for example, Donato Velluti, *La cronica domestica di messer Donato Velluti scritta fra il 1367 e il 1370*, ed. Isidoro Del Lungo and Guglielmo Volpi (Florence, 1914), pp. 296–97. "Paolo, figliuolo della detta monna Ginevera, diè vista d'essere buono garzone, stando al fondaco de' Covoni e faccendo bene: poi à seguito femmine e di non fare nulla, e cosi cattiveggiando perdè il tempo suo."

us vivid pictures of the aspiring merchants who set forth while still very young to challenge the world. According to his memoirs, Matteo di Niccolò Corsini formally emancipated his six sons, pushing them into adult careers, at the following ages: Piero in 1382, at age sixteen; Niccolo in 1383, at age ten; Ludovico in the same year, at age nine; Giovanni in 1388, at age twelve; Bartolomeo in the same year, at age nine; and Neri before his eighth birthday.[38] At the same time, he registered the boys, as the Statutes required, at the Office of the Mercanzia (the guild of merchants), which gave them a recognized status in the mercantile community and allowed them to seek employment. Matteo did not send his sons empty-handed into the world, but conveyed to them substantial properties, always in real estate. Piero, for example, the eldest, received two farms worth 1,500 florins,[39] while Matteo settled a dowry of 900 florins on his eldest daughter Caterina, when she married in 1380. Registration at the Mercanzia and conveyances of property enabled his sons to assume responsible positions in commercial enterprises, as their holdings served as a kind of bond, assuring their honesty and loyalty. Beginning in 1380, when Matteo was fifty-eight years old, he set about to substantially dismantle his patrimony and pass it on to the new generation, to his daughters in the form of dowries and as gifts to his many sons. Matteo was to live until 1402, but for two decades before his death he supported with sizable disbursements the careers of his children.

Matteo may have emancipated his sons at particularly early ages because he had been past forty when he married; perhaps he feared that death would prevent him from arranging for the future of his offspring. Still, it was not at all unusual for Florentine boys to begin a mercantile career at approximately age ten. Giannozzo Manetti, later to gain a reputation as a humanist, learned his letters at school and, "according to the custom of most Florentines" was sent "at a very young age" to master the abacus.[40] His formal education ended at age ten, when his father set him to work *al banco*, in a counting house. Within a few days, we are told, the gifted child was given charge of the *conto di cassa*, presumably the cash account, and shortly thereafter the *scritture*, the complex

38. *Il Libro di ricordanze dei Corsini* (*1362–1457*), ed. Armando Petrucci (Fonti per la storia d'Italia, 100; Rome, 1965), pp. 66–75 for the emancipations, and pp. 87–95 for the births.

39. Ibid., p. 67. The two farms were sold in 1389 for 1,150 and 450 florins respectively.

40. Vita di Giannozzo di Bernardo Manetti tratta da quella scritta da Naldo Naldi, *Principes scriptores*, ed. Galletti, p. 131. "Giannozzo di Bernardo Manetti nacque a di 5. di Guigno nel 1396., e dal padre, secondo il costume de' più de' Fiorentini, fu di pochissima età, doppo l'avergli fatto imparare i primi elementi, posto ad imparare l'abbaco; e di poi d'età di 10 anni messo al banco, in brevi giorni li fu dato il conto di cassa e di più le scritture."

books of the enterprise. Giovanni Boccaccio was also only a boy, not yet in adolescence, when his father launched him on a mercantile career; he lived unhappily as a merchant until he discovered *alma Poesis*, "dear poetry," at Naples, at age twenty-five.[41] Lamberto, son of Donato Velluti, was another child accountant, who kept the books of a wool shop "as if he were forty years old." Lamberto must have been very young when he began his service, as he had worked "many years" at his death in 1363, at age twenty-one.[42] Matteo Strozzi was not yet eleven when, in 1447, his mother took him from school, where he was learning the abacus, in order to place him in a merchant's office.[43]

The service of these child clerks and accountants in Florentine shops and offices earned them a salary, and it also gave them invaluable experience in conducting business and in communicating with merchants by word and by letter. It prepared them in sum, for their eventual, grand assault upon fortune. At about twenty years of age, many of them set forth from their native city in hopes of making a career in the international mercantile community. Matteo Corsini was twenty-one years of age when he left Florence for London, to work in the English mint. Buonacorso Pitti was only eighteen when he left Florence: "I was young," he recalls in his memoirs, "and inexperienced, and I desired to go through the world in search of fortune."[44] Niccolo di Matteo Corsini was nineteen when he set sail for Avignon in 1392, "with the spirit and intention of gaining experience in the career of merchant, among other merchants." Matteo and Battista, sons of Giovanni Corsini, were twenty-one and twenty years old respectively, when in 1429 they set out for the city of Buda in Hungary.[45]

In going abroad the young Florentines frequently joined older relatives,

41. Dantis, Petrarchae ac Boccaccii vitae ab Iannotio Manetto scriptae, *Principes scriptores*, ed. Galletti, p. 89. "Unde ex ludo Grammatici circa primos pueritiae suae annos ad scholam Arithmetici iuxta Florentinam consuetudinem traducitur. Inde paucis post annis nondum adolescentiam ingressus, ut ipse testatur, cuidam maximo eorum temporum mercatori traditur . . ."

42. Velluti, *Cronica domestica*, pp. 310–13. Lamberto was born on March 19, 1342 and died on December 16, 1363. His father reckons his age as twenty-two at death, but he had yet to reach his twenty-second birthday. He worked first at the *cassa*, ". . . e avendogli messo in mano il libro del dare e dell' avere, il tenea guidava e governava come avesse xl anni."

43. Alessandra Macinghi negli Strozzi, *Lettere*, p. 6. His mother relates: "Hollo levato dall'abbaco, e appara a scrivere; e porrollo al banco, che vi starà questo verno."

44. *Cronica di Buonaccorso Pitti con annotazioni, ristampata da Alberto Bacchi della Lega* (Collezione di opere inedite o rare dei primi tre secoli della lingua; Bologna, 1905), p. 36. "Nel Mccclxxv. essendo io giovane e sanza aviamento e desiderando d'andare per lo mondo a cierchare la ventura . . ." See p. 209, for a list of his many voyages.

45. For Niccolo, see Petrucci, *Ricordanze dei Corsini*, p. 78, "chon animo e intenzione d'avere aviamento di fare merchantantia con altri merchatanti." For Matteo and Battista, see pp. 130–31. Their father emancipated them on the eve of their departure.

or they continued to serve as factors or junior partners in established commercial houses. But they also sought their own profits, and they had to convert what resources they had into liquid capital. Donato Velluti, author of a rich set of memoirs in the fourteenth century, tells us that his elder brother Piccio mortgaged his share in their common patrimony in order to finance his trip to Naples.[46] In search of liquid capital, young merchants, it appears, frequently sold or mortgaged their real holdings, often to older relatives—men who had made profits abroad but now, in their declining years, wished to convert their resources into real estate or into mortgages based on real estate. The profits which Florentines made abroad tended to return abroad, but in the hands of the new generation.

Some Florentines returned from abroad with little profit, and some did not return at all. The brothers of Donato Velluti provide examples of both outcomes. The eldest brother, Filippo, came home to Florence from Palermo in 1342, immediately after the death of their father. Family policy required that at least one male in the lineage be married, and the death of a father, or older married brother, was a common occasion for summoning the young merchant home. Filippo was thirty-six, and he had served the company of the Peruzzi for "many years" at Pisa and for nine years at Palermo, without seeing his family at Florence. According to his younger brother Donato, he cut a brilliant figure upon his return, as he was "exultant in his wardrobe, stable, servants, and expenditures, more than can be described."[47] He had in fact hardly more than 25 florins in his purse, and his employers, the Peruzzi, were on the verge of bankruptcy; and still he spent. After marriage, he had difficulty assuming the staid ways of a paterfamilias. As his financial situation worsened, he became, in the judgment of his brother, "most miserly." But he remained a great drinker and eater, and he loved parties. When he died in 1348 at the age of forty-two, it was said at Florence that, although he died when the city was beset by plague, the plague had not killed him. Rather, he died from his own excesses—from the style of life he had adopted as a young merchant and could never abandon.[48]

Donato's second brother, Piccio, had been, as a young man, involved in a vendetta and a scandalous love affair at Florence.[49] After several

46. Velluti, *Cronica domestica*, pp. 145–46.

47. Ibid., p. 142, ". . . tanto borioso di vestimenta, di cavallo, e famiglia, e di spendere, quanto più si potesse dire . . ."

48. Ibid., p. 144. "E per quello si disse, non morì per cagione d'essa mortalità, nè di quella infermità, ma per molto affanno."

49. Ibid., pp. 144–48.

ventures abroad, he found success in the cloth trade linking Avignon, Marseilles, Pisa, and distant Rhodes. He acquired his own vessel, but fell sick aboard it in 1348, and came ashore to die in a tiny Tuscan port. Donato was never able to recover his brother's property from abroad, but he did bring home to Florence Piccio's illegitimate daughter, born in Sicily, then ten years old. He clearly felt responsible for the girl, although he was at first doubtful concerning her true parentage. But when he saw her, he recognized to his pleasure that her mannerisms were his brother's own.[50] Neither Piccio nor his property came back to Florence, but in the person of this little girl, part of him returned.

Some few young Florentines—we cannot guess how many—won in the race for fortune, and with their wealth they gained honor for and from their countrymen. In the proud words of a contemporary, these were "merchants, not of despicable, but of noble and honest wares, traversing France and England, trading in cloth and wool, as do all the greater and better men of the city; this profession is considered beautiful and grand, and he who pursues it is accepted and revered in the Fatherland."[51]

Such a merchant was Matteo di Niccolò Corsini, who for seventeen years worked in English mints and traded in the marts of Bordeaux, Lisbon, and Bruges. The first event he records in his memoirs was the date of his return to Florence—February 2, 1362, when he was thirty-nine years old.[52] This was for him a second birth, and we can well imagine the pride he experienced in having spent the flower of his youth so productively. His memoirs reveal his preparations for this second birth. For some time before 1362, he had remitted money from Bruges, at times in the form of cloth and furs, for the purchase of land near Florence. In 1360, while he was still in Bruges, his brothers in Florence found him a bride. After his return, he continued to invest money, from his own resources and also from his wife's substantial dowry, in real property, suitable for a mature, married citizen, responsible now for a household and a growing family. But he did not abandon commercial interests altogether; in 1366 he invested 2,000 florins in a wool shop, in which a junior partner, who doubtless also managed the

50. Ibid., p. 148. "... e lei vidi volentieri e trattai, io e la mia famiglia, come mia figliuola: e veramente fu figliuola del detto Piccio, avendo riguardo a le sue fattezze, e che in tutto il somigliava."

51. "... mercatanti, ma di mercatanzie nobili e oneste, non vili, passando in Francia e in Inghilterra, trafficando panni e lane, come fanno tutti li maggiori e migliori uomini della città: il quale esercizio è reputato bello e grande, e chi quello esercita, è accetto nella patria e riverito." The author is Lapo da Castiglionchio, cited by Petrucci, *Ricordanze dei Corsini*, p. ix.

52. Ibid., p. 3. Matteo was born on November 4, 1322.

shop, invested only 200.[53] In the following century, Giovanni Rucellai advised investors to prefer enterprises in Florence itself to dangerous ventures abroad.[54] This was the policy of older merchants, of Matteo himself, whose goals were shifting from the acquisition of money to its preservation. From 1380, he was engaged in conveying, as we have seen, substantial sums to his progeny. At his death in 1402, Matteo retained only modest holdings, but he had launched a new cycle in the history of the Corsini fortune.[55]

The strategy we have described generated at Florence distinctive patterns in the distribution of wealth, according to the age of its owners. To study property distribution by age, we shall first examine households and their properties within a rural community, the four quarters of the Florentine countryside in 1427, which included some 26,000 households (see Table 1.3). We shall group these households into categories according to the age of the male head, or, in the case of joint households, the age of the oldest head.[56]

In the Florentine countryside, the richest household heads are also the youngest—those who are less than eighteen years old. As they grow older, their wealth initially declines. Household heads at approximately age thirty-five are the poorest of all in the countryside. The reason for this early, gradual decline in the average wealth of rural households seems obvious. These young households included many joint heads, chiefly brothers holding their patrimony in common. As the brothers grew older, they married and had their own children, and this created pressures to divide the patrimony. Division in turn reduced the average wealth of the derivative households. Thereafter, the wealth of the family head tended to increase as he aged. We have a simple cycle here: accumulation of wealth as the male head ages; his death and the subsequent division of the inheritance; inevitable reduction in the average wealth of each new unit; and accumulation again. This would seem to be an almost predictable association of wealth and age, in the cycle of household development.

53. Ibid., p. 15. "E che fiorini ottociento d'oro ch'io gli avea mandati in due partite di Fiandra, cioè in panni e in pelateria . . . E che fiorini *** ch'io mandai da Brugia perchè si conperassono le posesioni . . . " For the wool shop, see ibid., p. 39.

54. See his comments on "Danari, possessioni, gravezze," *Giovanni Rucellai e il suo Zibaldone*, vol. I, *Il Zibaldone quaresimale*, ed. A. Perosa (London, 1960), p. 8.

55. This can be inferred from the diminished size of his *prestanza* or forced loan. See the comments of Petrucci, *Ricordanze dei Corsini*, p. xxviii.

56. Households headed by women are not included, because there are relatively few of them and changes in them cannot be traced across a full developmental cycle.

Table 1.3

The Distribution of Wealth According to Age of the Household Head, Countryside and City of Florence, 1427

Age of Head	*Number Households*	*Average Wealth Real Property*	*Average Wealth Movables*	*Average Wealth Public Debt*	*Average Wealth Total*	*Average Debts*
			Countryside of Florence			
0–17	287	86.31	29.09	1.39	116.80	16.13
18–22	559	54.41	10.32	0.00	64.73	10.23
23–27	1042	48.10	10.43	0.73	59.26	13.87
28–32	1714	46.21	13.21	0.74	60.16	15.83
33–37	1621	44.50	9.68	0.35	54.53	13.50
38–42	2768	50.60	14.80	0.24	65.64	16.51
43–47	1984	49.79	11.48	0.27	61.54	15.30
48–52	2720	54.32	11.66	0.59	66.58	14.15
53–57	1635	60.91	13.59	0.02	74.51	17.29
58–62	2688	62.82	11.37	0.10	74.29	14.29
63–67	1985	70.03	15.13	0.11	85.27	16.56
Over 67	4574	69.77	11.57	0.29	81.63	12.58
			City of Florence			
0–17	333	677.81	414.90	344.35	1437.06	271.11
18–22	350	403.18	246.51	256.24	905.93	194.02
23–27	563	430.56	161.07	225.97	817.59	203.92
28–32	898	447.73	314.45	288.28	1050.46	294.28
33–37	859	402.28	346.76	184.61	933.66	316.96
38–42	960	392.65	354.90	189.97	937.42	306.84
43–47	775	518.10	427.44	284.82	1230.35	356.61
48–52	823	463.66	505.09	319.69	1288.44	370.05
53–57	588	547.82	714.76	436.97	1699.55	473.02
58–62	617	482.14	457.67	294.97	1234.79	336.34
63–67	597	360.51	250.87	180.88	792.25	199.52
Over 67	735	395.02	358.11	332.83	1085.96	252.09

NOTE: Only households with a male head are included. Values are in florins.

This association is not, however, apparent in the city. Within Florence, to be sure, the youngest heads—children less than eighteen years old—also possess the richest households. Within the city as in the countryside, the heads—or rather, their households—grow poorer as they age. But in the city, the poorest of all heads are approximately age twenty-five, while in the countryside the poorest are about thirty-five. This indicates that coproprietors divided their patrimonies at younger ages in the city than in the countryside. The urban milieu favored individualism in property management. After age twenty-five, the family heads at Florence grow richer, but the richest of them all are not the oldest, men beyond age sixty-seven, as in the countryside. The Florentine paterfamilias reached the pinnacle of his wealth while he was still in his fifties—at approximately age fifty-five. The career of Matteo Corsini follows this pattern exactly. After his middle fifties, as his children approached maturity, the Florentine father began transferring to them substantial portions of his property, as dowries to daughters and as gifts to his emancipated sons. This, then, is the chief contrast between city and countryside in the developmental cycle of family fortunes: in the rural community, control over property rested primarily with the aged; in the city, that same control was vested in distinctly younger groups. At Florence, household heads over age sixty-seven owned only 9 percent of the total social wealth; in the countryside the same group of the aged controlled 22 percent.

There is another difference. The rural families certainly supported their youth, but they often rendered this help within the framework of an established household. Many sons who married remained within the parents' household; they shared its resources, but they also remained under the authority of the older generation. In the city, the paterfamilias more commonly emancipated his sons, allowing them to seek their way in life without his close supervision. While the urban family expected loyalty and discipline, it also allowed its sons great independence from an early age.

The composition of urban and rural domestic fortunes also differed. Not surprisingly, holdings in real property were always the most important component in the fortunes of rural households, usually accounting for 80 percent of all wealth, as opposed to roughly 40 percent in the city. Moreover, the rural household tended to increase its holdings in real property rather steadily as its head grew older. In the city, movable wealth and business investments were usually the largest and always the most variable component of family fortunes. The pattern here seems to have been the following. From approximately age twenty-five to age fifty-five, the urban household head substantially increased his wealth, primarily in movables. But he also continually diverted some profits into real-estate holdings, the value of which increases in absolute although not in relative terms. After age fifty-five, he was transferring both movables and real estate to his children, but movables in distinctly larger quantities. Probably too, as he aged, his business profits also diminished, a phenomenon that further reduced his liquid assets. The fortunes of the very old show a relative increase in holdings in the public debt, an investment that involved virtually none of the managerial responsibilities that the aged found onerous. The assets of family heads at Florence over age sixty-seven were almost evenly divided among movables and business investments, shares in the public debt, and land.

Debts too show a correlation with the age of the household head; it is best to consider them in relationship to the total assets of the age group, in order to measure the weight of indebtedness. In absolute sums, debts are much greater in the city than in the countryside, reflecting the need for substantial credits in the urban, commercial economy. But the countryside bore almost the same burden of debt, judged in relation to its total assets. In both city and countryside, young adults carried the heaviest debts, but the age of peak indebtedness was approximately twenty-five in rural areas and thirty in the city. Presumably, the city dweller required somewhat longer time than the peasant to achieve success in his profession. In both areas, debts decline as the family grows older; in their mature years, many family heads would in turn become the creditors of the young, lending as they once had borrowed. This was another channel through which the property of the aged flowed to support the energies of the young, for the good of the family and the benefit of the community.

How did the distribution and the management of wealth at Florence affect the culture of the Renaissance city? The possession of huge fortunes laid upon their owners the obligation to cultivate liberality and magnificence, and so to convert, as Pontano says, private wealth into public benefit and ornament. Then too, the great wealth of the city was under the control of comparatively young men. Male household heads forty-five or younger (in approximate terms) owned one-half the city's wealth; those fifty-five or younger possessed three-quarters. Did not this distribution of resources, favoring the young, help create a cultural style which catered to youthful tastes? At least in comparison with rural areas, Florence was a community dominated by its youth.

Finally, the rich in this society looked for the survival of their lineages to the youthful energies and skills of their offspring. They trained them superbly, supported them generously, and inspired within them an entrepreneurial drive, a willingness to develop their own particular talents, to seek out opportunity and accept risks. Perhaps the high skill, the originality and the verve of Florence's culture shares the spirit of its enterprising young, who with courage and competence accepted the challenge of preserving the fortunes of their families, and the honor of their city, for yet another generation.

2

Four Florentine Commercial Companies in Dubrovnik (Ragusa) in the First Half of the Fourteenth Century

Bariša Krekić

The history of the four great Florentine commercial companies—Bardi, Peruzzi, Acciaiuoli, and Buonaccorsi—is fairly well known and their activities in various parts of Italy and Europe have been rather thoroughly examined.[1] Still, one area close to Italy herself has been neglected. That is the eastern shore of the Adriatic Sea and, more particularly, the most active and important commercial center on that shore—Dubrovnik. Dubrovnik's role as intermediary between the Balkans and the West in the late Middle Ages was bound to attract the Florentines. Nevertheless, their presence in that city has been hardly touched upon in scholarly research and publications.[2] This article obviously is not designed to trace a complete picture of the Florentine presence in Dubrovnik or of Florentino-Ragusan relations. Instead, it attempts to outline the role of the Bardis, Peruzzis, Acciaiuolis, and Buonaccorsis in Dubrovnik on the basis of available Ragusan archival materials.

Dubrovnik in the first half of the fourteenth century was under Venetian protection, but it possessed internal autonomy and a large degree of freedom to maneuver in international affairs. It was in a stage of rapid economic growth and social and political consolidation. The economic

1. See, for example, R. Davidsohn, *Storia di Firenze* (Florence: Sansoni, 1965), IV/2, 347–407. A. Sapori, *La crisi delle compagnie mercantili dei Bardi e dei Peruzzi* (Florence: Olschki, 1926); A. Sapori, *Studi di storia economica* (*secoli XIII, XIV, XV*), vol. II (Florence: Sansoni, 1955). Y. Renouard, "Florence au temps de Laurent le Magnifique", "Affaires et culture à Florence au XIVe et au XVe siècle", "Le compagnie commerciali fiorentine del Trecento", *Etudes d'histoire médiévale* (Paris: S.E.V.P.E.N., 1968), pp. 452–53, 483–96, 511–45.

2. Yugoslav historians have made only passing references to the Florentines and their companies in their works dealing with thirteenth to fifteenth century Ragusan history. See B. Krekić, "Trois fragments concernant les relations entre Dubrovnik (Raguse) et l'Italie au XIVe siècle", *Godišnjak Filozofskog fakulteta u Novom Sadu 9* (1966), pp. 27–31, 34–35. Davidsohn, *Storia di Firenze*, IV/2, 774–78, has touched upon the Adriatic area, but only briefly and incompletely.

expansion was the result of maritime trade and, more importantly, of the Ragusan role in the exploitation of mines in Serbia, beginning in mid-thirteenth century, and in Bosnia somewhat later. (Both areas yielded silver, copper, iron, lead, and so forth). The Ragusans managed from the outset to make themselves indispensable as entrepreneurs and intermediaries in the transport and marketing of the Balkan minerals in the West, chiefly through Venice.[3] The booming economic activity in Dubrovnik and the multiple opportunities it offered attracted numerous foreigners. Apart from the Slavs from the Balkan hinterland and from Dalmatia, many Italians also came to Dubrovnik, principally from Venice. The Florentines and their commercial companies began showing interest in Dubrovnik in the second decade of the fourteenth century.

The activities of the Florentine companies were largely connected with the imports of cereals from southern Italy into Dubrovnik. Built in an arid and agriculturally poor area, the city constantly needed to import grains. Southern Italy, along with the Levant, was a vital source of these provisions.[4] The earliest mention of Florentine companies in Dubrovnik is connected with those imports: in May of 1318, "Feus Leonis, procurator Butini Benciuenni de societate Bardorum, Philippi Bagnesis de societate de Peruçςis et Bertini Andree de societate Açςaraliorum" sold to Dubrovnik a quantity of southern Italian barley.[5] As a representative of the Peruzzis, Feus also had to defend in the Ragusan court his right to dispose of a house in the city. The Ragusan patrician Petrus de Pabora alleged

3. On mining in the Balkans see M. Dinić, *Za istoriju rudarstva u srednjovekovnoj Srbiji/i Bosni*, 2 vols. (Belgrade: Srpska akademija nauka i umetnosti, 1955, 1962). D. Kovačević, "Dans la Serbie et la Bosnie médiévales: les mines d'or et d'argent", *Annales, Economies-Sociétés-Civilisations* (March-April 1960), pp. 248–58. On Dubrovnik's general development and position at this time see B. Krekić, *Dubrovnik in the 14th and 15th Centuries: A City between East and West* (Norman: University of Oklahoma Press, 1972).

4. On Ragusan nourishment and cereal trade see R. Jeremić and J. Tadić, *Prilozi za istoriju zdravstvene kulture starog Dubrovnika* (Belgrade: Biblioteka Centralnog higijenskog zavoda, 1938), I, 27–35. D. Dinić-Knežević, "Trgovina žitom u Dubrovniku u XIV veku", *Godišnjak Filozofskog fakulteta u Novom Sadu 10* (1967), 79–131; Dinić-Knežević, "Promet žitarica izmedju Dubrovnika i zaledja u srednjem veku", *Godišnjak Filozofskog fakulteta 12*/1 (1969), 73–87. On the importance of southern Italy and its grain for the Florentine companies see Davidsohn, *Storia di Firenze*, IV/2, 515–21, 797–98; also G. Yver, *Le commerce et les marchands dans l'Italie méridionale au XIII*[e] *et XIV*[e] *siècle*, (Paris: A. Fontemoing, 1903), pp. 107–26, 137–39.

5. Historijski arhiv u Dubrovniku [Historical Archives in Dubrovnik] (hereafter cited as HAD), *Diversa notariae* (hereafter cited as *Div. not.*), vol. III, ff. 2[v], 57–57[v]. Dinić-Knežević, "Trgovina", p. 83. On Philippus Bagnesi in southern Italy see R. Davidsohn, *Forschungen zur Geschichte von Florenz* (Berlin: E. S. Mittler u. Sohn, 1901) (Turin: Bottega d'Erasmo, 1964), III, 155, 156, 174. On the Bagnesi family see G. A. Brucker, *Florentine Politics and Society 1343–1378* (Princeton, N.J.: Princeton University Press, 1962), p. 43. On Bertinus Andree in southern Italy see Davidsohn, *Forschungen*, p. 151. On Butinus Bencivenni see Davidsohn, *Forschungen*, III, 181; also Sapori, *Crisi*, p. 260; Sapori, *Studi*, II, 736: "tenne la 'ragion' di Barletta dal 1318 al 1319." On the family, see L. Martines, *Lawyers and Statecraft in Renaissance Florence* (Princeton, N.J.: Princeton University Press, 1968), p. 68.

that the house "et omnia bona dicte societatis" (i.e., Peruzzi) were bound to him "pro certo naulo unius navis quod recipere debet a Donato, filio Giocti de Peruçςis de Florentia." Nevertheless, the court decided in favor of Feus, and he sold the house for 1,200 Ragusan hyperpers.[6] Later on, however, he had to give this money to the representative of two Venetians who "vigore jurium et actionum quas . . . habent a sociis de societate de Peruççis" had a prior right to the Pabora estate. The Pabora family was at the time in deep financial trouble, not only in Dubrovnik but also in Venice, and with the Peruzzi company.[7] As for Feus, he remained for a while in Dubrovnik and transacted business, sometimes as a Peruzzi representative,[8] sometimes as an agent of the Bardis,[9] and at times on his own.[10]

Sometime between June and October of 1319 Andreas del Seno took over as the new representative of the Peruzzis in Dubrovnik.[11] His work was again related to the tribulations of the unlucky Pabora family. Indeed, Del Seno protested still another sale of the Pabora possessions by their Venetian creditors.[12] The Paboras owed at this time a total of 305 "librarum venetarum grossarum" to the Peruzzis, and in November of 1319 all the documents pertaining to these debts, previously deposited in the Ragusan chancellery, were given "ex iure eis cesso a sociis societatis de Peruççis de Florentia" to the representatives of Paboras' Venetian creditors "qui habent jura et actiones a sociis dictarum societatum (i.e., Peruzzi) pro dictis debitis." The Venetian creditors collected the debts from the Paboras by selling their properties in Dubrovnik in 1319 and 1320.[13] Andreas del Seno meantime had developed businesses of his own,[14] but failure to pay his debts forced him to leave Dubrovnik in 1322.[15]

6. *Div. not.*, vol. III, f. 5.

7. Ibid., ff. 299ᵛ–300. Feus is called "procurator sociorum mercatorum florentinorum de societate Peruççorum de Florentia cui dicitur societas Tomaxii de Peruççis." Another document pertaining to the same group is *Div. not.*, vol. III, f. 26. An attempt by the Paboras in 1318 to pay off their debts to the Peruzzis by selling a house in Dubrovnik: *Div. not.*, vol. III, f. 7ᵛ. On the Pabora family see I. Mahnken, *Dubrovački patricijat u XIV veku* (Belgrade: Srpska akademija nauka i umetnosti, 1960), I, 352–53.

8. *Div. not.*, vol. III, ff. 26ᵛ, 315bis.

9. Ibid., ff. 49ᵛ, 75.

10. Ibid., ff. 41ᵛ, 149ᵛ.

11. Del Seno bought himself a vineyard and a lot near Dubrovnik in June 1319. In October of the same year he is listed among the witnesses for the payment of the annual Ragusan tribute to the Serbian King. Ibid., ff. 314bis, 157ᵛ, 207ᵛ.

12. Ibid., f. 326.

13. Ibid., ff. 218, 230, 231ᵛ, 255, 336. HAD, *Diversa cancellariae* (hereafter cited as *Div. canc.*) vol. VI, ff. 61ᵛ–62ᵛ.

14. *Div. not.*, vol. III, ff. 234ᵛ, 247ᵛ, 248ᵛ, 253. *Div. canc.*, vol. VI, ff. 33ᵛ, 92, 100ᵛ, 108ᵛ, 114ᵛ. Del Seno had money invested in credits to Ragusans and maintained contacts with southern Italy. *Div. canc.*, vol. VI, ff. 88ᵛ, 89, 90, 126, 130, 131. *Div. not.*, vol. III, f. 78.

15. *Div. canc.*, vol. VI, ff. 193ᵛ, 194.

In addition to the Peruzzis, members of the Acciaiuoli company from southern Italy, Bertinus Andree and Phylippus Ridolfi, had their agents in Dubrovnik. In 1318 it was "Heliseus Johannis de Florentia" who arranged a sale of wheat,[16] and next year a new agent, Tadeus Ricci, took over, acting for "Bertinus Andree et Bencius Johannis ... socii, mercatores de societate Açaralorum de Florentia Baroli commorantes" in another sale of wheat.[17] In the spring of 1320 Ricci sold to the Ragusan government part of the wheat and barley bought by the Venetian representative from the Acciaiuoli associates in Barletta.[18]

The failure of Andreas del Seno prompted the Peruzzi associates from southern Italy to send to Dubrovnik "Gregorius Johannis de Florentia" in April 1322, and he immediately engaged in the sale of cereals to the city.[19] The Bardis, however, had a much stronger representative in Dubrovnik in 1323–24 in the person of "Duccius Puccii de Florentia."[20] He dealt in financial transactions between Barletta, Dubrovnik, and Venice[21] and in the sale of cereals from southern Italy to Dubrovnik.[22] The transfer of money from Dubrovnik to the Bardi associates in Venice became a more frequent occurrence at this time and was not always connected with the company's south Italian members. Thus in 1324, in addition to Pucci, the

16. *Div. not.*, vol. III, ff. 40, 40v. Dinić-Knežević, "Trgovina", p. 84. Heliseus remained in Dubrovnik as a representative of the Acciaiuolis at least until May 1319. *Div. not.*, vol. III, f. 41. On Phylippus Ridolfi in southern Italy see Davidsohn, *Forschungen*, III, 133, 135. On the Ridolfi family see also Brucker, *Florentine Politics*, pp. 125, 203. L. Martines, *The Social World of the Florentine Humanists* (Princeton, N.J.: Princeton University Press, 1963), pp. 60, 63, 113.

17. *Div. not.*, vol. III, f. 200. On Bencius Johannis in Southern Italy in 1318 see Davidsohn, *Storia di Firenze*, IV/2 151, 156. On the Ricci family see Brucker, *Florentine Politics*, pp. 26, 33, 68, 124–27. Martines, *Social World*, pp. 41, 78; Martines, *Lawyers*, p. 187.

18. *Div. not.*, vol. III, f. 253v. In March 1320 Ricci was a guarantor for a Tuscan "qui inculpabatur quod debuerat retinere filiam cuiusdam sclavi." *Div. not.*, vol. III, f. 255v.

19. *Div. canc.*, vol. VI, f. 203v.

20. Interestingly, Duccius is not mentioned among the Bardi "fattori" in Sapori, *Crisi*, p. 261, or in his *Studi*, II, 730–54. On the Pucci family see Martines, *Social World*, pp. 73–5; Martines, *Lawyers*, p. 403, n. 33.

21. In July 1323, Duccius sent 216 hyperpers belonging to Cione de Lanfranchis from Barletta to Lunardo de Molino in Venice, through the good services of a Ragusan patrician. In March 1324, the same Ragusan received from Duccius 42 "libras bonorum denariorum venetorum grossorum de argento," property of the Bardi associates in Barletta, to be transfered to Giovanni Maffei, a member of the same company in Venice. *Div. canc.*, vol. VII, f. 11; *Div. not.*, vol. IV, f. 2v. On Giovanni Maffei see Sapori, *Crisi*, p. 267; Renouard, "Le compagnie", p. 529.

22. *Div. canc.*, vol. VII, f. 43v; *Div. not.*, vol. IV, f. 9. Dinić-Knežević, "Trgovina", p. 87, n. 73. The Bardi merchants mentioned in Barletta were "Andrea Portunari" and "Francischus Bonçii." On Andrea Portinari in southern Italy see Davidsohn, *Storia di Firenze*, IV/2, pp. 156, 174. Sapori, *Crisi*, p. 255; Sapori, "Il personale delle compagnie mercantili del medioevo", *Studi*, II, 718, 731; Renouard, "Le compagnie", p. 528—do not mention southern Italy. Davidsohn, *Storia*, IV/2, 775, maintains that the Bardis had a "fondaco per il grano" in Dubrovnik, but there is no proof for such an assertion either in his book or in archival materials of Dubrovnik.

Count of Dubrovnik himself three times sent money through the good services of some Ragusan patricians in the total amount of sixty-eight "libras . . . venetorum grossorum." It was to be given in Venice to "domino Johanni Buldu . . . et Dato, socio societatis Bardorum de Florentia Venetiis commoranti."[23] These were most probably payments for grains sold to Dubrovnik by the Bardis.

Duccius Puccii was relatively quickly replaced in Dubrovnik by another representative of the Bardis, Bonsignore Phylippi. In the latter part of 1324 he sold grains to the Ragusan island of Lastovo (Lagosta) and to Dubrovnik itself on behalf of the Bardi associates from Barletta.[24] Soon he became the representative of the Peruzzis from southern Italy as well[25] and simultaneously engaged in various business deals of his own.[26] Bonsignore is especially noteworthy as one of several Florentines who, in 1325, hired servants in Dubrovnik for long terms.[27] These servants were mostly from poor hinterland areas near, but outside of, the territory of the Ragusan state.[28]

The Bardi and Acciaiuoli companies remained active in Dubrovnik in 1325 and in subsequent years, always primarily in connection with their southern Italian trade.[29] There was, nevertheless, from time to time friction between the Florentines and the Ragusans, especially because of

23. *Div. not.*, vol. IV, ff. 2^v, 45^v, 52^v, 62.

24. Ibid., ff. 46^v–47, 53^v, 65^v. This "Buonsignore Phylippi" is probably the same man as the "Buono Filippi" mentioned by Sapori, *Crisi*, p. 260, as being between 1318 and 1345 in England and elsewhere, but not in Dubrovnik or in southern Italy. See also Sapori, *Studi*, II, 735–36; Renouard, "Le compagnie", p. 529. In December 1324 Buonsignore sold "magistro Maffeo Pellianico vetrario" a quantity "de çenere gatina," that had been shipped from Apulia. *Div. not.*, vol. IV, f. 73^v. On glass production and trade in Dubrovnik see Krekić, "Trois fragments", pp. 19–23, 32–33; V. Han, "Fifteenth and Sixteenth Century Trade in Glass between Dubrovnik and Turkey", *Godišnjak Balkanološkog instituta SANU 4* (1973), pp. 163–78; V. Han, "Problèmes relatifs à l'identification de l'ancienne verrerie ragusaine", *Godišnjak Balkanološkog Instituta 5* (1974), 215–33; V. Han, "Les relations verrières entre Dubrovnik et Venise du XIVe au XVIe siècle", *Annales du 6e Congrès de l'Association Internationale pour l'Histoire du Verre* (Liège 1975), pp. 159–67.

25. *Div. not.*, vol. V, f. 81.

26. Ibid., vol. IV, ff. 99^v, 101; *Div. canc.*, vol. VIII, f. 2.

27. In February and March of 1325 Buonsignore engaged a young man from Trebinje, not far from Dubrovnik, for six years, another man for twenty years, and a girl for twelve years. *Div. not.*, vol. V, ff. 35^v, 39^v, 43.

28. Apart from Buonsignore, other Florentines hired servants in Dubrovnik for their companions in Italy as well as for themselves. Ibid., ff. 32, 39. On servants in Dubrovnik, see R. Samardžić, "Podmladak dubrovačkih trgovaca i zanatlija u XV i XVI veku," *Zbornik studentskih stručnih radova* (Belgrade, 1948), pp. 64–78.

29. *Div. canc.*, vol. VIII, ff. 3, 19. In 1325 the most prominent Florentine in Dubrovnik, Bencius del Buono, appeared on behalf of the Acciaiuolis in a sale of barley. *Div. canc.*, vol. VIII, f. 14. Dinić-Knežević, "Trgovina" p. 88 n. 76.

financial problems. In 1326, for example, Phylippus Bagnesis, the Peruzzi associate in Barletta, had taken by force a Ragusan ship in that harbor as payment of a debt of 400 hyperpers that two Ragusan patricians owed him. The Ragusan government responded to this act of violence by sequestering the debt.[30] Such occurrences, however, did not discourage business between the Ragusans and the Florentine companies, both in Dubrovnik and in southern Italy.

A significant indication of Dubrovnik's new importance emerged in 1327 and concerned that city's role in the Florentine contacts with the Levant. Representatives of the Peruzzis and the Acciaiuolis, as well as a merchant from Pisa, had hired, in 1323, the ship of a Ragusan patrician for a trip to "Tuniço de Barbaria." In 1327, the Ragusan shipowner was going to Venice to claim the money that the Florentines still owed him.[31] Although our information on this aspect of Florentine use of Dubrovnik is still rather scarce, there is, as we shall see, enough to conclude that the document of 1327 indicates the beginning of a trend, rather than an isolated case.

The reappearance in Dubrovnik, in 1329, of the former Bardi representative Duccius Puccii, this time as a factor of the Acciaiuolis, was connected with considerable transfers of Acciaiuoli monies from Dubrovnik to Venice. In the first half of that year, using four Ragusan patricians as intermediaries, Duccius sent over 130 "libras venetorum grossorum" and 712 hyperpers to Johannes Petri, an Acciaiuoli associate in Venice.[32] The next year, Duccius sent to Venice, this time through Bencius del Buono, the prominent Florentine merchant in Dubrovnik, and through a Ragusan patrician, over 90 "libras venetorum grossorum." This Acciaiuoli money was to be delivered to "Bonacorso Giani, socio dicte societatis Veneciis commoranti."[33] Simultaneously, Duccius engaged in sales of Acciaiuoli barley and wheat from southern Italy[34] and, having also become a representative of the Peruzzis in Dubrovnik, he sold their wheat to the city.[35] Toward the end of 1330, however, Duccius must have left Dubrovnik, for

30. *Div. canc.*, vol. VIII, ff. 106, 107ᵛ.

31. Ibid., ff. 157–157ᵛ. In the same year a Florentine, mentioned as "habitator Jadre" and "habitator Ragusii," together with another man from Zadar, received 79 bags of flax from Clarentia. *Div. canc.*, vol. VIII, ff. 144–144ᵛ. On Clarentia's importance for the Florentine trade, see Davidsohn, *Storia di Firenze*, IV/2, 772–73. On a conflict between Zadar and the Peruzzis in 1313, see Davidsohn, *Forschungen*, III, 126.

32. *Div. canc.*, vol. IX, ff. 23, 24, 26, 35, 41, 48.

33. Ibid., f. 207ᵛ. See Davidsohn, *Storia*, IV/2, 865.

34. *Div. canc.*, vol. IX, f. 208. Dinić-Knežević, "Trgovina" p. 90.

35. *Div. canc*, vol. IX, f. 212ᵛ.

the Acciaiuolis were represented there by "Pone cancellarius Ragusii."[36] The Peruzzis, incidentally, had another man in Dubrovnik at this time, who also was taking care of their affairs, particularly those concerning continued sales of wheat and related financial matters.[37]

Much more interesting and important, however, were the events in 1330 involving the Bardi company and its presence in Dubrovnik. The troubles started in April of that year, when a letter from the Venetian Doge arrived in Dubrovnik, ordering that "debeamus habere, tenere et capere omnes de societate Bardorum et eorum bona." This resulted in a conflict between the Ragusan patricians, constituted in their three councils, and the Venetian Count of the city and, through him, the Doge. A unanimous decision of the Major Council stated that the Count, "nobis ignorantibus, fecit capi et detineri Johannem Fei uti factorem societatis Bardorum de Florentia," in accordance with Doge's orders. This decision ran against one of the same Major Council of February 1, 1330, according to which "quilibet possit tute et secure in avere et persona venire, stare et reddere Ragusii cum blavo, frumento et grascia qualibet, non obstantibus aliquibus represaliis, contradictionibus, preceptis, factis vel faciendis per aliquam dominationem, rectorem, universitatem vel locum." For Ragusans, the matter obviously involved much more than just the arrest of a Florentine merchant. It concerned the jurisdiction of the Venetian Count; it endangered the reputation of Dubrovnik as a safe commercial center, and it menaced its source of essential foodstuffs. Ultimately, the whole relationship between Dubrovnik as a protégé and Venice as a protector was at stake.[38]

The Ragusan Major Council, therefore, by unanimous vote decided "pro bono civitatis, non obstantibus dictis licteris" (i.e., from the Doge) to set Fei and his property free and to send an explanatory letter to Venice. The protests of the Count's companion—also a Venetian—were of no avail, although the Ragusans must have been aware of the basic truth of his warning that "ipsi debebant obedire preceptis domini Ducis et quod non faciant contra sibi precepta." They therefore decided to send an embassy to Venice.[39] In spite of, or perhaps because of, the delicate nature

36. Ibid., f. 209.

37. HAD, *Apthay*, vol. II, f. 16.

38. HAD, *Reformationes* (hereafter cited as *Ref.*), vol. IX, f. 51. For the causes of the Venetian action against the Bardis see Davidsohn, *Storia di Firenze*, IV/2, 863; Yver, *Le commerce*, pp. 268–69. On Veneto-Ragusan relations at this time see B. Krekić, "Le relazioni fra Venezia, Ragusa e le popolazioni serbo-croate," *Venezia e il Levante fino al secolo XV* (Florence: Olschki, 1973), pp. 396–97.

39. *Ref.*, ibid. vol. IX, f. 51.

of their business, the two elected ambassadors took a long time leaving Dubrovnik. Their instructions were approved in the Major Council only at the beginning of June and they left the city on June 15, 1330, returning there on July 23. They were supposed to make excuses "de relaxatione quam fecimus fieri de mercatore qui fuerat detentus per dominum Comitem contra Deum et justitiam et contra fidem."[40] In a letter sent to them during their stay in Venice, the Ragusans explicitly forbade the ambassadors from asking any "misericordia de eo quod non sumus cupabiles [*sic*!]" and specified that an earlier letter to the Doge should not be interpreted as asking forgiveness, "cum que fecimus, cum quo fecimus, non credimus nec credimus aliquid fecisse quod sit contra dominum Ducem et formam pactorum et quod non petent aliquam misericordiam."[41]

The Doge, of course, rejected such Ragusan contentions and ordered them—through the returning ambassadors in July—to send to Venice within three months 115 "libras grossorum et extimationem seu utilitatem" of 800 staria of wheat and 500 staria of barley. He considered these to be Fei's property, which should have been confiscated in Dubrovnik. The Major Council sent another embassy to Venice to explain that there were no goods belonging to Fei in the city at the time the Doge's orders arrived, except for the 115 "libre grosse." It was, also, to be stressed that "the wheat and barley did not belong to Johannes nor to the Bardis," but that it belonged to an Anchonitan on whose ship these grains had been transported. That being so, they could not be confiscated, because "res que non erant dicti Johannis vel societatis Bardorum non reperitur [*sic*!] interdictum."[42]

The new embassy left for Venice on August 29 and returned on November 13, 1330. From its instruction it is evident that the Venetians were very irritated by the Ragusan attitude in this affair. Not only was the Doge "agravatus" because Fei had been freed from jail, but "multo magis agravari poterat de verbis explicatis coram Ducali Excellentia per ambaxatores Ragusii." This was especially true considering the contents of several letters sent in the meantime to Venice by the Count and "communitas" of Dubrovnik. The Venetians were insisting that Dubrovnik deposit the above mentioned money and cereals, or their value, in Venice. The Ragusan Major Council, for its part, maintained its original position,

40. Ibid., ff. 52^v–53.

41. Ibid., f. 56^v.

42. Ibid., ff. 58^v, 75. Dinić-Knežević, "Trgovina," p. 90, n. 100, has a brief and erroneous note on this case. The Fei case is also mentioned briefly and with errors by Davidsohn, *Storia di Firenze*, IV/2, 775–76.

but used a milder tone: the new ambassadors were to tell the Doge that Fei had been jailed by the Count "sine aliqua examinatione si erat de Bardis vel non." When the Major Council decided to free Fei, it was stressed that they acted "cum reverentia Ducali, non credendo facere contra eius precepta." At that time Fei had only 115 "libras grossas," which were deposited with the Ragusan "massarii bladorum," and no wheat or barley. The Count had confiscated that money and it was set free, together with Fei, by the Major Council "semper credendo salvare Ducalem preceptum et rationes." The two reasons for such action had been already explained to the Doge: "prima quia pro Bardo cognitus non fuit" and second "propter securitate [*sic*!] et fidem que . . . dedimus cuilibet venienti Ragusium cum blado dum civitas Ragusii erat in ultima necessitate blade."[43]

The seriousness with which this whole situation was treated by the Ragusans is illustrated by the following events: the same day that the two ambassadors were elected to go to Venice, August 14, 1330, another embassy was elected to go and congratulate the Serbian King "pro triupfo [*sic*!] et gloria quam ad presens . . . recepit per victoriam quam habuit de domino Imperatore Bulgarie." This was the famous battle of Velbužd, in which the Serbian army of King Stevan Dečanski crushed the Bulgarian army of Tsar Michael Šišman. This victory changed the balance of power in the Balkans, and the Serbs were predominant in the area for the next four decades, especially during the rule of their greatest Tsar, Stevan Dušan (1331–55). For the Ragusans, who had very strong economic links with Serbia and whose interests in Serbian mines were already very substantial, this victory called for an especially high-level congratulatory embassy, which might be able to assess the new situation and to take advantage of it through negotiations and other means. Nevertheless, the chancellor of the city was not sent to Serbia. Since it was obviously unusual for this key figure not to be included, the Major Council felt it necessary to explain that he was being kept in Dubrovnik "until the return of the ambassadors from Venice"—an additional indication of the importance attributed to the conflict with the Doge.[44]

43. *Ref.*, vol. IX, ff. 59–59^{v}.

44. Ibid. On the battle of Velbužd and its importance see K. Jireček, *Istorija Srba* (Belgrade: Naučna knjiga, 1952), I, 206–07; *Historija naroda Jugoslavije* (Zagreb: Školska knjiga, 1953), I, p. 380; G. Ostrogorsky, *History of the Byzantine State* (Oxford: Blackwell, 1968), p. 505; W. Temperley, *History of Serbia* (New York: Howard Fertig, 1969), pp. 60–62. V. Dedijer, I. Božić, S. Ćirković, M. Ekmečić, *History of Yugoslavia* (New York: McGraw-Hill, 1974), p. 85.

In early October 1330, letters arrived from the ambassadors in Venice. Their contents are unknown, but they must have been important, because once again "septem sapientes" were appointed to draft an answer and a few days later the ambassadors were authorized "ad obligandum comune et homines Ragusii et omnia eorum bona."[45] It is not stated that this authorization was directly connected with the case of Johannes Fei, and the accompanying detailed note has been lost. Still, in view of the fact that the ambassadors had been sent to Venice to plead the Ragusan case in the conflict over Fei and the Bardi property in Dubrovnik, and in view of their previous activities and the general tone of the authorization, it seems safe to assume that the ambassadors had not been able to convince the Doge and the Venetians to change their minds. The result probably was that Dubrovnik had to make the payments demanded by Venice. Since no further information on this case exists in the archival documents, such a conclusion seems even more justified. Besides, in other similar cases, before and after this one, the Venetian government usually had its way.[46]

The existence of Bardi and Peruzzi activity in the small but important Serbian coastal city of Kotor, south from Dubrovnik, is recorded in local documents in 1331. The Florentine representative there, Gerius Soderini, received from the "communitas Catharensis" 2,500 Serbian "perperorum de cruce" on behalf of the Peruzzis and the Bardis.[47] In 1335 Soderini was again in Kotor, but this time was no longer mentioned as an agent of Florentine companies.[48] Although there is no direct indication that the operations of Soderini in Kotor were linked to those of the Florentine representatives in Dubrovnik, it is reasonable to assume that the Florentines in the two cities had close contacts. In view of the geographic setting, the importance of the two centers, and their very intense mutual relations, it is plausible to presume that the activities of the Florentine agents in Kotor were channeled through, or at least closely connected with, those of their counterparts in Dubrovnik.

Meanwhile, the Florentine companies continued their work in Dubrovnik. The Acciaiuolis remained active through their southern Italian

45. *Ref.*, vol. IX, ff. 68ᵛ, 76ᵛ.

46. For example, only two months later, in December 1330, the Ragusans complied with "precibus et rogaminibus" of the Doge that "drapparia cuiuscumque conditionis laborata in civitate Florentie, comitatu et districtu, et similiter quelibet merçaria in civitate eidem [*sic*], districtu etiam commitatu laborarata [*sic*]" should not be imported into Dubrovnik by anyone. *Ref.*, vol. X, f. 1.

47. A. Mayer, ed., *Kotorski spomenici* (Zagreb: Jugoslavenska akademija znanosti i umjetnosti, 1951), p. 259. For Geri di Stefano Soderini, see Sapori, "Storia interna della compagnia mercantile dei Peruzzi", *Studi*, II, 669, 693.

48. Mayer, *Kotorski spomenici*, pp. 415, 437–38.

members and continued supplying wheat to Dubrovnik in the early 1330s.[49] Duccius Puccii reappeared in Dubrovnik in mid-1333, engaging in wheat sales and sending company money to the Acciaiuoli representative in Venice.[50]

A new company came upon the scene at this time—the Buonaccorsi. In May 1333, "Fortebraccius Charmontesis, actor et negotiorum gestor" for Nerius Balducii, the Buonaccorsi associate from Barletta, came to Dubrovnik and sold various quantities of southern Italian wheat to the government.[51] Chiarmontesi quickly established himself as a respected businessman in Dubrovnik[52] and continued to sell Buonaccorsi grains to the city in 1334.[53] At the same time, he acted on behalf of other merchants from Barletta.[54] Toward the end of 1334, Chiarmontesi, like agents of other companies, engaged in sending Buonaccorsi money—part of it originating with associates in southern Italy—through Dubrovnik to Venice.[55] He continued these operations in 1335, ordinarily using Ragusan patricians as intermediaries.[56] Simultaneously, Chiarmontesi continued selling Buonaccorsi cereals from southern Italy[57] and engaged in business of his own.[58] He stayed on in Dubrovnik in 1336, but apparently switched his allegiance. He joined with "Pone cancellarius Ragusii," and they became agents "Phylippi Rugerii, socii societatis Bardorum . . . Barulo

49. *Div. canc.*, vol. X, f. 28. There were, however, conflicts. In December 1332, the Ragusan government asked the Acciaiuoli associates in Barletta to return within one month "unçiam unam de Karlinis" that they had taken forcibly from a Ragusan patrician when he visited Apulia as Ragusan "sindicus." Should the Acciaiuolis refuse to return the money, the Ragusan government will reimburse its man, but then "habet regressum super ipsos socios et societatem predictam."

50. Ibid., f. 104v. Dinić-Knežević, "Trgovina," p. 91, n. 108. In November 1333, Duccius sent 505 ducats, the property of the Acciaiuoli associates in Barletta to "Johannes Petri," member of the same company in Venice, through the good services of a Ragusan patrician. *Div. canc.*, vol. X, f. 106.

51. *Div. canc.*, vol. X, ff. 20, 28, 89, 105. On the Chiarmontesi family see Martines, *Social World*, p. 222.

52. For Chiarmontest as arbiter among Florentines in Dubrovnik, see *Div. canc.*, vol. X., ff. 115, 115v; as a witness at the payment of the Ragusan tribute to the Serbian King in 1334: *Div. canc.*, vol. XII, f. 11v; Davidsohn, *Storia di Firenze*, IV/2, p. 776. For other cases, see *Div. canc.*, vol. X, ff. 153, 207, 211; vol. XII, f. 18.

53. *Div. canc.*, vol. X, f. 204; vol. XII, f. 3. Dinić-Knežević, "Trgovina", p. 92.

54. *Div. canc.*, vol. X, f. 226v.

55. Ibid., vol. XII, f. 17v. This shipment consisted of 176 ducats and was to be given in Venice to Nerius Balducii, who had obviously been transfered there from southern Italy.

56. Ibid., ff. 51, 65, 69, 72, 82v, 96, 118v, 124, 138, 138v. The total amount for 1335 was 306 Ragusan hyperpers, 10 "libre denariorum venetorum grossorum," and 2,010 Venetian ducats. One of these transfers was effected through Bencius del Buono.

57. Ibid., f. 82. Dinić-Knežević, "Trgovina", p. 91, n. 108. In this activity Chiarmontesi was assisted by "Pone cancellarius."

58. He dealt in wheat and arms sales. *Div. canc.*, vol. XII, ff. 56, 57v. Dinić-Knežević, "Trgovina," p. 118, n. 325.

commorantis et ipsius societatis," selling wheat from southern Italy to Dubrovnik.[59] The Bardis, incidentally, had another representative in the City in 1337, Gregorius Johannis de Florentia who was also involved in the wheat trade.[60]

The last mention of the activity of the Peruzzis in Dubrovnik occurs in 1334. Their representative, Vicentius Fiorini de Florentia, sent at the time some company money "caporalibus societatis Peruççiorum comorantium Baruli" and sold Peruzzi wheat to Dubrovnik.[61] The Bardis reemerged for the last time in 1339–40 in a rather peculiar way: the distinguished Florentine merchant in Dubrovnik, Bencius del Buono who had previously had brief contacts with the Acciaiuolis and the Buonaccorsis, in 1339 and 1340 sent several couriers to Constantinople with letters for the Venetian Marino Michel and others "de societate Bardorum de Florentia" in the Byzantine capital.[62] Although Bencius himself is not mentioned as a Bardi agent, it is clear that the Bardi company was happy to take advantage of his prestigious position in Dubrovnik in order to enhance its contacts with Constantinople, since Dubrovnik was already a well-established link in communications with the Levant.[63]

Thus the agents of the Florentine companies ceased their activities in Dubrovnik by 1340, only a short time before the companies met their downfall.

Several observations are called for in reviewing the work of the four Florentine companies in Dubrovnik. In the first place, it is clear that they did not all remain in the city for an identical length of time. The Bardis had the longest tenure, from 1318 to 1339–40. The Peruzzis are mentioned from 1318 to 1334; the Acciaiuolis, from 1318 to 1333. The Buonaccorsis were active in Dubrovnik only from 1333 to 1335.

Over the years, the Peruzzis had the largest number of agents in Dubrovnik, nine altogether, but only five remained loyal exclusively to them, while the others shifted their allegiances to other companies. The Bardis had five representatives, four of whom also worked for other companies. The Acciaiuolis had four men, two of whom divided their loyalties, while the Buonaccorsis were represented by one man, who eventually switched

59. *Div. canc.*, vol. XII, f. 261^{v}. On Phylippus Rogerii see Davidsohn, *Forschungen*, III, 174, 181. Sapori, *Studi*, II, 738, lists him as a Bardi "fattore" in southern Italy in 1336. See also Renouard, "Le compagnie," p. 529.

60. *Div. canc.*, vol. XII, f. 260^{v}.

61. Ibid., vol. X, ff. 160, 194^{v}.

62. *Div. not.*, vol. V, ff. 58^{v}, 139^{v}; vol. VI, ff. 91, 139^{v}, 189.

63. B. Krekić, "Kurirski saobraćaj Dubrovnika sa Carigradom i Solunom u prvoj polovini XIV veka," *Zbornik radova Vizantološkog instituta SANU 1* (1952), 113–20.

to the Bardis. It seems that the longer an agent stayed in Dubrovnik, the greater the chances were that he would switch loyalties. Thus, for example, Duccius Puccii, a representative of the Bardis in 1323 and 1324, switched to the Acciaiuolis in 1330 and then joined the Peruzzis in the same year, only to reappear as an Acciaiuoli agent in 1333. Sharing of loyalties, however, was not always a matter of successive allegiances. In some cases a man worked for more than one company at the same time. Feus Leonis, for example, was the representative of the Bardis, Peruzzis, and Acciaiuolis in Dubrovnik in 1318, and Duccius Puccii in 1330 worked for both the Acciaiuolis and the Peruzzis.

Almost all the representatives of Florentine companies in Dubrovnik were Florentines. There are only two minor exceptions: Bencius del Buono lived for a prolonged period in Dubrovnik, was prominent in local life, became a resident and then a citizen of Dubrovnik and, as we have seen, did some favors for the Acciaiuolis, Buonaccorsis, and Bardis. But he too was a Florentine by origin.[64] The other case is "Pone cancellarius Ragusii," who did minor work for the Acciaiuolis, Buonaccorsis, and Bardis. However, although he was not from Florence itself, he was from Pistoia, a neighboring city whose turbulent history was intimately linked with that of Florence.[65]

As for the Ragusans with whom the Florentines principally dealt, governmental functionaries aside (e.g., the "massarii bladorum," who were always patricians), it is clear that the preference went to local patricians. This is especially true in the case of the delicate operations of money transfers. Out of twenty-nine such cases that I was able to establish, twenty-six were handled by Ragusan patricians, two by Bencius del Buono, and only one by a local merchant. It is interesting that, out of the twenty-nine cases, eleven involved two members of the Bodaça (Budačić) patrician family, one of whom—Thoderus de Bodaça—was responsible for eight transfers of Bardi and Acciaiuoli money to Venice over a period of nine years.[66] All of this indicates that the Florentine companies relied mainly on their own men to control their affairs in an important commercial

64. Bencius del Buono, known also as Bencius del Buono Sacchetti, was the father of the famous novelist Franco Sacchetti, who probably was born in Dubrovnik between 1330 and 1335. Davidsohn, *Storia di Firenze* IV/2, 776–78, and n. 3, has an incomplete and partly erroneous discussion of Bencius's stay in Dubrovnik. Unfortunately, neither E. Ligotti, *Franco Sacchetti, uomo discolo e grosso* (Florence: Sansoni, 1940); nor L. Caretti, *Saggio sul Sacchetti* (Bari: Laterza, 1951), has anything interesting to say on his origins. Most recently, I. Voje, "Bencio del Buono," *Istorijski časopis, 18* (1971), 189–99, considers Bencius to be Franco's father.

65. On Pistoia see Davidsohn, *Storia di Firenze*, vol. III, passim. D. Herlihy, *Medieval and Renaissance Pistoia. The Social History of an Italian Town, 1200–1430* (New Haven, Conn.: Yale University Press, 1967).

66. On the Bodaça family see Mahnken, *Dubrovački patricijat*, I, 140–44, esp. 143.

center such as Dubrovnik. At the same time, however, they did not systematically exclude local elements from their business dealings and were willing to entrust them even with some of the more sensitive operations.

As mentioned earlier, the most important single trade activity of the Florentine companies in Dubrovnik was the sale of grains from southern Italy. According to my calculations, the four companies contracted to import into Dubrovnik close to 13,000 salmas of cereals between 1318 and 1336. Of this, wheat constituted more than 89 percent, and the remainder was barley. The most active were the Acciaiuolis, with more than 4,100 salmas, followed by the Bardis with almost 4,000 salmas, the Buonaccorsis with 2,500 salmas, and finally the Peruzzis with over 2,300 salmas. The single most active year as far as contracts for the sale of these grains are concerned was 1330, with a total of 3,550 salmas. There were several years when Florentine companies contracted to import 1,500 salmas (for example, in 1334 and 1336) or 1,000 salmas into Dubrovnik (for example, in 1323, 1333; in 1318 the contracts totaled 1,360 salmas).

It should be pointed out, however, that these numbers reflect the contracts made with Florentine representatives in Dubrovnik by the Ragusan massarii bladorum, or contracts between the Ragusan "sindici" in southern Italy and members of various companies. They do not necessarily show the exact amount of cereals actually brought to Dubrovnik. There were instances when the quantities imported into the city fell short of quantities specified in the contracts and in such cases the Florentines were penalized. On the other hand, there were instances when they brought into Dubrovnik larger amounts than the ones they contracted for, in which case the Ragusans usually accepted them and sometimes allowed them to be reexported.

What was the importance of the Florentine companies' imports of grains in the overall Ragusan provisioning in that essential foodstuff? What was the Florentine share in the Ragusan imports of cereals? To find the answers, one should first determine the Ragusan need for grain and the size of Dubrovnik's imports in the first half of the fourteenth century. Dušanka Dinić-Knežević, the only scholar who has studied in detail the Ragusan grain trade, thinks that Dubrovnik's annual consumption of cereals at the time amounted to about 10,000 staria, that is, about 3,800 salmas.[67] She assumes that, out of this amount, 5,000 to 7,000 staria were imported through governmental intervention, the rest by private

67. My calculation is based on numerous data from documents, giving an average of 2.62 staria for one salma.

enterprise. For the second half of the fourteenth century the same author sees a rise of grain consumption to over 20,000 staria (about 7,600 salmas) annually, and ascribes this increase to the growth in population.[68] Dinić-Knežević cautiously remarks that "we cannot be sure the consumption was exactly of that size" and adds that her calculation is only "approximate." Indeed, it seems appropriate to revise upward her figures for the fourteenth century.

Philippus de Diversis de Quartigianis, the headmaster of the Ragusan secondary school, in his description of Dubrovnik in 1439–40 stated, "there is such a multitude of consumers [in Dubrovnik] that the city and its district need 70,000 staria of grains and even more than that."[69] Even taking into account Dubrovnik's very fast growth at the time, it is hardly credible that the consumption—and, by implication, the population—rose three and a half times between the second half of the fourteenth and the first half of the fifteenth century. One must, therefore, assume that the consumption was higher than 20,000 staria annually in the second half of the fourteenth century. This inevitably leads one to reject as too low the 10,000 staria estimated by Dinić-Knežević for the first half of that century. Indeed, it seems strange that there would be a doubling (or more) of consumption—and population—between the first and second half of the fourteenth century, especially in view of the fact that Dubrovnik had suffered severely from the Black Death of 1348–49.[70]

Furthermore, a comparison between the quantities imported by the Florentine companies and Dinić-Knežević's calculations will, in my opinion, strengthen the case for an upward revision. If the average annual consumption amounted to about 3,800 salmas, and the average government-regulated imports were between 1,900 and 2,670 salmas, then according to Dinić-Knežević's estimates at least in one instance (1330) over 93 percent of the consumption needs of Dubrovnik were satisfied by the Florentine companies' imports—a very doubtful circumstance, to

68. Dinić-Knežević, "Trgovina," pp. 128–29. The other work dealing, among other subjects, with Ragusan eating habits, Jeremić and Tadić, *Prilozi za istoriju*, gives no information on quantities.

69. Philippus de Diversis de Quartigianis, "Opis položaja, zgrada, državnog uredjenja i pohvalnih običaja slavnoga grada Dubrovnika," translated from Latin into Serbo-Croatian by I. Božić, *Dubrovnik*, vol. III, 1973, p. 42.

70. On the Black Death in general see Y. Renouard, "L'événement modial le plus important du XIVe siècle, la Peste Noire de 1348–1350"; Renouard, "Conséquences et intérêt démographiques de la Peste Noire de 1348", both in *Etudes d'histoire médiévale*, pp. 143–64. For Dubrovnik see Jeremić and Tadić, *Prilozi za istoriju*, I, 66–68. M. D. Grmek, "Quarantäne in Dubrovnik," *Ciba Symposium*, vol. 7, pt. 1, (1959), pp. 30–31. V. Bazala, *Pregled povijesti zdravstvene kulture Dubrovačke Republike* (Zagreb: Dubrovački horizonti, 1972), pp. 30–32. Krekić, *Dubrovnik*, pp. 97–98.

say the least. On the other hand, the average amount of Florentine imports contracted for in the twelve years between 1318 and 1336 for which we have information is 1,080 salmas annually. This amount would cover about 28.5 percent of Dubrovnik's needs in those years. Considering the fact that the Ragusan government imported grain from other sources and areas and that there were considerable private imports, it seems rather unlikely that the city would depend to such a degree on one source of supply. It seems especially questionable that in a few particular years the Florentine companies could play such preponderant role in satisfying Ragusan needs in cereals.[71]

For these reasons I believe that the overall consumption in Dubrovnik was higher than 10,000 or 20,000 staria a year in the fourteenth century. Consequently, the Florentine imports, while very important, were not as substantial as Dinić-Knežević's calculations imply. The assumption of higher consumption leads naturally to the conclusion that there was a larger population in the city. Unfortunately, I am not in a position to offer any precise or even approximate estimate of the population at this time. Because I am unable to offer any revised estimate for cereals consumption in Dubrovnik in the fourteenth century, I do not feel it is possible to venture into population estimates until further study of that very important and complex problem is undertaken.[72]

The role and importance of Dubrovnik in the overall activities of the Florentine commercial companies can only be tentatively approached. It is obvious from the number of their representatives, from the quantities of money, and, especially, from the amounts of grain involved that Dubrovnik was not a major operation for the Florentines. If one compares our numbers with some of those estimated for example, by Sapori,[73] it becomes evident that Dubrovnik represented a relatively minor investment of the companies' money and manpower. Nevertheless, the quality of some of the Florentine agents, the consistency and sensitivity of some of their operations indicate that Dubrovnik was not regarded lightly by the Florentines. Its main appeal for them certainly was as a link between their activities in southern Italy and their interests on the eastern shore of the Adriatic and in Venice. If one keeps in mind the great importance of Dubrovnik as an intermediary between the mineral-rich Balkans and

71. The Florentine companies would have supplied Dubrovnik with 39 percent of its cereals in 1334 and 1336; with 35 percent of them in 1318; with 26 percent of them in 1323 and 1333, and so on.

72. There is no study of Dubrovnik's population at this time. It is generally assumed that the city had 5,000 to 6,000 inhabitants toward the end of the fifteenth century. See Krekić, *Dubrovnik*, pp. 33, 54–55.

73. Sapori, *Crisi*, pp. 215–21, 228, n. 2; Sapori, *Studi*, II, 672–80.

Italy at this time, it is easier to understand the Florentines' interest. Further research, both in Dubrovnik and in Florence, might very well show that the companies, as well as individual Florentines, had considerable vested interests in that aspect of Dubrovnik's economy, but for the time being that must remain only a hypothesis.

3

The First Infidelities of the Venetian Lire

Frederic C. Lane

Because urbanization occurred in Italy much earlier than in England, many problems of commercial and industrial life that became acute in seventeenth century England were anticipated by developments in Italy in the thirteenth and fourteenth centuries. This observation is strikingly true of monetary history. In the commercial life of such cities as Genoa, Florence, and Venice, there was intense need for a medium of exchange which could pass readily from hand to hand, as well as a need for dependable standards of value in determining obligations. Severe difficulties arose in establishing both in law and in practice desired relations between the coins which passed from hand to hand as a means of payment and the moneys of account which were used as standards of value.

There were three such moneys of account in Venice at least as early as 1300; England throughout its history has had only one money of account, the pound sterling. Because Venice had a number of different pounds (*libre* or *lire*) with different names, the changeability of their relations to coins in use is an obvious problem. Because England had only the pound sterling, there is a temptation to regard it as lacking any independence in its relations with coin. Against such a simplistic view, A. E. Feavearyear summarized its history by saying: "The pound [sterling] in the Middle Ages was as much a unit of account as it is today, with a value varying with considerable independence of the value of the metal." He emphasizes that it was the same pound in spite of these variations: "There has been no break in the sequence of contracts in which pounds, shillings, and pence have been the consideration from those times [Anglo-Saxon] to the present day [1931]. Though at one period based upon a silver standard, later upon a gold standard, and in three periods upon no metallic standard at all, the pound has a continuous history and never ceased to be accepted in any period in full settlement of debts incurred in the pounds of an earlier period."[1]

1. A. E. Feavearyear, *The Pound Sterling: A History of English Money* (Oxford, 1931), pp. 2, 6.

Description of the changing values of moneys of account by saying that they were "based on" silver or gold, or "tied," "linked," or "attached" to some particular coin, involves the use of figures of speech. The title's reference to "infidelities" as a way to characterize the changing relations of the Venetian moneys of account to the coins in circulation may be excessively fanciful, but it serves to emphasize the metaphorical nature of all such phrases. A precedent for such usage is Carlo Cipolla's use of figurative language in calling moneys of account "ghosts."[2] That metaphor has its advantages, but hardly does justice, it seems to me, to the extent to which moneys of account remained alive and begat offspring, as this essay's tracing of the genealogy of the many Venetian lire will show.

More important than the choice of descriptive metaphors is the analysis of the effects on prices and incomes produced by changes in coinage and in the relations between coins and moneys of account. In the late nineteeth and early twentieth centuries, these effects explain the passion with which the gold standard was denounced and defended. Many centuries earlier in western Europe, silver, rather than gold, had been considered the standard of value, the basis of moneys of account. A "return to gold" began in the thirteenth century but moneys of account attached to gold coins were adopted only gradually and intermittently, spreading from the south and east to the north and west.[3]

Venice was in the middle of this movement, being like Genoa and many southern Italian cities a focal point in the intensifying trade between Western Christendom and the Byzantine and Islamic lands across the Mediterranean. Venice's monetary systems developed during the twelfth and thirteenth centuries in conditions that sharply contrasted with those in England of that period. England was an extensive kingdom populated almost entirely by farmers, while Venice was a city with a population that did not exceed 100,000, with perhaps half again as many people inhabiting the surrounding lagoons and islands. Their commercial enterprises had expanded from harvesting salt and fish in the lagoons and the marketing of such products in northern Italy to obtaining silks and spices overseas and paying for them, at first with slaves and lumber, and later with woolen cloth and metals. The supply of cloth depended on exchanges with France

2. Carlo M. Cipolla, *Money, Prices and Civilization in the Mediterranean World* (Princeton, N.J., 1956), pp. 38 et seq.

3. Robert Sabatino Lopez, "Back to Gold, 1252," *Economic History Review*, ser. 2, *9*, no. 2 (1956), 219–40; Lopez, "Il ritorno all'oro nell' Occidente duecentesco," *Rivista storica italiana, 65* (1953), 172 et seq.; A. M. Watson, "Back to Gold—and Silver," *Economic History Review*, ser. 2, *20*, no. 1 (1967), 14–26.

and Flanders. Among the metals, which were brought to Venice mainly by German merchants, the most important were gold and silver. Venetian monetary problems were complicated by the city's dependence on other regions with many diverse coinage systems, a dependence evident on the one hand in its food supplies and on the other in its flourishing bullion market and the intense traffic at the Rialto in precious wares from distant lands.[4] Under these circumstances it is not surprising that Venice very early developed a monetary system more complex than that of England. In spite of this contrast, and in spite of the much fuller documentation about the relations of moneys of account and means of payment in seventeenth century England, or in eighteenth and nineteenth century America, we do find some striking similarities, especially in regard to the shift from a silver to a gold standard.

As a first step toward understanding these similarities and differences, it is necessary to explain the monetary developments in twelfth century Venice. Venice's position as a leading bullion market had not yet been secured, but the city encouraged the import and export of precious metals, while making provision to have them refined in Venice. There was no ban in principle on the circulation of foreign coins. Until about 1180 there were more coins from foreign mints circulating quite legally in the city than there were products of the Venetian mint. The oldest indigenous money of account was the pound (libra or lira) composed of 240 of the Venetian pennies (*denari*). Under Doge Sebastian Ziani (1172–78) these pennies, the largest coins then minted at Venice, weighed .37 grams and contained only 27 percent silver. Those of the succeeding doge weighed .39 grams and had the same fineness. Accordingly the silver content of the *libra venecialis* in the later years of the twelfth century was about 24 grams fine.[5]

With the technique of coinage then in use, even freshly minted coins of the same denomination differed enough in weight so that money changers found it worthwhile to save the heavier specimens for export or melting down. After they had been worn by use for twenty years or more and clipped or "sweated," and after all those that were of full weight had been culled out, coins in circulation had an average value at least 5 to 10 percent

4. Robert S. Lopez, *The Commercial Revolution of the Middle Ages* (New York, 1971), chaps. 3, 4, 5; Frederic C. Lane, *Venice, A Maritime Republic* (Baltimore, Md., 1973), chaps. 5–12.

5. Nicolo Papadopoli-Aldobrandini, *Le Monete di Venezie* (Venice, 1893–1907), I; Louise Buenger Robbert, "The Venetian Money Market, 1150–1229," in *Studi Veneziani, 13* (1971), 16.

less than the mint standard.[6] When Doge Enrico Dandolo (1192–1205) began coining pennies, he had good reason to fear that any he issued at the same weight and fineness as those of Sebastiano Ziani would disappear from circulation. His issue of pennies contained slightly less fine silver than had those of Ziani.

But that kind of debasement was quite contrary to the policy that Enrico Dandolo shortly adopted and that Venetian governments followed thereafter. The intrinsic metallic content of all the main coins issued with identical designs and names was kept remarkably constant. The main exceptions were small and fractional, quasi-token coins. According to that principle, Dandolo met the need for large quantities of coin both for domestic use (to pay shipwrights, for example) and for buying supplies overseas, as in financing the Fourth Crusade, by issuing new types of coin. Some were of smaller denominations than the denari, and contained a smaller percentage of silver. More important were Dandolo's new big coins, each worth 26 denari, which were as purely silver as the techniques of coinage made practical. They were called *grossi* to distinguish them from the earlier pennies, which were hereafter called *parvi* or *parvuli*.

The acceptance of the grossi was assured by giving them a value as legal tender higher than could be justified by comparing their silver content with that of the parvi. The content of the grossus in fine silver was 2.1 grams and it was worth 26 denari parvi, whereas 26 of the kind of denari parvi Dandolo had issued at the beginning of his reign contained 2.4 grams fine (.25 × .37 × 26). This comparison shows that the grossus was "bad money" in the sense in which "bad" is used in "Gresham's Law." If the minting of both coins had continued, the grossi would have driven the parvi out of circulation. The Venetians avoided such an unprofitable and useless operation of their mint by ceasing for more than sixty years the issuance of any coins valued as one denarius parvus.

Thus, for more than sixty years after the issuance of the grossus, it was the only silver coin minted in Venice. A little silver, but very little, went into the fractional coins, the bianco, worth a half or a third of a denarius parvus, and the quatarolo, worth a quarter thereof. They contained at best only 1/20th of their weight in fine silver; they were mainly copper, black money. The coinage of denari was not resumed until the time of Doge Lorenzo Tiepolo (1268–75).[7]

6. Abbott Payson Usher, *The Early History of Deposit Banking in Mediterranean Europe* (Cambridge, Mass., 1943), I, 196–98. Feavearyear, *Pound Sterling*, pp. 84, 110, 124.

7. Papadopoli, *Monete*, I, 89–109; Robbert, "Venetian Money Market," pp. 29, 38, 45.

Meanwhile the traditional Venetian libra was sometimes called the libra denariorum parvorum because it was conceived as composed on 240 of the old denari, now called also parvi. Clearly distinct was a new money of account called the *libra grossorum*, conceived as composed of 240 of the large coins, the grossi (sometimes called denari grossi, since denari was then a generic term). But references to this new money of account for high denominations are rare for that period. When "lib. ven." appears without further specification, one may assume the *libra denariorum parvorum*, the traditional Venetian libra, is meant.

During about sixty years the value of this Venetian libra compared to the moneys of other countries depended on the grossi. In that sense one may say that the Venetian libra was tied to the grossi. Since the grossi contained 2.1 grams of fine silver and were being coined in large quantity with the value as legal tender of 26 denari, this Venetian libra contained 19.38 grams of fine silver $(\frac{2.1 \times 240}{26})$, somewhat less than it had had when based on pennies freshly coined by Sebastian Ziani.[8]

I am tempted to call this shift in the attachment of the Venetian libra from the denari to the grossi the first infidelity of the Venetian lire, even if it was only a minor flirtation. Probably it is more helpful to say that during this period the traditional Venetian libra was based on both types of coin, on the old denari surviving from earlier coinages and on the newer grossi. Either might be used in paying a debt recorded in the traditional libra. After the pennies of Ziani's time had been worn, clipped, and culled for twenty to sixty years they may well have averaged even less than 90 percent of their weight when first issued, so that there is no substantial contradiction in thinking of the Venetian libra of this period as based on both of the silver coins in circulation, the new grossi and the old denari parvi. Presumably the common way of paying one Venetian libra was to hand over 9 grossi and 6 denari ($9 \times 26 + 6 = 240$).

Reference to payment involving the use of both grossi and parvi is found in connection with a law of 1254. This reference specified that one libra ad grossos had the value of 9 grossi and 5 parvi. That equation had the effect of giving to one grossus the value of 26 1/9 denari parvi. The introduction of this awkward fraction suggests that the grossus was beginning to rise in

8. Papadopoli, *Monete*, I, 86; Louise Buenger Robbert, "Reorganization of the Venetian Coinage by Doge Enrico Dandolo," *Speculum*, *49* (1974), 49.

value compared to the parvus and that an effort was being made to prevent the rise.[9]

Certainly a rise in the value of the grossi compared to the parvi was going on in the 1260s. In 1269 the grossus was declared officially worth 28 parvi; in 1282 it was officially worth 32 parvi. The denarius parvus kept that value, 1/32 of a grossus, for many decades although the silver content of the parvus was reduced in 1282–89 so that it was about 10 percent less than 1/32 of the silver in a grossus.[10]

When the denarii parvi were thus devalued from 1/26 to 1/32 of the grossus, the traditional Venetian libra began to lead a double life and acquired two distinct names. If its value was based on the small pennies it was called the libra denariorum parvorum. If its value was based on grossi, it was called the *libra ad grossos*. To distinguish it more clearly from the libra grossorum, the libra ad grossos was sometimes called the libra parvorum ad grossos.[11]

9. The fraction of $\frac{1}{9}$ was reached by subtracting from the 240 denari in a libra the 5 denari parvi. That left 235 of these denari still due. To pay those 235 denari, 9 grossi sufficed. 235 divided by 9 gives $26\frac{1}{9}$.

The exact date and language of the law is doubtful. Compare *Deliberazioni del Maggior Consiglio di Venezia*, ed. R. Cessi, in R. Accademia dei Lincei, *Atti delle Assemblee Costitutionali Italiane*, (Bologna, 1931), II, 222, 369; Archivio di Stato di Venezia, Giudici al Piovego, Busta I, Cap. I, first entry after the formal oath of the magistrates; and *Novissimum Statutorum ac Venetarum legum volumen duabus in partis divisum Aloysio Mocenigo* (Venice, 1729), p. 221. But a legal specification that 9 grossi and 5 parvi equaled 1 libra is the only satisfactory explanation of the awkward fractional valuation of the grossus as $26\frac{1}{9}$ denari ad grossos. See Frederic C. Lane, "Le vecchie monete di conto veneziani ed il ritorno all'oro," in *Atti dell' Istituto Veneto di Scienze, Lettere ed Arte*, vol CXVII, (Venice, 1958–59), pp. 55–56, in an article which analyzes pertinent passages in a manuscript of Thomas E. Marston subsequently given to the Library of Yale University. The Marston manuscript was published as the *Zibaldone da Canal*, ed. Alfredo Stussi (in Fonti per la Storia di Venezia, sez V. Fondi Varii, Venice: Il Comitato per la Pubblicazione delle Fonti relative alla Storia di Venezia, 1967).

10. Lane, "Le vecchie monete," pp. 53–57; Papadopoli, *Monete*, I, 109–10. 120–23, 138. After 1289 the denarius parvus weighed .292 grams and was 19.8 percent fine silver.

11. Reference to the libra denariorum parvorum or libra parvorum are found as early as 1212 and 1223 but only to distinguish that libra from the libra grossorum, although references to the latter are rare before 1229. When lib. ven., without other specification is used before 1252 one may assume that it refers to the libra parvorum. Robbert, "Venetian Money Market," pp. 47, 47n, 48; Papadopoli, *Monete*, I, 128.

I have found no reference to libre ad grossos in the commercial documents published by Morozzo della Rocca and Lombardo but in 1245 there was a promise of "libras denariorum venecialium quattuormille in denariis grossis." R. Lombardo and R. Morozzo della Rocca, *Documenti del commercio veneziano nei secoli xi-xiii* (Turin, 1940), vol. II, doc, 776, 777.

The earliest clear reference I have found to "libra ad grossos" is in 1276 in the papers of the estate of Marco Querini, son of Giovanni, in Archivio di Stato di Venezia (cited hereafter as ASV), Procuratori di San Marco, Busta 113. Its use earlier seems implied by the regulation for paying customs in Cessi, *Deliberazioni del Maggior Consiglio*, II, 285, April 9, 1271. Early but not precisely datable references to it are in the Capitulare Visdominorum Ternarie, Biblioteca Nazionale Marciana, Venice, MS Lat. Cl. V, Cod 6, Coll. 2380, f. 1, 10. After 1280, references to libre ad grossos in the estate papers in the archives of the Procuratori are common. It is called the "libra parvorum ad grossos," in Elena Favaro, ed., *Cassiere della*

This change seems to me best described as a splitting of the old Venetian libra into two separate moneys of account, the libra ad grossos and the libra parvorum. Carlo Cipolla's terminology suggests characterizing the change as the creation of new ghost moneys. Calling it a split in the standard of value seems to me better because it suggests the right answer to a vital question: What happened to obligations, wages, and prices which had previously been set in the Venetian libra? Were they paid as if the traditional libra had become a libra ad grossos or as if it had become a libra parvorum?

In the course of the next twenty years, how those questions were answered made a difference of about 30 percent. A holder of 100 libre of government bonds (*imprestiti*) would after 1282 receive coin containing 144 grams of silver if the "libre" were considered libre parvorum or 193 grams of silver if they were considered libre ad grossos. A seaman or a shipwright whose wages remained at a customary rate that added up to make 50 lire due him in a year would receive 72 grams of silver if the "libre" were considered libre parvorum or 96½ grams of silver if they were considered libre ad grossos. Clearly it was to the interest of creditors to have their credits recognized as libre ad grossos. It was in the interest of employers to have the wages they were accustomed to paying calculated as if in libre parvorum. To some extent these interests dominated both in practice and in the provisions made by the government to regulate the transition.

An important body of creditors were the holders of government bonds. The bonds had been floated by imposing loans on the well-to-do. Venice's rulers were men of wealth. It is not surprising therefore that the libre veneciales recorded in the loan office (Camera degli Imprestiti) were considered libre ad grossos.[12]

The salaries of government officials were at about the same time also fixed in a money of account based on the grossi, either by interpreting the traditional salary of the office in libre as meaning libre ad grossos or by

---

Bolla Ducale, Grazie—Novus Liber (1299–1305), in Fonti per la Storia di Venezia, sez. I Archivi Pubblici (Venice, 1962), no. 62 (1300).

Roberto Cessi, *Problemi Monetari Veneziani* (*fino a tutto il sec. xiv*) in *Documenti finanziari della Repubblica di Venezia* (hereafter cited as *Doc. Finan.*), ed. Commissione per gli Atti delle Assemblee Costituzionali Italiane, R. Accademia dei Lincei, Serie IV, vol. I (Cedam, 1937), p. xxxiv, described the lira a grossi as a lira di piccoli calculated on the basis of the original value of the piccoli relative to the grosso. I suggest modifying Cessi's statement only so as to indicate that the value

$$1 \text{ grossus} = 26\tfrac{1}{9} \text{ denarii}$$

was not "the original value" but a value fixed by law about the time that the grossus began rising in value compared to the denari parvi.

12. Gino Luzzatto, *Il debito pubblico della Repubblica di Venezia* (Milan, 1963), pp. 8*n*, 150.

specifying the salary for new offices in a designated kind of libre. For the latter purpose, the libra grossorum was used as well as the libra ad grossos.[13] Whether a salary or account was recorded in libra ad grossos or libra grossorum, payment would be made in grossi, or, if made in other coin, in an amount determined by the values of these coins compared to the grossus.

Payments at the loan office and the payment of salaries to high officials were not the only transactions in which the old money of account, libre venecialis, were transformed at the end of the thirteenth century into libre ad grossos. The same development probably occurred in most other accounts in which payments had in practice been in grossi. This seems to have been true of all payments made in the Levant and it is significant that in 1275 the Great Council ordered that all payments made for the commune "beyond the sea" be made in grossi, even those to sailors and oarsmen.[14] Within Venice some tax payments were levied in denarii parvi, but when the tax on the butcheries was auctioned in 1285, the payment was specified as in libris ad grossos and most taxes thereafter were in libra ad grossos.[15]

Most private commercial investments were in the form of *collegantiae* and were investments for a single season or voyage. When the two kinds of libre began to pull apart, a new contract would specify which kind of Venetian libre or foreign money was involved.

For retail trade within the city, prices were set in libre parvorum. A law of December 11, 1269 ordered that all transactions (*mercate*) of 50 libre or less except those in gold, silver, pearls, and precious stones be made ad denarios parvos, naming the amount in libre and *solidi*.[16] This law of 1269 might almost be said to have created the libre parvorum (later called the *lira di piccoli*). This libra could be considered a new sort of ghost, a money of account based on the new (i.e. devalued) denari parvi, while the old Venetian libra clung to the grosso and continued its life as the libra ad grossos. Certainly the libra parvorum became the usual money of account used in setting prices in the retail trade. The libra parvorum was used also in setting wages within Venice.[17] And because it was sometimes used in setting rents, it was sometimes also employed in evaluating real

13. *Documenti finanziari della Repubblica di Venezia*, ser. I, vol. I, pt. I, doc. 6, 9, 11 and others of about 1300.

14. *Doc. Finan*, ser. IV, vol. I, doc. 23.

15. *Bilanci Generali* in *Doc. Finan*, ser. II, vol. I, parte I, doc. 55. In 1339 the tax on wool was fixed in libre ad grossos (ibid., doc. 64). Many provisions of that year specified whether taxes were in grossi or piccoli.

16. Cessi, *Deliberazioni del Maggior Consiglio*, II, 393. This law was enacted immediately after the law of December 6, which set the current price of the grossus as 28 denarii parvi.

17. Of stonecutters, for example. Rudolfo Gallo, "Marco Polo, il sua famiglia e il suo libro," in *Nel centenario della nascita di Marco Polo* (Venice: Istituto Veneto di Scienze, Lettere ed Arti, 1955), p. 112.

estate, even very valuable buildings, although some rents are also recorded in libra grossorum. For purposes of taxation real estate was valued also in libre ad grossos.[18] And the libra ad grossos was the most used in foreign trade, shipping, and government finances.

That the libra ad grossos was so widely used in spite of its mathematically inconvenient relations to the coins in use and to the other moneys of account seems to have been due to the fact that this libra alone combined the two qualities of (1) being derived from the traditional pound of Venice so that it was regarded as a continuation of the age-old standard of value and (2) being based on the grossus, a coin kept at unchanged weight and fineness and associated in the minds of the Venetians with national success, prosperity, and financial soundness.

The change in the relative values of the grossus and the denarius parvus affected in a minor way the money of account for large denominations, namely, the libra grossorum. Its relation to the traditional Venetian libra had been established as 1 libra grossorum = 26 libre venecialis. If it kept that relationship with the libra ad grossos, after the libra ad grossos was declared worth 9 grossi and 5 parvi, then the libra grossorum could be figured to be worth only 239 grossi instead of 240. for 26 times 9 grossi plus 26 times 5 parvi works out to only 239 grossi in all.

This difficulty was solved by distinguishing two kinds of libre grossorum or *lire di grossi*, to use their Italian name. One, called the *lira di grossi manca* (the short pound) was equal to 26 *lira a grossi* (libre ad grossos) and to 239 grossi. In contrast, the libra grossorum of 240 grossi was called the *lira di grossi complida*.[19] Thus there were four kinds of libre to be distinguished, which will be referred to hereafter by their Italian names:

lira di piccoli = libra parvorum
lira a grossi = libra ad grossos
lira di grossi manca } = libra grossorum
lira di grossi complida }

The relationship among these four moneys of account between 1282 and 1328 may be summarized as follows:

1 lira di piccoli	= 240 piccoli	= 7.5 grossi coins
1 lira a grossi	= 1.22 lire di piccoli	= 9.15 grossi coins
	= (1 lira, 4 soldi, 6 denari)	
1 lira di grossi manca	= 26 lire a grossi	= 239 grossi coins
1 lira di grossi complida	= 32 lire di piccoli	= 240 grossi coins

18. Gino Luzzatto, *Studi di storia economica veneziana* (Padua, 1954), p. 82; Luzzatto, *Il debito pubblico* (Milan, 1963), p. 146.

19. Lane, "Le vecchie monete," pp. 53–57.

It is to be noted that each lira was divided for purposes of calculation into 240 denari, but the *denaro a grossi*—the denaro of which 240 equaled a lira a grossi—was not represented by any coin. The denaro a grossi was purely a denomination of account, a quite disembodied example of what Carlo Cipolla suggests calling a ghost. It might even be called a phantom, if not a phantasma. Its value was not tied to that of any coin, past or present, called a denaro; for the denaro coin, the *piccolo* (denarius parvus) was worth only about 5/6 of the denaro a grossi. The value of a denaro a grossi was determined by the grosso—by the fact that 240 denari a grossi formed a lira a grossi and 26 lira a grossi were worth 239 grossi coins. Through this complicated relationship, lire, soldi, and denari a grossi were all based on the grosso.

The next major change in Venetian moneys of account was connected with the shift from a silver standard to a gold standard. This change, which occurred in the fourteenth century, resembled in many ways the change from a silver standard to a gold standard that occurred in England between 1650 and 1750.[20] In both cases the change was gradual, was preceded by a deterioration of the silver coinage, and was in part an unexpected by-product of efforts to bring nearer to mint standard the silver coins in circulation. In both cases, also, it came at a time when silver was relatively scarce. That is, it came at a juncture when the value of gold, after having for decades been rising relative to silver, was falling.

Gold coins from Byzantine, Neapolitan, Genoese, and Florentine mints were widely used in Venice before the Serenissima issued a gold coin of its own, the ducat, in 1284–85. When payments were made with any of these gold coins in the thirteenth century, they were given values in the moneys of account mentioned above, which were all based on silver coins.[21] The most widely circulating gold coin in 1284 was the florin. When the Venetian government in that year authorized the coinage of gold, it specified that the Venetian ducat be of the same weight and fineness as the florin and that the ducat cost no more than 18 grossi.[22] The next year it specified that the ducats have value as legal tender for 40 soldi a grossi (about 18 1/2 grossi).[23]

Since gold had been rising in value relative to silver before 1284, the

20. Feavearyear, *Pound Sterling*, pp. 121–42; J. K. Horsefield, *British Monetary Experience* (Cambridge, Mass., 1960), pp. 81–90.

21. Robbert, "Venetian Money Market," pp. 19–20, 65, 92–93; Lane, "Le vecchie monete," pp. 76–78.

22. Lane, "Le vecchie monete," pp. 58–60.

23. Lane, "Le vecchie monete," pp. 60–72.

instruction to the mint masters to coin ducats at a cost of no more than 18 grossi per ducat was probably given with the intention of preventing the Florentine florin from rising in value compared to the Venetian grosso. Accordingly, Robert Cessi has described it as a part of a long campaign in "defense of the grosso."[24] Success in this "defense" was helped in the late thirteenth century by the arrival on the Venetian market of a great deal of gold from Hungary.[25] At the same time, much gold in the form of Levantine gold coins may have been drawn to Venice to be reminted into ducats. In 1284, the same year in which coinage of ducats was ordered, Venetian officials were forbidden to accept any such gold coins as worth more than 40 soldi a grossi,[26] the value set on the ducat, and in 1287 the mint was authorized to offer a special high price for gold derived from melting Byzantine and Neapolitan coins.[27]

Although the ducat was thus launched in a way that temporarily gave the grosso the relatively high value of 1/18th or 1/18.5 of a ducat or florin, the grosso soon fell to much less. Even in 1284–85 the bimetallic ratio in Italy generally was 11.3 to 1, although the rules of the Venetian mint concerning the content of pure gold or silver in the ducat and grosso established a ratio of 10.9 to 1, assuming that 1 ducat equalled 18.5 grossi. Putting such a low value of gold soon became utterly unrealistic. Large production of silver by Bohemian mines drove the bimetallic ratio up to 13:1 or 14:1. Consequently ducats rose in value. The laws of 1284 and 1285 regulating the ducat specified a minimum value for it as legal tender but set no maximum at which it might be received. By 1305, if not before, and certainly by 1310, the ducat had risen to 24 grossi,[28] and in one reference it is given as worth 28 grossi before 1314 and at that time 24 grossi plus 12 parvi.[29] Under these conditions, coinage of ducats would have ceased

24. Cessi, *Problemi Monetari*, in *Doc. Finan*, IV, pp. xxxix–xlii.

25. Balint Homan, "La circolazione delle monete d'oro in Ungheria del x al xiv secolo e la crisi europea dell'oro nel secolo xiv," in *Rivista italiana di numismatica*, ser. 2, *5* (1922), 128–31, and Homan, *Geschichte des ungarishen Mittelalters* (Berlin, 1943), II, 353–54.

26. *Doc. Finan.*, ser. IV, vol. I, doc. 35, 45.

27. The indications given in my "Le vecchie monete," pp. 61, 66 may need correction since they were based on *Doc. Finan.*, ser. IV, vol. I, doc. 46, which gives 132 libre as the price of a marc of gold, whereas Cessi, *Deliberazioni del Maggior Consiglio*, III 167 gives 132½, a figure confirmed by checking the original, A.S.V., Maggior Consiglio, Deliberazioni, Zaneta, f. 24^v. The libre 132½ (= 2650 soldi) was the price of a marc of pure gold obtained by melting down "perperi seu tari sive alia moneta."

28. Watkins, "Return to Gold—and Silver," p. 24; Lane, "Le vecchie monete, pp. 76–78; Josef Janáček, "L'argent tchèque et la Méditerranée (xiv et xv siècles)" in *Histoire économique du monde méditerranéen, 1450–1650, Mélanges en l'Honneur de Fernand Braudel* (Toulouse, 1973), I, 247–48.

29. In statutes for goldsmiths in C. Monticolo, ed., *I capitolari delle arti veneziane sottoposte alla Giustizia Vecchia*, 4 vols. (Rome, 1896–1914), III, 320.

if the only way for the mint to obtain gold bullion was to pay for it in silver at the rates specified in 1284–85. But in fact the coinage of gold was not only maintained but increased, because the law of 1285 permitted the mint to pay for gold bullion by using the gold coin minted from the bullion. While using that provision of the law of 1285 for all it was worth, the masters of the mint used other provisions of the law of 1285 to reduce the seigniorage changes from 3 percent to .75 percent.

Payment in ducats became more and more common, especially when arrivals of gold increased and supplies of silver became relatively less. This occurred first in the 1320s, partly because gold from the Sudan became very plentiful in Egypt, and partly because more gold from Hungary found its way to Venice. The resulting fall of the bimetallic ratio from 14 : 1 or 13 : 1 back to 11 : 1 or 10 : 1 occurred first in southern Europe and spread northward at a considerably later date. Gold coins, which had been rising generally, took a sharp turn downward in Italy in 1326–32.[30]

During this period when gold was becoming more plentiful, a law of 1328 made the ducat legal tender for 24 grossi.[31] Too many scholars have described this law of 1328 as raising the value of the ducat in money of account from 40 soldi a grossi to 52 soldi a grossi (the equivalents of 18 1/2 and 24 grossi),[32] whereas, as has just been explained, the ducat had been accepted commercially as worth 24 grossi (52 soldi a grossi) or more, for twenty to thirty years before 1328. What the law of that year did was to raise the official minimum value of the ducat during a crisis in which the ducat was falling rapidly. Had there been no law increasing

30. Lane, "Le Vecchie monete," pp. 61–68, 72, 76–78. Watkins, "Return to Gold," p. 26, concentrates his attention on the continued rise of the value of gold north of the Alps until the middle of the century and ignores the evidence I used on an earlier drop in Italy in the 1320s. On possible causes of such a drop see Homans, "La circolazione," pp. 146–54; Eliyahu Ashtor, *Les Métaux précieux et la balance des payments du Proche Orient à la basse époque* (Paris, 1971), pp. 18–28; R. H. Bautier, *The Economic Development of Medieval Europe* (New York, 1971), pp. 164–69.

31. The omission of this decree from the documents printed by Cessi in his supplement to his *Problemi monetari* is an example of the incompleteness of the *Doc. Finan.*, ser. IV, vol. I. The degree was printed years ago by Papadopoli (*Monete*, I, 380*n*) from a copy of the Capitolare dei Signori delle Notte. It can be found also in the Capitolare degli Estraordinarii, f. 19^{v}, cap. xliv, which was Miscellanea codici of ASV, cod. 131, recently reclassified as Cinque Savii alla Mercanzia, busta 23, f. 19^{r}.

32. Gino Luzzatto in his "L'oro e l'argento nella politica monetaria veneziana dei sec. xiii-xiv," in *Rivista storica Italiana* (1937) reprinted in his *Studi di storia economica veneziana* (Padova, 1954), pp. 259–70, gave a lucid and enlightening explanation of material worked over by Cessi's *Problemi Monetari*, and cited a few additional, and very significant documents. However, Luzzatto assumed, as a matter of logic (cf. p. 265) but without specific evidence on the point, that because a ducat was legal tender for 40 soldi, a holder of ducats would part with them at that valuation and (p. 267), that the government insisted on that relationship until 1328. Against such an assumption are the many quotations of the ducat at 24 grossi in 1305–23 cited in my "Le vecchie monete," pp. 76–77.

its value as legal tender, the ducat would have gone down below 24 grossi in the 1320s.

The law of 1328 which prevented the fall of the ducat below 24 grossi (52 soldi a grossi) came at the end of a vigorous effort to raise the silver coinage in circulation up to the mint standard. The silver coinage had been deteriorating for a long period. Grossi had been coined in large quantities for more than a century but there had been no recoinage, that is, the old coins had never been called in. There is no record of any demonetizing of grossi bearing the names or images of early doges in order to force their exchange for grossi bearing the image or name of a later doge. There were complaints of much wear and tear, clipping and culling, and counterfeiting. Particularly objectionable were the large number of coins minted in the South Slav states of Bresnova and Rascia from silver from Bosnian and Serbian mines. Some of these Balkan issues resembled the grossi sufficiently to pass from hand to hand as if they were grossi, although they contained less silver.[33] Not all foreign silver coins were banned. Import of some issues called pieces of twenty and twenty-two were for a time encouraged.[34] But the issues of Rascia and Bresnova were for a time treated as counterfeit. Merchants or workmen who had to accept them in order to get paid passed them on as quickly as possible, as they did worn or clipped grossi of Venetian mintage. As a result the best of the grossi, especially the heavier pieces in new issues, were culled out for export.

In England in the seventeenth century similar processes reduced drastically the average weight of silver coin in circulation. When there had been no recoinage since 1601, an expert estimated in 1652 that the average silver coins in circulation were only 70 to 80 percent of the mint standard, and in 1695 "mixed silver . . . received in the ordinary course at the Exchequer over a period of three months weighed 51 percent of the standard weight."[35] The deteriorated condition of England's silver coinage and the chaos it caused is vividly described by contemporaries. There are no similar descriptions for thirteenth century Venice; sources of that kind are lacking for both the thirteenth and fourteenth centuries. But there is reason to believe that a hundred years without recoinage had had somewhat similar effects in Venice by the beginning of the fourteenth

33. *Doc. Finan.*, ser. IV, vol. I, doc. 60. The Marciana MS above cited, Capitolare Ternarie, f. 51, 59, September 3, 1305, shows that some coins were actually being melted down in order to remove them from circulation.

34. *Doc. Finan.*, ser. IV, vol. I, doc. 91, Germans importing "denarios de XX et de XXII" were exempted from the 5 percent import tax in 1332.

35. Feavearyear, *Pound Sterling*, pp. 84, 110, 124.

century. Culling for export, the process by which good new money was promptly driven out by bad old money, must have been more intense in Venice than in England, because in Venice the export of silver coin was not only permitted but encouraged. Proceedings at the mint were sometimes modified for the avowed purpose of enabling merchants who had supplied the mint with silver to receive the minted product in time to send east on scheduled galley voyages.[36] Another major difference between the English and the Venetian situations was that Venice, as a good market for the products of German miners, received almost continually a large inflow of silver bullion.

This century-long deterioration of Venetian silver coinage culminated during the decade of the 1320s in a financial crisis linked to monetary reforms. The men dominating Venetian policy—fiscal, monetary, and commercial—at the beginning of the crisis formed a group which Robert Cessi characterized as hard-money, budget-balancing protectionists.[37] The first step toward reform of the currency was an enlargement of the mint in 1319–20[38] and orders to mint more piccoli (denari parvi).[39] About the same time the size of the bonds that bankers were required to post was raised.[40] Then in October and November 1321 the ruling councils took measures which precipitated a squeeze, perhaps inadvertently, perhaps deliberately. On October 19, 1321, customs officials and other government agencies were forbidden to accept payments in any form except good grossi. They could accept other silver or gold coin as security that payments would be made but only if the security was worth 10 percent more than the amount due.[41] This did not result in simply placing a 10 percent premium on good grossi. Since debtors of the government had solid claims to receive back the coin or jewelry they had given as security, the government bureaus and the central treasury could not freely transfer or spend the coin deposited with them. As a result they could not meet their own obligations or turn in their accounts for auditing at the times

36. In July 1328 special provision was made to enable merchants who had put silver in the mint to receive the mint's product in time to send by the galleys. ASV, Avvogaria di Comun, Deliberazioni del Maggior Consiglio, Brutus, f. 84 t.

37. Cessi, *Problemi Monetari*, pp. li-liii.

38. ASV, Maggior Consiglio, Deliberazioni, Fronesis, f. 13 (Jan. 7, 1318/9) and *Doc. Finan.*, ser. IV, vol. I, doc. 76.

39. F. Nani-Mocenigo, ed., *Capitolare dei Signore di Notte* (Venice, 1877), no. 180.

40. *Doc. Finan.*, ser. IV, vol. I, doc. 75.

41. This decree of the Quarantia is recorded as cap. xxvii in the Capitolare degli Straordinarii, at the ASV, formerly Miscellanea codici 131, reclassified as Cinque Savii alla Mercanzia, busta 23. It is not published in the *Documenti Finanziarii*, although these *Documenti* (ser. IV, vol. I, doc. 77) include the decree of the Maggior Consiglio of October 27, 1321, which refers to it.

legally specified. The state treasurers and other officials were granted more time.[42]

Moreover, because the merchants importing wares on the state-owned galleys lacked grossi with which to pay freights in order to get their wares unloaded, the Great Council voted on November 24, 1321 that they be permitted to unload as soon as customs officials received adequate security of future payment. This law contained no mention of security being in the form of coin nor of security being 10 percent more than the freight due.[43] In practice, either immediately or some time later, bankers were providing the "security" under arrangements that were, in effect, a form of paying by transfer of bank credits.[44]

The state and other shipowners might be satisfied by payment in bank credits, but crews demanded wages in coin. To meet their demands, the treasurers were ordered to transfer enough of what they had received as security, which totaled more than 24,000 lire, to the Procurators of San Marco in order to receive in return, from the funds in the hands of the Procurators, enough coins so as to pay the crews.[45]

Ordering customs duties paid in good grossi was only a first step towards banning underweight grossi entirely from circulation. Hitherto, inferior grossi had been valued according to their weight. On November 26, 1321 the Great Council declared circulating grossi at values determined by their weight to be illegal. All grossi that had been clipped or sweated ("cum ferro vel aqua vel aliter malo modo") were to be destroyed. Others could circulate but no one could accept them as worth less than 32 piccoli (denari parvi).[46] Since the piccoli which had been coined in substantial amounts since 1318 contained about .058 grams of pure silver and the mint standard for the grossi was unchanged (2.1 grams of fine silver), a full weight grosso contained more than 10 percent more silver than 32 full weight piccoli.[47] In effect the decree allowed for continuing the circulation at par of grossi which by reason of variations in minting or of wear and tear were less than the mint standard but within 10 percent of it. Those below that standard were to be destroyed.

These provisions against circulation of deteriorated grossi stimulated

42. ASV, Maggior Consiglio, Deliberazioni, Fronesis, f. 81 t and 82 t, f. 83 r.

43. Ibid., f. 82 t, and Avvogaria di Comun, Deliberazioni del Maggior Consiglio, Neptunus, f. 166 t.

44. Reinhold C. Mueller, "The Procuratori di San Marco and the Venetian Credit Market, A Study of the Development of Credit and Banking in the Trecento" (Ph.D. diss., Johns Hopkins University, 1969), pp. 215–18.

45. ASV, Avvogaria di Comun, Deliberazioni del Maggior Consiglio, Neptunus, f. 166 t and Maggior Consiglio, Deliberazioni, Fronesis, f. 83, November 24, 1321.

46. *Doc. Finan.*, ser. 4, vol. I, doc. 79.

47. Papadopoli, *Monete*, I, 154–55.

the use of other means of payment. To meet the situation, new restrictions were placed on the use of foreign coins[48] and on drafts by one banker on another.[49] Provisions for the acceptance of pledges instead of grossi were renewed.[50] It seems that there were not enough good grossi to meet the demand for coin and the measures taken in the fall of 1321 were having a deflationary effect.

Change to a more liberal policy began in 1325[51] and was made fully effective in 1328 by the law already mentioned which provided that ducats would be accepted by the government and must be accepted by others as worth 24 grossi. This marked the beginning of the abandonment of the grosso as Venice's basic coin and standard of value. Combined with the banning of all grossi more than 10 percent below mint standard, it made payment in gold coin easier than payment in silver coin.

Three or four years later the abandonment of the grosso as standard was made more complete by the issuance of new silver coins, the *mezzanino* and *soldino*. They were given official values in money of account higher than was justified by the relation of their silver content to the silver content of the grosso. The more important of the new coins, the soldino was made legal tender for 12 piccoli. With the grosso worth 32 piccoli, the soldino was accordingly legal tender for 12/32ds of a grosso, although it contained only 9/32ds as much silver in 1332 and about 8/32ds in 1350–79.[52]

The combined effects of the new official values for the ducat and the new silver coinage was to drive the grossi out of circulation. Already in February 1334 the Senate adjusted some shipping regulations to allow for the fact that grossi were hard to find.[53] In November 1335 the Great Council ordered the state treasurers and the mint masters and other officers into whose hands grossi might come not to use them to pay their

48. Nani, *Capitolare dei Signori di Notte*, no. 204, February 26, 1321/2 in Quarantia.

49. *Doc. Finan.*, ser. IV, vol. I, doc. 80.

50. R. Cessi and P. Sambrin, eds., *Le Deliberazioni del Consiglio dei Rogati* (*Senato*), *serie Mixtorum*, in Monumenti storici pubblicati dalla Deputazione di Storia Patria per le Venezie, n.s., vol. XV, (Venice, 1960), p. 254, no. 92 (June 1322).

51. Cessi, *Problemi Monetari*, p. lv.

52. Papadopoli, *Monete*, I, 158–64, 173–82. The exact date of the inception of the new silver coinage (mezzanini and soldini) is not clear, but circulation of these coins prior to November 1332 is evident from Trevisan sources. Cessi, *Problemi Monetari*, pp. lxi-lxii; and Guido Antonio Zanetti, *Nuova raccolta delle monete e zecche d'Italia*, 5 vols. (Bologna, 1775–89), IV, 187–89. Already in March 1333 their circulation was being pushed also in Crete and other colonies. ASV, Senato Misti, reg. 15, f. 66 t.

53. Transport of coin on "unarmed" ships had been limited to the amounts that ship captains and merchants might take for their personal expenses, the limits being fixed in grossi. In February 1334 these limits were more loosely and broadly defined because, the law states, "grossi male possint habere." ASV, Senato Misti, reg. 16, f. 48 r.

own salaries but to sell them for the profit of the commune and to pay their own salaries with "the money now current, namely ducats or soldini" ("monetis que current hodie, scilicet de ducatis vel duosinis").[54]

The supply of ducats and the new issues of silver relieved the earlier scarcity of coin. By 1338, senatorial decrees referred to money as plentiful, although many counterfeits were still circulating.[55] Grossi were still minted until about 1350 at the old standard, but by that date they were being issued by the mint as worth 48 denari piccoli. Much silver arrived for minting about 1350 but most of it went into new types, into the mezzanini and soldini that began to be issued with the same decree of fineness as had long been traditional for the grossi, .965. The new type of soldini weighed .552 grams, just a trifle more than 1/4th of the old grossi.[56]

What under the conditions existing after 1334 determined the values of the lira a grossi and the lira di grossi relative to each other and to the standards of value in use in other countries? These Venetian moneys of account had been based on the grossi, which were no longer circulating in Venice. The hope of the government seems to have been that the moneys of account would be based on both the gold ducat and the silver soldino simultaneously. For this to be in fact the case, the quantity of silver in the soldino had to be adjusted so that its official value compared to the ducat agreed with the bimetallic ratio determined by the bullion market.

For many years in the middle of the fourteenth century, official values agreed fairly well with intrinsic metallic values. For some decades government bureaus probably paid and received gold ducats and silver soldini both at their official values, which were expressed by rating the ducat as worth 64 soldi di piccoli, as well as 2 soldi di grossi and 52 soldi a grossi. But changes in the relative values in the marketplace of gold and silver could make ducats sell at a premium, as did old-style grossi. An appropriate increase in the amount of fine silver in the soldino might have prevented the ducat from rising above 64 soldi di piccoli when the price of gold bullion went up. But such adjustment of coins to market fluctuations reflecting changes in the bimetallic ratios would have been difficult and

54. ASV, Avvogaria di Comun, Deliberazioni del Maggior Consiglio, Philippicus, f. 7. The significance of this decree in showing that grossi were no longer circulating in Venice at their value as legal tender but could be sold at a premium was well stressed by Gino Luzzatto in his "L'oro e l'argento," reprinted in his *Studi*, p. 269.

55. *Doc. Finan.*, ser. IV, vol. I, doc. 94.

56. Papadopoli, *Monete*, I, 176, 181–82, 187, 196, 216; Antonio Lombardo, ed., *Le Deliberazioni del Consiglio dei XL della Repubblica di Venezia*, vol. II, in Monumenti storici, n.s., vol. XII (Venice, 1958), nos. 348, 365, 385.

may have seemed unnecessary as long as the rise of gold was moderate. In 1331 the ducat was quoted at 70 soldi, and in 1345 again it was almost at 70 soldi; but in the years between it had dipped; and in 1349–50 it was back down to 64 soldi.[57] So long as the fluctuations were within this range, the lira a grossi and the lira di grossi could be thought of as based on both ducat and soldino equally.

A change came in the 1350s. The ducat threatened to go below 64. A new type of soldino was then issued containing less silver than earlier issues.[58] After this decrease in the metallic value of the soldino, the next time the vicissitudes of the bullion flows raised the value of gold relative to silver, the ducat went as high as 74 soldi and in the 1360s it went even higher.[59]

This rise in the market value of the ducat led to a splitting of the lira di grossi. Very soon after 1332, in some accounts a distinction was made between *lire di grossi in monete* and *lire di grossi a oro*.[60] The lira di grossi in monete was based on the soldino and other silver coins such as the piccolo and the mezzanino. The lira di grossi a oro was based on the ducat.

Before this split had occurred, even before the monetary crises of the 1320s, while grossi coins were still fully in circulation, the lira di grossi had become used more and more as a money of account. Its popularity grew while the ducat was worth 24 grossi, either by decision of the market as in many years before 1328, or by law after that year. There was then an easily calculated relationship between this money of account and the coins then in use: 1 lira di grossi = 10 ducats, and 1 soldo di grossi = 1/2 ducat or 12 grossi. On accounts kept in lire di grossi smaller sums were recorded by setting up in the account books a fourth column for "piccoli," as subdivisions of the grosso according to the ratio legally established since 1282: 1 grosso = 32 piccoli. Accordingly, because each lira di grossi was equal to 240 grossi, each lira di grossi was equal to 240 × 32 piccoli, or 7,680 piccoli.

After the monetary reforms of 1328–32 the grosso which was 1/240th

57. Zanetti, *Nuova raccolta delle monete*, IV, 169–76.

58. Ibid.; Papadopoli, *Monete*, I, 173–82.

59. Zanetti, *Nuova raccolta delle monete*, IV, 169–76; *Doc. Finan.*, ser. IV, vol. I, p. lxxxi; Papadopoli, *Monete*, I, 210.

60. The accounts of the estates of Tommaso Querini, kept by the Procuratori di San Marco, Citra, busta 260, before 1341 convert into lire a grossi sums entered originally in lire di piccoli or lire di grossi. Beginning in 1341 all sums are converted into lire di grossi a monete. Only in the 1350s are there signs that sums recorded in lire di grossi a monete were later converted into lire di grossi a oro. The accounts of Jacobelli Gabriel (ASV, Procuratori di San Marco, Misti, busta 67), from 1361 on, clearly convert sums initially recorded in other lire into lire di grossi a oro. I am indebted to Reinhold C. Mueller for indicating to me the usefulness of the records of these particular estates.

of the lira di grossi was no longer the same as the grosso coin. It had become a "ghost," a mere accounting unit, because its value was not that of the coin of the same name. Its value was 1/240th of that of the lira di grossi, dependent on whatever coin determined the value of the lira di grossi.

When the lira di grossi split, the metallic value of the lira di grossi in monete was determined by the metallic content of the soldini and similar silver coins issued after 1332. Since the soldini were worth 12 piccoli, as their name proclaimed, and the lira di grossi equalled 7,680 piccoli, the metallic value of the lira di grossi in monete was that of 640 soldini ($\frac{7680}{12}$).

The metallic value of the lira di grossi a oro was determined by the metallic content of the ducat, of which the lira di grossi a oro was worth 10. In calculations, this lira di grossi a oro, like all other lire, was divided into 240 denari. They were denari grossi, called simply grossi for short, but their metallic value was not that of the coins of the same name. The metallic value of these grossi of the lira di grossi a oro was 1/24th of a gold ducat. Similarly the value of the piccoli of the lira di grossi a oro was not that of the coins called piccoli. Their metallic value was 1/768th of a ducat (24×32).

When the lira di grossi split, and especially when the split widened in the 1360s, it became important whether the salaries, prices, and debts of various kinds that had been recorded in lira di grossi were considered as in monete or a oro. Since the ducat kept on rising until, about a century later, it reached 124 soldi, in the long run it made a great difference whether accounts were kept in lira di grossi in monete or lira di grosso a oro.[61]

In the 1340s, when the ducat ranged between 64 and 70, the distinction may not have seemed vital. After the 1360s, however, the distinction became necessary and the lira di grossi a oro came to be most widely used.[62] In fact the lira di grossi in monete was nothing more than a rather cumbersome multiple of the lira di piccoli, since both were based on the same silver coins, before 1379 primarily on the soldino.[63] A new kind of silver coin was issued in 1379 and given the respected name "grosso,"

61. Papadopoli, *Monete*, vol. I, appendix I, table II.

62. In the accounts of the estate of Jacobelli Gabriel (ASV, Procuratori di San Marco, Misti, busta 67) conversion from "monetis" into lire di grossi a oro was made by deducting "la lazio de superscriptis monetis." The lazio is given as a specified number of soldi per ducat. Reworking the figures reveals that a lazio of 9 soldi meant that the ducat was worth 73 soldi instead of the minimum legal figure of 64. In 1362 the lazio rose to 10 soldi. In the fifteenth century an account in lire di grossi can generally be assumed to be "a oro," as in the account books of Andrea Barbarigo, unless otherwise specified; but Reinhold Mueller informs me that the grain office was ordered to keep accounts in lire di grossi in monete.

63. According to the equations:

1 lire di grossi in monete = 32 lire di piccoli

1 lire di piccoli = 20 soldini

1 lira di grossi in monete = 640 soldini

although no grossi had been minted for twenty-four years. The new issue was distinguished from the earlier issues by a star next to the figure of Christ on the reverse. The new grosso contained only 1.86 grams of fine silver, just four times as much silver as the soldini, also with a star, issued at the same time.[64] Thus the grosso as a coin was assimilated into the series of silver coinages begun in 1331. The grosso of the lira di grossi a oro on the other hand remained purely a denomination of account. Its value compared to the silver grosso coin depended on the exchange rate that the marketplace established between gold ducats and the silver coins. That was expressed in *soldi di piccoli*. If the ducat was valued at less than 96 soldi di piccoli, the grosso a oro was worth less than the new silver grosso coin; if the ducat was valued at more than 96 soldi di piccoli, the grosso a oro was worth more than the grosso coin. The grosso in monete on the other hand was always worth exactly two-thirds of the new grosso coin (with star).[65] This contrast between grossi a oro and grossi in monete emphasizes the split of the old lira di grossi.

A similar split occurred in the lira a grossi, which had once been Venice's most important money of account in spite of the cumbersome fractional values encountered in its use. There were no such cumbersome fractions in the relations between the coins in use and the lira di grossi in monete, and it was mathematically relatively easy to convert lire, soldi, and denari a grossi into lire, soldi, and denari di grossi in monete. The conversions involved multiplying by 26, for the piccolo of which there were 7,680 in a lira di grossi in monete were considered each equal to 26/32ds of the denari of which there were 240 in a lira a grossi. In this respect the lira di grossi in monete took the place of the disappearing lira di grossi manca, which had also been 26 times the lira a grossi. A lira a grossi a oro, however, continued in use in the fifteenth century because the state debt was recorded in that money of account.[66] In such accounts, 1 ducat always equalled 52 soldi a grossi a oro, so that 10 ducats or 1 lira equalled 26 lire a grossi a oro. Thus, multiplying by 26 also served to convert figures from lire a

64. Papadopoli, *Monete*, I, 207–08, 215–16.

65. If the ducat was at 96, as in 1410 and probably earlier, it was then worth not only 24 grossi a oro, as it had been ever since 1330 in money of account, but also 24 of the new style grossi coins. Thus the new coinage of 1379 made possible the same relation between the gold ducat and the silver grossi coin that had prevailed before 1330, when the grosso coin had been heavier.

66. Accounts of estates administered by the Procurators of San Marco leave some doubt concerning the date at which the loan office paid in silver (monete) or in gold (a oro)—see note 62—but after 1385 clearly it added an aggio (lazio) when paying in monete. See Luzzatto, *Il debito pubblico*, pp. 240–41, 250. On the uses of the various lire 1336–40 see also Giulio Mandich's introduction to Armando Sapori, ed., *Il libro Giallo dei Covoni* (Milan, 1970), pp. cviii–cix.

grossi into lire di grossi when both were a oro, that is, when both were based on the gold ducat.

The disappearance of the lire a grossi and the lire di grossi in monete left Venice in the fifteenth century with only two widely used moneys of account, the lira di piccoli and the lira di grossi a oro. The former, based on silver, was used in retail trade and in calculating wages figured by the day. The lira di grossi, now firmly based on gold ducats, was the standard of value used in wholesale trade, banking, and foreign exchange, and in recording and paying the public debt and salaries of high officials. Its use "a oro" climaxed Venice's "return to gold." The sixteenth century was to shatter this gold standard. But that is another story.

Summarizing in the terms used in the title of this essay, we may say that both the lira di piccoli and lira di grossi had already before the fifteenth century experienced changing attachments. Although the lira di piccoli had always been thought of as 240 piccoli, its metallic value had been determined mainly by the grossi during about sixty years in the thirteenth century when no piccoli were minted and was determined in the middle of the fourteenth century more by the soldino than by the piccolo. In this sense the lira di piccoli had formed liaisons with several silver coins. The lira di grossi had been through a more dramatic change, an irrevocable separation. It still carried the name derived from its first attachment, which showed that it had once equaled 240 grossi coins. But Venice's monetary crisis of 1321–32 had divorced it from the grosso coin. By 1400 it was firmly wedded to the ducat. By that wedding it had shifted Venice from a silver standard to the use of a gold standard in large monetary transactions.

4

A Plague Doctor

Carlo M. Cipolla

The Medieval and Renaissance city was afflicted with a problem which was essentially ecological in nature, namely a violent disequilibrium between the density of the population and the prevailing levels of hygiene and public health. The dire result of this disequilibrium was the recurrence of epidemics, mostly of bubonic plague, which at closely spaced intervals wiped out a large portion of the population. Ever since the outbreak of the great pandemic of 1347–51 people recognized the infectious nature of plague, but because they were totally ignorant of the sequence rat→rat's flea→man they overrated the possibility of man to man infection. Thus it was not easy in time of epidemic to find doctors willing to treat plague patients. On the other hand, if the plague were so highly contagious, a doctor visiting a patient—it was argued—would not only easily contract the infection but would also carry it to other people or to patients suffering from other ailments. The solution to this double-edged problem was found with the institution of the community plague doctors. These were physicians or surgeons, especially hired by an infected town or village in time of an epidemic, who were responsible for the treatment of the plague patients only and had to refrain from intercourse with the rest of the population. Their job was not only particularly dangerous but also very unpleasant because the plague doctor was quarantined, so to speak, for the entire period of the epidemic and some time thereafter. Those who applied for such positions were normally either second rate doctors who had not been particularly successful in their practice or young doctors trying to establish themselves. Texts of agreements between town administrations and plague doctors are not difficult to find in the archives and some have been published.[1] Although they inform us about the terms eventually agreed

1. See, for instance: A. Chiappelli, "Medici e chirurghi in Pistoia nel Medioevo," *Bullettino Storico Pistoiese, 10* (1908), 147; L. Guerra-Coppioli, "Capitolati medici dei tempi andati," *Rivista di Storia delle scienze mediche e naturali, 3* (1912), 129 ff.; L. Couybà, *La Peste en Agenais au XVIIe siècle* (Villeneuve sur Lot, 1905), pp. 260 ff.; and P. Delunay, *La Vie médical* (Paris, 1935), pp. 266 ff. .

upon by the parties involved, the cold and detached juridical prose of the notaries hardly reveals the bargaining which always preceded the final settlements. The bargaining was often hard. On May 10, 1630, the town council of Torino considered the conditions requested by one Dr. Maletto to serve as a plague doctor. After some discussion the council instructed its representatives "to deal promptly with Dr. Maletto. They should try to reduce his pretenses and extract the best possible deal for this community but they ought to be careful not to lose the opportunity of hiring Dr. Maletto because it would be difficult to find a substitute at the same salary."[2]

In the Communal Archive at Pavia (Lombardy)[3] there is the original draft of an agreement reached between the community and a plague doctor. The document is of special interest because it shows a series of corrections and additions to the original text that are suggestive of the bargaining that took place.

The document is dated May 6, 1479, and it contains the "conditions agreed upon between the magnificent Community of Pavia and the doctor of medicine Giovanni de Ventura in order to treat the patients suffering from the plague."

The first clause deals with the salary. The community promised to pay to the doctor a monthly salary of 30 florins, which, as we shall see, had to be net of living expenses.

The second clause originally provided that the community would pay the salary two months in advance. This amounted to an interest-free deposit equivalent to two months' salary in favor of the doctor. However, in the bargaining that followed, the clause was modified, and the town's representatives managed to cut the advance to one month's salary.

Obviously the doctor had some doubts about the solvency of the community, and he was not satisfied with the advance payment. He wanted more guarantees, and the third clause of the contract stipulates that the community had to give the doctor an adequate pledge for the payment of his salary. On this point there seems to have been no further discussion.

A fourth clause also raised no difficulties. It was common practice in the hiring of an immigrant community doctor, whether plague doctor or not, that the community would provide him with a convenient house free of charge or at a reduced rent. In this particular case, the community of Pavia promised to provide Dr. Ventura with "an adequate house in an

2. Archivio Civico, Torino, *Ordinati*, busta 179.
3. Archivio Civico, Pavia, busta 443.

adequate location," completely furnished, at the community's expense. The clause suggests that Dr. Ventura had not been living in Pavia.

Disagreement must have flared up again on the fifth clause. Originally it had been stipulated that the city administration would continue to pay the doctor his salary for two months after the termination of his employment. Later on, however, the town's representatives backed out, and in the subsequent bargaining, as in the matter of the advance, they managed to reduce the extra pay to one month's salary.

In both clause two and clause five, the final text is less favorable to Giovanni Ventura than the original draft. Were the administrators beginning to feel some doubts about the quality of the doctor's services? Or, having brought the doctor to the verge of acceptance, did they feel that toughness might extract from him an even better deal? We shall never know, but the modifications to the original text of clauses six and seven seem to favor the first hypothesis. The sixth clause originally specified the duties of the doctor, emphasizing the limits of his obligation. It stipulated that "the said master Giovanni shall not be bound nor held under obligation except only in attending the plague patients." Later on, however, the town's representatives felt that they needed a better guarantee of a satisfactory performance and pressed for an addition which specified the doctor's duties in more positive terms: "namely, the doctor must treat all patients and visit infected places as it shall be found to be necessary." With the seventh clause the town's administration committed itself to give a free grant of Pavian citizenship to the doctor in appreciation for his good services. But again, at the time of the final draft, it was felt necessary to qualify the original text by the conditioning clause "according to how he shall behave himself."

What kind of man was Master Giovanni Ventura? We have no information on him and all we can do is to speculate on the limited basis of the agreement he made with the town of Pavia during a time of a social tragedy. He was ready to risk his life for some 30 florins a month, and it is doubtful whether he assumed this risk for purely humanitarian reasons. He was obviously anxious to obtain the citizenship of Pavia. One is tempted to think of him as an uprooted adventurer. But I doubt that that was the case. More likely he was an obscure doctor from the countryside, and the fact that he was normally addressed as "master" clearly shows that he was of humble social standing. There were in the villages young men who, thanks to scholarships or to the economic sacrifices of their parents or to both, managed to obtain a university degree. But it was not easy for them to practice in the cities because the city doctors did not welcome competition, and they therefore resisted the immigration of more doctors. On the other hand, as the memoirs of Jerome Cardano testify, toward the end of the fifteenth century a physician did not fare well in the countryside where peasants often had recourse to barbers and quacks. The dream of a young country doctor was to be admitted to the city. Perhaps Dr. Ventura was such a one, and when the plague hit the city, he played his version of Russian roulette: if all went well, he would have obtained the citizenship of Pavia, thus establishing there both his residence and practice.

Did Dr. Ventura have a family? In all likelihood he had neither wife nor children; otherwise their presence would have been mentioned in the clause referring to the house that the community had to provide for him. Yet Dr. Ventura must have had relatives in mind when he made the stipulations in the agreement. The chances of survival of a plague doctor during an epidemic were not high, and in clause eight, with obvious reference to the advance payment granted by clause two, Dr. Ventura obtained the promise that "in the event—may God forbid it—that the said Master Giovanni should die in the exercise of these duties, that then and in that case his heirs should not be required to make restitution of any part of his salary that might remain unearned." Was he thinking of his parents?

The institution of the community doctor in the Italian cities dated back to at least the end of the twelfth century. The idea behind the institution was to make available free medical treatment and care for the poor. The community plague doctor was but a special kind of community doctor and clause nine is similar to the analogous clauses that one finds in all agreements relating to the hiring of community doctors: "the said Master Giovanni shall not be able to ask a fee from anyone, unless the plague victim himself or his relatives shall freely offer it."

A plague epidemic was not only a human tragedy for a city; it was also an economic disaster. All too often, enormously swollen expenditures on public health measures were accompanied by drastic diminution of revenues, and all this meant bankruptcy for the frail public finances. Reading the agreement, one has the impression that Master Giovanni was more worried about the solvency of the city than about his chances of survival. With clause two he had obtained an advance payment. With clause three he had obtained from the city a special pledge to guarantee his salary. With clause ten he obtained that "whenever and however it shall come about—God forbid that it should—that because of a plague of this kind the city may be brought so low that Master Giovanni cannot have his wage nor the things necessary to his existence, that then and in that case Master Giovanni may be released from his obligation without any penalty."

By the end of the fifteenth century the gulf between physicians and barber-surgeons was widening in Italy; the physicians were more and more regarded as upper class while the barber-surgeons were increasingly considered part of the lower orders. By the end of the sixteenth century a physician was no longer addressed as "master"; that title being normally reserved to the barber-surgeons. In 1479, things had not yet gone so far, although even then it would have been unusual for a high-ranking, distinguished physician to be addressed with the title of "master." Dr. Ventura was obviously neither distinguished nor high-ranking. However, he was a physician and not a barber-surgeon, because clause eleven stipulates that "the Community is under obligation to maintain a barber who should be at least adequate and capable." The reason for the clause is obvious: a main task in the treatment of plague patients was lancing their suppurating bubos and the operation was normally performed by a barber-surgeon and not by a physician.

A city infected with plague was quarantined by all other places; trade and communications were halted, victuals became scarce and difficult and expensive to obtain. Many of those who were spared by the plague could hardly escape starvation. Dr. Ventura protected himself against these unpleasant events with clause twelve, which stipulates that "the Community has and is under the obligation to provide said Master Giovanni with all and everything which is necessary for his life, paying and exbursing the money therefore." Master Bernardino di Francesco Rinaldi obtained a similar clause when he was hired as plague doctor by the city of Volterra in 1527.[4]

With clause four Dr. Ventura had already secured for himself free housing facilities: clause eleven took care of all other living expenditures. Thus the 30 florins of the monthly salary could be left untouched and put aside. When one's life is at stake, it is hard to decide whether pecuniary compensation is adequate or not. As we shall see below, however, by the standards of the time, the financial terms extracted by Dr. Ventura were reasonably adequate. But he kept worrying about the solvency of the community. He had already obtained the promise of an advance payment (clause two). He wanted a special pledge to guarantee his salary (clause

4. Guerra-Coppioli, "Capitolati medici," p. 135.

three). He had made certain that in case of insolvency he would be released of his obligation (clause ten). But these guarantees were seemingly not enough to set his mind at rest. In a final assault on the problem he extracted clause thirteen, which stipulates that "however the community would not observe the previously agreed conditions, either partially or totally, then and in that case it would be possible to said Master Giovanni to be totally free from any engagement, notwithstanding the previous clauses or others to be made." Clause thirteen practically repeats what was already established by clause ten. What the town's administrators thought of this obsession of Dr. Ventura and of his being more concerned with the possible insolvency of the Community than with the probability of his catching the plague we shall never know. We know, though, that after they had accepted clause thirteen and had recognized the doctor's right to leave the job under the aforesaid conditions, the administrators pressed to have this addition inserted: "that the doctor should notify the community at least ten days in advance so that the Community would be in the condition to provide (for a substitute)."

While Giovanni could not take his mind off the community's possible insolvency, the town's administrators kept worrying about the kind of service that the doctor would provide to the patients. The minds of the two parties were following different logics and as the doctor persistently returned to his own point, the administrators felt that they had to reiterate their own. They had already managed to add to clause six the condition that "the doctor must treat all patients and visit infected places as it shall be found to be necessary." They had also succeeded in emphasizing that the grant of citizenship would be dependent on "how shall he behave himself" (addition to clause seven). But they were still uneasy. They therefore requested the insertion of clause fourteen, which stipulates that "said Master Giovanni would have and should be obliged to do his best and visit the plague patients, twice, or three times or more times per day, as it will be found to be necessary."

The town administrators were understandably concerned with the capacity of the doctor to resist the assault of the infection and to deliver his services. This concern was not motivated by pure humanitarianism. Clause fifteen stipulates that "in the case—may God forbid it—that the said Master Giovanni would fall ill, and could not perform his office, that then and in such case he should receive a salary only for the time of effective service."

The last clause stipulated that "said Master Giovanni will not be allowed to move around the city in order to treat patients unless accompanied by a man especially designated by the Community." The explanation offered is that Dr. Ventura when accompanied by the deputy would be "identified as the doctor appointed to that office," but the real reason behind the clause was to ensure that the doctor would not intermingle with other people. The deputy's function was to monitor Giovanni's movements. In Prato, in December 1527, the community made an inquiry on the behavior of the local plague doctor Stefano Mezzettino. It was noticed that, according to the rules, "when the community plague doctors move around they always have to be accompanied by a custodian especially appointed, but said Master Stefano went to treat a patient in Pinzidemoli and went there alone, without the custodian, with great danger for all concerned." He was reprimanded and fined.[5] A plague doctor was regarded as a contact and all contacts had to live in isolation.

From the remarks I have made on some of the clauses, it will be apparent that the agreement made between Dr. Ventura and the city of Pavia was not dissimilar from analogous agreements made in other cities. One has, indeed, the distinct impression that by the last quarter of the fifteenth century a standard formula had evolved. This formula was adopted, with minor variations, in places as different as Turin in Piedmont, Pavia in Lombardy, and Volterra and Prato in Tuscany. The pecuniary reward, however, varied considerably from place to place, largely depending on the quality and prestige of the doctor, the availability of substitutes, the severity of the epidemic, and the urgency of the town's needs. Dr. Ventura, we have seen, was granted 30 florins per month, the free use of a house, and his living expenses.

The florins mentioned in the contract were units of account. Thirty such florins corresponded to 11 1/2 gold florins and therefore to approximately 40 grams of pure gold. What this meant in terms of purchasing power is difficult to say because the price structure of those days was totally different from the price structure of today. Books of medicine were then valued in Lombardy between 5 and 13 florins each, with many having the value of 6.5 florins.[6] Thus the 30 florins that Dr. Ventura received each month hardly bought five books of medicine. But manuscripts cannot be compared with the printed books of today, and few doctors owned more than some dozen books. Compared to other salaries, the salary of Dr. Ventura was not at all bad. A skilled worker, if he managed

5. Archivio di Stato, Prato, *Fondo Comunale* 4042, c. 14 v (December 13, 1527).

6. T. Gasparini Leporace, "Due biblioteche mediche del Quattrocento," *La Bibliofilia, 52* (1950), 205–20. In this work values are quoted in gold ducats. In 1479, a gold ducat was equivalent to 83 shillings while a florin of account corresponded to 32 shillings.

to be employed 200 days a year—which was virtually impossible—hardly made 60 florins in a year. The accountant of the community made 84 florins a year. The mayor of the city made 540 florins. At the university there were two or three famous professors who earned more than 1,000 florins per year, but 75 percent of the lecturers earned less than 200 florins per year.[7]

A contemporary living in a developed country may think that 40 grams of gold per month do not represent an exceptionally attractive salary. But in fifteenth century Europe gold was a scarcer commodity. Life was often brutish and short, and death was a more familiar event. Our story proves that a monthly salary of 40 grams of gold plus living expenses was high enough to attract a doctor to a job which bordered on suicide.

7. On all that precedes see: D. Zanetti, "A la Université de Pavie au XVe siècle," *Annales: économies, sociétés, civilisations* (1962) p. 432.

5

The Genoese Notaries of 1382: The Anatomy of an Urban Occupational Group

Benjamin Z. Kedar

On an autumn day in the year 1382, the officials of the Genoese Guild of Notaries presided over a remarkable drawing of lots. The name of each son of a notary was written on a separate slip. The names of the legitimate sons of living notaries were then deposited in one bag, while those of the sons of deceased notaries, as well as those of the illegitimate sons of living notaries, were put in another. Subsequently, the slips from the first bag were drawn by lot one by one, then those from the second bag, and the names were registered in the order of the draw. The resulting list of 481 sons of notaries was to determine the order of accession to fill future vacancies in the Guild of Notaries. Henceforth, so it would seem, membership in the guild was to be the exclusive prerogative of members' sons.[1]

The restrictionist policy which prompted the preparation of this list did not carry the day. In the coming decades, a large number of notaries whose names do not figure in the list practiced their craft in Genoa. The laws of 1403, enacted under the stern rule of Genoa's French governor, Boucicaut, expressly subjected admission to the Guild of Notaries to the regulation of the commune, and documents of subsequent years testify that Genoa's rulers created new guild members at their will.[2] But while

1. For the text describing the procedure of the draw and for the resultant list of notaries' sons, see Giovanna Balbi, "Sul collegio notarile genovese del 1382," in *Miscellanea di storia ligure in onore di Giorgio Falco* (Milan, 1962), pp. 286–98. For a photocopy of the first page of the text see D. Puncuh, "Il notaio nella vita politica economico-sociale del suo tempo," *Atti della Società Ligure di Storia Patria* (hereafter cited as *ASLSP*), *78* (1964), 163. On the purpose of the draw see D. Puncuh, "Gli statuti del collegio dei notai genovesi nel secolo XV," in *Miscellanea di storia ligure in memoria di Giorgio Falco* (Genoa, 1966), pp. 271–72; G. Costamagna, *Il notaio a Genova tra prestigio e potere* (Rome, 1970), p. 162.

2. For the first point, see, for example, the names of the notaries in the 1396 list, in E. Jarry, *Les origines de la domination française à Gênes, 1392–1402* (Paris, 1896), pp. 496–501; for the two latter see Puncuh, "Gli statuti," pp. 273–74 and n. 19. For the parallel creation of notaries by the Genoese counts-palatine see Gabriella Airaldi, *Studi e documenti su Genova e l'Oltremare* (Bordighera, 1974), chap. 4.

the list of 1382 may reflect merely an episode in the constitutional history of the guild, it constitutes a promising point of departure for the study of the demographic and social characteristics of the Genoese notaries of the time.

As the list specifies not only the names of each son of a notary but also that of the father, it allows for the construction of a list of the notaries whose sons figure on the original list. Of these there are 232: 152 were living in 1382 and 80 were dead. The 152 living notaries should not be considered as the full roster of the Guild of Notaries on that date, however. Not all notaries necessarily had sons: some might have been unmarried, others childless, and some might have had only daughters. Still others might have had grown-up sons who either had already acceded to the notariate or did not aspire to it. At any rate, three of the fifteen guild officials who in 1382 presided over the drawing of lots do not appear as fathers on the list:[3] they evidently fit into one of the above categories. Also absent from the list are sixteen Genoese notaries who are known, from other documents, to have lived in 1382.[4] Thus it is evident that there were at least 171 notaries in Genoa at that time. It may not be farfetched to assume that the total number stood at about 200. This is not a shot in the dark: back in 1258, and again in 1267, and in 1288, there were 200 notaries in Genoa, and in 1399 the Genoese Council of Elders confirmed a resolution of the Guild of Notaries which stipulated that the guild's membership was not to exceed that number.[5]

In other words, the evidence points to the conclusion that about the same number of notaries served Genoa in the days of her demographic and commercial apogee in the late thirteenth century, as did during the demographic shrinkage and commercial depression in the latter part of

3. These are Germanus de Castilliono, Anthonius de Pestina, and Anthonius de Multedo de Monelia.

4. The names of the following fourteen notaries appear in the register of the deliberations of the doge and the Council of Elders which took place during the year 1382: Anthonius de Fontanegio f. Johanis, Anthonius de Fontanegio Nicolai, Anthonius Gallus, Anthonius Panizarius, Constantinus de Palacio, Johannes Bayrus, Martinus de Tholomeo, Maximus de Judicibus de Rappallo, Nicolaus Acornerius, Nicolaus de Paverio, Nicolaus de Tellia, Raffael de Casanova, Raffael de Goasco, Theramus Pich(?). Archivio di Stato, Genoa (hereafter cited as ASG), *Diversorum Registri, No. 497 (1382)*, ff. 10^{v}, 20^{v}, 22^{r}, 27^{v}, 30^{r}, 37^{v}, 42^{r}, 105^{v}, 149^{v}. The notaries Ilarius Carpenetus and Theramus de Maiollo de Rappalo appear in a notarial act as giving testimony in March 1382: Léone Liagre-de Sturler, *Les relations commerciales entre Gênes, la Belgique et l'Outremont d'après lès archives notariales génoises, 1320–1400* (Brussels and Rome, 1969), doc. 394, pp. 526–29.

5. Costamagna, *Il notaio a Genova*, pp. 153, 168–69; for the datum for 1288, see D. Herlihy, *Pisa in the Early Renaissance: A Study of Urban Growth* (New Haven, 1958), p. 10, n. 23. On the other hand, the guild statutes of 1462—and possibly before them the lost laws of 1403—put the maximum number of guild members at 150: Puncuh, "Gli statuti," pp. 300–01; also 273–75. In 1698, the number was reduced to 140: Costamagna, *Il notaio a Genova*, p. 199.

the fourteenth century. The size of Genoa's overall population throughout this period remains a matter of conjecture; but if one posits 100,000 inhabitants for the 1290s, and 60,000 for the 1380s,[6] it follows that, since the absolute number of notaries remained constant, the ratio of notaries to inhabitants rose from 1:500 to 1:300. This does not necessarily imply that the Genoese of the depression era were more likely to have recourse to the services of notaries. Quite the contrary, one may assume that in the later Trecento many Genoese were capable of writing their own documents and that private demand for notarial assistance therefore decreased. On the other hand, the burgeoning communal bureaucracy of the latter part of the fourteenth century required the services of an ever-growing number of notaries. In 1376, for instance, the one office of the Ambasciata Anglie—a customs agency probably established to raise the money needed to cover the expenses of a mission to England—employed three notaries simultaneously.[7] In about 1382, perhaps fifty notaries were employed by the commune. In addition, notaries were sent to the castles situated in the countryside of Genoa; they did duty as scribes of the commanders of the Genoese galley fleets; they accompanied the city's ambassadors on their missions abroad; and they served on the staff of the *compere*, the important creditor organizations of Genoa, of which no less than twenty were established between the years 1333 and 1407.[8] At the same

6. For an estimate that Genoa may have reached the 100,000 mark about 1300, see, for example, R. S. Lopez, "Market Expansion: The Case of Genoa," *Journal of Economic History*, *24* (1964), 448. Data on the Genoese taxes on cereals collected by J. Day (*Les douanes de Gênes, 1376–1377* [Paris, 1963], I, table IV, xxviii) suggest that in 1382 the population of Genoa was only about 60 percent of what it had been in 1341.

7. These are Nicolaus de Ricobono, Gabriel Judex, and Symon de Ingibertis: Day, *Les douanes de Gênes*, I, 309. The last two appear among the 152 living notaries of the 1382 list of notaries' sons, while the first is among the 80 deceased by that date. Gabriel Judex was a member of the Council of Elders in 1386 and of the General Councils of 1395 and 1396. In 1384, 1385, and 1395 he farmed various income-sources of the commune, while in 1392 he served as "colector pro comune Janue drictus Catalanorum": *Liber Iurium Reipublicae Genuensis*, vol. II (= *Monumenta Historiae Patriae*, vol. IX), col. 1054d; Jarry, *Les origines*, pp. 436, 499; ASG, San Giorgio, *Securit. Avall. comper. novorum S. Pauli*, a. 1384, f. 47^{v}, 54^{r}; a. 1385, f. 16^{r}, 42^{v}; Archivio Segreto, no. 3021 (= *Diversorum Comunis Janue*, filza 1), no. 120; Rosa Callura Cecchetti et al., *Genova e Spagna nel XIV secolo. IL "Drictus Catalanorum", 1386, 1392–*93 (Genoa, 1970), pp. 101, 394–95, and passim. On his involvement in commerce see below. Symon de Ingibertis was a member of the 1382 General Council, and in 1392 he seems to have served in the Genoese customs office that dealt with the Catalans: ASG, *Div. Reg. 497* (*1382*), f. 7^{v}; Rosa Callura Cecchetti et al., *Genova*, p. 101.

8. In 1411, the commune employed sixty-six notaries, in 1419 fifty-three: Puncuh, "Gli statuti," p. 272, n. 15. On notaries accompanying Genoa's ambassadors see F. Gabotto, "Come viaggiavano gli ambasciatori genovesi nel secolo XIV," *Giornale storico e letteraric della Liguria*, *9* (1908), 18, 29; also, ASG, *Antico Comune*, *Magistrorum rationalium*, nos. 119 (the notary Johannes de Dominico, on a mission of 1378) and 120 (Dominicus de Campis, 1386). For the 1344 injunction that required a fleet commander to employ a scribe "qui sit de collegio notariorum Janue" see L. Sauli, ed., *Imposicio officii Gazarie*, in *Monumenta Historiae Patriae*, vol. II (Turin, 1838), col. 337.

Table 5.1

Notaries of Various Italian Cities, 13th–15th Century

Genoa	1258–88	200
	1399	200
	1462	150
Milan	1288	1,500[a]
Florence	1338	600[a]
Bologna	1294	ca. 2,000
Padua	1254	86
	1294	ca. 500
	ca. 1320	ca. 600
Perugia	1310	431
	1343	289
Piacenza	1351	ca. 400
	1420	186
Pisa	1293	232
Spoleto	1318	213
Treviso	1327	487
Roman Curia[b]	1483	72
	1506	101

Sources: G. Barraclough, *Public Notaries and the Papal Curia: A Calendar and a Study of a "Formularium Notariorum Curie" from the Early Years of the Fourteenth Century* (London, 1934), p. 25 and n. 4; D. Herlihy, *Pisa in the Early Renaissance: A Study of Urban Growth* (New Haven, 1958), p. 10 and n. 23; J. K. Hyde, *Padua in the Age of Dante* (New York, 1966), pp. 49, 162; C. Guttinger, "Le collège des notaires de Spolète aus XIV[éme] siècle," *Mélanges d'archéologie et d'histoire de de l'Ecole française de Rome, 79* (1967), 681; R. S. Lopez and I. W. Raymond, *Medieval Trade in the Mediterranean World: Illustrative Documents* (New York and London, 1955), pp. 65, 72; C. Pecorella, *Statuti notarili piacentini del XIV secolo* (Milan, 1971), pp. 8, 33–35.

[a] Data from narrative sources.

[b] Numbers of notaries allowed to practice at the seat of the curia.

time, at least two notaries were employed by the archbishop of Genoa.[9] In short, one may assume that perhaps one half of Genoa's 200 notaries were, by the latter part of the fourteenth century, in the service of an organization of some kind.[10]

How does the number of Genoese notaries compare with the number in

9. These are Felixius de Garibaldo and Antonius Folieta: Thomas Rymer, *Foedera*, vol. III, pt. 2, 2d ed. (London, 1830), pp. 907, 923, 1009; D. Cambiaso, "Sinodi genovesi antichi," *ASLSP, 68* (1939), 87–88, 90–91. Only the first-named notary appears in the list of 1382. Priest-notaries, so common in contemporary Venice, have not been encountered in Genoa.

10. By 1324, a similar situation already prevailed in Pisa: Herlihy, *Pisa*, p. 20. Around 1350, Pisa engaged about 150 notaries: O. Banti, "Ricerche sul notariato a Pisa tra il secolo XIII e il secolo XIV. Note in margine al *Breve Collegii Notariorum* (1305)," *Bolletino Storico Pisano, 33–35* (1964–66), 173. The commune of Padua, which in 1276 had employed 91 notaries, by 1362 engaged 106: J. K. Hyde, *Padua in the Age of Dante* (New York, 1966), p. 162.

other Italian cities? Table 5.1 reveals that it was surprisingly small. Not only Milan, Florence, Bologna, and Padua far surpassed Genoa in this respect, but even small inland cities like Treviso and Spoleto had more notaries. The relative numerical smallness of the Genoese notariate becomes even more pronounced when one takes into account that Genoa's 200 notaries had to serve not only the city but its overseas colonies as well. A law of 1304 expressly provided that the scribes of the Genoese courts at Pera and Caffa, as well as those of the courts in Cyprus, must be members of the Genoese Guild of Notaries.[11] In fact, of the 171 Genoese notaries who are known to have lived in 1382, at least 11 had practiced their profession overseas at one time in their careers,[12] while 11 more had been active abroad in other capacities.[13]

11. V. Promis, ed., "Statuti della colonia genovese di Pera," *Miscellanea di storia italiana, 11* (1870), 777. According to an enactment of 1316, the scribe of the Caffa consulate must be a Genoese notary: *Imposicio officii Gazarie*, col. 397. For the 1363 enactments concerning the Genoese notaries at Caffa and Pera, see col. 362.

12. Ambroxius de Flachono, Anthonius de Castilliono, and Anthonius de Clavaro served as scribes of the court of Pera: L. T. Belgrano, "Prima serie di documenti riguardanti la colonia di Pera," *ASLSP, 13* (1877), 152, 157, 173. Anthonius de Credentia in 1374 drew up in Famagusta the peace treaty with Cyprus: *Liber Iurium Reipublicae Genuensis*, vol. II, col. 814. Bartholomeus Villanucius, who stayed in 1360 in Famagusta, served in the 1380s and the 1390s as dragoman of the commune of Pera: A. Lombardo, ed., *Nicola de Boateriis, notaio in Famagosta e Venezia, 1355–1365* (Venice, 1968), doc. 37, pp. 42–43; Belgrano, "Prima serie," pp. 139, 140, 146, 151, 157. In 1387 Hector de Allineriis drew up a convention at Pera; in 1390 he negotiated a treaty with Aragon: Belgrano, "Prima serie," p. 146; Maria Teresa Ferrer i Mallol, "La pace del 1390 tra la Corona d'Aragona e la Repubblica di Genova," in *Miscellanea di storia ligure in memoria di Giorgio Falco* (Genoa, 1966), p. 186. Jacobus de Monelia was elected in 1382 as *scriba curie Syi*: P. P. Argenti, *The Occupation of Chios by the Genoese and their Administration of the Island, 1346–1566* (Cambridge, 1958), II, 386. Johannes de Bardi served in 1383 as notary and chancellor of the commandor of the Genoese fleet in Cyprus and the eastern Mediterranean: Liagre-de Sturler, *Les relations commerciales*, p. 549; Stefania Mangiante, "Un consiglio di guerra dei Genovesi a Cipro nel 1383," *ASLSP, 77* (1963), 256. Jullianus Panizarius acted in 1383 as notary in Caffa: C. Desimoni, "Trattato dei Genovesi col Chan dei Tartari nel 1380–81 scritto in lingua volgare," *Archivio storico italiano*, ser. 4, *20* (1887), 161. On the notarial acts which Nicolaus de Bellignano drew up in Caffa in 1381–82 see G. G. Musso, "Gli Orientali nei notai genovesi di Caffa," *Archivi e cultura, 7* (1973), 97–110; Gabriella Airaldi, *Studi e documenti*, Chap. 1. Raffael de Casanova was probably active at Chios in 1359: D. Gioffrè, "Atti rogati in Chio nella seconda metà del XIV secolo," *Bulletin de l'Institut belge de Rome, 34* (1962), 320.

13. Badasal Vegius is mentioned in 1371 as "emptor introytus pondis et ponderis de Caffa": H. Sieveking, *Genueser Finanzwesen mit besonderer Berücksichtigung der Casa di S. Giorgio* (Freiburg im Breisgau, 1898), I, 201. The lawyer and notary Bartholomaeus de Jacopo was in 1362 a member of the Council of Elders, and in 1365 consul of Caffa; in 1369 he appeared as witness to a Genoese-Venetian alliance against Egypt; in 1380 he was elected to the consulate of Caffa and as *emendator cabellarum*, and in 1386–87 he served as one of the *sapientes* of the commune: Argenti, *The Occupation of Chios*, II, 57; Giorgio Stella, *Annales Genuenses*, ed. Giovanna Petti Balbi, in *R.I.S., new series*, vol. XVII, part 2 (Bologna, 1975), p. 159. 31–32; G. Golubovich, *Biblioteca bio-bibliografica della Terra Santa e dell'Oriente francescano*, II (Quarracchi, 1913), p. 198; ASG, *Div. Reg., No. 496 (1380)*, f. 38^v, 157^r; Liagre-de Sturler, *Les relations commerciales*, doc. 498, p. 651. For additional details see G. Pistarino, "Bartolomeo di Jacopo," in *Dizionario biografico degli italiani*, vol. VI

At least one contemporary had been aware that the Genoese notariate was numerically small. This was the Florentine notary ser Lapo Mazzei who, in a letter of 1401, remarked that there were not as many lawyers and notaries in Genoa and in Venice as there were in Perugia, Bologna, Florence, and elsewhere. Mazzei attributed this difference to the limited knowledge of law in Genoa and in Venice.[14] His assessment might not have been too far from the truth. If one remembers that Pisa, too, had only a relatively small number of notaries, one may hypothesize that as overseas commerce intensified in Venice, Genoa, and Pisa in an age in which legal and notarial services had not yet become widespread, commercial practice evolved in these cities relatively independent of lawyers and notaries. Therefore, even when professional services became easily available, the citizens of these major centers, who had become accustomed to conducting their affairs with comparatively limited reliance on professionals, tended to resort to lawyers and notaries less readily than the inhabitants of cities where the intensification of urban and commercial life more or less coincided with the diffusion of Roman law and the spread of the notariate. Of course, it is possible that the reasons for the disparity in the number of notaries should be sought in areas to which Mazzei did not allude. Thus, it is possible that literacy was more widespread in Genoa and in Venice, and therefore laymen were capable of filling governmental posts elsewhere manned by notaries. Or perhaps the administration of these cities was more economically structured and thus necessitated less notarial services. Again, the notarial guilds of the various cities might have differed in their exclusiveness. At any rate, the size of the Guild of Notaries may prove to constitute an important variable in the comparative study of administrative and cultural developments of the Italian city-states. For instance, as

---

(Rome, 1964), pp. 727–28. Dominicus de Cornilia appointed proctors in Famagusta on August 19, 1383: ASG, *Notari, N. 381* (Giovanni Bardi, 1382–85), f. 158ʳ. Johannes de Alegro and Johannes de Bozolo were at Pera in 1382 and 1387 respectively: Belgrano, "Prima serie," pp. 139, 146. In 1382 Nicolaus de Paverio was elected to serve as *massarius Famaguste:* ASG, *Div. Reg., No. 497* (*1382*), f. 105ᵛ. Paulus Savina witnessed an act at Chios in 1381, and was a member of the General Councils of 1395 and 1396: Liagre-de Sturler, *Les relations commerciales*, docs. 381, 388, pp. 508, 518. On Bartholomaeus Pindeben de Vernacia, Janonus de Bosco, Leonardus de Montaldo, and Raffael de Reza, see notes 21, 29, 35, 43, 44 below.

14. " . . . e' sono terre per lo mondo che si passano d'ogni mandato e d'ogni general procura, perché non sanno in quelle parti molta legge: e questo è vero, e hollo provato a Genova e Vinegia, che non v'ha molti giudici o notai. Altrove, come s'è a Perugia, a Bologna e a Firenze, e altrove, chi ha a pagare, non pagherebbe mai se le carte de'mandati o delle procure non fossono fondate in sul punto della ragione." *Lettere di un notaro a un mercante del secolo XIV*, ed. C. Guasti (Florence, 1880), II, 224, quoted in C. Bec, *Les marchands écrivains: Affaires et humanisme a Florence, 1375–1434* (Paris and The Hague, 1967), p. 220, n. 481.

notaries played a major role in the spread of early humanism, one may adduce the numerical smallness of the Genoese notariate as one of the reasons why Genoa lagged in the adoption of humanist culture.

Like those in Bologna and in Padua (but unlike those in Florence), Genoa's notaries and lawyers belonged to two distinct guilds.[15] Both guilds—together with the guild of the physicians and the guild of the grammar teachers—enjoyed a higher status than the other guilds of the city: the statutes of the early fifteenth century subjected these four guilds to the direct supervision of the communal syndics and not to that of the regular supervisors of guilds.[16] Nevertheless, the differences between lawyers and notaries were considerable. The lawyers, who received their schooling at a university, were professionally more highly esteemed than the notaries, who normally apprenticed under a practicing notary.[17] Most lawyers belonged to the higher echelons of Genoese society: of the twelve Genoese who received their law degrees at Bologna between 1378 and 1405, seven were nobles and two belonged to the *cappellazzi* families which gave to Genoa many of her commoner doges. In 1390, fifteen of the twenty-four members of the lawyers' guild bore old and noble names like di Negro, Fieschi, d'Oria, and Spinola, while one belonged to a family of cappellazzi.[18] But whereas the Guild of Lawyers served as a meeting ground for nobles, cappellazzi, and ordinary commoners, the Guild of Notaries was an all-commoner association.[19] Moreover, many of the notaries were newcomers to the city: of the 171 notaries of 1382, 94 bear toponymic surnames of the *de N.* type, which points to a non-Genoese origin.[20] On the other hand, only one of the 171 is a cappellazzo: he is Leonardo Montaldo, the fleet

15. On the two systems of organizing the legal profession, see Hyde, *Padua*, p. 122.

16. *Leges Genuenses*, in *Monumenta Historiae Patriae* (Turin, 1901), vol. XVIII, col. 724–25; cf. Costamagna, *Il notaio a Genova*, p. 169.

17. On the professional role of the Genoese lawyers in communal affairs, see B. Z. Kedar, *Merchants in Crisis: Genoese and Venetian Men of Affairs and the Fourteenth-Century Depression* (New Haven and London, 1976), pp. 70–72. On the differences between lawyers and notaries in Florence see L. Martines, *Lawyers and Statecraft in Renaissance Florence* (Princeton, 1968), pp. 34–35, 55–56, 400.

18. A. Sorbelli, ed., *Il'Liber Secretus Iuris Caesarei' dell'Università di Bologna*, vol. I, *1378–1420*, (Bologna, 1938), pp. 2, 4, 6, 15, 17, 22, 31, 65, 92, 144, 152, 165; L. Isnardi, *Storia della Università di Genova* (Genoa, 1861–67), I, 312.

19. For a similar situation in Padua, see Hyde, *Padua*, p. 158.

20. On the evidential value of surnames of this type see R. W. Emery. "The Use of the Surname in the Study of Medieval Economic History," *Medievalia et humanistica 7* (1952), 43–50; R. S. Lopez, "Concerning Surnames and Places of Origin," ibid., *8* (1954), 6–16; R. W. Emery, "A Further Note on Medieval Surnames," ibid., *9* (1955), 104–06; B. Z. Kedar, "Toponymic Surnames as Evidence of Origin: Some Medieval Views," *Viator*, *4* (1973), 123–29. In Florence, "65 percent of all notaries who held communal office between 1343 and 1382 came from families recently migrated to the city." M. B. Becker, "Florentine Popular Government (1343–1348)," *Proceedings of the American Philosophical Society 106* (1962), 370, n. 53.

commander and lawyer who was to become Genoa's doge one year later.[21] Montaldo was undoubtedly a member of the Guild of Notaries—four of his sons appear on the 1382 list of notaries' sons, and when he died of the plague on June 6, 1384, one hundred taper-bearing notaries surrounded his bier.[22] And yet Montaldo had been merely a nominal member of the guild. Genoa's chronicler of that age, Giorgio Stella—a notary and a notary's son, who figures together with his three brothers on the 1382 list—expressly relates that Montaldo had never practiced the notarial art, and hints that he joined the guild only to enable him to represent the artisan guilds of the city on a crucially important committee.[23] Thus, the one member of prominent origins who entered the Guild of Notaries did so with the objective of furthering his political career.

Leonardo Montaldo is titled in the 1382 list as *iurisperitus et notarius*, lawyer and notary. He is not the only member of the guild to be styled that way: Bartolomeo di Jacopo also has this title, while Master Manuele *de Lagneto* appears in the list as *notarius et phisicus*. Evidently the Genoese notaries allowed simultaneous membership in two guilds. In this respect they were more tolerant than their Florentine counterparts: the 1344 statutes of the Florentine Guild of Lawyers and Notaries barred the admission of physicians.[24] The relative openness of the Genoese guild finds expression also in its policy vis-à-vis candidates of illegitimate birth: while the Florentine and Placentine statutes prohibited the admission of bastards,[25] the Genoese list of 1382, which was supposed to regulate the accession of candidates to the guild, contains the names of legitimate as well as natural sons of notaries.

Genoa's notaries were not recruited from among the nobles or the leading commoners of the city; nevertheless, many notaries played an important role in the public affairs of the community. Table 5.2 shows that the Guild of Notaries, probably just 200 members strong, supplied from 10 to 16

21. For biographical details see L. M. Levati, *I dogi perpetui di Genova, an. 1339–1528. Studio biografico* (Genoa, 1928), pp. 94–107; R. di Tucci, "Costruzione di galee genovesi durante il dogato di Leonardo Montaldo," in *Ad Alessandro Luzio: Miscellanea di studi storici*, vol. I (Florence, 1933), pp. 331–33.

22. Stella, *Annales Genuenses*, p. 190. 26–27.

23. ". . . qui et collegio notariorum aggregari voluit, quamvis notarii non exerceret operam," ibid., p. 186. 13–14. Whether there were other nominal members in the Genoese Guild of Notaries must remain an open question. Obviously, nominal membership would have reduced the number of notaries to whom Genoese citizens could resort for professional services. Nominal membership, which served as a springboard to participation in communal politics, is well known in other cities: Martines, *Lawyers*, pp. 25–26; Hyde, *Padua*, p. 22.

24. Martines, *Lawyers*, p. 28. In Padua, membership in the Guild of Notaries and in the College of Lawyers was mutually exclusive during the communal period: Hyde, *Padua*, pp. 122, 132–33.

25. S. Calleri, *L'Arte dei Giudici e Notai di Firenze nell'età comunale e nel suo statuto del 1344* (Milan, 1966), p. 31; Martines, *Lawyers*, p. 28; C. Pecorella, *Statuti notarili piacentini del XIV secolo* (Milan, 1971), pp. 29, 93.

Table 5.2

Membership of Notaries in the General Councils of Genoa, 1386–96

Year	*Nobles*	*Commoners*	*Notaries*[a]	*Percentage of Notaries out of all Commoners*
1367	75	150	15	10.0%
1368	86	194	22	11.3%
1380	160	199	30	15.1%
1382	170	160	19	11.8%
1395	174	236	38	16.1%
1396	277	330	51	15.5%

SOURCE: *Liber Iurium Reipublicae Genuensis*, vol. II (=*Monumenta Historiae Patriae*, vol. IX), col. 760–62, 777–80; Archivio di Stato, Genoa, *Diversorum Registri, No. 496* (*1380*), f. 2ʳ–9ʳ; *No. 497* (*1382*), f. 7ʳ–12ᵛ; E. Jarry, *Les origines de la domination française à Gênes, 1392–1402* (Paris, 1896), docs. X, XVII, pp. 433–36, 496–501.

[a] The lists of the General Councils do not specify the occupation of all of their notary members, but comparison with other documents leaves little doubt as to their profession.

percent of all the commoners who sat on Genoa's General Councils in the latter part of the fourteenth century. This amounts to a remarkable overrepresentation, as there must have been at the time many thousands of adult commoners in the city. Moreover, the presence of notaries in the General Council was impressive in other ways. Minutes of a General Council session held on November 10, 1395, reveal that twelve commoners and six nobles took to the rostrum; no less than three of the commoners were notaries.[26] Notaries were similarly prominent in other deliberative assemblies of those years.[27] And in the Council of Elders (*consilium antianorum*), the most important Genoese body after the doge, one seat was almost always reserved for a notary, whereas lawyers were only rarely members.[28] Notaries were also entrusted with the government of Genoese possessions: Bernabò di Carpena, for instance, was in 1361 consul of Chilia,

26. They were Badasal de Pineto, who opened the discussion, Dagnanus Carpenetus, and Simon Joardus: Jarry, *Les origines*, doc. X, pp. 425, 428.

27. In a convocation of commoner Ghibellines, held on July 8, 1396, four of the thirteen speakers were notaries, and in a Ghibelline assembly of July 28, 1398, there were three notaries among the eleven commoners who spoke: Ibid., docs. XIV, XXXVIII, pp. 450–51, 578–80.

28. For lists of members of the Council of Elders between 1362 and 1402 see *Liber Iurium Reipublicae Genuensis*, vol. II, col. 715ᵇ, 736ᵃ, 746ᵈ, 775ᵈ, 815ᵈ, 848ᵃ, 851ᵇ, 911ᵃ, 937ᵃ, 950ᵈ, 1014ᵃ, 1044ᵇ, 1051, 1054ᵈ, 1108ᵈ, 1116ᵈ, 1127ᵇ, 1147ᵈ, 1158ᵃ, 1174, 1191ᵇ, 1195ᵈ, 1203ᵃ, 1206ᵃ, 1214ᵈ, 1279, 1304ᶜ; Belgrano, "Prima serie," pp. 176, 179, 315; Argenti, *The Occupation of Chios*, II, 57, 81, 158, 177, 199; Rymer, *Foedera*, III, pt. 2, 906, 1008; Liagre-de Sturler, *Les relations commerciales*, pp. 454, 460; Ferrer i Mallol, "La pace del 1390", p. 186. In one Council of 1389, there were two notaries: *Liber Iurium*, vol. II, col. 1158ᵃ. However, none of the Elders elected on February 20, June 20, and October 21, 1382, was a notary, although on all three occasions several of the electors were members of the Guild of Notaries: ASG, *Div. Reg. No. 497* (*1382*), f. 31ᵛ–32ʳ, 89, 133.

the Genoese settlement in the Danube estuary; while Giannone Bosco, the father of the future lawyer Bartolomeo Bosco, in 1374 served as captain of Genoa's Riviera di Levante and in 1380 headed the important colony of Caffa as well as Genoa's other possessions in the Crimea; and Vincenzo Gallo was in 1398 put in charge of the castle of Montebello.[29] Evidently the notaries, who were the best-educated and most articulate element of the lesser *popolo*, attained political prominence under the commoner regime which prevailed in Genoa after 1339.

Besides the influence notaries could exert through membership in the elected bodies of the commune or through election to posts to which all citizens were eligible, they could also make their presence felt by filling crucial executive posts for which only they were professionally qualified.[30] Thus the laws of 1363 provided that the two subchancellors of the commune must be members of the Guild of Notaries. The three chancellors, on the other hand, were to be chosen by the doge and the Council of Elders at their will, but in practice the choice must have been limited to notaries, for all the chancellors found in the documents of the period are styled *notarius et cancellarius.*[31] (The laws of 1413 made this limitation explicit: all four chancellors, and two of the four subchancellors, had to be members of the guild).[32] Outside the chancery, notaries were appointed to diverse clerical positions. But it would seem that while many notaries were nominated to posts which required their professional skills, even more notaries were elected to positions which were open to all citizens. The examination of the register of the deliberations which were held by the doge and the Council of Elders during the year 1382 discloses that four notaries served as chancellors, one as subchancellor, and seventeen were elected to serve as scribes. In addition, forty-six were elected to posts which did not require notarial skills.[33]

29. G. Pistarino, ed., *Notai genovesi in Oltremare: Atti rogati a Chilia da Antonio di Ponzò, 1360–61* (Genoa, 1971), docs. 21, 31, 40, 45, pp. 35, 51, 66–67, 77; M. Buongiorno, *Il bilancio di uno stato medievale: Genova, 1340–1529* (Genoa, 1973), p. 92; S. de Sacy, "Pièces diplomatiques tirées des archives de la république de Gênes," *Notices et extraits des manuscrits de la bibliothèque du roi, 11*, (1827), 53–54, 59; Jarry, *Les origines*, doc. XXXV, p. 570.

30. The fact that notaries had access to two parallel avenues to political influence did cause resentment: cf. Martines, *Lawyers*, p. 47.

31. The following of the 171 notaries of 1382 are styled *notarius et cancellarius:* Anthonius de Credentia, Anthonius Panizarius, Badasal de Pineto, Conradus Mazurrus, Georgius de Clavaro, Jullianus Panizarius, Maximus de Judicibus de Rappallo, Petrus de Bargalio, Raffael de Casanova, Raffael de Goasco, Ricobonus de Bozolo and Aldebrandus de Corvaria.

32. Costamagna, *Il notaio a Genova*, p. 163.

33. In Perugia, during the same year, fifty notaries were nominated to perform strictly notarial tasks; twenty-nine were elected to posts open to all citizens, and twenty-nine others were appointed to both notarial and nonnotarial positions. This breakdown is based on the list of elected notaries published by R. Abbondanza, *Il notariato a Perugia* (Rome, 1973), doc. 89, pp. 120–32.

Was political participation equally open to all guild members? A search of the rosters of the General Councils of 1367, 1368, 1380, 1382, 1395, and 1396 suggests that this was not the case: only 76 of the 171 notaries of 1382 were members of these councils. To these seventy-six, one should add Leonardo Montaldo, the future doge; the two *viceduces* of 1382, Antonio *de Pessina* and Federigo del Poggio;[34] and twelve notaries who are known to have been members of the Council of Elders but not of the General Councils in question. Of this total of eighty-eight, twenty-nine were elected to two General Councils or more, and at least twenty-one served both in a General Council and on the Council of Elders. Bartolomeo Pindeben da Vernazza, Giorgio *de Via*, and Pietro della Grotta were probably politically the most active of the 171 notaries of 1382. Pindeben, who figures on the 1382 list of notaries' sons first as one of the nine councillors of the Guild of Notaries, and then as father of four sons, was elected to the General Councils of 1368 and 1396. In 1376 he was podesta of Pera. Sometime before May 20, 1382 he did duty as treasurer of the Office of Maritime War and on October 21 of the same year he served as one of the electors of the new Elders. In 1383 he was a councillor of the Genoese fleet commander in the eastern Mediterranean. In 1392 he was sent as ambassador to the king and queen of Sicily. Between 1384 and 1399 he was a member of the Council of Elders during at least four different terms of office.[35] Giorgio *de Via*, the father of six sons according to the 1382 list, was a member of the General Councils of 1368, 1382, 1395, and 1396 and served on the Council of Elders in 1393 and 1399. In 1382 he was a candidate for the office of the podesta of Chios and a member of a fiscal committee. In 1398 he examined the registers of the communal loans and in 1404 he was a magistrate of the Cyprus *mahona*.[36] Pietro della Grotta, who figures on the 1382 list as a father of

34. ASG, *Div. Reg.*, *No. 497* (*1382*), f. 35^{v}, 115^{v}.

35. In 1360 Pindeben was at Chios: Argenti, *The Occupation of Chios*, III, 540; in 1397 he was a member of the Officium octo additorum: Jarry, *Les origines*, p. 551. He was an *antianus*, or Elder, in 1384, 1390, 1396, and 1399: *Liber Iurium*, vol. II, col. 937^{a}; Ferrer i Mallol, "La pace del 1390," p. 186; Belgrano, "Prima serie," pp. 179, 315; Jarry, *Les origines*, p. 443. On his podestate at Pera, see Belgrano, "Prima serie," p. 131; for his other offices in the years 1382–92 see ASG, *Div. Reg. No. 497* (*1382*), f. 78^{r}, 133^{r}; *Notari, N. 381* (*Giovanni Bardi, 1382–85*), f. 152^{r}; Archivio Segreto, no. 3021 (= *Diversorum Comunis Janue*, filza 1), no. 69. For his (and others') membership in the General Councils see the lists quoted in table 5.2.

36. ASG, *Div. Reg. No. 497* (*1382*), f. 41^{r}; Archivio Segreto, no. 3021 (=*Div. Com. Jan.*, filza 1), no. 88; *Div. Reg.*, *No. 498* (*1398*), f. 33^{v}; *No. 499* (*1399*), f. 12^{r}; Argenti, *The Occupation of Chios*, II, 385; G.G. Musso, *Navigazione e commercio genovese con il Levante nei documenti dell'Archivio di Stato di Genova* (*Secc. XIV-XV*), (Rome, 1975), doc. 20, p. 260. By 1417 he was dead: Renée Doehaerd and Ch. Kerremans, *Les relations commerciales entre Gênes, la Belgique et l'Outremont d'après les archives notariales génoises, 1400–1440* (Brussels and Rome, 1952), doc. 236, p. 264. Three of Giorgio's sons, Thomas, Christoforus, and Barnabas, appear as beneficiaries in the 1416 will of Antonius de Via, notary and official at Pera: L. T. Belgrano, "Seconda serie di documenti riguardanti la colonia di Pera," *ASLSP*, *13* (1884), 972. For the career of Antonius, see Belgrano, "Prima serie," pp. 146, 151, 157, 160.

five sons, was elected to all of the above General Councils, and served on the Council of Elders in 1373, 1378, 1393, and 1394; in 1375 he was a member of the Officium Monete; on September 24, 1382, he was appointed to hear the ambassadors of Florence and on October 8 to determine the tax quotas of Genoa's commoners.[37] But while several of the notaries of 1382 were intensively involved in communal politics and while many were appointed to more than one political office, some fourscore of them are not known to have been elected to a General Council or to the Council of Elders. One may surmise therefore that a sizable proportion of the notaries did not hold any political office whatsoever.[38]

Were local-born notaries more active in communal politics than notaries who had immigrated from Genoa's countryside or from more distant regions? The career of Bartolomeo Pindeben da Vernazza, whose toponymic surname points to non-Genoese origin, suggests that newcomers could make good in the volatile politics of late-Trecento Genoa. And indeed Pindeben's was not an isolated case. A breakdown of the 171 notaries of 1382 into old-timers and newcomers—with individuals being considered newcomers on the basis of their foreign toponymics—discloses that the percentage of membership in the above General Councils is well-nigh identical for the two groups: thirty-four out of seventy-seven old-timers, or 44.2 percent, versus forty out of ninety-four newcomers, or 42.6 percent.

To what extent did Genoa's notaries participate in the city's trade? Several notarial acts, as well as other documents, concern notaries who were involved in business. The notary Giovanni *de Guasco*, son of the late Simone, dictated his testament on April 12, 1377, before embarking on a commercial trip to the eastern regions of Romania.[39] In 1382 Bartolomeo Pindeben joined with other underwriters in the insuring of merchandise dispatched to the Sicilian harbor of Catania; in 1383, and again in 1385,

37. On his service on the Council of Elders, see Argenti, *The Occupation of Chios*, vol. II, p. 81; *Liber Iurium*, vol. II, col. 848[a]; D. Gioffrè, ed., *Liber Institutionum Cabellarum veterum* (*Communis Janue*) (Milan, 1967), p. 191; ASG, Archivio Segreto, no. 3021 (*Div. Com. Jan.*, filza 1), no. 104. *Officium Monete:* Liagre-de Sturler, *Les relations commerciales*, p. 455; see also pp. 413, 427, 438, 474, 486, 721 (where his name is spelled *de la Grotta*), 753. *1382:* ASG, *Div. Reg.*, *No. 497* (*1382*), f. 125[r], 130[r].

38. Since most of the lists of the General Councils and Councils of Elders are not extant, it is impossible to specify the exact number of notaries who had played no role in these bodies. However, the fact that the notaries who appear in the extant lists often fulfilled more than one political role suggests that the total absence of a notary from all extant lists, as well as from the other pertinent documents which had come under study, may indicate in many cases that that notary indeed did not participate in politics.

39. ASG, *Notari, N. 380* (*Giovanni Bardi, 1376–84*), f. 61. The same *Johanes de Guasco not. q. Symonis* figures in the 1382 list of notaries' sons as the father of two. He may be identical with *Johannes de Goastho not.* (or *Johannes de Goasco not.*) who served in 1382 as *scriba imposicionis et exactionis mutui florenorum:* ASG, *Div. Reg. No. 497* (*1382*), f. 41[r], 107[v].

Pindeben participated in the insuring of cargoes bound for England.[40] Another notary, Giannino *de Frescheto* da Chiavari, appears as insurant of ships in acts of 1382, 1384, and 1385.[41] A sum Pietro della Grotta had given in *commenda* gave rise to a dispute which was settled by arbitration in March 1376. A month earlier, the notary Antonio da Finale, son of the late Andriolo, entered into a *societas* with one Antonio Sacco, and then, with the sum of £.Gen. 1, 125 of the partnership, left to do business in Paris and elsewhere.[42] In 1372, at Chios, a local inhabitant owed 444 ducats, the price of 12 pieces of Châlons cloth, to the Genoese notary Raffaele *de Reza*; Jacopo da Moneglia, whom the doge and the Council of Elders had elected in 1382 to serve as scribe at the court of Chios, appears there in 1388 as co-owner of a quantity of alum which was to be sent to Middelburg.[43] Giannone Bosco, who served as consul of Caffa in 1380 and went in 1387 on a diplomatic mission to the countries bordering the Black Sea, figures in an act of 1384 as *civis et mercator Janue* and as owner of six-and-a-half carats of a cog named *Sancta Maria*. The act reveals that the cog touched at the port of Genoa after eight consecutive years of commercial sailing in the Mediterranean and, as the shipmaster tarried before presenting his financial report, Giannone and another co-owner of the cog lodged a complaint against him.[44] And in 1391 Raffaele Villanucio and his associates imported 1,500 *mine* of corn from Agrigento, Sicily, to Genoa.[45]

40. ASG, *Notari, N. 380 (Giovanni Bardi, 1376–84)*, f. 130ʳ; Liagre-de Sturler, *Les relations commerciales*, docs. 406, 472, pp. 543, 620–21.

41. Liagre-de Sturler, *Les relations commerciales*, docs. 399, 427–29, 463, pp. 534–35, 572–74, 612–13. In the list of 1382, this notary appears as *Janinus de Frescheto de Clavaro;* in the insurance contracts, as *Janinus de Frescheto, notarius*, or *Jane de Frescheto de Clavaro notarius* or *Jane de Frescheto civis Janue*. But the comparison of other details of the contracts suggests that all forms refer to the same individual.

A *Johannes de Bozolo habitator Levanti* appears as insurant in a contract of 1395: Ibid., doc. 592, pp. 786–87. It is not clear, however, whether he is identical with the notary Johannes de Bozolo of the 1382 list.

42. Ibid., doc. 347, pp. 470–72; doc. 345, pp. 468–69. Is this *Anthonius de Finario, notarius, q. Andrioli* identical with the *Anthonius de Finario q. Andree* of the 1382 list? And which—if any—of them is the *Anthonius de Finario notarius* who added a sheet to the 1377 cartulary of the Ambasciata Anglie (Day. *Les douanes de Gênes*, p. 786, n. 3), or the *Antonius de Finario, notarius*, who took to the rostrum in the council of 1396 (Jarry, *Les origines*, p. 491)?

43. Liagre-de Sturler, *Les relations commerciales*, docs. 333, 526, pp. 449–50, 695; Argenti, *The Occupation of Chios*, II, 386. Guillelmus, the son of the notary Lodisius de Monterubeo—father and son appear in the 1382 list—received in 1384 a loan to be repaid at Bruges; the father, who gave the security, had to repay the sum in 1393, because his son had died in the meantime: Liagre-de Sturler, *Les relations commerciales*, doc. 578, p. 765.

44. R. di Tucci, *Studi sull'economia genovese del secolo decimosecondo. La nave e i contratti marittimi. La banca privata* (Turin, 1933), doc. XXVI, pp. 35–37. In 1385, Giannone quarrelled with Giovanni Spinola on account of the deterioration of a cargo which had arrived from Romania: Musso, *Navigazione*, p. 157. An entry of the same year refers to Giannone as to a *bancherius:* ASG, Antico Comune, r. 17 (*Massaria comunis Janue, 1385*), f. 39.

45. ASG, Archivio Segreto, no. 3021 (*Div. Com. Jan.*, filza 1), no. 59.

Thus, there can be no doubt that some notaries were involved in commerce and that some even engaged personally in trade. But how typical were the nine notaries whose involvement in trade emerges from the acts which have been examined? To arrive at an approximation of the percentage of the notaries who were involved in business one must not rely on the extant acts, since the proportion they represent of all the original acts is unknown. There exists, however, an alternative method which—although not devoid of pitfalls—allows for a more reliable gauging of the commercial involvement of Genoa's notaries. This method consists of searching the Genoese customs cartularies of 1376–77 for the names of the 171 notaries of 1382.[46] The results are quite unequivocal. Out of the 171 notaries only 21 appear in the cartularies as liable to pay duties for goods imported or exported. Out of these 21, only 9 appear as liable both in 1376 and in 1377: 8 are only in the register of 1376, and 4 only in that of 1377.[47] Their involvement in the overseas commerce was rather slight and casual. The commoners who appear in the 1376 cartulary shipped goods through the harbor, on the average, on 3.4 different occasions, while the average for the 17 notaries who paid customs during that year stood at merely 1.8. Moreover, the average amount of customs duties a commoner paid in 1376 was four times higher than that paid by a notary: £.Gen.

46. Two of the pitfalls of this method should be mentioned. First, it is not certain that all of the 171 notaries of 1382 were in Genoa in 1376–77: Pindeben, for one, was podesta of Pera in 1376. Second, in most cases the customs cartularies do not identify an individual as a notary. (The lawyers, on the other hand, are easily recognized by the *dominus* which precedes their name). To avoid an under-estimation of notaries, all individuals bearing names identical with those which appear in the 1382 list of notaries' sons have been regarded as notaries.

The reliability of the method is enhanced by the fact that four or, with Anthonius de Finario, five, of the nine notaries whose involvement in business has been established on the basis of notarial acts appear as customs-payers in the cartularies of 1376–77, which have been edited by Day, *Les douanes de Gênes*.

47. Ambroxius de Olliverio was liable in 1376 to pay £.Gen. 2.14.6 in customs; Anthonius de Finario in 1376, 0.2.3; Dagnanus Carpenetus in 1376, 0.4.8; Dominichus de Bracellis in 1377, 0.17.5; Gabriel Judex in 1376, 0.5.0; Gandulfus de Fossato de Lavagna in 1376, 0.7.5, and in 1377, 0.9.3; Georgius de Via in 1377, 0.14.6; Illarius Gambarus in 1376, 0.6.6, and in 1377, 2.16.7; Janinus de Frescheto de Clavaro in 1377, 0.14.3; Janonus de Bosco in 1376, 1.10.0, and in 1377, 0.4.0; Johannes de Albario in 1376, 0.10.0, and in 1377, 0.12.3; Leonardus de Montaldo in 1377, 0.5.10; Martinus de Tolomeo in 1376, 0.1.7; Nicolaus de Lazaro in 1376, 3.14.1, and in 1377, 1.8.0; Nicolaus Fatinanti in 1376, 0.1.6, and in 1377, 0.14.5; Petrus Venerosus in 1376, 0.5.3; Philipus Noytoranus in 1376, 1.5.4, and in 1377, 1.2.3; Quilicus de Naa in 1376, 0.2.2; Raffael de Reza in 1376, 1.3.4, and in 1377, 0.5.0; Raffael Villanucius in 1376, 0.6.8, and in 1377, 0.13.0; Thomas Mastrucius in 1376, 1.2.8. In addition, the following seven notaries paid customs in the name of other Genoese: Gaspal de Testana, Jullianus Grollerius, Jullianus Tarighus, Lucianus de Castello, Leonardus Barosus, Nicolaus Muscha, Raffael de Zoalio. Five of the eighty notaries who were dead by 1382 paid customs for their own goods. All sums have been computed from entries in Day, *Les douanes de Gênes*.

2.14.5 versus 0.13.6. But even these averages do not give the full picture, because they are skewed by the duties of one notary, Niccolò di Lazaro, whose involvement in commerce was substantial: on seven different occasions he shipped or received goods for which he had to pay £.Gen. 3.14.1 in customs. Therefore the median seems to be more revealing an indication than the average; it amounts to only 1.0 for the occasions on which goods did pass through the harbor, and only £.Gen. 0.7.5 for the customs duties paid.[48] Thus, one may assume that the notaries were far less conspicuous in Genoa's commerce than in the city's politics.

But the relationship between the notarial involvement in politics and in commerce can be further scrutinized. It is significant that eighteen of the twenty-one notaries liable to pay customs in 1376–77 are known to have played a political role: Leonardo Montaldo ascended to the dogate; Giannone Bosco assumed crucial offices on behalf of the commune; Tommaso Mastruccio in 1382 served as an elector of the Elders and as one of the *XL consiliarii civitatis Janue*; and fifteen others were members of General Councils or of the Council of Elders, or of both.[49] Similarly, out of the nine notaries whose business ties are revealed by the documents, four or five were elected to a General Council;[50] a sixth, Jacopo da Moneglia, was sent to serve in a vitally important possession overseas; the seventh was the above-mentioned Giannone Bosco. Again, of the four notaries who in 1375 participated in the company which had been established for the governance and exploitation of Famagusta—Andreolo Maniscalco, Gandolfo *de Fossato* di Lavagna, Raffaele *de Reza*, and Giannone Bosco[51]—the last three were liable to pay customs in 1376–77. And of the thirteen notaries of 1382 who are known to have farmed communal income-sources

48. It is possible, though, that the *Nicolaus de Lazaro* who appears in the customs cartularies is not identical with *Nicolaus de Lazaro not.*, the commoner who represented the quarter of San Lorenzo in the General Council of 1382, but should be considered a member of the noble family *de Lazaro*. (For a list of Genoese noble families see Kedar, *Merchants in Crisis*, pp. 137–38.)

The respective average and median values for the thirteen notaries who appear in the cartulary of 1377 are 1.8 occasions and £.Gen. 0.16.8 (averages), and 1.0 occasions and £.Gen. 0.9.3 (means). For a comparison of the customs payments of Genoa's nobles and commoners in 1376, see Kedar, *Merchants in Crisis*, pp. 51–56.

49. On Janonus de Bosco see notes 29, 44, 51, and 52; on Thomas Mastrucius see ASG, *Div. Reg.*, *No. 497* (*1382*), f. 89ʳ, 155ʳ.

50. On Pindeben and Grotta see notes 35 and 36 above; Raffael de Reza was member of the General Councils of 1380, 1395, and 1396, and elected Elders on February 20 and June 20, 1382 (see note 28 above); Raffael Villanucius was Elder in 1379 and member of the General Councils of 1382 and 1396; Anthonius de Finario might have been a member of the General Council of 1395 (see note 42 above).

51. Giovanna Petti Balbi, "La maona di Cipro del 1373," *Rassegna storica della Liguria*, *1* (1974), 269–85, esp. pp. 274–77.

in the years 1371, 1384, and 1385,[52] no less than eleven were elected to a General Council or to the Council of Elders, the twelfth being the ubiquitous Giannone Bosco. Therefore one may conclude that while many notaries did not play an active political role and while most notaries did not engage in trade, a small minority was prominent both in politics and in business.

Could a notary who was deeply involved in political and economic activities find the leisure to pursue the notarial craft itself, entering acts and contracts in his registers? The notarial acts preserved in Genoa's Archivio di Stato provide a clue. It is true that many acts were destroyed when the French navy bombarded the Genoese archive in 1684, and therefore the present-day absence of a notary's acts does not prove that he did not practice the notariate. In other words, the fact that the acts of only 27 out of 171 notaries of 1382 are extant does not indicate that only these 27 individuals exercised the notarial profession. Nevertheless, it can be hardly accidental that none of the four notaries who in 1375 participated in the Famagusta Company and only one—Chilico *de Naa*—of the thirteen farmers of communal income-sources appears among the twenty-seven notaries whose acts have been preserved. On the other hand, none of the twelve notaries of 1382 who are known to have served as chancellors appears among the Genoese who were liable to pay customs in 1376–77, although seven of them were members of a General Council.[53] Consequently one may assume that, at any given moment, the Genoese Guild of Notaries included members who were notaries pure and simple; members who exercised the notarial craft and held elective political offices as well; members who did not practice the notarial profession at all but devoted their energy to politics and business; and members—probably a small minority—who were simultaneously active in all three areas. One may also conjecture that, in the course of their careers, some notaries shifted their emphases from one area to another.[54]

The Genoese Guild of Notaries presents therefore a wide spectrum of

52. In 1371, they were Anthonius de Gavio, Badasal Vegius, Germanus de Casteliono, and Nicolaus Oberti. See Sieveking, *Genueser Finanzwesen*, I, 200–01. In 1384, they were Anthonius de Sancto Matheo q. Guillelmi, Badasal de Zoalio, Bartholomeus Pindeben, Gabriel Judex, Janonus de Bosco, Julianus Grolerius, Leonardus Barosus, and Raffael de Zoalio. See ASG, San Giorgio, *Securit. Avall. comper. novorum S. Pauli*, a. 1384, f. 7^v, 14^v, 18^v, 19^v, 24^r, 47^v, 51^v, 53^v, 54^r, 56^v, 57^v, 62^v, 67^v. In 1385, they were Badasal de Zoalio, Bartholomeus Pindeben (and his son Johannes), Chilicus de Naa, Gabriel Judex, and Julianus Grolerius. See *Securit. Avall. comper. novorum S. Pauli*, a. 1385, f. 8^v, 10^v, 16^r, 16^v, 42^v, 50^v, 55^v, 56^v.

53. For the list of chancellors see note 31 above.

54. For a similar conclusion with regard to Genoa's notariate in the thirteenth century, see R. L. Reynolds, "In Search of a Business Class in Thirteenth-Century Genoa," *Journal of Economic History*, suppl. V (1945), p. 17. Cf. Hyde, *Padua*, pp. 159, 161; Martines, *Lawyers*, p. 38.

individuals who differed not only in political power and economic versatility but probably also in their day-to-day routine. In addition, there must have been considerable differences in wealth. In an interrogation held in Genoa in March 1382, the notary Illario Carpeneto, then more than twenty-eight years old, declared his possessions to be worth £.Gen. 100, while Teramo di Maggiolo, many of whose notarial acts are extant, assessed his worth at £.Gen. 200.[55] Simone dei Inghiberti, a notary employed by the customs office of the Ambasciata Anglie, received in 1377 an annual salary of £.Gen. 40;[56] a generation later, Giorgio Stella, notary and chronicler, served as scribe with the prestigious Massaria generalis communis Janue at an annual salary of 100 pounds Genoese.[57] Bartolomeo Villanucio, the notary who was employed as dragoman of the commune of Pera, received in 1390–91 a salary of 250 hyperpers, while Domenico di Pace, notary of the treasurers of the commune, earned a mere 100 (and even this was 25 hyperpers more than the salary of Master Tommaso, the *doctor grammatice* who held school at Pera).[58] The notaries who engaged in business surely commanded more assets than Illario Carpeneto and Teramo di Maggiolo did in 1382. Antonio da Finale, the notary who went to Paris on business in 1376, had invested in that venture £.Gen. 562.10.0. Bartolomeo Pindeben undertook to insure woad and wine worth 100 florins and 125 pounds Genoese respectively. The worth of the goods Illario Gambaro shipped or received through the harbor of Genoa amounted to £.Gen. 325 in 1376, and to £.Gen. 2,827 in 1377; he was liable to pay for them £.Gen. 0.6.6 and 2.16.7 respectively. Even the value of the goods of Chilico *de Naa*, which were taxed only £.Gen. 0.2.2 in customs, amounted to £.Gen. 108. Obviously, participation in the overseas trade must have been beyond the means of notaries who earned but £.Gen. 40 per annum, or whose worth was assessed at 100 pounds Genoese.

Where did Genoa's notaries make their abode? Did they spread evenly all over the city or did they show preference for certain neighborhoods? The lists of the General Councils of 1380 and 1382 provide a partial answer to this question, since they include not only the names of forty-nine notaries

55. Liagre-de Sturler, *Les relations commerciales*, doc. 394, pp. 527, 529. Theramus de Maiollo was a member of the General Councils of 1380, 1395 and 1396.

56. Day, *Les douanes de Gênes*, p. 736. On the same day, the customs official Pambelus de Cassali received £.Gen. 100 as salary for two years; Day, loc. cit.

57. Giovanna Balbi, "Giorgio Stella e gli 'Annales Genuenses,'" *Miscellanea storica ligure 2*, (1961), 128. In addition, Stella owned some property at Triora, his father's place of origin: ibid., pp. 130–31, 210–14. From 1384 onward, Genoa's doges received an annual salary of £.Gen. 1,000 as well as £.Gen. 7,625 for expenses: M. Buongiorno, "Gli emolumenti dei dogi perpetui genovesi," *Studi Genuensi*, *5* (1964/65), 59.

58. Belgrano, "Prima serie," pp. 157–58.

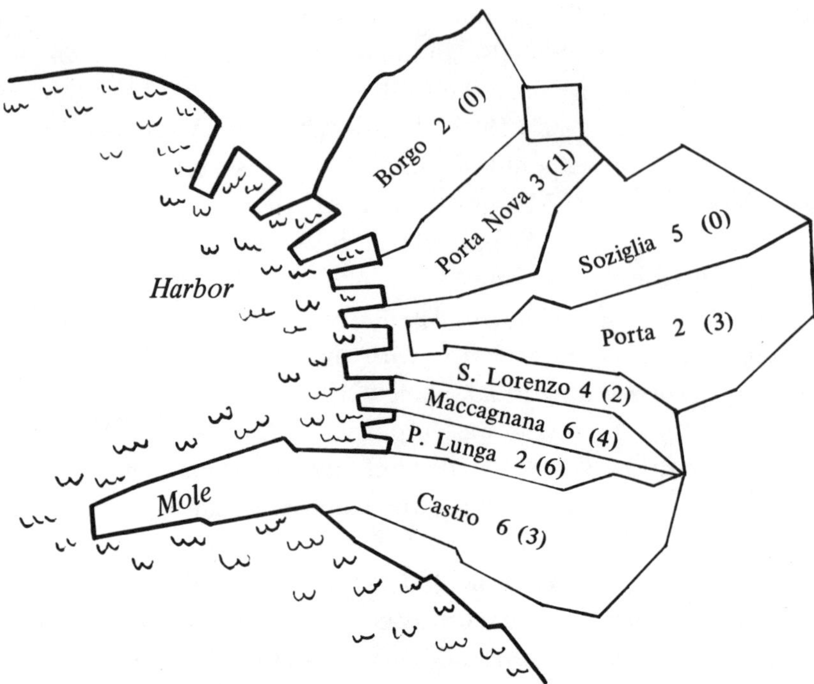

Figure 5.1 Genoese Notaries Representing City Quarters, 1380 and 1382

NOTE: For each quarter, the number of notaries who represented it in the General Council of 1380 is given first; the corresponding number for 1382 follows in brackets. The division into quarters is taken from J. Heers, "Urbanisme et structure sociale à Gênes au Moyen Age," in *Studi in onore di Amintore Fanfani* (Milan, 1962), I, 407.

but also indicate the *compagne*, or quarters of the city, which they represented. Figure 5.1 reveals that while there were notaries in every quarter, the majority of notaries came from Castro, Piazza Lunga, Maccagnana, and San Lorenzo. These were Genoa's oldest quarters, which had been enclosed by the city walls back in Carolingian times.[59]

The time has come to turn from the notaries of 1382 to their sons. The 152 notaries who appear in the list of 1382 fathered 345 sons. Their distribution is shown in table 5.3. The average number of sons per notary stands at 2.27. But this is not necessarily the true number. Some notaries might have had grown-up sons who either had already joined the Guild of

59. On the evolution of Genoa's quarters see J. Heers, "Urbanisme et structure sociale à Gênes au Moyen Age," in *Studi in onore di Amintore Fanfani* (Milan, 1962), I, 373–81. On the domiciles of the sixty-nine notaries who appear in the tax list of 1440, see H. Sieveking, "Aus Genueser Rechnungs- und Steuerbüchern. Ein Beitrag zur mittelalterlichen Handels- und Vermögensstatistik," *Sitzungsberichte der Kais. Akademie der Wissenschaften in Wien, phil.-hist. Klasse*, vol. 162, fasc. 2 (1909), p. 67.

Table 5.3

152 Members of the Genoese Guild of Notaries and Their Sons, 1382

No. of Sons per Notary	*No. of Notaries*	*Total No. of Sons*
1	60	60
2	42	84
3	24	72
4	10	40
5	9	45
6	5	30
7	2	14
Total	152	345

Notaries or who had decided to follow another profession. Such sons would not appear on the 1382 list. This is not mere guesswork. Lucchino da Corniglia, a member of the General Council of 1368 and a councillor of the Guild of Notaries in 1382, appears on the list as the father of four sons: Raffaele, Galeazzo, Leonardo, and Jacopo. However, it transpires that a fifth son, Domenico, appears on the list not as a notary's son but as a notary in his own right. This Domenico made the list only because he had already sired a son, Barnabà; otherwise his name would not have appeared and Lucchino da Corniglia would have been counted as the father of only four sons.[60] Thus there is no way to determine how many notaries' sons were not included in the list, and therefore the average of 2.27 must be regarded as a minimum.[61]

In addition to sons, the notaries surely also had daughters. Their number may be estimated. On the basis of data supplied by Giovanni Villani, one may assume that in the Florence of the 1330s the ratio of males to females stood at about 115:100 at time of baptism. In Siena the sex ratio at birth varied during the years 1386 to 1399 between 141.9:100 and 96.5:100, exceeding 120:100 in seven different years. In Pistoia the sex ratio for

60. In 1383 the notary Dominicus de Cornilia appointed as proctors his father Luchinus, his brother Georgius, and his wife Catalina (see note 13 above). Thus it would seem that Luchinus de Cornilia had a sixth son, Georgius. (Both Dominicus and Georgius have been counted among the 345 notaries' sons).

61. It is noteworthy that notaries whose age in 1382 must have been greater than thirty-four had a higher average of sons: the sixteen notaries who had been members of the General Council of 1368 and appear as fathers in 1382 have fifty-one sons, or 3.19 on the average. Likewise, the twelve guild officers who presided over the 1382 draw, and who probably were among the older members of the Genoese notariate, have thirty-six sons in the list, or 3.0 on the average. (The name of the guild treasurer *Anthonius de domino Marthino quondam Oberti* should be corrected to *Anthonius de Sancto Matheo q. Oberti*: cf. the photocopy in Puncuh, "Il notaio," p. 163).

children fifteen years and younger stood in 1427 at 125 boys to every 100 girls. Such high ratios probably reflected, in part, an underreporting of female children.[62] Nevertheless, it may be safer to posit for the offspring of the Genoese notaries of 1382 a sex ratio as high as 120:100. Consequently, the average number of daughters per notary would stand at 1.89, and the combined average of sons and daughters sired by one notary at 4.16.

This 4.16 average per notary should be considered as very high. A previous study, based on Genoese testaments, has ascertained that the testators who had children at the time their wills were drawn up had, on the average, 3.18 children in 1343, but only 1.83 in 1348 and 2.3 in 1358 to 1361. In 1451 to 1458 the average was 3.0.[63] Consequently one may assume that the notaries, who belonged on the whole to the wealthier segment of the lesser popolo, had more children than the average Genoese.

The positive correlation between wealth and number of children has already been established for early fifteenth-century Pistoia and Florence.[64] The same correlation seems to obtain within the Genoese notariate of 1382: the 20 fathers who appear in the cartularies of 1376–77 as liable to pay customs—and who may be regarded therefore as relatively wealthy—had 65 sons, or 3.25 on the average; the 132 fathers not liable to pay customs had an average of only 2.12.

An overwhelming majority of notaries, and notaries' sons, bear the names of saints: 85.5 and 84.3 percent respectively. At the same time, only 57.1 percent of the 170 noble members of the General Council of 1382 and only 75.9 percent of the 141 commoner members who were not notaries had been named after saints. Apparently the trend toward saints' names was more pronounced among the notaries than among the population at large.[65]

Perhaps the most intriguing piece of evidence which emerges from the 1382 list is the high percentage of natural sons. There are at least 64 of them,[66] and they constitute 18.6 percent of all the sons. Moreover, Table 5.4 reveals that of the 152 fathers no less than 54, or 35.5 percent, had natural

62. Lopez and Raymond, *Medieval Trade*, p. 72; R. Mols, *Introduction a la démographie historique des villes d'Europe du XIVe au XVIIIe siècle* (Louvain, 1955), II, 288–89. D. Herlihy, *Medieval and Renaissance Pistoia: The Social History of an Italian Town, 1200–1430* (New Haven and London, 1967), pp. 80–84.

63. J. Heers, *Gênes au XVe siècle: Activité économique et problèmes sociaux* (Paris, 1961), pp. 27–28. The study was based on a limited number of wills, just 134 for all four periods.

64. Herlihy, *Medieval and Renaissance Pistoia*, pp. 97–99, 118; Herlihy, "Viellir à Florence au Quattrocento," *Annales, E.S.C., 24* (1969), 1349, n. 6; 1350, n. 1.

65. On this trend and its possible significance see Kedar, *Merchants in Crisis*, pp. 97–104.

66. The number might have been even higher. The 1382 list does not indicate the spot at which begins the registration of the slips from the bag which contained the names of sons of deceased notaries, and of natural sons of the living. In the present study, all sons of living notaries who appear after the first case of a son of a deceased one (No. CCCV), are considered as illegitimate. However it is possible that the first slips drawn from that bag bore the names of illegitimate sons—if so, their total would exceed sixty-four.

Table 5.4

152 Genoese Notaries, by the Legal Status of Their Sons, 1382

No. of Sons	*Legitimate Sons*	*Natural Sons*	*Legitimate and Natural Sons*	*Total*
1	33	27	–	60
2	31	5	6[a]	42
3	14	1	9[b]	24
4	10	–	–	10
5	6	–	3[c]	9
6	3	–	2[d]	5
7	1	–	1[e]	2
	98	33	21	152

[a] 1 legitimate, 1 natural son.
[b] in seven cases, 2 legitimate and 1 natural; in two cases, 1 legitimate and 2 natural.
[c] 4 legitimate, 1 natural.
[d] 5 legitimate, 1 natural.
[e] 5 legitimate, 2 natural.

sons. Of these, 33 had natural sons only, and 21 had natural as well as legitimate ones. These figures are staggering: the only comparable data come from Siena, where there were, between 1381 and 1419, always more than 1,600 legitimate children for every illegitimate one.[67] Of course, one may assume that the Sienese had every reason to underreport illegitimate children, whereas the Genoese notaries had an obvious incentive to register theirs, because registration was considered imperative for ensuring the natural son's admission to the guild. But the gap between the Genoese and the Sienese data is too wide to be regarded merely as a result of differential reporting. Surely some of it reflects a genuine dissimilarity. Now, should one assume that illegitimacy was widespread in Genoese society at large, or was it rather a characteristic of the notaries? In the absence of relevant data this remains an open question. It should be noted, however, that in 1381 there were some 5,000 slaves in Genoa,[68] and as in other Italian cities, the overwhelming majority of them were females. The existence of illicit relationships between female slaves and their Genoese owners, and between the slaves and other Genoese, is well-documented.[69] Also, it is a

67. Mols, *Introduction*, II, 301.

68. According to the calculations of Domenico Gioffrè, their number was 5,056 in 1381, 4,100 in 1384, and 3,092 in 1387. D. Gioffrè, *Il mercato degli schiavi a Genova nel secolo XV* (Genoa, 1971), p. 80, n. 23.

69. G. Pistarino, "Tra liberi e schiave a Genova nel Quattrocento," *Anuario de estudios medievales, 1* (1964), 353–74; Gioffrè, *Il mercato*, pp. 96–101. For the 1384 legitimation of the son of a Genoese noble and of "Margarita de proienie seu genere Tartarorum, libera a coniugio," see Gabriella Airaldi, *Studi e documenti*, pp. 249–55, 325, 333; on the problem in general, pp. 331–32.

well-attested fact that among Genoa's slave owners, notaries were particularly numerous.[70] It is tempting to assume that some of the natural sons on the 1382 list were born out of liaisons with female slaves. At any rate, illegitimate offspring did not carry a stigma among the notaries of late-Trecento Genoa. In 1382, one of the treasurers of the Guild of Notaries was the father of a natural son, as were no less than seven of the nineteen notaries elected to the General Council of that year. The indifference with regard to illegitimacy, so focal to the Burckhardtian image of the Renaissance, seems to have found some of its earliest exponents among the Genoese notaries of 1382. Their sixty-four natural sons may be regarded as the undistinguished precursors of one of the towering figures of the coming age—Leonardo da Vinci, the illegitimate son of a peasant girl and a notary.

70. Pistarino, "Tra liberi e schiave," p. 355, n. 12; Gioffrè, *Il mercato*, pp. 82–83; R. Delort, "Quelques précisions sur le commerce des esclaves à Gênes vers la fin du XIVe siècle," *Mélanges d'archéologie et d'histoire publiés par l'Ecole française de Rome*, *76* (1966), 247. In 1360, the notary Bartolomeus Villanucius (see notes 12 and 58 above) sold his female slave at Famagusta: Lombardo, *Nicola de Boateriis*, doc. 37, pp. 42–43. A young Tatar slave named Margarita was sent to Theramus de Maiollo from Pera: Delort, "Quelques précisions", p. 248. After Giorgio Stella's death, his sons manumitted the Tatar slave Marta, declaring that she had served well both their late father and themselves: Balbi, "Giorgio Stella," p. 215.

6

Kinsmen and Neighbors in Medieval Genoa

Diane Owen Hughes

An intricate relationship between blood ties and territorial ties stands out as an intrinsic and defining feature of the medieval city. Unlike the ancient city, where "only the clan-less politically illegitimate *plebs* were organized in terms of local residence,"[1] the medieval commune from its origins used territorial association for purposes of urban organization. In Genoa the commune's roots were imbedded in a group of voluntary territorial associations called *compagne*, which had evolved from three basic divisions within the early medieval city: *castrum*, the Carolingian fortress on the site of the original Ligurian town; *civitas*, the Carolingian walled city outside the castrum; and *burgus*, a district of settlements to the northwest of the Carolingian city, outside the wall. By at least 1130, seven compagne had emerged, four within the wall and three outside it: Palazzolo (later called Castro) and Piazzalunga in castrum; Macagnana and San Lorenzo in civitas; and Porta, Soziglia, and Borgo in burgus. A balance between the Carolingian city and the medieval was achieved in 1134 when Borgo was divided to give the newer, unwalled district its fourth compagna, Portanuova.[2] As the similarity of name suggests, the *compagna communis*, a sworn association which from the late eleventh century drew all of Genoa's residents into a common action group on the basis of territorial rather than social, professional, or kin ties, may have originated in a formal union of individual compagne, whose members

This paper was written while I was a visiting fellow of the Society for the Humanities at Cornell University. It is a pleasure to thank its director, Henry Guerlac, for his generous anticipation of the fellows' needs and the genial and elegant surroundings he provided. I should also like to thank the Canada Council for a grant which let me microfilm many of the notarial cartularies on which this study is based.

1. Max Weber, *The City*, ed. and trans. Don Martindale and Gertrud Meuwirth (New York, 1958), p. 101.

2. Ubaldo Formentini, *Genova nel Basso Impero e nell' Alto Medio Evo* (Milan, 1941), pp. 95–100; Luigi Tommaso Belgrano and Cesare Imperiale di Sant' Angelo, eds., *Annali genovesi di Caffaro e de' suoi continuatori* (Rome, 1890–1929), I, 24–25, 27.

agreed to unite for limited periods or for specific enterprises.[3] Although the compagna communis eventually became a permanent body of citizens, it never lost its original territorial bias: the ease with which a resident of its territory could become a citizen distinguished Genoa from most other important Italian communes, whose views of citizenship were more exclusive.[4]

Genoa's eight compagne manifested physically the egalitarian spirit that seems to have conditioned the compagna communis. Their earliest boundaries are nowhere described, and it is likely that they had changed somewhat by the fifteenth century when an extant map and numerous administrative documents begin to define them as narrow strips running from the outlet at the port to the wall that enclosed the city. Early traditions of settlement had undoubtedly made their original boundaries less regular. The port, gates, markets, and churches were nodes of spontaneous precommunal settlement whose social, economic, and military ties later compagna organization probably respected. In the Carolingian castrum, for example, the district of the militia—called Prione—at the important Porta Sant'Andrea and the quarter of San Donato around that eleventh-century church were probably both halved only late in the Middle Ages to regularize the boundary between the compagne of Palazzolo (Castro) and Piazzalunga.[5] But there is evidence that the government had always sought to allot to the campagne roughly equivalent shares of the benefits inherent in the city's plan: Portanuova, the eighth compagna, created in 1134 outside the Carolingian wall, may initially have lacked direct access to the sea; but it received a gate in 1155 when Genoa constructed a new wall.[6] An indication of their equality can perhaps be seen in population

3. For a review of scholarly debate over the compagna, see Vito Vitale, *Breviario della storia di Genova* (Genoa, 1955), I, 13–18 and II, 16–18, whose views I follow here. The first compagna communis recorded in the Annals was sworn in 1099 and lasted for three years. It was renewed annually after 1122, by which time it is generally equated with the commune.

4. Genoese citizenship was granted after a year's residence in the city and seems never to have had the contentious political and economic overtones that citizenship assumed in other communes. From the beginning we find in Genoa that single, undifferentiated citizenship toward which Siena moved in the fourteenth century and which some communes, like Venice, never achieved: William M. Bowsky, "Medieval Citizenship: The Individual and the State in the Commune of Siena, 1287–1355," *Studies in Medieval and Renaissance History*, 4 (1967), 193–243; Brian Pullan, *Rich and Poor in Renaissance Venice* (Oxford, 1971), pp. 100–01. Nor were the rights of new citizens limited in Genoa, as they sometimes were in Florence, for example, in times of intense social competition: G. A. Brucker, *Florentine Politics and Society, 1343–1378* (Princeton, 1962), pp. 116–20.

5. For the regular boundaries of the fifteenth century, see Jacques Heers, "Urbanisme et structure sociale à Gênes au Moyen-Age," in *Studi in onore di Amintore Fanfani* (Milan, 1962), I, 394–402.

6. Belgrano and Imperiale di Sant' Angelo, *Annali genovesi*, I, 27.

statistics. Each compagna seems to have had a fairly balanced population containing citizens of all social and professional groups. Genoa's first tax assessments show that even in the fifteenth century, when the patriciate's abandonment of the ancient district within the castrum had begun to alter earlier settlement patterns, all eight compagne of the medieval city still housed varied populations and even the poorest contained significant patrician establishments.[7]

The associative spirit which seems to have animated these territorial divisions in the precommunal period, when the members of a district may have organized naval expeditions against the Saracens and commercial ventures in the Levant,[8] had declined by the mid-twelfth century when Genoa's extant notarial records begin. Although the compagna remained more than a lifeless bureaucratic district, it did not frequently foster significant social bonds among those whom it joined in formal civic relationships. Since the city's military, political, and judicial activities were organized around it, the compagna's corporate life was kept alive through ties created during military service, in the hurly-burly of compagna-centered elections, and in appearances at court—or even through the buying and selling of shares in the communal debt, divided, like the commune itself, into compagne.[9] Such corporate life took theatrical form in the compagna's distinctive arms and banners and in the public ceremonies at which they were distributed.[10] More pragmatic concerns are revealed by occasional demands for particular concessions: in 1190, for example, a year of political crisis that ended with the appointment of Genoa's first podesta, the compagne secured the hearing of pleas on a rotating basis in castrum, civitas, and burgum rather than in a central location.[11]

Yet the hostile rivalry between regions that became institutionalized in many Italian cities was absent in Genoa. There are no records of battles or contests among Genoese compagne to rival the *elmora* or *pugna* contests

7. Heers, "Urbanisme et structure sociale," pp. 394–402.

8. The name compagna is exclusive to Genoa. Deriving from *cumpanis*, it is closely tied to notions of commensality, perhaps, as some have suggested, with particular reference to the provisions of ships, so called *compagna* or *compaina:* see Teofilo Ossian de Negri, *Storia di Genova* (Milan, n.d.), pp. 233–34. In the twelfth century the compagna seems to have organized the galleys for war: Belgrano and Imperiale di Sant' Angelo, *Annali genovesi*, II, 192.

9. Michel-Giuseppe Canale, *Nuova istoria della Repubblica di Genova* (Florence, 1860), II, 148–51.

10. Belgrano and Imperiale di Sant' Angelo, *Annali genovesi*, III, 70–71; A. Ascheri, *Notizie intorno alla reunione delle famiglie in alberghi in Genova* (Genoa, 1846), p. 3.

11. Belgrano and Imperiale di Sant' Angelo, *Annali genovesi*, II, 34.

among the *terzi* of Siena, which often degenerated into the regional stone-throwing battles from which they had probably arisen and which were common throughout Tuscany.[12] Nor did the compagna encourage constructive bonds among its members. Few significant patterns of interaction among men and women of the same compagna emerge from the extensive Genoese notarial acts of the thirteenth and fourteenth century. If we except those whose common compagna membership was reinforced by other ties, such as kinship or guild membership, and those who lived together in the small, enclosed neighborhoods that we shall consider below, members of the same compagna acted together with not much greater frequency than they did with other citizens. They did not do business together more often; they did not frequently intermarry; and, to judge from their testamentary bequests and their selection of arbiters, executors, and guardians, their *compagni* did not regularly become their friends.[13]

The failure of this politically important regional association to forge the social and economic ties of community should be seen in the light of patrician reaction to compagna organization and patterns of immigrant settlement in the city. The history of both is encased in the neighborhoods that the patriciate and the immigrants created.

Genoa's urban patriciate had countered territorial association through systematic territorial control. At a time when kinship ties—at least at the level of the aristocracy—were being strengthened and extended throughout Europe, it is hardly surprising that aristocratic families in Genoa asserted their territorial claims and sought to maintain their status by common family action. The greatest families had rushed in the twelfth century to secure stategic urban property throughout the city—at important markets, at the port, and at the city's gates. The 1186 survey of Genoa's three major markets shows them encircled by the houses of the city's patriciate: all of the twenty-one listed owners were members of

12. Ferdinand Schevill, *Siena* (New York: Harper Torchbook, 1964), pp. 340–44; Daniel Waley, *The Italian City-Republics* (New York, 1969), p. 199.

13. This and other general statements in this study are based on an assessment of all the printed twelfth- and thirteenth-century Genoese cartularies, complete reference to which can be found in Diane Owen Hughes, "Toward Historical Ethnography: Notarial Records and Family History in the Middle Ages," *Historical Methods Newsletter*, 7 (1974), 69–70, n. 12, and of selected unprinted cartularies and filze of the thirteenth and fourteenth centuries housed in the Archivio di Stato, Genoa (hereafter cited as ASG), namely Cartularies 8, 12, 33, 41, 43, 48–52, 77, 78, 88, 93, 119, all catalogued in *Cartolari notarili genovesi: Inventario*, Pubblicazioni degli Archivi di Stato, XXII and XLI (Rome, 1956–61), and Bartolomeo Bracelli e Francesco de Silva, Andreolo Caito, 1–3, Tommaso Casanova, 1–12, Oberto Foglietta, Sr., 1, Giovanni Gallo, 1–3, Therami de Maiolo, 1–2, Bartolomeo Manarolo, Leonardo Osbergerio, and Giannino Vataccio. The method of analysis in this study is the largely geographical and prosopographical one described in the article cited above.

the consular aristocracy, and most were of viscontal origin.[14] The attraction of a diversity of holdings may have been balanced initially by the desire to concentrate familial property within a particular compagna. The Doria, for example, consistently acquired and developed the land around San Matteo where the family had its central establishment and later extended these activities to the more rural lands that rose behind it toward the wall on the hills, thus becoming the single greatest holder in the compagna of Porta.[15] Genoese governmental structure provided clear incentive to such concerted compagna control in the early twelfth century when each compagna seems to have elected leaders to the governing council.[16] Although elections remained compagna-based, by the thirteenth century that direct relationship between the compagna and the governing council had been lost: members of the Council of Eight Nobles were selected without regard to compagna. In the emergency election of 1264, called in response to growing political unrest in the city, 200 men (50 from each compagna) elected 32 (4 per compagna) who then, with regard not to compagna but rather to political-familial alliance, elected the 8 nobles, 2 each from the Grimaldi, Fieschi, Doria, and Spinola factions.[17] The growing political detachment of the compagna allowed Genoa's patrician families to become territorially diversified. By the thirteenth century the city's politically active families had established patterned holdings in Genoa's important commercial and strategic districts. The Grimaldi's early settlement with the Spinola at San Luca was complemented in the mid-thirteenth century, for example, by extensive real-estate holdings at the westernmost Porta dei Vacca; at Molo, Genoa's recently extended port area in the southeast; and at Canneto, a central commercial district. They gave the Grimaldi influence in three compagne: Borgo, Macagnana, and Palazzolo—one from each of the city's orginal divisions of castrum, civitas, and burgus.[18] The Grimaldi and Doria were among Genoa's greatest families; but other aristocrats, some in an attempt to secure an independent political base, others attaching their holdings to those of their

14. Cesare Imperiale di Sant' Angelo, ed., *Codice diplomatico della Repubblica di Genova* (Rome, 1936–42), II, 293–95.

15. Such activity had begun as early as the twelfth century, see Mario Chiaudano and Mattia Moresco, eds., *Il cartolare di Giovanni Scriba* (Rome, 1935), nos. 713, 1093; and Francesco Podestà, *Il colle di S. Andrea in Genova* (Atti della Società Ligure di Storia Patria, xxxiii, 1901), pp. 125–49.

16. In the full list of consuls given by the annalist for 1130, for example, all of those whose residence can be traced represented their own compagne: Belgrano and Imperiale di Sant' Angelo, *Annali genovesi*, I, 24–25.

17. Ibid., IV, 63–65.

18. ASG, cartulary 119, ff. 15^{v}–16^{r}.

political allies through an intricate net of alliances, also conformed to this pattern on a smaller scale.[19] Such considerations were important in Genoa where political survival could depend on territorial strength—as it did in 1335, for example, when the Ghibelline alliance led by the Doria and Spinola was sealed off by its enemies in the areas of the city over which the two families exerted territorial control.[20]

Just as the patriciate met the challenge of territorial association through territorial control, so did it try to mitigate the social and military threat of geographic proximity by transforming the neighborhood into a kin association. At its center was the fortified enclave where, under the shadow of commonly held towers, members of a lineage group lived in adjoining or neighboring houses, conducted business in family shops or in the common *curia* before the great house that belonged to the family's head, and worshipped in the private family church, or—when they could not manage that—in a parish church to which they had attached a private chapel.[21] This was the shape of the della Volta settlement at the Mercato San Giorgio (the ancient Roman forum near the port). In the twelfth century it contained common shops, warehouses, and baths for perhaps a dozen della Volta houses which huddled round the family church of San Torpete. Like the dozens of other noble settlements that can be reconstructed from thirteenth-and fourteenth-century notarial evidence, it bears remarkable resemblance to the more famous and substantially restored Doria settlement at San Matteo. In that intensely private urban district the great adjoining houses turn away from the central city toward the tiny square with its central church of San Matteo, which Marino Doria had secured as a private church in 1125 and which by the fourteenth century enshrined the bones and memories of generations of Doria ancestors. It was an enclave that was closed behind barricades when Genoa's incessant factional strife threatened its security—but an enclave into which were crowded the impressive palaces of certain affinal relatives and allies as well as alleys of less substantial dwellings that housed poor relations and clients.[22]

19. The tendency of allied families to form consolidated holdings throughout the city was encouraged by the frequency with which secondary urban property (that is, property that lay outside the central enclave) was awarded to daughters in their dowries.

20. Georgius Stella, *Annales* (Rerum Italicarum Scriptores, xvii), col. 1068.

21. Ennio Poleggi, "Le contrade delle consorterie nobiliari a Genova tra il XII e il XIII secolo," *Urbanistica*, 43–44 (1965), 17–25; Mattia Moresco, "Le parrocchie gentilizie genovesi," in *Scritti di Mattia Moresco* (Milan, 1959), pp. 1–27.

22. Diane Owen Hughes, "Urban Growth and Family Structure in Medieval Genoa," *Past and Present*, 66 (1975), 9; Jacopo d'Oria, *La chiesa di San Matteo in Genova* (Genoa, 1860); and see the plan reconstructed by Cesare Imperiale di Sant' Angelo, *Jacopo d'Oria e i suoi annali* (Venice, 1930), appendix.

Through the extension of kinship and patronage the aristocratic enclave became an urban neighborhood. Although the streets that stretched outward from these central enclaves were among the most cosmopolitan in the city—containing Genoese from up and down the Riviera, colonies of foreign merchants, and artisans in a variety of guilds—aristocratic initiative refined their social bonds. And for social purposes their residents can be divided into two groups: those who were drawn effectively into the orbit of the noble enclave through the extension of ties of kinship and patronage and those who were not. Prosperous merchants, notaries, and occasionally even rich artisans who owned neighboring property were frequently absorbed by the aristocratic family that dominated the district. Although the family's leaders might occasionally sacrifice their sons and daughters in marriage to these neighbors in return for the receipt of an inflated dowry or the chance to give a reduced one, their more usual way of extending kin ties outward into the neighborhood was to marry their poor relations to their neighbors. And, as in the case of Ogerio Nocenzio, a neighbor and traveling partner of the della Volta in the twelfth century who married a distant and impoverished relative of the great Ingo, marriage ties complemented commercial ones.[23] Patrician women of later centuries who brought small dowries to their marriages with men of humbler station were frequently marrying their neighbors, and their husbands can often be found in subsequent notarial acts as partners and agents of the family.[24] Furthermore, the great popular families whose houses formed part of, or bordered on, a noble district in the fourteenth century were often linked to it by one or more marriage ties. Indeed, when the Boccanegra and Adorno families (both of which led popular regimes in Genoa in the fourteenth century) married into the patriciate, they usually favored marriage with their neighbors.[25]

Patronage was also important, if harder to measure. It certainly attracted particular groups to the patrician neighborhood. The most important communities of merchants from abroad and from other Italian cities generally established themselves as a group within a noble enclave, drawn there both by its central location and by the ties of patronage that noble families could extend. The Piacenzans, for example, had been among the first merchants to frequent Genoa and had settled permanently within the aristocratic enclave of the Malocelli near the mercato San

23. Chiaudano and Moresco, *Il cartolare di Giovanni Scriba*, nos. 35, 64, 214, 503.

24. See, for example, in the Lercari family, ASG, Notary Tommaso Casanova, 9, ff. 126^{v}–127^{v} and Notary Therami de Maiolo, 1, f. 204^{r-v}.

25. Natale Battilana, *Genealogia delle famiglie nobili di Genova* (Genoa, 1825–33); Notary Tommaso Casanova, 9, ff. 13^{v}, 15^{r-v}.

Giorgio; but they transferred their *loggia* to the Grimaldi district at the other end of the city after Lanfranco Grimaldo had served as podesta of Piacenza in 1253.[26]

Patronage also helps to explain how the crowd of obscure neighbors who frequently appear as witnesses to patrician contracts, as minor legatees in patrician wills, and as messengers and agents of patrician women were tied to the patrician neighborhood. Buongiovanni da Voghera, who lived at San Matteo in the house of Oberto Doria, was but one of many from that city, for example, who were drawn into the Doria orbit in the mid-thirteenth century, witnessing the family's most solemn acts, securing patronage for their friends and relations, acting as Doria emissaries in small business concerns outside the enclave, serving in battle on Doria ships.[27] Patrician patronage went beyond the fairly permanent commercial relationship it established. The patrician family rented such neighbors their apartments and shops and the land on which they built their homes; it also leased them on good terms land on family estates in the countryside, creating a bond that extended over city walls.[28]

Patrician marriage with neighboring *popolani* and patronage of humbler neighbors may help to explain how the Genoese patriciate escaped so lightly during the popular regimes of the fourteenth century, how it maintained its district strength in spite of long absences from the city during the intense factional strife of the thirteenth and fourteenth centuries, and finally how it could depress the kind of territorial association that might pose a threat to its inherited position.

Such aristocratic initiative could occasionally give the compagna unusual associative life. The compagna Borgo fostered social bonds in the fourteenth century, for example, that cut across isolated family enclaves, artisan districts, and enclosed neighborhoods. Dominated politically by the powerful and often opposed Spinola and Grimaldi, who had settled at San Luca in the twelfth century,[29] its patrician families formed through an active policy of intermarriage a particularly close social and economic network—one which extended ties of kinship to the prosperous merchant

26. Arturo Ferretto, *Codice diplomatico delle relazioni fra la Liguria, la Toscana e la Lunigiana ai tempi di Dante* (*1265–1321*) (Atti della Società Ligure di Storia Patria, xxxi, 1903), II, 1, n. 1.

27. Giacomo Gorrini, *Documenti sulle relazioni fra Voghera e Genova* (*960–1325*) (Biblioteca della Società Storica Subalpina, xliii, 1908), nos. 140, 156, 161, 256, 281, 303, 308, 386.

28. See, for example, the Embriachi lease of country estates whose borders were contiguous with the lands of their aristocratic urban neighbors at Castro: ASG, Notary Giovanni Gallo, 3, f. 219^{r-v}.

29. They had intermarried by the late twelfth-century when they joined to found the family church of San Luca: see Mattia Moresco, "Note sulla fondazione della chiesa gentilizia degli Spinola nel 1188 in Genova," in *Scritti*, pp. 397–411.

families whose houses bordered on the patrician enclaves and economic and social patronage to its humbler neighbors. In Borgo it was patrician settlement and patrician social connections that linked the compagna's separate *piazze* and *contrade*. The joint Grimaldi holdings throughout Borgo—at San Luca, at Porta dei Vacca, at San Siro, and elsewhere—had parallels in the smaller, double settlements of other aristocrats—those of the Lomellini, for example, at Fossatello and at their new district at Sant' Agnese.[30] And marriage, which linked the Grimaldi with every patrician family in the compagna and which, to take the example of just one family, linked the Oltremarini at Fossatello in the 1340s with the Grimaldi at San Luca, with the Lomellini at Fossatello and Sant' Agnese, with the Bestagno and Gentile at San Siro, and with the Cibo at San Siro and Sant' Agnese,[31] made each of the compagna's patrician enclaves aware of—or at least curious about—the most intimate activities of the rest. Since economic ties almost inevitably complemented ties of kinship, the relations among the patrician enclaves at Borgo reached deep into their neighborhoods. When Venturino Mayrana, an artisan from San Siro, went up to Sant' Agnese in 1342 to find a wife, he was following paths established by the district's patricians.[32] And behind the frequent and intimate relations among popular families at Sant' Agnese and Fossatello, a common bond of Lomellini patronage can usually be detected.[33]

But the relatively intense compagna ties at Borgo in the 1340s, which were fostered by the cohesion of the patrician families there and the expansion of their settlements within the compagna, are harder to find elsewhere in Genoa. Patrician patronage and marriage ties more frequently broke down the structure of the compagna as they linked patrician enclaves throughout the city, Furthermore, the tendency of the aristocracy to concentrate its settlements in particular areas of the city, especially around its central markets and at the port, left the higher, hilly districts of most compagne, if not free from patrician control, at least less touched by its physical proximity. Fifteenth-century surveys give a crude sense of the differences in demographic texture. In contrast to the low-lying districts that housed many patrician settlements and whose densities ranged from

30. ASG, Notary Tommaso Casanova, 5, nos. 19, 147, 152–53; 10, ff. 121^{v}–122^{v}; 11, f. 64^{r}; Notary Therami de Maiolo, 2, f. 216^{r-v}.

31. ASG, Notary Tommaso Casanova, 3(i), ff. 97^{r}–98^{r}; 9, f. 131^{r}; 10, f. 113^{v}; 11, ff. 8^{r}–9^{r}, 50^{r}, 223^{r-v}.

32. ASG, Notary Tommaso Casanova, 9, ff. 55^{v}–56^{r}.

33. Behind the marriage gift that Antonio Rondana of Sant' Agnese left in his will of 1345 to the daughter of Leonardo Scala, a spice merchant of Fossatello, for example, stands long association of both with the Lomellini and their aristocratic relatives and neighbors: ASG, Notary Tommaso Casanova, 2, unnumbered document dated Nov. 1325; 9, ff. 132^{r-v}, 160^{v}–161^{r}; 10. f. 194^{v}.

twenty to sixty houses per acre, the hillside districts that extended up to the wall had densities that were less than eight houses per acre.[34] And the difference in population density, given the much more generous scale of many houses near the port, was undoubtedly even more striking. Their sparse population, an absence of patrician association, and the nature of their settlement—all contributed in these districts to a sense of physical isolation that robbed the compagna of social life.

The hilly districts felt the impact of the steady flow of immigrants who came to the city from the towns and villages of the eastern and western Riviera in the twelfth and thirteenth centuries as Genoa extended its authority along the coast.[35] Two things are striking about the immigrants: their absence of effective kin ties within the city and their remarkable devotion to their native villages. Unlike the patriciate, who consciously created kin districts and sought to maintain power through the extension of kin ties, the small merchants and artisans who settled on the hills seem to have settled on their own. If their brothers, sisters, cousins, aunts, or uncles came to Genoa with them, they almost never bought property in the same neighborhood, rarely did business together, and seldom relied on one another in moments of crisis. Women found it hard to produce kinsmen to act as their legal counselors and, as the notaries were careful to record and as the law allowed, turned instead to neighbors.[36] Men often approached priests, fellow craftsmen, or neighbors to act as executors of their estates or guardians of their children.[37]

Most of the property holders in these districts came from the property-holding class of the villages of the Ligurian countryside.[38] If they had sold part of their holdings in the countryside to secure a place for themselves in the city, they seem to have been reluctant to break with their village past. Indeed, their retention of ties with their villages qualified the urban nature of their lives. They often continued to hold property in the countryside and houses in the village, which were passed on to their children and their children's children. They continued to give charitable donations to the village church and often remembered villagers in their wills.[39] And finally, they frequently returned to the village to find wives or married Genoese women whose parents had come from the same town or village.

34. Heers, "Urbanisme et structure sociale," pp. 396–97.

35. Vito Vitale, *Il comune del podestà a Genova* (Milan, 1951), pp. 60–120.

36. Hughes, "Urban Growth and Family Structure," pp. 20–21.

37. The earliest contracts showing such a tendency are those of Oberto Scriba in 1190, and he was a notary whose clientele was largely drawn from the new immigrant population.

38. Erik Bach, *La cité de Gênes au XIIe siècle* (Copenhagen, 1955), pp. 133–39.

39. For early examples, see ASG, ms. 102 (Diversorum), ff. 201^{r}, 222^{v}, 239^{r-v}, 248^{r}.

For example, when Oberto, the son of a barrelmaker from Chiavari, decided to take a wife in 1313, he went to the house in Fossatello of a merchant from Chiavari and arranged to marry his orphaned niece. The four witnesses, two from Chiavari and two others from neighboring villages, seem to have been summoned to secure for the match the weighty and collective approval of home.[40] And when a certain Simone di Collo died in 1307, leaving a generous bequest to provide dowries for twenty-five poor Genoese maidens, his money was used to unite men and women whose roots were planted in the same countryside. In at least seven of the nine extant contracts the bride and groom came from, or had their origins in, the same or an immediately neighboring village.[41]

In some instances they were simply marrying their neighbors. For if the absence of an effective network of kin ties among immigrants gave to the relations among neighbors an intensity they might otherwise have lacked, the tendency of villagers to settle together in the city made many Genoese neighborhoods the physical extensions of particular villages. In most areas of the city neighbors were more likely to share village than craft ties. A district of artisans in Genoa was usually no more than a few houses on a short street, and even these often contained people pursuing other trades. The woolworkers who gathered into compact districts near the fast streams of Bisagno and Polcevera at either side of the city were exceptional. Their sense of unity with their fellow craftsmen can be seen at a personal level in the appointment, for example, of a senior craftsman as an "official" estate executor for his neighbors and fellow artisans.[42] And it assumed political significance when their united force helped to elect a popular regime in 1257.[43] The scattered artisan settlements elsewhere in the city, however, made their trades less coherent. At a personal level, the attraction of different trades in the same neighborhood helps to explain both the frequency with which sons were apprenticed in different trades and the variety of crafts found within individual Genoese families. At a governmental level, their lack of a geographic base may help to explain why even during the popular regimes of the thirteenth and fourteenth centuries the crafts in Genoa exerted so little political influence.[44]

Neighborhood ties were repeatedly strengthened, however, by village

40. ASG, cartulary 77, ff. 166^r–167^r, 204^r.

41. Ibid., ff. 118^v–222^v.

42. Roberto Lopez, "Le origine dell'arte della lana," in his *Studi sull' economia genovese nel Medio Evo* (Turin, 1936), pp. 196–97.

43. Vitale, *Breviario della storia di Genova*, I, 95–97.

44. On the character of anti-magnate legislation in Genoa, see Gina Fasoli, "Ricerche sulla legislazione antimagnatizia nei comuni dell' alta e media Italia," *Rivista di storia del diritto italiano*, 12 (1939), 102–05.

ties. The popular neighborhood of San Donato, for example, was filled in the thirteenth century (as the adjacent neighborhood of Chiavica had been in the twelfth) with men and women from Recco.[45] These ties, constantly reinforced by their ownership of land in their common village, by their search for local wives, and by a stream of new immigrants, were intensified by the neighborhood's physical confinement. If the compagna never became an effective district, the five or six much smaller *conestagie* into which each compagna was divided and which developed banners and bureaucracies all their own never became effective neighborhoods.[46] For the Genoese who lived outside the noble enclave and its district, the neighborhood was not an administrative unit but a *contrada* or *vicinia* of a few streets, whose center was often a local church. In fact, the most vigorous neighborhoods seem to have been those that were centered on a church, whose small square was used to transact neighborhood business and whose priests were active in community affairs. At San Donato the priests were constantly involved in the neighborhood: witnessing acts, arbitrating disputes, and trading actively with their neighbors. Giovanni, a dyer of San Donato, not only did a flourishing business with his neighbor priests, but he also assured the canons of that church in 1226 that he would guarantee that an absent canon would agree to the election regulations that they had just drawn up; it was undoubtedly common knowledge that the canon owed him money.[47]

Upon the hills and in the other areas of the city free of patrician enclaves, men and women tended to confine themselves to a tight network of personal relationships centered on the neighborhood, which were supplemented less by other urban ties than by ties with the village from which they and many of their neighbors had come. Necessities of business often worked against this cohesion as crafts, markets, and the port pulled the neighborhood into the city. But even in a neighborhood like Sant' Agnese village ties could vie with an aristocratic presence as a stimulant to the formation of social bonds. The two Viale brothers who lived there in the mid-fourteenth century, for example, were related by marriage to at least one patrician family at San Siro and were active in trade with and alongside their patrician neighbors. They seem, nevertheless, to have formed their

45. Mario Chiaudano and Raimondo Morozzo della Rocca, eds., *Oberto Scriba de Mercato (1190)* (Turin, 1938), nos. 301, 305, 583; M. W. Hall, H. C. Krueger, and R. L. Reynolds, eds., *Guglielmo Cassinese (1190–2)* (Genoa, 1938), nos. 369–70; Ferretto, *Codice diplomatico*, II, 137, 139, n. 2, 408.

46. Stella, *Annales*, col. 1193; Heers, "Urbanisme et structure sociale," pp. 381–82, 394–402.

47. Arturo Ferretto, ed., *Liber magistri Salmonis, 1222–6* (Atti della Società Ligure di Storia Patria, xxxvi, 1906), pp. 550–51.

closest social bonds with neighboring families whose roots lay in Quarto, where the Viale also held land and houses.[48] And the case of two builders from Sant' Agnese who took as their partner in 1342 a craftsman who lived in a distant district of Genoa—but who had come originally from a little town in Lavagna whose natives also filled the streets of Sant' Agnese—shows how subtly village and neighborhood connections insert themselves into apparently the most urban of arrangements.[49]

Urban growth and a slowing of immigration began in the fourteenth century to change the nature of many of these enclosed neighborhoods, and from the mid-fourteenth century neighborhood ties may less often have joined men and women in common activities. The calls upon popular governments to create more suitable neighborhood meeting places in popular areas, although they may be signs of neighborhood identity, may also reveal a growing need to organize what had once worked on its own. As early as 1365 the popular government had persuaded Pope Urban V during a visit to Genoa to donate to the commune some church houses. These were demolished to create the Piazza Nuova as a meeting place for the popular neighborhood around Sant' Ambrogio, and by the following century many popular neighborhoods were allowed to construct squares and loggie.[50] At San Donato a new and frequently embellished loggia was the outward sign of neighborhood activity that led to the formation in 1447 by the heads of 102 neighboring families of a formal neighborhood association, which continued to meet for at least two decades. Led by four elected leaders who were to care for the preservation of the vicinia, the association admitted only neighbors who met the approval of three-quarters of the group's membership. If a member left the neighborhood, he was dropped from the rolls.[51]

The formation of such an association of neighbors was in part an attempt to cope with social and political strife within Genoa, which by the fourteenth century had begun to divide popular neighborhoods. The only clear oath of the membership at San Donato was to put aside all distinction of party.[52] Such a need was felt throughtout the city, which was rent each year by partisan strife so fierce that it left large districts in ruin. Benzo

48. ASG, Notary Tommaso Casanova, 10, ff. 3^{v}–6^{r}, 9^{r-v}, 23^{r-v}, 187^{v}–188^{r}; 11, ff. 173^{r}–174^{r}, 176^{r}–177^{r}, 200^{r-v}.

49. ASG, Notary Tommaso Casanova, 9, ff. 84^{r-v}, 87^{v}.

50. Podestà, *Il colle di S. Andrea*, p. 150; Luigi Tommaso Belgrano, *La vita privata dei Genovesi*, 2d ed. (Genoa, 1875), pp. 46–47.

51. Jacques Heers, *Le clan familial au Moyen Age* (Paris, 1974), pp. 149–51.

52. "Nullo colore infringere volumus."

of Alessandria's pessimistic prediction of a Genoa so increasingly deformed by ruins that later passersby might say, "This was Genoa,"[53] is supported by less literary records. Boniface VIII had given a canon and schoolmaster of Genoa permission in 1297 to spend his declining years in Chiavari rather than in Genoa because the houses and cloister of San Lorenzo had been reduced to ruins.[54] The cathedral was particularly vulnerable because it was surrounded by the houses of the aristocracy, who fomented the wars which paralyzed the city and whose neighborhoods became battlefields. In a day's minor skirmish in the summer of 1398, for example, fighting moved from the piazza of the Lercari into the neighboring square of the Malocelli, and on to the enclave of the Squarciafichi, leaving the charred remains of twenty-two houses in its wake.[55]

In their desperate struggle for political dominance, certain aristocratic families turned to their neighborhoods and converted territorial into kin ties to create what came to be called in Genoa an *albergo*. It is significant that the Genoese annalist first used the term in 1265 to describe the Spinola, who were then trying to overthrow the government.[56] By the 1270s the notarial records contain references to the members of at least three families from the Spinola neighborhood at Luccoli who had assumed the Spinola surname and who had joined with them in a permanent social and political alliance.[57] In the thirteenth century, the albergo sometimes reunited members of a lineage group whose identity had become fragmented. Many of those who formed the Spinola albergo may indeed have belonged to cadet lines which had taken different surnames.[58] Such a reunion was the stated reason for the creation of the albergo Squarciafico in 1297, at which time five separate, agnatically related lines agreed to take the name of the most prominent, Squarciafico.[59] By the first decades of the

53. "Hec fuit Janua," cited by Joseph R. Berrigan, "Benzo d'Alessandria and the Cities of Northern Italy," in *Studies in Medieval and Renaissance History*, 4 (1967), 188.

54. Ferretto, *Codice diplomatico*, II, 19, n. 1.

55. Stella, *Annales*, col. 1165.

56. Belgrano and Imperiale di Sant' Angelo, *Annali genovesi*, IV, 71.

57. Ferretto, *Codice diplomatico*, II, lxxiv, 134, 145, 224, 238, 266, 279, 280, 369, for the Dugo, Biscia, and Baione families, who were still in the albergo in the fifteenth century. Some members of these families remained outside the albergo, however, as did Gabriele Dugo, a merchant who had taken up residence in Constantinople, where he made his will in 1315. His connections with Genoa remained very strong, and his sons returned there after their father's death. But although Gabriele was closely associated with the Spinola in business, he does not seem to have been a member of their albergo: ASG, Notary Tommaso Casanova, 1, ff. 149^{v}–152^{r}; 2, unnumbered document.

58. As suggested by Edoardo Grendi, "Profilo storico degli alberghi genovesi," *Mélanges de l'Ecole française de Rome* (*Moyen-Age-temps modernes*), 87 (1975), 276–77.

59. ASG, cartulary 146, f. 65^{r}.

fourteenth century, however, the principle of albergo formation had become more clearly territorial and the agnatic tie, more commonly fictive. In the case of the city's greatest families, such as the Doria and Spinola or the Grimaldi and Fieschi, the albergo could be more an exaggeration of patronage ties than an association of aristocratic neighbors. Indeed the attempt on the part of the Grimaldi and Spinola at San Luca to form a single albergo failed because the small group of Spinola at San Luca, divided from their kinsmen at Luccoli, feared domination by the Grimaldi, whose concentrated strength was at San Luca.[60] Among those removed from the highest social and political plane, however, the albergo was often a union of equals, like the albergo Cattaneo, which at the beginning of the fourteenth century joined the della Volta and Mallone families and enclaves at San Giorgio, or the Gentile albergo, which in the 1330s began to unite the Avvocati, Pevere, Pignoli, and Turca at San Siro.[61]

In the creation of alberghi, territorial ties vied with blood ties as a principle of association. Although lineage bonds remained strong, geography served to give them definition. The albergo almost always united neighbors. It was usually for geographic reasons that an entire lineage failed to unite within one albergo, as when the Spinola at Luccoli and San Luca or the di Mari at San Pietro and Luccoli divided to form separate alberghi.[62] As neighboring patrician families united within an albergo, they merged their enclaves, often demolishing buildings, as the Doria had done in the late thirteenth century at San Matteo, to design larger central squares. And they pulled in their client neighbors, who, like the man at Santa Maria delle Vigne who signed himself Bartolomeo Camilla, "formerly a woolworker," took the albergo's aristocratic surname.[63]

A faltering economy and a demographic crisis were undoubtedly spurs to the albergo's rapid formation in the fourteenth century. Both were clearly in the mind of Leonia di Mari when she stipulated that two emigrant kinsmen must return to take up their citizenship rights in Genoa alongside others of the albergo di Mari if they wished to receive their legacies.[64] But it was the city's political turbulence that overwhelmingly determined the albergo's architectural form and social attitudes, encourag-

60. Grendi, "Profilo storico," pp. 263, 271–72.

61. For the albergo Cattaneo, see ASG, cartulary 48, ff. 85^{v} and 105^{r} (for the presence of the Mallone), cartulary 50, ff. 13^{r}, 19^{r-v}, 21^{v}, 23^{v}, 29^{r}, cartulary 77, f. 174^{r} (for the presence of the della Volta). For the albergo Gentile, see ASG, Notary Tommaso Casanova, 9, ff. 11^{r}, 39^{v}, 108^{r}–109^{v}; 10, ff. 36^{r-v}, 47^{v}–51^{r}.

62. Ascheri, *Notizie intorno*.

63. Gabriella Airaldi, ed., *Le carte di Santa Maria delle Vigne di Genova (1103–1392)* (Genoa, 1969), p. 225.

64. ASG, Notary Therami de Maiolo, 1, ff. 167^{v}–168^{r}.

ing its increasingly private and enclosed nature. Branca Doria, who led his family in the fourteenth century, seems seldom to have conducted his business outside the secure walls of the Piazza San Matteo. And when he moved through the city, he usually went in formal company, or slipped away from hostile factions in the dead of night.[65] And Rabella Grimaldo, the leader of his albergo at San Luca later in the same century, appears in most notarial acts within sight of his house and the fortifications of his enclave.[66] If other members of their families and their alberghi appeared more frequently in other parts of the city, their interests too were becoming more localized within the albergo, where client members acted as agents and noble members as business partners. The albergo's poor began for the first time in the late fourteenth and early fifteenth century regularly to assume precedence over the poor at large in the wills of the albergo's aristocratic leaders. And the remarkable lineage exogamy practiced in medieval Genoa began to break down at the same time as men stayed in the albergo for their wives.[67]

In their constant efforts to construct better towers, dungeons, and other fortifications to secure the albergo, patricians expressed their fear of its violation, a fear that was intimately connected with their sense of honor. Honor was bound up in the family district—in its houses, in the bones of its ancestors,[68] and, at least by the fourteenth century, in the chastity of its women. Unlike women from popular families, who moved relatively freely about the city, patrician women conducted their business almost without exception within the enclave.[69] The ultimate penetration of the patrician quarter and dishonoring of its family was the violation of its women. The chronicler Giorgio Stella even expressed surprise that in 1327 the Ghibellines did not molest the women of their defeated Guelf

65. See, for example, ASG, Cartulary 127, ff. 150^{v}, 172^{r-v}, 176^{r}, 177^{v}, 178^{r}, 207^{r}, 231^{r}, 239^{v}, 258^{r}, 259^{r}, 260^{r}, 286^{v}; cartulary 130, ff. 1^{v}, 5^{v}, 6^{r}, 22^{r}; Arturo Ferretto, "Branca Doria e la sua famiglia," in *Codice diplomatico*, I, 45–46.

66. His dealings in the 1340s are recorded in the acts of Tommaso Casanova, 9–11.

67. ASG, Notary Oberto Foglietta, Sr., 1, nos. vi and xxxiv; Notary Therami de Maiolo, 1, ff. 167^{v}–168^{r}.

68. The chief reason advanced by the Grimaldi and Spinola for their founding of San Luca in the twelfth century was that it offered better security for burial than neighboring San Siro: Hughes, "Urban Growth and Family Structure," p. 10. A similar concern was expressed in the fourteenth century by Violante, the widow of Francesco degli Oltremarini, who chose burial in the Oltremarini chapel at San Siro, stipulating that if that chapel fell into the hands of another family, her remains were to be removed: ASG, Notary Tommaso Casanova, 2, unnumbered document dated 27 January 1338.

69. Older widows with children were granted greater freedom, however. See Diane Hughes, "Domestic Ideals and Social Behavior: Evidence from Medieval Genoa," in *The Family in History*, ed. Charles E. Rosenberg (Philadelphia, 1975), pp. 139–42.

opponents, who had been left behind in their urban enclaves.[70] As aristocratic concern for honor filtered down to the popolani, whose women were both more vulnerable to attack and more exposed to temptation, they turned not to kinsmen but to neighbors. The fifteenth-century association of neighbors at San Donato had four matrons to care for the morals of the women of the neighborhood.[71]

Neither the patrician neighborhoods in the densely settled districts of Genoa nor the popular areas in the more sparsely settled hills survived the fourteenth century without change. The patrician lineage could not survive the political, economic, and demographic crises of the later Middle Ages without the territorial strength that it found in formal union with neighbors. In popular areas the kin ties that inevitably developed among long-settled families and the increasing opportunity to participate in urban affairs with the introduction of popular government in 1339 undoubtedly began to dissolve the natural, close-knit neighborhoods of an earlier age. But the early isolation of both the patrician neighborhood, whose focus was at once the fortified enclave and the aristocratic lineage, and the popular neighborhood, whose focus was at once a local church and a distant village, contributed to medieval Genoa's peculiarly anarchic social and political life. The nature of these neighborhoods should help us to see that the reasons for Genoa's political incapacity lay less in any kind of individualism than in corporate exclusiveness and isolation.

70. Stella, *Annales*, col. 1055.

71. Heers, *Le clan familial au Moyen Age*, p. 149.

7

Pars, Parte: Dante and an Urban Contribution to Political Thought

Edward Peters

Of all the constituent parts of political communities, none has had to overcome as intense and enduring an opposition on the part of political and constitutional thinkers, from antiquity to the nineteenth century, as the institution of party. On the other hand, none has seemed so essential in the eyes of political analysts for the effective functioning of modern republican or democratic governments and political communities. Ignored or condemned by classical political theorists from Aristotle to Cicero, the concept of party was semantically tainted by association with such terms as *factio* and *secta.* Later, it was set systematically in opposition to such compelling images as *unitas*, *concordia*, and *corpus* by medieval political theorists.[1] The very idea of organized, constructive political conflict

1. On the development and terminology of social and political conflict in the Roman Republic, see P. A. Brunt, *Social Conflicts in the Roman Republic* (London, 1971) and A. W. Lintott, *Violence in Republican Rome* (Oxford, 1968). The most thorough study of the semantics of the Roman usage of "pars" and "factio," however, is the study of Lily Ross Taylor, *Party Politics in the Age of Caesar* (Berkeley and Los Angeles, 1949), esp. pp. 7–24, 176, 188–90. Under Augustus and afterward, both pars and factio "became practically synonymous with *seditio*" (Taylor, p. 190, n. 40). My colleague Robert E. A. Palmer has kindly informed me that the terms long retained this meaning in Latin belles lettres. In his *Etymologiae*, ed. W. M. Lindsay, 2 vols. (Oxford, 1911), Isidore of Seville defines *factiosus* (X, 106) as "inter opprobria, cum seditiosum accipi volumus: cum vero gratiosum ac potentem et quasi magnae factionis." *Seditio* (V, xxvi, 11) is defined as "dissensio civium, quod seorsum alii ad alios eunt." In Book VIII, *De ecclesia et sectis*, (VIII, iii, 4–5) both *secta* and schisma, particularly the latter, are regarded as fundamentally pejorative: "Schisma ab scissura animorum vocata. Eodem enim cultu, eodem ritu credit ut ceteri; solo congregationis delectatur discidio." With Isidore, factio, secta, seditio, and schisma have become virtually identical, pejorative terms. St. Augustine's treatise *Contra partem Donati*, written in 397 and no longer extant, suggests that among the Church Fathers the social sense of pars too had gone the way of factio and secta. For Byzantium, see Jacques Jarry, *Hérésies et factions dans l'Empire Byzantin du IVe au VIIe siècle* (Cairo, 1968), esp. pp. 95–188. On the vocabulary of society and its parts, see Pierre Michaud-Quantin, *Universitas: Expressions du mouvement communautaire dans le moyen-âge latin* (Paris, 1970), particularly pp. 271–80 for a discussion of another, and perhaps related usage of pars, that in ecclesiastical elections. There is further literature and discussion in Walter Ullmann, *The Individual and Society in the Middle Ages* (Baltimore, 1966), pp. 34–35. There is an extensive literature on the ecclesiastical concept of *unitas*, from Cyprian on.

within a single community failed to acquire theoretical respectability until it was taken up (cautiously, to be sure) first by English thinkers of the seventeenth and eighteenth centuries and then (even more cautiously) by political theorists in the North American colonies and the new republic, notably James Madison. In spite of a growing willingness to tolerate a politics of parties in the work of such thinkers as Barrington, Hume, Burke, and Madison, political theorists' acceptance of the idea of party was slow and tangled in semantic difficulties. Even into the nineteenth century theories of party oppositon and party government made difficult headway against what both theorists and the political public persisted in conceiving of, and indeed experiencing, as factionalism—divisive, corroding, and ultimately destructive of the unity of the state.

The history of the idea and institution of party has been further obscured by historians' and political scientists' reluctance to agree on the nature of party and faction, the nature of organized political conflict, and the social origins of the modern party system. In this essay I propose to take a position far less rigid and analytical than is often found in discussions of the nature and history of parties and approach the history of the idea in terms of both semantics and political theory, particularly as they offer evidence for the concept of the term in two different periods and places, the first in the northern Italian cities between 1200 and 1500, and the second in England and North America between 1649 and 1800. For only once in European history before the English and North American experiments of the eighteenth and early nineteenth centuries had anything resembling a theory of the legitimacy of party acquired any currency. This phenomenon occurred in the northern Italian city-republics between the thirteenth and the fifteenth centuries. Its opening phase was signaled by the use of the term *pars* (*parte* in Italian) in reference to the Guelf and Ghibelline conflicts early in the thirteenth century. Its closing phase was typified by the brooding political meditations of Machiavelli and Guicciardini in the first half of the sixteenth. After the mid-seventeenth century, political factionalism in England, colored in some quarters by the attraction of republican political ideals, gained ground slowly as political thinkers were once again compelled to face the question of conflict and opposition not only as a theoretical problem, but as an enduring fact of political life. I shall risk the suggestion that in the experience of party the world of Dante and his contemporaries and successors anticipated in several important ways the problems of political conflict and opposition within the civil community and in some instances, particularly in the writings of

Leonardo Bruni and Niccolò Machiavelli, came close to finding a rationale for party conflict and conciliation that was not dissimilar from the views of several eighteenth-century constitutional theorists.[2]

Dante, "a great scholar in almost every branch of learning, albeit he was a layman," was also, as he once called himself, "a man preaching justice," a prophet. The motif of prophecies, adumbrated, partial, misguiding, obscure, and malevolent, constitutes one of the great themes connecting Heaven and Hell. In the *Paradiso* most of the earlier prophecies are finally stated explicitly, in both love and sorrow, and none of them is more troubling than that made by Cacciaguida in *Paradiso*, 17. Dante has said,

> While I was in Vergil's company upon the mountain that heals the souls, and descending into the dead world, grave words were spoken to me of my future life, though I feel myself set foursquare against the blows of chance; so that my desire would be met if I knew what approaches me, for an arrow foreseen comes more gently.

And Cacciaguida, addressed in the first place because he is a respected relative, a saint, and one "who sees contingent things before they are in themselves," "without dark sayings," as in pagan antiquity, and "in plain words and express terms," out of Christian love, utters the memorable, sonorous prophecy of Dante's exile, a prophecy that reflects Dante's sense of his own solitude as he had expressed it to the Italian cardinals in his letter of 1313: "*una sola vox, sola pia, et hec privata, in matris Ecclesie quasi funere audiatur*":

> And that which will weigh heaviest on thy shoulders is the wicked and senseless company with which thou shalt fall into that valley, which shall become wholly ungrateful, quite mad and furious against thee; but before long they, not you, shall have the brows red for this. Of their brutish folly their doings shall give proof, so that it shall be thine honor to have made a party by thyself.

In spite of Dante's twenty years of philosophical and political solitude, Cacciaguida's prophecy is still painful. And the content of that prophecy, "Si ch'a te fia bello/averti fatta parte per te stesso," that Dante will

2. See Frederic C. Lane, "At the Roots of Republicanism," *American Historical Review 71* (1966), 403–20, for a discussion of other relationships between Italian and American republicanism and the citation of extensive literature. See also Ullmann, *The Individual and Society in the Middle Ages*, esp. pp. 101–51.

make a party unto himself, is *not* honorific. It is certainly not, as some commentators have read it, a kind of paean to Dante's romantic political individualism. Dante's becoming a parte is of a piece with the salty taste of other men's bread, the steepness of other men's stairs, and the bestiality of the exiled White Guelfs. Being a parte will be to Dante's honor, because in the upside-down moral world of early fourteenth-century, there is no hope of a restored political community. Parte, which is used in an unremittingly pejorative sense throughout the writings of Dante, Remigio de' Girolami, Compagni, and Villani, is a condemnation to continued political impotence, an ironic commentary on the political divisiveness that Dante so uniformly condemns throughout the *Commedia*.

A party was not even a legitimate part of a *popolo*, and, as Dante remarks in *Paradiso*, 31, the only "popol giusto e sano" is that of Heaven, where there are no parties. The honor of which Cacciaguida speaks in *Paradiso*, 17, is the honor that exists in the face of the shame of factionalism, not an honor that justifies it. It was this sense of pars, parte, and factio that the citizens of the northern Italian city-republics sharpened and tasted first, and yet could not avoid. Other before and after Dante had perceived and denounced the evils of factionalism, but few put their denunciations into great poetry, and few could work it as sharply into the counsels of Heaven as Dante. "Questo tuo grido" (this cry of yours), Dante's "molesta voce," Cacciaguida says, was not made to benefit Dante himself, but to lacerate Dante's world. In that perverted world, Dante's own future could be at best dismal, and the badge of "parte per te stesso" was not a badge otherwise worn in honor.

The apparatus of Dante's assault on the concept of parte as the sign of civic discord appears early in the *Inferno*, probably as early as the whirling banner and its aimless followers in canto 3. In canto 6, the bestial Cerberus introduces a number of motifs that are developed in Dante's discussion with the Florentine Ciacco, and Florence, "la città partita," full of discord, is divided by "la parte selvaggia" and "the other." Throughout much of the *Commedia*, bestiality is associated with civil discord, probably from the frequency of the image in Aristotelian sources and commentaries, and very frequently it is associated with the form of discord taken by party and factional opposition.[3] Ciacco's is one of the prophecies taken up and expanded by Cacciaguida in *Paradiso*, 17. Farinata, in *Inferno*, 10, speaks of Dante's ancestors' hostility "to me, to my forebears, and to my party,"

3. See, e.g., Pierre Michaud-Quantin, *Études sur le vocabulaire philosophique du Moyen Age* (Rome, 1970), p. 51, citing Jean Buridan's *Quaestiones in decem libros Ethicorum Aristotelis*, VII, q. 1.

and is saddened by his own party's failure to have learned the *arte* of returning to power. Farinata too, dimly prophesies Dante's inglorious future, and with him in the tombs of the heretics are other great Ghibellines, including Frederick II and Cardinal Ottaviano degli Ubaldini, the *sectae* of the heretics here explicitly identified with the *pars Gebellina.* In canto 15, Brunetto Latini, who himself had inveighed against partisanship in his *Livre dou Trésor*, takes the divisions of Florence still further back in time. Ciacco had spoken of the Black and White Guelfs, Farinata of the Guelfs and Ghibellines, and Brunetto of the legendary beginnings of factionalism in Florence, the intrusion of new people from Fiesole, an "ingrato popolo maligno . . . tiene ancor del monte e del macigno." "Thy fortune holds for thee such honor," Brunetto tells Dante, "that one party and the other shall be ravenous against thee." In canto 16, the three Florentine sodomites elicit yet another condemnation of factionalism from Dante. Thus, halfway through the *Inferno*, Dante's condemnation of party strife and its origins has been repeatedly and extensively articulated. In canto 19, Dante, having explored the domestic, political, and social origins of civil discord, begins his depiction of the Church's role in fomenting and extending party divisions. In canto 28, the party feuds of Dante's own Italy are linked with ecclesiastical and domestic schism, through Mohammed, Piero de Medicina, Curio, Mosca, and Bertran de Born. Ecclesiastical schism and family discord are here linked to the political struggles in Florence and in other city-republics. Even the association of the giants, in canto 31, with the towers of city factions, particularly in the image of linguistic discord in Nimrod, echoes Dante's systematic depiction of party rivalry in its multiple dimensions. The reference in canto 31 completes its exposition in the *Inferno*.

The *Purgatorio* takes up the theme of discord on a grander scale, from Dante's majestic invective in canto 6, with its references to Marcellus and partisanship and the perversions of rapid and contrary changes in law and custom, and with the reference to *rinovate membre*, a grotesque image of recalling citizens that echoes some of the physical transformations in the lower *bolge* of the *Inferno*. In canto 14 and canto 15, Guido del Duca and Vergil discuss communal affection in the context, first, of the politics and rivalries of the Romagna, and, second, in the larger context of charity in Vergil's discourse. Canto 16, extending Brunetto Latini's discourse in *Inferno*, 15, and pointing toward Cacciaguida's revelations in *Paradiso*, 17, answers the last of Dante's civic questions, and when, in canto 27, Vergil "crowns and mitres" Dante over himself, he anticipates Cacciaguida's prophecy of Dante's becoming a "party unto himself" in *Paradiso*, 17.

In *Paradiso*, discord and party strife appear in sharper contrast to the background, partly because of their inappropriateness, both in Paradise itself and in the long political meditation that runs through the *Commedia*, with its beginnings in *Inferno*, 6. In *Paradiso*, 6, Justinian scornfully describes the futile and avaricious competition waged by the yellow lilies against the *pubblico segno* on the one hand, and the imperialists' claiming the *segno* itself as an emblem of a mere party cause. Carlo Martello in *Paradiso*, 8, reconciles the diversity among individuals and explains the biological violations committed by the divided society of Florence. In *Paradiso*, 15–17, of course, the discussion of parties is taken up at its most extended level and traced back to Florence's fall from "il buon tempo antico" and the intrusion of new people with lower standards. St. Peter's invective in *Paradiso*, 27, accuses the papacy and echoes Justinian's earlier denunciation:

Non fu nostra intenzion ch'a destra mano
 de' nostri successor parte sedesse,
 parte dall'altra del popol cristiano;
nè che le chiavi che mi fuor concesse
 divenisser signaculo in vessillo
 che contra battezzati combattesse;
nè ch' io fossi figura di sigillo
 a privilegi venduti e mendaci,
 ond' io sovente arrosso e disfavillo.

Paradiso, 27, 46–54

Dante, it should be pointed out, like many other medieval writers, knew many uses of "pars" and its synonyms and cognates. His most frequent usage of the terms are not, in fact, in the pejorative political sense, but in that range of geographical, philosophical, logical, and geometrical terminology in which the word had a strictly neutral meaning. The contrast between Dante's commonest use of the term and his pejorative use of parte in politics is striking precisely because Dante rarely uses factio or secta. When he denounces civil discord, it is parte he denounces, almost as if the word took on a stronger meaning in contrast with its more frequent subordination in spatial and logical discourse. It is the parte that the poet attacks, and indeed it is Dante's perception of the party as the chief object of his denunciations that suggests the particularly odious connotations the term, and the institutions it designates, have for him. Parte, the product of the Devil, of avarice, of biological and genetic mishaps, of injustice in all its forms, and of social degeneration, bears the semantic brunt of Dante's outrage.

Dante's invective against parte was not simply the result of his philosophical ideas, but a direct attack upon the use of the term to designate political opposition in the city-republics themselves. For the term pars had come into wide use in the thirteenth century to designate political opposition, and contending groups on opposite sides of issues and cities used the term to refer to both themselves and their enemies.[4]

Many scholars have studied the origins of political conflict in twelfth- and thirteenth-century Italy, and many have observed Dante's particularly intense and unremitting invective against civil discord, which echoes similar expressed attitudes on the part of other writers, most frequently Remigio de' Girolami, Dino Compagni, and Giovanni Villani.[5] Few, however, have paid much attention to the terms pars and parte in themselves and to their appearance in the thirteenth century to designate political groupings. What is particularly striking about the term pars is its initially value-free usage. It is one thing to denounce party universally, as Dante does, or to use the term only as a epithet to describe one's enemies, as did many writers in seventeenth- and eighteenth-century England and the North American colonies. The partes in thirteenth-century Italy appear to have been the first to apply the term *both* to themselves and to their opponents, thus using it to designate subgroups within a wider political community. Many historians have properly observed that the content of the terms Guelf and Ghibelline waxed and waned between the early thirteenth and the early fourteenth centuries, possessing various meanings that could be understood only in terms of particular localities and particular times (even Bartolus threw up his hands in distraction when it came to explaining the differences between Guelf and Ghibelline). Nevertheless, the use of the term pars to designate the two groups and the survival of pars as a political construct well beyond the age when Guelfism and Ghibellinism had wholly lost the last of their ideological content has a great deal of significance.

4. The standard collection of references is Robert Davidsohn, *Forschungen zur Geschichte von Florenz* (1908; reprint ed., Turin, 1964), III, 29–67. See also R. Caggese, "Sul l' origine della parte guelfa e le sue relazioni col Comune," *Archivio storico italiano*, 5th series, *23* (1903), 265–309; G. Glotz, ed., *Histoire générale: Histoire du moyen age* (Paris, 1939), vol. IV, pt. 1, E. Jordan, *L'Allemagne et l'Italie aux XIIe et XIIIe siècles.*

5. Most recently, Charles T. Davis, "Ptolemy of Lucca and the Roman Republic," *Proceedings of the American Philosophical Society, 118* (1974), 30–50; Charles T. Davis, "An Early Florentine Political Theorist: Fra Remigio de' Girolami," *Proceedings of the American Philosophical Society, 104* (1960), 662–76; L. Minio-Paluello, "Remigio Girolami's *De Bono Comuni*," *Italian Studies, 11* (1956), 56–71; Louis F. Green, *Chronicle into History: An Essay on the Interpretation of History in Florentine Fourteenth-Century Chronicles* (Cambridge, 1972).

Few scholars now accept the older views of class conflict and urban-rural rivalries that were once invoked to explain the factionalism of the Italian cities from the eleventh to the fourteenth centuries. The growth of town populations, wealth and physical fabric, and autonomy increased dramatically from the tenth century on. The unpredictable rivalries fashioned and discarded throughout the Investiture Conflict altered not only traditional town authority relationships, but also the relative importance of different groups within each town. From the early twelfth century on, the towns of northern Italy created a kind of social, material, and political life that had not before been seen in the history of the West. Not the city-states of Greece or Rome, not even the closely governed cities of Byzantium or the Islamic east, had been quite like them, and a number of their unique circumstances deserve re-emphasis.

First, after the early twelfth century, the distance between the Italian cities and their nominal legal overlords, the Holy Roman Emperors, varied considerably. Deprived of the ultimate authority of state organization, many of their institutions were developed to deal with practical problems on a level that put the question of absolute authority to one side. They and their territories were compact, densely populated, and extraordinarily diversified socially. These three features set them apart from other contemporary political structures, which were hampered by problems of communications, size, and social homogeneity. Finally, the city itself took a long time to attract and hold the loyalty and identification of its citizens, partly because the question of urban governmental authority was always ambiguous, and partly because most city-dwellers felt more loyalty to the innumerable *societates*, the lesser communities from the neighborhood to the *arte*, to the military association, to the clan, or to the religious confraternity than they did to the city itself. The fractionalization of loyalty, economic interests, status, and family generated much dissension and insecurity, as well as civic instability, and political turbulence was a constant of life under these conditions.

It is one thing to look back at the history of the towns from this side of the watershed constituted by the modern theory of the sovereign state and regard them as politically incomplete communities. It is another to look at the problem of political power within the towns from the point of view of those who had to live with it and possessed virtually no political theory at all to justify their public activities. In a brilliant study, Nicolai Rubinstein has shown how, in the case of Florence, political theory grew up in the chronicles concerning the origins of the city and was the result of several writers' attempts to understand the rapid economic, social, and political changes that had taken place during the thirteenth century.[6] Although several chroniclers attributed much to Fortune and to cycles of progress and decline determined astrologically, Rubinstein has elsewhere shown how, in the case of Albertino Mussatto's account of Paduan history, "by blending Roman ideas on history with contemporary astrological speculations and the political experience of changes and instability, Mussatto was able to present his contemporaries with an interpretation of Paduan history which would help to explain the fateful events of the last years of the Paduan republic."[7]

Neither Mussatto's nor Dante's dismay at the prospect of understanding the rapidly changing course of local history, with the confines of the city as its object, is surprising, considering the rapidity of that change, the diversity of the elements active in it, and, until quite late, the lack of any widely accepted theory or institutional structure supporting the organic polity. In the eyes of neo-Aristotelians and other theorists of the organic polity, discord and factionalism seemed the only explanations for turbulent histories in city after city. In the eyes of those who, in the late twelfth and thirteenth centuries, lived through the changes that later histories tried to make sense of, discord and factionalism were hardly objectified at all, but were rather the normal horizons of political life.

The terms by which the various societates acquired a voice in affairs that they saw as touching *them* alone, far more than as touching the city as a whole, usually entailed deference to some group of nobles and division among groups of nobles themselves. Within the cities there was virtually no limit to the extent to which division on these terms could occur. The multiple affiliations and interests of the nobles (whether older nobility, *magnati*, or *popolani grassi*) were continued in the oligarchies that replaced them and ruled the governments of the popolo. Within these successive governments, there was room for rivalries, but hardly for opposition on a "constitutional" basis.

Within this framework of family, societates, confraternities, and even more amorphous interests, the administrative officials of the cities, the *podestà*, sought to maintain both the rights of the communes and the stability of the public order. Commune, *consorterie*, arti, *vicinanze*, popoli—such subsocieties as these made the medieval Italian city rather like a nest of ill-fitting Chinese boxes, no one of which was able to turn the *civitas*

6. Rubinstein, "The Beginnings of Political Thought in Florence," *Journal of the Warburg and Courtauld Institute*, 5 (1942), 198–227.

7. Rubinstein, "Some Ideas on Municipal Progress and Decline," *Fritz Saxl: A Volume of Memorial Essays* (London, 1957), pp. 165–83, at 183.

itself into a political unit. In this world, whose political conditions pointed toward the experience of later territorial states, civil administration did little to create a state framework except by trying to prevent the undue exercise of informal power by one contending group or another. Thus the appearance of Guelf and Ghibelline parties in the early years of the thirteenth century is less important as a chapter in the history of the papal-imperial conflict than as the opportunity to grasp the form of a societas that could claim a degree of legitimacy denied to the contending groups within the city itself.

Édouard Jordan, in his account of the origins of the Guelf-Ghibelline struggle, shrewdly remarked:

> We must recall that at the beginning the Italians were not set to fighting one another because they supported the Empire or the Church; it was because they were already struggling for local interests that they had chosen in different ways between two powers who fought each other over and around their heads. It is necessary to be a bit more sceptical of that reproach, addressed since the thirteenth century at the popes and above all at the emperor for having set discord into Italy. It existed there already.[8]

The attractions of the Guelf and Ghibelline causes were many. Each side could claim the sanction of a superior authority and count on the aid of people of like sympathies in other towns. Each could attack the other with new and formidable weapons, new arms, confiscated property, declarations of enemies as traitors, if Guelfs, or as heretics, if Ghibellines. These larger causes offered a wider base of support than the more parochial societates. Nevertheless, they did not become identical with the civitas itself, and they emerged, as Romolo Caggese long ago put it, "as two great associations which joined themselves to the skeleton of the organism of the commune as a vertebral column."[9] With local, particularistic antagonisms translated to a larger sphere, both parties organized themselves so successfully that whichever of them dominated a city could determine communal policy while remaining separate from the commune itself. However unstable particular communal governments might be, the resouces of one of the great partes provided both a degree of stability and a powerful force for instituting change. In short, the partes offered another channel for the political life of the divided communes, one with greater claims to

8. Jordan, *L'Allemagne et l'Italie*, p. 257.

9. Caggese, "Sul l' origine", p. 281.

legitimacy, greater financial and juridical strength, and a wider basis of participation. Because the commune had failed to reconcile the diverse interests of its multiple subcommunities, the partes came to dominate the commune. Finally, during the period of Dante's youth, when organic notions of the civitas were beginning to be circulated, the ideology of the partes, particularly of the *parte guelfa*, played no small role in shaping the idea of a complete and ordered community. Thus, in spite of the distracting aspect of papal or imperial sympathies and the tangle of foreign relations, the multiplicity of interests that made up each party in each city, and the garbled versions of party opposition that later chroniclers laid out, the partes, particularly the Guelf party, played a role in urban political development that contributed substantially to the organization of the civitas as it emerged in Dante's lifetime and was reflected in the preaching and the writing of such powerful civic theorists as Remigio de' Girolami.[10]

By significantly expanding the character and composition of their support, however, the partes actually intensified the contentious character of urban life at the same time as they strengthened the legitimacy of their claim to a larger and larger role in communal affairs. Not only did party ideology and propaganda run the risk of deepening political opposition within the towns, however, but party affiliation with papal or imperialist causes, however nominal and intermittent, could not fail to be affected by shifts on the larger political scene. Papal attempts to control the Angevins of Naples after the astonishing successes of the 1260s, the arrival of Henry VII in 1310, the new round of papal-imperial conflicts between John XXII and Louis of Bavaria, and the papal rapport with Charles IV are the major shifts of alliances and intensifications of conflicts on the larger scale that influenced the policy of parties within the towns themselves. In spite of the vulnerabilities and risks that party domination of the communes entailed, however, it is hard to avoid the conclusion that the appearance and development of the partes themselves constituted a new arena for political awareness and political activity in the north Italian city-republics. At the very least, the partes offered a rationalization for the control of communal institutions, laws, and policies considerably stronger than any

10. The best general survey of this period is that of Marvin B. Becker, *Florence in Transition*, 2 vols. (Baltimore, 1968–69). In the wider context of the world of the city-republics, see J. K. Hyde, *Society and Politics in Medieval Italy* (New York, 1973), pp. 65–152; D. P. Waley, *The Italian City Republics* (New York, 1969), pp. 164–220. On the specific problem of political and social conflict, see J. K. Hyde, "Contemporary Views on Faction and Civil Strife in 14th Century Italy," in *Violence and Civil Disorder in Italian Cities, 1200–1500*, ed. Lauro Martines (Berkeley and Los Angeles, 1972), pp. 273–307, as well as the other studies in that volume; Lauro Martines, "Political Conflict in the Italian City States," *Government and Opposition, 3* (1967/68), 69–91.

political movement before the growth of an organic theory of political unity. As Jordan concludes, emphasizing the strength of party organs, particularly in Florence:

> The factions that the labels designated were not spontaneous and diffuse groups analogous to our modern parties; but, by a transformation that had as one of its gravest consequences the continuation of that division, they constituted themselves as *partes*, associations powerfully organized, highly disciplined, provided with administrative organs, governed by regularly elected chiefs, ruled by statutes, disposing of considerable resources, animated by a lively *esprit de corps*, and, banished or readmitted, understood the need to remain distinct from the commune in order to control it.[11]

Surely the remarkable organization of the parte guelfa in Florence, for example, influencing as it did the political life of virtually the whole of Tuscany, constitutes something more than mere factionalism, constitutes, in fact, a new kind of political organization that influenced the shape of political consciousness as much as the neo-Aristotelianism that has often received much of the credit.

"Political culture" in the Italian cities was, of course, an inseparable part of the rest of civic culture, and as a number of important and stimulating studies have recently shown, the cultural life of the cities was also rapidly changing during Dante's lifetime. The religious experience of the cities, long considered separately from their political and economic life, the optimism that marked much of civic life and institutions, and the glowing paeans to communal solidarity reflected in sources as diverse as the works of Remigio and Lorenzetti were all part, with formal political theory, of the new intellectual development of the idea of a *vita civile*.[12] The solidarity and broad diffusion of Guelf or Ghibelline party membership contributed to such a movement, although that contribution is often not recognized. But the last years of the thirteenth century and the first decades of the fourteenth saw such a notion of civic solidarity develop only slowly, and up through the beginnings of the critical period 1343–78, the institution of party took up the slack in the constitution of the polity that endured into the second half of the fourteenth century.[13]

11. Jordan, *L'Allemagne et l'Italie*, p. 330.

12. Generally, see John Larner, *Culture and Society in Italy, 1290–1420* (New York, 1971); Marvin Becker, "Dante and His Literary Contemporaries as Political Men," *Speculum*, *41* (1966), 665–80; Charles T. Davis, "Education in Dante's Florence," *Speculum*, *40* (1965), 415–35.

13. For the period, Gene A. Brucker, *Florentine Politics and Society, 1343–1378* (Princeton, 1962).

The rapid development, organization, and rise to power of the Guelf and Ghibelline parties and, in the famous case of Florence, the division between the Black and White Guelfs gave a structure, a new source of legitimacy and power, and a new direction to major elements in the cities, even though their opposition derived more from the particular and varied alignments of interests in the city-*contado* and from the unique constitutional structure of governmental authority than from the great conflicts between the Hohenstaufen and the papacy. Dante's denunciation of parte recognizes both the local and the external pressures that helped to create the parties, but his subordination of political theory to moral and philosophical vision only made him condemn the factionalizing all the more fiercely. Of all the villains in Dante's political world, only Henry VII is spared the poet's denunciation of the divisive and avaricious forces within the urban ruling classes and the Church for having usurped the pubblico segno and the papal keys for use as mere party emblems.

Dante was one of the first, and one of the most articulate writers to challenge the factionalism of the parties in the name of the organic polity. Although Dante's ideal polity was the universal Empire, other writers conceived of it as the city itself. And slowly in the course of the fourteenth century in Florence, the parte guelfa both strengthened that new idea of polity and came to be a component part of it. While fifteenth-century writers looked back to the Guelfs with a lack of sympathy and understanding, they also expressed a nostalgia reminiscent of Dante's nostalgia for "il buon tempo antico." Furthermore, in the invective with which later writers, from Dino Compagni to Villani and Marchionne di Coppo Stefani, denounced party and factional conflict, the Guelf achievement came to be denounced indiscriminately with other manifestations of civil discord. And in areas as diverse as eschatology, political theory, law, historiography, and art, and, as some scholars have suggested, the changing social and political circumstances within such cities as Florence itself, the concept of the importance of the parte guelfa as a party waned in the later fourteenth and fifteenth centuries, surviving only as a vaguely understood element in Florentine political ideology, as a constituent part of what Donald Weinstein has recently called "The Myth of Florence," and in the white shields with red crosses of the Guelf party that were absorbed into Florentine political iconography.[14]

14. Donald Weinstein, "The Myth of Florence," in *Florentine Studies: Politics and Society in Renaissance Florence*, ed. Nicolai Rubinstein (Evanston, 1968), pp. 15–44, with extensive literature cited. See also George Holmes, "The Emergence of an Urban Ideology at Florence, 1250–1450," *Transactions of the Royal Historical Society*, 5th series 23 (1973), pp. 111–34.

Weinstein's important study traces the historical development of the eschatological Florentine political and religious ideology around the time of Savonarola. According to this ideology, Florentine religion, civic order, and virtue would soon constitute a compelling model for the whole world. As Weinstein convincingly demonstrates, elements of this view had been present even in the earliest thirteenth-century chronicles of Florentine history and had been kept alive and developed by various writers and groups, from lay and clerical religious visionaries to humanist historians like Bruni. The external threats from Milan and the internal turmoils of the late fourteenth century had combined to create an elaborate vision:

> So it was that under the double pressure of civic strife and foreign aggression the mythic Florence of the Guelfs tended to coalesce with the prophetic Florence of the Ciompi. Good government and piety, social justice and power, temporal and religious leadership—Rome and Jerusalem—were blended in a single vision which seems to have functioned both as a model of a civic ethos and as a promise of ultimate rewards.[15]

Florentine civic humanism and "the new assertion of Florence's mystical destiny to religious and political supremacy" served as diverse political powers, as Weinstein notes, as Cosimo de' Medici, his opponents in the 1460s, Lorenzo the Magnificent, the post-Laurentian reactionaries, Savonarola, and the restored republic of the early sixteenth century.

If eschatology is at once the most capacious and the vaguest area in which the decline of party legitimacy may be traced, legal theory may be considered the most narrow and precise. Yet the views found in both between 1300 and 1400 are remarkably similar. In the various works of Bartolus, particularly in the well-known treatise *De Guelphis et Gebellinis*, the question of the legitimacy of party power is treated as both a historical and a juridical reality. One of the first writers to suggest a twelfth-century origin (and perhaps a kind of prescriptive right) for the party feuds of the thirteenth century, Bartolus argues that both parties represent "duas affectiones, quiddam . . vocatur Guelphi, quiddam Gebellini," and these

15. Weinstein, "The Myth of Florence," pp. 34–35. On the origins of the Black-White feud, see Gino Masi, "La struttura sociale delle fazioni politiche fiorentine ai tempi di Dante," *Giornale dantesco, 31* (1928), 1–28; Masi, "Sull'origine dei Bianchi e Neri," *Giornale dantesco, 30* (1927), 124–32. On the use of the term pars in other cities, as well as an account of party organizations under other designations, see J. K. Hyde, *Padua in the Age of Dante* (New York, 1966), pp. 193–219; Gina Fasoli, "Guelfi e Ghibellini di Romagna nel 1280–1281," *Archivio storico italiano, 94* (1936), 157–180; Davidsohn, *Forschungen*, III, 39–45; William Bowsky, "Florence and Henry of Luxemburg: The Rebirth of Guelfism," *Speculum, 33* (1958), 177–203.

affectiones in turn derive from the *magna discordia* between Frederick Barbarossa and the Roman Church. Bartolus's particular concern, however, is to determine whether or not the legislative enactments taken by the council of a city (specifically, the commune of Todi), from which the members of one of the two parties are absent, are valid. Bartolus asks whether the missing party's absence was voluntary or involuntary, whether, if the absence is involuntary, the absent party had the *ius condendi statuta* or not, and, if it had, whether its absence was *ex justa causa* or not. In Bartolus's view, each party appears to have shared some part of the total public authority of the commune of Todi, and, if one party was exiled, even though the other, or both, were *collegia approbata* and lawful as long as they tend to further the *bonum publicum*, it was nearly impossible for a single party to rule legally. Bartolus goes on to say that no honorable man in any case should assume a party name or affiliation, *nisi ex magna causa*. There is, according to Bartolus, a theoretically legal justification for parties, but the weight of experience suggests that in practice and, more important, in law, extensive party power is dangerous and raises serious constitutional questions.[16]

The successors of Bartolus, including Baldus, continued to maintain the technical legality of party authority, but increasing juridical hostility grew up in the course of the fourteenth century. Walter Ullmann has suggested that lawyers increasingly swung toward the opinion that all political parties were illegal. He cites the remarkable opinion of the jurist Raynerius de Forlivio, who took that view, because, as Ullmann puts it, "[parties] were disruptive of political unity and stability within the body politic; that, in other words, they were factors disturbing the smooth and peaceful internal development and, consequently, might unduly upset the political and social balance within the state."[17]

The sweeping and vague claims of eschatology, on the one hand, and the narrow technical world of juridical opinion, on the other, both reflect a similar rejection of the legitimacy of party in the political life of the north Italian city-republics during the course of the fourteenth and fifteenth centuries. The immediate historical experience of the early fourteenth century turned other kinds of thinkers toward a similar opinion. The most famous of these is Marsiglio of Padua, whose *Defensor Pacis*, completed in 1324, also focused directly upon the causes of discord within the city-

16. See the discussion in C. N. S. Woolf, *Bartolus of Sassoferrato* (Cambridge, 1913), pp. 189–95 and John H. Mundy, *Europe in the High Middle Ages, 1150–1309* (New York, 1973), pp. 440–42.

17. Walter Ullmann, "The Mediaeval Theory of Legal and Illegal Organizations," *Law Quarterly Review, 60* (1944), 285–91.

republics of northern Italy. In Marsiglio's analysis of the ideal state, the very word pars is functional, describing various offices within the republican regime, not contending groups or a single triumphant group in power. The organic political theories of Aristotle, passed through St. Thomas, Remigio de' Girolami, and Ptolemy of Lucca (and, as Nicolai Rubinstein has pointed out, through the Lorenzetti frescoes in the Palazzo Pubblico in Siena) and urbanized to suit the particular character of the city-republics in the process, could be set over against the theme of discord and faction and invoked to justify either a republican or a signorial regime.[18] In Marsiglio's eyes, as in Dante's, the intervention of external powers, particularly the interference of the papacy, had fomented discord within the cities and prevented the collective authority of the citizens from disposing of executive power within its proper limits. Neither party nor signory satisfy the constitutional requirements of the *Defensor Pacis*. Marsiglio instead develops a sophisticated and articulate expression of the idea of a common good and of the institutional details that supervise its maintainance.

The new emphasis upon the organic character of the political community was reflected in historiography as well as political theory. In the *Chronica* of Giovanni Villani, both the Guelfs and the Ghibellines come under heavy attack, the former because they have forfeited their right to rule by the avarice of their members, and the latter because their actions lead toward inevitable tyranny. Later in the century, the chronicle of Marchionne di Coppo Stefani attacks both parties equally and sees in them nothing more than factionalism and occasions for civil strife, reflecting, far more than even Villani, the view that parties represent a division of an originally unified people. He thus reverses Dante's thesis of the mingling of two separate peoples, but emerges with no less devastating a criticism of party politics.[19]

By the first half of the fifteenth century, when Leonardo Bruni undertook to write the history of Florence on a larger scale and from a more complex point of view, he recognized for the first time the essentially competitive character of republican institutions and the danger of the republic's tendency to dissipate its energies in factional struggles for power. Envy

18. Nicolai Rubinstein, "Marsilius of Padua and Italian Political Thought of His Time," in *Europe in the Late Middle Ages* ed. John Hale, Roger Highfield, Beryl Smalley (Evanston, 1965), pp. 44–75; Rubinstein, "Political Ideas in Sienese Art: The Frescoes by Ambrogio Lorenzetti and Taddeo di Bartolo in the Palazzo Pubblico," *Journal of the Warburg and Courtauld Institutes*, *21* (1958), 179–207; Helène Wieruszowski, "Art and the Comune in the Time of Dante," *Speculum*, *19* (1944), 14–33.

19. Green, *Chronicle into History*, is a good general introduction.

and contention, Bruni admitted, are a necessary accompaniment of liberty, and in the good republic they will be kept under control. The discord among noble families, the accessibility of an arena for the demonstration of outraged honor and social influence, and the absence of a constitution that could control the competitive spirit of the magnates and release the psychological energies of the citizens—all accounted for Florence's grim history of party domination. The determination of public policy by private interests, social passions, and factionalism were for Bruni the results of a failure to control the dangers of republicanism. Bruni goes on to point out that bringing in foreign lords, excluding large segments of the powerful from office, and the widespread practice of imposing exile on dissidents do not merely suppress fundamental discords. They weaken the city, while strengthening its enemies. For Bruni, then, factionalism and party preponderence are the result of the commonwealth's failure to control the human passions that threaten to erupt while it preserves a constitution that encourages eruption but brings other political and cultural advantages. Bruni's aphorism sums up his criticism of factionalism: "Cives enim sic odendi sunt, ut tamen cives illos esse meminerimus".[20] The *inane partium studium*, Guelf or Ghibelline, is no proper passion of the constitutional state nor a proper outlet for republican civic concerns. Yet Bruni, as Donald Wilcox has shown, recognized better than any earlier writer the coincidence of factionalism with republican liberties. On a number of occasions Bruni speaks against the excesses of factionalism rather than against factionalism and competition for honors (what earlier writers had called the *gara d'ufici*) itself. Neither private gain nor private injury must take place if factions are to be balanced. In short, unlike his predecessors who praised the virtues of the organic polity, from Brunetto Latini to Marchionne di Coppo Stefani, Bruni is sufficiently perceptive to see the intimate, tangled relationship between various forms of political conflict and the good of the republican state itself. For all of his reverence for the polity, however, Bruni does not scorn the parties as his predecessors had, and his appreciation of the parte guelfa strongly suggests that he is coming to terms with a theory that accorded the parte a place in the republic.

Casual and frequent denunciations of factionalism appeared throughout the late fifteenth and early sixteenth centuries, heightened, surely, by the vicissitudes of Florentine internal history, particularly the circumstances surrounding the career of and contributing to the impact of Savonarola.

20. See the extended discussion in Donald J. Wilcox, *The Development of Florentine Humanist Historiography in the Fifteenth Century* (Cambridge, Mass., 1969), pp. 71–83. See also Franco Gaeta, *Il vescovo Pietro Barozzi e il trattato "De factionibus extinguendis"* (Rome, 1961).

Once again a historian, this time Machiavelli, was one of the few voices that echoed Bruni's recognition of the close relationship between faction and republican government. In his analysis, Machiavelli tried to account for a positive containment of contention; he did not condemn it categorically.[21] Yet Machiavelli, careful as he is, envisions nothing on the scale of the earlier parte guelfa; indeed, he rarely uses the term *parte* at all, favoring *sette*, and attempting to distinguish those organized conflicts that preserve the republic by balancing rival interests from those (usually factions and sects) that threaten to undermine it. Machiavelli may represent one of the earliest attempts to secularize the term *secta*. Machiavelli's *divisioni*, unlike Dante's, have two meanings, one productive and the other destructive. In his repeated proposals for a framework of laws and institutions that could check the destructive aspects of political conflict and his emphasis upon the competing interests of all citizens and the equal distribution of offices and state rewards, Machiavelli touched on two of the most striking developments of the next three centuries, a new concept of the constitution and an expanded political public.

The society of fifteenth- and sixteenth-century Florence, in spite of the leads offered by Bruni and Machiavelli, looked more toward division-free concord and political autonomy. It regarded the city not only as *sibi princeps* but as *sibi magister* and perhaps, as Weinstein suggests, *sibi salvator*. Increasingly, a more sophisticated awareness of economic and social differences replaced the mechanistic moral denunciations of Dante and Villani. And the names as well as the natures of old political divisions, Guelfs and Ghibellines, Blacks and Whites, Amidei and Buondelmonte, were eventually relegated to the status of moral exempla in the archaic history of Florence. In other respects, of course, much of the earlier rationale

21. The best study of Machiavelli's concept of division and political conflict is the work of Alfredo Bonadeo, *Corruption, Conflict, and Power in the Works and Times of Niccolò Machiavelli* (Berkeley and Los Angeles, 1973), esp. pp. 35–71, 98–105. Bonadeo cites most of the relevant primary and secondary literature. In addition to Bonadeo's work, however, it is useful to note two studies of other justifications of factionalism in late fifteenth- and early sixteenth-century Florence: Felix Gilbert, "Florentine Political Assumptions in the Period of Savonarola and Soderini," *Journal of the Warburg and Courtauld Institutes, 20* (1957), 187–214, and Felix Gilbert, "Bernardo Rucellai and the Orti Oricellari: A Study on the Origin of Modern Political Thought," *Journal of the Warburg and Courtauld Institutes, 12* (1949), 101–31. On Machiavelli and the early period of Florentine history, see Nicolai Rubinstein, "Machiavelli e le origini di Firenze," *Rivista storica italiana, 79* (1967), 952–59. There are a number of interesting studies on Machiavelli by modern political scientists in Martin Fleischer, ed., *Machiavelli and the Nature of Political Thought* (New York, 1972). The paper by Harvey Mansfield, Jr., "Party and Sect in Machiavelli's *Florentine Histories*," (pp. 209–66) deals directly with the problem addressed in this essay, but does so very unfortunately. See the comments of Mark Phillips and J. A. Gunn following Mansfield's paper, pp. 277–81.

for the emergence of parties had become unnecessary by the late fifteenth century. A complex view of the polity, the resurgence of religious groups linking different social ranks and channeling ecclesiastical and devotional influences throughout Florentine society, and the depoliticization of much of public life under the Medici had reduced the grounds for division and factional strife. The restoration of Medici rule in the person of Cosimo the Younger slowly transformed the contentious republic of Bruni and Machiavelli, "the worn-out republic," as Eric Cochrane calls it, "into a well-run monarchy."

With Machiavelli's concept of *vivere civile* and his dogged insistence on the legitimacy of party opposition in a well-ordered state, even in the last Florentine republic, battered by Fortune, Frenchmen, Spaniards, and popes, the first extended European experience of party and polity came to an inglorious end. The city itself became the principality, and the adventurous monarchies of the sixteenth century had little use for Machiavelli's delicate orchestration of competing powers within the small political community. Machiavelli himself became the symbol, ironically, of the destructive and cynical attempts to divide the political community that sixteenth- and seventeenth-century writers and rulers identified with parties and factions.[22]

The political experience of sixteenth- and seventeenth-century Europeans intensified the revulsion against divisions within the polity. The social tensions that most political structures of this period only seemed to exacerbate produced *ligues*, *frondes*, and rebellions, movements against which virtually every political theorist and political authority savagely turned. The Reformation, by once more raising in its original sense the specter of schism and sectae, particularly in political and ecclesiastical polemics, contributed further to the unrelievedly discordant character that any concept of party or faction possessed.

Sixteenth- and seventeenth-century dictionaries reveal these attitudes as sharply as any polemics, perhaps, because of the commonplace character of their definitions, more sharply. As Alison Gilbert Olson has pointed out, the 1559 edition of *Bibliotheca Eliotal, Eliotes Dictionarie* offers a characteristic definition:

22. See Mario Praz, "The Politic Brain: Machiavelli and the Elizabethans," reprinted in *The Flaming Heart* (New York, 1958), pp. 90–145; Felix Raab, *The English Face of Machiavelli* (Oxford, 1964); Friedrich Meinecke, *Machiavellism* (reprinted., New York, 1965).

> Factio factionis, f.g. a division of people in sundry opinions ... also a companie or bande of men, sometyme rychesse, authoritee, or estimacion in a citee. Factionum principes, the heads of rebellion or sedition ...[23]

Many other similar definitions could be cited from other dictionaries of the same period and for much later. Not until the eighteenth century did the opprobrium in which the concept of party was held, which included Machiavelli as one of its chief targets, begin to give way to a new concept of *vivere civile.* Ultimately, something of the Florentine secretary's guarded enthusiasm for the constructive virtures of controlled opposition within the state acquired greater strength and ultimately won a major place within eighteenth- and nineteenth-century political communities. Of Machiavelli's intellectual legacies to later political theory, the themes of *raison d'état* and anti-Machiavelism have received by far the most attention from historians. Yet Machiavelli's unremitting attention to the nature of the political societies he observed in ancient Rome and in his own Florence had seen something legitimate in the character of conflict in these societies that acquired new meaning, not for the princely states of the sixteenth and seventeenth centuries, but for the contentious civil communities of eighteenth-century England and the North American colonies. Between the implacable hostility universally felt toward the idea and the term party and faction as late as the end of the seventeenth century and the general acceptance of both a century later, there lies a complex process of transformation. The political experience and constitutional theory of this period has generated a large and competent but often diffuse and conflicting literature. A brief discussion of some of the circumstances that led to the legitimation of the concept of party in the political communities of England and North America in this period may suggest one further instance in which the experience of the medieval city anticipated that of its later and larger political successors.

The very proliferation of the various forms of sectae in sixteenth and early seventeenth-century Europe may well have contributed to one aspect of the grudging acceptance of faction and sectarianism by seventeenth-century political theorists. Not only did the Reformation and its social and political consequences not disappear, as many theorists seem to have hoped they would, but even the principles of the Peace of Augsburg, "cuius regio, eius religio," became strained almost beyond the resources of many political communities between 1550 and 1650. The general ap-

23. Olson, *Anglo-American Politics, 1660–1775* (Oxford, 1973), pp. iv-viii.

proaches toward a degree of toleration on essentially utilitarian grounds, first adumbrated by the Politiques during the French wars of religion, soon made their way into the pamphlet literature of seventeenth-century England. It appears, in fact, that the first steps toward the acceptance of religious sectarianism, a fundamental condition for the tolerance and legitimation of political parties, were taken by theologians in the seventeenth century.[24] As J. A. W. Gunn has convincingly demonstrated, one of the earliest and most sophisticated of such approaches was that of John Shute, later Viscount Barrington, who early in the eighteenth century urged the rights of full citizenship for Nonconformists in order to ensure their loyalty to the Crown. Barrington then went beyond the familiar contemporary notions of balancing competing interests to argue something very close to the idea of the *concordia discors* of Machiavelli, Sidney, and Montesquieu:

> The constitution of England consists in a ballance of parties as the libertys of Europe do in a Ballance of power. . . . So when we allow one of the parties in England to be above the check of the other, we bid farewell to its liberties too.[25]

Against the familiar eighteenth-century notion of balance and concordia, on which several of his principles are based, Barrington set the much more active image of the essential conflict of undeniable and indestructible elements—religious Conformity and Dissent—"in the context of the party struggle." And he appears to have emerged with a doctrine of the legitimacy and necessity of party politics that anticipated those promulgated at the end of the eighteenth century.

Barrington is one figure of several whose view of politics was of sufficient

24. Although it focuses primarily upon the debates over the nature of sovereignty on the part of English thinkers of the seventeenth century, J. H. M. Salmon, *The French Religious Wars in English Political Thought* (Oxford, 1959) suggests the importance of theories of natural law and toleration, the exhaustive discussions of political liberties in the tracts of the 1670s and 1680s, and the new role of the individual and his rights in the theory of Sidney and Locke in the complex political theory that emerged in England in the late seventeenth century, particularly in their cosmopolitan origins: "[The strands of thought woven into the pattern of liberalism] have been regarded as the specifically English products of the seventeenth century, but at every stage of their English formulation it has been possible to trace the debt of English politics to the examples and ideas of the French Religious Wars" (p. 170). More recently, J. A. W. Gunn, "Party Before Burke: Shute Barrington," *Government and Opposition, 3* (1968) offers a detailed study of the complex intellectual origins of Barrington's theories of party legitimacy in the early years of the eighteenth century.

25. Gunn, "Party Before Burke," p. 228. For other aspects of the legitimation of the idea of party in seventeenth-century England, see Caroline Robbins, "'Discordant Parties': A Study of the Acceptance of Party by Englishmen," *Political Science Quarterly, 73* (1958), 505–29. Both Robbins and Gunn cite an extensive literature, and further documents may be found in Alan Beattie, ed., *British Party Politics* (London, 1970), I, 1–57.

width to embrace social and religious divisions and to force their solutions into the political arena. For what characterizes many of Barrington's views, as it does those of later political thinkers, is as much a new image of the psychology of the political community as a new theory of politics per se. Much has been written of Machiavelli's and Guicciardini's cynicism regarding the possibility of concord within a fractious and passionate polity. However, less note has been taken of the revival of this and analogous views of human society in the late seventeenth and eighteenth centuries. In the writings of Algernon Sidney, for example, the same view of an imperfect, potentially brutalized and licentious human condition that had led Hobbes to posit the authority of a centralized monarch is turned inside out and made the rationale of effective, productive republican government.

The new psychological orientation of eighteenth-century political theorists from Montesquieu on suggests a new image of *homo politicus*, one perhaps adumbrated by Machiavelli and Hobbes (and perhaps more sympathetically conceived by the former). This view's essential characteristics are a degree of voluntarism, a belief in the endemic nature of social conflict, and the conviction that opposing elements must be balanced. Such a new *imago hominis* makes its appearance in other fields as well, from biography to the historical study. Montesquieu's political theory depends upon such a view of the human passions and the role of social conflict in adjusting them to suit the needs of the political community at large.[26]

Such transformations of political theory did not, of course, occur in a social vacuum. If the devastating sectarianism of the sixteenth and seventeenth centuries instilled an absolute, undeviating horror of faction and division within political and religious communities, it may also have made thinkers receptive to the fact that such divisiveness could never be suppressed and that it must needs be contained in some sort of commodious political framework. The insertion of religious toleration into the constitutional framework of European states, with England in the lead, widened the concept of constitutionalism and thus prepared the way for a broader role for political diversity. Thus, political and social experience, new attitudes toward the psychology of human behavior and its relation to the collective character of the political community, and a new theoretical appreciation of social conflict, later embodied in the theory of contending political parties—all contributed toward the legitimization of the theory

26. On these and the following remarks, see Neal Wood, "The Value of Asocial Sociability: Contributions of Machiavelli, Sidney, and Montesquieu," in Fleischer, *Machiavelli and the Nature of Political Thought*, pp. 282–307, and Wood, "Some Reflections on Sorel and Machiavelli," *Political Science Quarterly*, *83* (1968), 76–91.

of party in the period between 1660 and the beginning of the nineteenth century. The course of this history, from Algernon Sidney and Barrington to Burke, is reflected in the experience of real political parties in the political life of England under the last Stuarts and the first Hanoverians.[27]

Britain's North American colonies were also involved in the theory and practice of party opposition and conflict during the same period. The first colonists were, if anything, even more scornful of party and faction than their English contemporaries. John Winthrop, with John Smith's *Advertisements for the Inexperienced Planters of New England* in hand and mind, appears to have designed his colony specifically to avoid that propensity to factionalism that Smith had denounced as the greatest danger to colonial stability and success. For Winthrop, faction and division were devices used only by those political forces he detested the most, "the rules of Matchiavell and the Jesuits," the Devil, and "the council of England and other states who walk by politic principles only." Harmony, mediation, compromise, and, above all, the Covenant dominated the thought and language of seventeenth-century colonial political figures from Winthrop to Mather and beyond.[28]

Yet, as Dante and Machiavelli had long ago remarked of Florence and other city-republics, factions in the colonies existed and even made their impact upon the mother country. Similarly, after 1649, English political factionalism made its own impact upon the life of colonial society. Various aspects of colonial life, in fact, generated factionalism even more quickly and intensely than life in England itself. Mobility produced dissenting factions under many colonial administrations. The multiple interests and roles of the colonial gentry tended to make quarrels and rivalries in one area of activity spill over into others, including politics. Dissidents and factions could look to sympathizers in neighboring colonies and in England, and until 1765 colonial interests often served as a focus for English opposition to the government.

The philosophical acceptance of political opposition in England and the pragmatic experience of factionalism in the colonies stands at the beginning of the historically and historiographically complex problem of the modern history of parties, particularly as that history has been regarded by scholars who take the nineteenth-century norms of English and

27. The literature on the subject of parties in English political life in the eighteenth century is extensive. Most of it is available in the studies of A. S. Foord, *His Majesty's Opposition, 1714–1830* (Oxford, 1964), Clayton Roberts, *The Growth of Responsible Government in Stuart England* (Cambridge, 1966), and J. H. Plumb, *The Growth of Political Stability in England* (London, 1967).

28. In general, see Olson's controversial and provocative study, *Anglo-American Politics, 1660–1775.* For Winthrop, see T. H. Breen, *The Character of the Good Ruler* (New Haven, 1970).

American political parties as their primary—and sometimes sole—criterion for the definition of party. According to such a view, party and faction are separate and distinct, thus leaving the political organization and groupings of the early nineteenth century virtually without a past, springing fully armed, as it were, out of the circumstances of political life in the first quarter of the nineteenth century. Many scholars have tirelessly pointed out that factions were too ephemeral, too oriented toward single issues, and tied too firmly to deferential politics to qualify as true parties. In one of the fundamental works on the idea of party in revolutionary America, Richard Hofstadter elaborated upon this argument. He considered the importance of the fact that whole legislative programs were not necessary in the eighteenth century; the role of the politics of deference in selecting leaders because of family, status, character, generosity, or personal reputation; and the lack of a sustained commitment to issues or policies, and concluded that political parties had no history, in effect, before the 1790s.[29] Hofstadter's conclusion is supported by the work of many scholars, and indeed by much of the language of the sources, in which the terms party and faction are virtually interchangeable and consistently pejorative. Even Madison, when read in this light, can appear to be interested in controlling conflict rather than in recognizing an integrated role for political opposition within a constitutional framework.

Yet much of the support for this view of the rise of parties depends upon a very narrow focus upon party experience after the beginning of the nineteenth century. Such a view was once responsible for the theory of "New Monarchies" that were alleged to have arisen in the sixteenth century, as well as a view that once held, largely by misreading the impressionistic and tantalizing works of Max Weber, that capitalism appeared in Europe as an inevitable consequence of the character of the Protestant concept of vocation. Ronald Formisano, in a critique of the scholarship in the history of parties, criticizes both the celebrants of party and its critics as possessing "an exaggerated view of parties as electoral machines unrelated to conflicts over values and social belief-systems. . . . The critics tend to empty party politics of its social, cultural, and ideological content."[30] Parties, even in the early nineteenth century, played a partial role in government, and were largely dependent, during their emergence,

29. Richard Hofstadter, *The Idea of Party* (Berkeley and Los Angeles, 1969). A short abstract of Hofstadter's arguments has circulated widely: "A Constitution Against Parties: Madisonian Pluralism and the Anti-Party Tradition," *Government and Opposition, 4* (1969), 345–66, reprinted in *Political Parties in American History*, ed. Winfred E. A Bernhard, I, *1789–1828* (New York, 1973), 34–58.

30. Ronald P. Formisano, "Deferential-Participant Politics: The Early Republic's Political Culture, 1789–1840," *American Political Science Review, 68* (1974), 473–87. I am grateful to my colleague Richard R. Beeman for suggesting this study to me.

on changing modes of patronage from clients and family to interest groups and constituents, on the spirit of subcommunity unity as exemplified by such voluntary associations as militia companies, and perhaps on the increased popular interest in politics and the diversity of those interested. In these terms, the history of party, freed from the narrow constraints of focus upon electoral issues, may be regarded as a direct continuation of that often denounced factionalism of the eighteenth century. Freed from the narrow and restrictive focus upon electoral and organizational forms after 1800, the history of parties may well be more productively considered as a chapter in the history of how lesser communities within larger communities reconciled their immediate, temporary, parochial needs with the problem of the government of the larger community as a whole. In this light the history of modern political parties touches the history of the violent conflicts of opposing forces in the Italian city-states in the thirteenth and fourteenth centuries, for they too faced the same problem, although with very different conceptual frameworks and social and economic resources. Both societies were, after all, a part of what some historians have come to call "traditional Europe," and in both the heady experience of the proximity of public power to private needs, wants, and aims was remarkably similar.

In a sophisticated and extensive review article of the historiography of early American politics, Jack Greene suggested "a rough typology of political forms into which, after the elimination of certain individual variants, most pre-1776 colonial political activites can be fitted":

> . . . *chaotic factionalism*. . . . involved a ruthless competition for dominance, power, and economic advantage among rival groups of leading men, groups which were largely ad hoc and impermanent. . . . *stable factionalism* . . . was distinguished by the emergence of two semi-permanent opposing interest groups with relatively stable memberships and representing explicit regional . . . economic, religious, or kinship rivalries. . . . *domination by a single, unified group* . . . [involved] all the avenues to political power and most of the primary sources of wealth . . . monopolized by a dominant elite. . . . *faction free with a maximum dispersal of political opportunity within the dominant group* . . . depended upon a homogeneity of economic interests among all regions and all social groups, a high degree of social integration, and a community of political leaders so large as to make it impossible for any single group to monopolize political power.

Greene remarks, "[this typology] may by providing a general frame of reference at least make it easier to discuss early American politics. Hopefully, it may also be a first step toward the development of new, less abstract categories which will more accurately reflect the political life they seek to describe."[31] Such forms could well, it may be suggested, be extended to the period before 1776 to help break the semantic and conceptual barriers that now exist between faction and party in contemporary historical literature and thought.

After 1745 the coalition governments of England drew heavily upon party distinctions and cooperation, and at the same time they brought colonial affairs more prominently into the forefront of governmental concerns. In turn, English interest in them sharpened party rivalries within the colonies themselves. But the inability or willingness of royal officials to support favorable loyalist parties in North America and the demise of colonial affairs as a rallying point of opposition in English government led to a separation between English and American parties that turned out to be irreparable. By 1769 some Americans could assume naturally that parties were fundamental and essential parts of English government. At the same time, the American experience of faction became, as it were, independent of English forces. The political public in the colonies had expanded beyond the narrow framework of governors and assemblies and embraced the "out of doors," where the role of colonies as pawns of British factions declined. In addition, "the longer tradition of legitimate opposition to royal authority [in the North American colonies] gave the colonists more experience than their British counterparts in working with political factions."[32] Without the experience of factions, and except for those lesser groupings formed for hosts of different reasons, unstable and short-lived, the acceptance of party a quarter-century later might have turned out differently. Emotions, wills, and experience of loyalty to small groups in a political context, with the experience of success, failure, and impact of those groups on the larger political community was, for the Americans, as for the Italians and British before them, a prerequisite to more sophisticated and precisely defined party organizations.

In this respect, it is possible to read such documents as *The Federalist*, X and L, in a different light. Could Madison's views on party have depended less up on his reading of English political theory than upon his and others' experience of "faction"? The hard and bitter disputes that raged on, and often increased in intensity after 1783, may well have been weathered, not primarily by innovation and invention, but by the very

31. Jack P. Greene, "Changing Interpretations of Early American Politics," in *The Reinterpretation of Early American History: Essay in Honor of John Edwin Pomfret*, ed. Ray Allen Billington (San Marino, Cal., 1966), pp. 151–84. I am grateful to my colleague Vincent Conti for pointing out Greene's study to me.

32. Olson, *Anglo-American Politics*, pp. 142–82, at 180.

experience of hated faction that American writers, no less intensely than their Italian predecessors, had denounced so bitterly.[33]

Machiavelli's Florence had not weathered its own storms, although it had succeeded for four centuries partly through a skillful diffusion of political powers. Indeed, it is anachronistic to expect that it might have. It existed at the beginning of an age of princes, just as the United States was created at that age's end. Yet the experience of both societies had much in common. Intrasocietal rivalry, the proliferation and confused interaction of many lesser, often overlapping communities within the larger community of the colony or the city-republic, and the communications between local dissidents and like-minded supporters in other regions were certainly common to both societies. The fragmentation of dominant oligarchies in the face of social, religious, and economic pressures and the deferential attitudes toward the leaders of individual families and *consorterie* made groups in both societies seek out larger communities of interest, effective factions or temporary parties. Troublesome citizens or disenfranchised magnates might be sent into exile or made to stand surety for their good behavior, and the *fuorusciti* of Massachusetts made as much difficulty in London as did those of Florence in Pisa or in imperial or papal camps. Superior authorities could and did often intervene in local disputes, and religious conflicts often spilled over into the political arena. At times exiles could threaten to drain off so much population or economic strength as to weaken the remaining society. There were few barriers between the intensity of family quarrels and the wide scope of civic polity. In both societies thinkers recognized that political factionalism only represented one aspect of more fundamental social divisions, and, most important of all, both societies experienced that shortened distance between private and public conflicts that made conflict itself an endemic characteristic of political life.

Finally, in both societies, an absolute, unquestioned, unambiguous, single-willed authority was absent. In these circumstances, the role of faction and party offered strength and a kind of superior legitimacy to a constitutionally incomplete polity, transcending the narrow constraints of local, sectarian, or purely private interests, at least in theory, and remaining

33. On Madison, see Marvin Meyers, "Founding and Revolution: A Commentary on Publius-Madison," in *The Hofstadter Aegis: A Memorial*, ed. Stanley Elkins and Eric McKitrick (New York, 1974), pp. 3–35, and Meyers, *The Mind of the Founder: Sources of the Political Thought of James Madison* (Indianapolis, New York, 1973). A different approach to the similarities, if not the links, between Machiavelli and Madison is that of David E. Ingersoll, "Machiavelli and Madison: Perspectives on Political Stability," *Political Science Quarterly*, *85* (1970), 259–80.

vulnerable to claims made on behalf of the higher authority which gave it its legitimacy in the first place. In the period between 1783 and 1840, the United States witnessed a similar ambiguity in the character of central governmental authority. And that milieu shaped the later system of party opposition and gave it a new organization and legitimacy. This experience, like Britain's in the eighteenth and nineteenth centuries, turned out far differently from that of Florence and the other medieval towns. Nevertheless, medieval cities were among the first, and most adventurous polities in modern European history. In the role of faction and party as well as in other aspects of the exploration of the variety and range of human political and social experience, they launched the political adventure of modern Europe.

The Eastern City

8

A Tale of Two Cities: Commercial Relations between Cairo and Alexandria During the Second Half of the Eleventh Century

A. L. Udovitch

An abundance of urban entities was one of the distinguishing features of the medieval Islamic world. The existence of cities and towns was neither limited to intermittent periods of the eight or so centuries which we designate as medieval Islam, nor was their continued presence restricted or distinctive to one or several geographic areas in the vast and variegated area which the Islamic world of the Middle Ages encompassed. Rather, urbanism was a characteristic feature of the entire period and of all of its parts. Medieval Islamic civilization was predominantly an urban civilization. However, it was not only the considerable number of cities and towns which made it so, but also the fact that the spiritual, material, and political culture of medieval Islam was an almost exclusively urban creation.

Historians of or from the West, in whose tradition "medieval" is associated with the contraction—if not absence—of city life, were impressed not only with the prominence of cities, but also by what appeared to be a veritable explosion in the number of urban entities beginning shortly after the major Islamic conquests in the mid-seventh century. Consequently, the subject of cities was one of the first aspects of medieval Islamic social life to attract the systematic attention of scholars. Thus, compared to the literature on many other problems of Islamic social history, we now possess a respectable historical literature on the medieval Islamic city.[1] Although pre-existing cities and towns were encountered by

1. A full bibliography on medieval Islamic urbanism would require an essay in itself. Among the more recent works, all of which contain either extensive bibliographies or copious references to earlier works, cf. Ira M. Lapidus, *Muslim Cities in the Later Middle Ages* (Cambridge, Mass., 1967); A. H. Hourani and S. M. Stern, eds., *The Islamic City* (Philadelphia, 1969); Ira M. Lapidus, ed., *Middle Eastern Cities*, (Berkeley and Los Angeles, 1969); Oleg Grabar, "Cities and Citizens: The Growth and Culture of Urban Islam," in *The World of Islam*, ed. Bernard Lewis (London, 1976), pp. 89–116; Michael E. Bonine, "Urban Studies in the Middle East," *Middle East Studies Association Bulletin, 10*, no. 3 (October 1976), 1–37.

the Muslim conquerors in the course of their expansion in northern Africa and western Asia, they founded many more towns themselves, which provides at least a partial justification for using the epithet "Islamic" to designate the cities and towns of the medieval Near East.[2] A partial list of the cities founded in the first century and a half of Islamic rule would include Kūfa, Basra, Wāsiṭ, Mosul, Baghdad, and Shīrāz in the east and Fustat (Old Cairo), Qayrawān, Al-Mahdiyya, Fez, Marrakesh, and Rabāṭ in the west. This is an impressive achievement indeed, and it has motivated one scholar to remark that one scarcely encounters another civilization with an equal ardor for the founding of new cities.[3]

An examination of the distribution of Islamic cities in the Near and Middle East during the Middle Ages reveals a rather striking fact. No major political or administrative center was located on the seacoast. Furthermore, even though there were numerous Islamic coastal towns of some economic and commercial importance, the major entrepôts of trade and economic life were invariably located some distance inland. This is particularly noticeable in that portion of the Mediterranean coastline which came under Islamic domination, especially when contrasted with the Byzantine and Roman periods: Caesarea of Syro-Palestine gave way to Damascus and Ramle; Alexandria to Fustat-Cairo; and Carthage to Qayrawān.[4]

While we do not possess a comprehensive naval and maritime history of the Islamic Middle Ages, the consistent ambivalence, if not wariness, of the pre-Ottoman Muslim polities in the Mediterranean with regard to the sea and other maritime matters has been noted by a number of scholars. The sea was a menacing frontier to the Muslim rulers of the Near East. This view of the sea and the cautious and defensive policies which it engendered are a motif of Islamic political and military thinking from the earliest years of Islamic hegemony in the Near East until the advent of the Ottomans in the early sixteenth century. The few instances in which Islamic rulers adopted a relatively sustained, confident and aggressive naval policy in the Mediterranean are only the exceptions which prove the rule. The sea was not feared primarily because of the unpredictable dangers of its

2. Cf. A. H. Hourani, "The Islamic City in the Light of Recent Research," in *The Islamic City*, ed. Hourani and Stern, pp. 23–24, for brief and judicious remarks on the significance of the term "Islamic" as used to designate the urban entities of the medieval Near East.

3. W. Marçais, "L'Islamisme et la vie urbaine," in *Comptes Rendus de l'Académie des Inscriptions et Belles Lettres* (1928), p. 86.

4. Cf. S. D. Goitein, "Cairo: An Islamic City," in *Middle Eastern Cities*, ed. Lapidus, p. 82.

winds, storms, and waves. These dangers and risks were, after all, common to all men—regardless of creed—who went down to the sea in ships. The threat of the sea to the medieval Islamic world of the Mediterranean was a "strategic" one. The sea was the one vulnerable frontier from which Islamic domination of the lands bordering on the Mediterranean could be seriously threatened.

In the early years of the Islamic conquests, the Caliph 'Umar recommended "that the Muslims be kept away from seafaring. No Arab travelled by sea save those who did so without 'Umar's knowledge or they were punished by him for it. 'Umar thus punished 'Afrajah b. Harthamah al-Azdī, the chief of the Bajīlah. He sent him on a raid against Oman, and he learned (later) that he had raided it by sea. He disapproved of his having made the raid by sea, and told him so in no uncertain terms."[5] 'Umar refused the repeated requests of Mu'āwiya, his military commander in Syria, for permission to raid the Byzantine-held outposts on Cyprus, which, in the words attributed to Mu'āwiyah, were so close to the Muslim-held Syrian coast that the Muslims could hear "the barking of the dogs of the Christians." Our sources abound with many other instances of the Caliph 'Umar's displeasure and distress at any attempt of Arab tribal warriors to traverse large bodies of water in the pursuit of their conquests. Ibn Khaldun attributes 'Umar's policy to his recognition of the fact that "the Arabs were not skilled in navigation and seafaring,"[6] skills which their adversaries at that time, the Byzantines and European Christians, possessed to a high degree.

In subsequent centuries, the Muslims of the southern and eastern coasts of the Mediterranean did acquire many of the maritime skills of their predecessors and adversaries and ventured forth, with intermittent boldness and success, onto the waters of the great middle sea. Nevertheless, the ambivalence toward the sea and naval activity persisted. Throughout the Middle Ages, the coastal towns of Syria, Palestine, and Egypt were regarded as frontier outposts. Tyre, Sidon, Ascalon, Damietta, and Alexandria are usually designated by the term *thaghr* (frontier fortress) the identical term used to designate the march areas of raids and counter raids on the shifting borders separating Islam from Christendom. Crete, Cyprus, Sicily, and other Mediterranean islands held by the Muslims were similarly called *ath-thughūr al-jazariyya* (island frontier fortresses).

5. Ibn Khaldun, *The Muqaddimah: An Introduction to History*, trans. Franz Rosenthal (Princeton, 1967), II, 39, where the earlier sources for this episode are given in detail.

6. Ibn Khaldun, *Muqaddimah*, II, 39.

Even such points as Alexandria and Damietta, where the Mediterranean coastline for hundreds of miles in either direction had been firmly under Muslim control for many centuries, the hostile and threatening area was perceived as beginning at land's end.

In his monumental history and geography of Egypt, the *Khiṭaṭ*, the fifteenth-century Egyptian chronicler Al-Maqrīzī devotes nine very compact pages to a summary of the naval history of the Islamic world up to his time, with a particular emphasis on the Muslim principalities bordering on the Mediterranean.[7] While Maqrīzī's discussion contributes no startling new detailed information or illuminating insights into medieval Muslim naval activity, his overview does indicate a very significant general pattern. The naval efforts of the successive Muslim states bordering on the Mediterranean were sporadic in character. For long periods there was no permanent navy or fleet. Throughout the medieval period, the coasts of Syria, Egypt, and North Africa were not only vulnerable but were actually attacked frequently by Christian raiding parties.[8] In the face of this persistent menace, Muslim policy was reactive. Flurries of naval activity, which occurred, for example, in Egypt during the reign of Caliph Al-Mutawakkil (847–861) or in the early Fatimid period, were followed by periods of indifference.[9] The central and successful role of naval power in first establishing and then maintaining a Christian European presence in the Levant for approximately two centuries of the Crusades not only reinforced the Muslim wariness of the sea, but gave rise, in the eastern Mediterranean, to a policy by which the Muslim powers of that area in effect expressed their unwillingness and inability to meet the challenge of the rising European maritime power. Beginning with Saladin in the late twelfth century and culminating in the period of Mamluk rule (1250–1517), the attitude of neutrality and indifference to the sea turned into one which D. Ayalon has aptly characterized as "decidedly negative." The Mamluks embarked on a systematic policy of destroying the fortifications of the cities and towns of the Syro-Palestinian coast, thereby denying to any potential enemy a coastal foothold from which he might then penetrate inland and threaten the very foundations of

7. Al-Maqrīzī, *Al-mawā'iẓ wal-i'tibār bi-dhikr al-khiṭaṭ wal-āthār* 2 vols., (Bulaq, 1270 A.H.), II, 189–97.

8. Cf. David Ayalon, "The Mamluks and Naval Power—A Phase of the Struggle between Islam and Christian Europe," *Proceedings of the Israel Academy of Sciences and Humanities*, *1*, no. 8 (1965). This brief, lucid paper is the single most brilliant and insightful discussion of the medieval Near Eastern Islamic attitudes toward naval matters. Although Ayalon, in his article, focuses on Egypt between 1250 and 1500, many of his ideas are relevant to earlier periods as well. In the first part of this essay, I have drawn liberally from Ayalon's pioneering work.

9. Maqrīzī, *Khiṭaṭ*, II, 19.

their power. Ports and coastal towns of Egypt were not as severely affected by this policy as those on the Syrian coast.[10]

In a section of his *Muqaddimah* devoted to requirements for town planning, Ibn Khaldun writes as follows:

> In connection with coastal towns situated on the sea, one must see to it that they are situated on a mountain or amidst a people sufficiently numerous to come to the support of the town when an enemy attacks it. The reason for this is that a town which is near the sea but does not have within its area tribes who share its group feeling, or is not situated in rugged mountain territory, is in danger of being attacked at night by surprise. Its enemies can easily attack it with a fleet and do harm to it. They can be sure that the city has no one to call to its support and that the urban population, accustomed to tranquility, has become dependent on others for its protection and does not know how to fight. Among cities of this type, for instance, are Alexandria in the East, and Tripoli, Bone and Salé in the West. . . . Alexandria was designated a 'border city' [*thaghr*] by the 'Abbāsids although the 'Abbāsid sway extended beyond Alexandria to Barqah [in Libya] and Ifrīqiyah [Tunisia]. The designation of Alexandria as a 'border city' expressed 'Abbāsid fears that attacks against Alexandria could be made from the sea. Such fears were justified in the case of Alexandria because of its exposed situation. This situation was probably the reason why Alexandria and Tripoli were attacked by the enemy in Islamic times on numerous occasions.[11]

In the passage just quoted, Ibn Khaldun was expressing an insight distilled from the medieval Islamic experience, to wit, that the sea and its coastline were totally dependent on the hinterland for their safety and protection. This notion was basic to the Islamic attitude and policy vis-à-vis naval and maritime matters in the Mediterranean area throughout the Middle Ages. This view had not only military and naval implications but also affected the pattern and organization of trade—especially in the eleventh and later centuries, which was a period of expansion for international trade in the Mediterranean.

Militarily it meant that in Fatimid Egypt, for example, Cairo rather than Alexandria would serve as the primary naval base for warships

10. Ayalon, "The Mamluks and Naval Power," pp. 7–11.

11. Ibn Khaldun, *Muqaddimah*, II, 248–49. I have slightly altered Rosenthal's translation in some places.

and that in its commercial relations throughout the Mediterranean, including those with Italy, Spain, and Byzantium, Fustat-Cairo was the pivot of commerce rather than Alexandria, even though Alexandria was the port through which most of the goods constituting this trade were carried.[12]

The geographic disjunction between Egypt's financial, commercial and economic center, Fustat-Cairo, and its major port, Alexandria, created particular problems for its medieval traders, primarily in the field of communication and commercial organization. How merchants adjusted to this particular circumstance and how this reality affected institutions of trade and other relationships between those involved in trade is revealed to us in very vivid terms by the letters of the Cairo Geniza.

I have chosen to present here four Geniza letters which bear on this problem. They all date from the latter half of the eleventh century—a period during which the already flourishing international trade of the Mediterranean was undergoing even greater expansion. The primary center of activities had moved from North Africa, especially Tunisia, eastward to Egypt. These letters are drawn from a group of documents that relate to the career of the versatile Nahray b. Nissīm, a scholar, merchant, and banker. The largest corpus of Geniza documents pertaining to any one man are those connected with his activities. Over 300 letters, most of them addressed to him but also some written by him, have been preserved, as have numerous notes and accounts connected with his business, communal, and personal affairs. Nahray came to Egypt from Tunisia—as did many other eleventh-century merchants represented in the Geniza. He was born in Qayrawān, Tunisia, probably about 1025. As early as 1045, he was already traveling to do business in Egypt and in about 1050, he settled in Fustat where he married into a local Egyptian family. He seems to have prospered as a merchant and gained prominence as a scholar and community leader. He died in Fustat in 1096 or 1097 and the more than three hundred documents concerning him are distributed over the entire fifty years of his active commercial career.[13]

12. A. M. Fahmy, *Muslim Naval Organization in the Eastern Mediterranean* (Cairo, 1966), pp. 48–50; S. D. Goitein, *A Mediterranean Society* (Berkeley and Los Angeles, 1967), I, 296; Maqrīzī, *Khiṭaṭ*, II, 193. This last source contains a detailed description of the Fatimid war fleet—its assembly, departure, and return to base at Al-Maqs, slightly north of Cairo.

13. For further details concerning the biography of Nahray b. Nissīm and the significance of his corpus of letters, see S. D. Goitein, *Letters of Medieval Jewish Traders* (Princeton, N.J., 1972), pp. 145–46; Goitein, *Mediterranean Society*, I, 153–59, 247–48. Regarding the shift in Mediterranean trade from Tunisia eastward to Egypt, cf. Goitein, "Medieval Tunisia—The Hub of the Mediterranean," in Goitein, *Studies in Islamic History and Institutions* (Leiden, 1968), pp. 308–28.

All four letters presented here passed between Fustat and Alexandria. One is from Nahray's cousin and associate Nathan b. Nahray who was a resident of Alexandria; the other three are part of Nahray's correspondence with Yeshūʿa b. Ismāʿīl, also a resident of Alexandria, who was a frequent partner and business associate of Nahray b. Nissīm's. In addition to the letters presented here, both of these men are represented in the Geniza documents by many other letters to Nahray and other merchants as well.

I. A letter from Alexandria from Nathan b. Nahray, a first cousin of the recipient Nahray b. Nissīm addressed to the latter in Fustat. It is to be dated in the 1060s. The original is in the University Library, Cambridge Taylor-Schechter Collection, TS 10J 16 folio 17.

This letter highlights the importance of Alexandria as a major Mediterranean port attracting ships and merchants and goods from North Africa, Italy (including Genoa), and Spain. In addition to the information about shipping and related matters, the letter, in a manner characteristic of the business correspondence of the Geniza, alludes to a wide variety of personal and business items, important and petty, of mutual concern to the correspondents. Their significance will be discussed in the concluding portion of this essay.

> May God lengthen the life of my master, the elder, and preserve his support, well-being and grace and may he subdue his enemies. I am writing with eight days remaining in the month of Av, may God turn it [i.e., the month] into an occasion of joy. I am writing, after having dispatched to you several letters with Baruch. I hope that these have reached you. In these letters I informed you that a ship arrived from Al-Mahdiyya. As yet, no one has arrived from Tripoli or from Sfaqs.[14] I spend my entire day waiting on the seashore and I pray that God, in his mercy, will not disappoint our hopes.
>
> Together with this letter of mine, I am sending to you the letter of Abū Sahl ʿAṭā and the letter of Nissīm.
>
> I have acquired for you a quarter of a *mann*[15] of camphor from the total amount that has arrived. Neither the loss of weight resulting from packing and shipping [*naqs*] nor the transportation expenses [*ma'ūna*] were, as yet, charged to you. When the elder, Abū ʿImrān, arrived, we informed him of the nature of the situation and he said, "I will not take the goods against which the loss of weight resulting

14. Al-Mahdiyya was the major port of medieval Tunisia; Sfaqs was another Tunisian port some eighty miles to the south of Al-Mahdiyya on the eastern coast of Tunisia; the Tripoli meant here is Tripoli, Libya.

15. The mann was a measure of weight which in Egypt was equivalent to approximately two pounds. Cf. W. Hinz, *Islamische Masse und Gewichte* (Leiden, 1955), p. 16.

from packing and shipping and the transportation expenses are still to be charged." The *naqs* of the entire amount of camphor was approximately 25 dirhams [......] two dinars and two-thirds. I have informed you of this.

Abū 'Imrān[16] mentioned that he left with you the reed basket [*ṣuft*] which he purchased for me. Would you please return it to its owner [i.e., the seller], even if you have to offer a discount of a *qīrāṭ*[17] or two qīrāṭ. Act as you see fit, for I have already purchased another one.

In your letter, you adverted to the situation with respect to the sale of your goods and the needed repairs to your house. In recent days, I have, by God, been subjected to the kind of concerns and anxieties which only God knows, and I pray that He, in His mercy, will provide me with some relief.

This week, a Spanish ship arrived from Spain, namely from Denia. A group of our colleagues were on this ship including Mukhtār al-Ḥalabī, David b. Samḥūn, and the son of Ibn Lakhtūj and Ibn ash-Sharābī. They did not stop at Al-Mahdiyya at all and they have no news about it. The Spanish ship contains a great deal of silk and many other goods.

Ships have arrived from the Land of the Rūm,[18] from Genoa and from other places. It is said that three other ships will be arriving from Spain. I have informed you of this.

Could you please send the linseed oil to me with a suitable person. Otherwise, keep it until someone will be coming through the canal [*khalīj*][19]; for the time when it will be passable is not far off.

I read your letter to the wife of the late 'Awwāḍ, and they are very grateful.

The elder, Abū 'Imrān, is in difficult straits with his partner.

16. The reference here is to Abū 'Imrān Mūsā b. Abī al-Hayy. He was an intimate business and personal associate of Nahray b. Nissīm and had the same relationship with the latter's cousin, Nathan b. Nahray, who is the author of this letter. For further details concerning Abū 'Imrān and translations of some of his commercial correspondence with Nahray b. Nissīm, see A. L. Udovitch, "Formalism and Informalism in the Social and Economic Institutions of the Medieval Islamic World," in *Individualism and Conformity in Classical Islam*, ed. Speros Vryonis (Wiesbaden, 1976), pp. 42–56, esp. n. 10, 11.

17. The qīrāṭ (English: carat), was a money of account equivalent to a twenty-fourth part of a gold dinar; cf. Hinz, *Islamische Masse und Gewichte*, p. 27.

18. The term Rūm as used in the Geniza documents and by many medieval Arab geographers designates not only the Byzantines, but also the Italians and others from Christian lands. In this particular case, Genoa is considered as part of the Land of the Rūm. Cf. Goitein, *Mediterranean Society*, I, 43.

19. The canal connecting Alexandria to the eastern arm of the Nile was navigable only for part of the year; cf. Goitein, *Mediterranean Society*, I, 298–99.

May God improve his situation as well as our own. I have sent to you, with Maymūn, the servant of Abū al-Bishr Azhar, the cloth [*maqṭa*ʿ][20] belonging to you. I hope that it will reach you.

Abū ʿImrān claims that he paid you two dinars and he said, "Deliver the camphor belonging to my master [i.e., Nahray] to me and I will then deliver it to him." I have informed you of this.

Could you please send to me the rose-water jam [*ward murabbā*], a small amount of which Abū ʿImrān says he left with Ibn Ṭībān.

My best regards to you and regards to Nissīm, may God protect him. I delivered your letter to my master, the elder Abū al-Ḥasan, and he sends you his regards. And the old woman sends you her greetings. Convey my regards to R. Yeshūʿa and inform him of my longing for him. And peace.

II. A letter from Nahray b. Nissīm in Fustat to his colleague and business associate Yeshūʿa b. Ismāʿīl in Alexandria. Even though he traveled to Fustat frequently, Alexandria was the home base of Yeshūʿa b. Ismāʿīl.

This is one of the few letters written by Nahray which survive. Most of the correspondence which has come down to us consists of letters addressed to him. In addition to business and related matters, much of this document is concerned with the passage of letters and merchants between Fustat and Alexandria, highlighting the importance and the difficulties in the intense communication and exchange of people and information between these two cities. Nahray's frequent references to his anxieties caused by the difficult days and to the uncertainty of communications create a strong presumption that this letter was written during the unsettled period of civil and military strife which prevailed in Egypt during the late 1060s. The original is in University Library, Cambridge, Taylor-Schechter Collection, TS 13J 14 folio 2.

May God lengthen the life of my master, the elder, and preserve your well-being, happiness and prosperity. I am writing to you from Fustat at the end of the month of Tammūz. The situation here is fine, but I am nevertheless full of anxiety; it is the will of God, the Creator of the world, blessed be His name, and praise and gratitude to him for all His deeds.

I received your letter and from it I learned of your well-being. I rejoiced at this news, and also offer praise to God for the safe arrival

20. Alexandria was noted for the production of maqṭaʿ, cloths or garments which were woven from linen or from linen and cotton; cf. Goitein, *Letters of Medieval Jewish Traders*, p. 134.

of the elder, Abū al-Faḍl b. Faraḥ. He caused some serious difficulties for me, but I am prepared to ignore these and give precedence to the maintenance of our established relations. Give him my regards, therefore, and congratulate him on his safe arrival. Please do the same for all our colleagues who arrived in the same ship. Were it not for my anxiety and distraction, I would write letters to each one of them. Please convey my apologies to them.

I have sent you the letters that arrived from the West [i.e., North Africa] with Harūn al-Zajjāj al-Yahudī. A number of letters also arrived for the elder, Abū al-Faḍl, and I am enclosing them with this letter of mine. Please transmit them to him. If, however, I should encounter Abū Sa'd, the son of the sister of the *ḥaver*[21] R. Yeshū'a, I will give the letter to him instead, and he [i.e., Abū al-Faḍl] will be able to ask him for it.

I have been hoping that the heavy baggage will be recovered; I pray that God will soon replace this loss for us.

I do not know whether or not you have returned on the boat of Ibn Dīsūr the bale of brazilwood[22] which was on the account of our partnership of last year. Please inform me concerning this matter. Similarly, let me know whether you have shipped the bale containing the myrobalan[23] belonging to our partnership of this year.

In your letter you mention the names of the ships that set out on the high seas and of those that remained behind. I pray that God, in His mercy, will bring us news of their safe passage.

Please let me know what is happening with you for I am very worried.

In your previous letter you mentioned that if letters for you were not getting through, you then wished them to be sent overland. On my part, I do not know whether letters for me have been getting through or not. If you find someone with whom to send letters overland, please find out who has the letters intended for me and then please have them sent together with the letters you yourself are dispatching.

With respect to my inquiry regarding the incident related to the iron[24] belonging jointly to us and which was in the package on the ship

21. Cf. n. 30, below.

22. Brazilwood was an Indian red dyeing material; cf. *Encyclopaedia of Islam*, 2d ed., I, 961, s.v. *bakkam*.

23. Myrobalan was a medicinal herb used for intestinal maladies.

24. The word for iron is rendered here by the Hebrew *barzel* rather than the Arabic *ḥadīd*. Iron was an uncommon commodity in the Mediterranean trade of the Geniza merchants. Use of a Hebrew instead

of Al-Hamdānī. Write, telling me to whom it is all to be sold and to whom the proceeds are to be delivered. I have not mentioned this matter to anyone in my letters.

I had already opened the packing mattress and spread out the wool before the arrival of your letter. I will put up for sale the Sūsī cloth,[25] the *afrākh*,[26] and all the other items you mentioned after the difficult days pass. The city is at a complete standstill. There is no buying or selling, and no one is spending a single dirham. All the people's eyes are turned toward the Nile. May God in His mercy raise its waters.

Mastic is worth thirty dinars per *qinṭār*.[27] I hope that you will conclude the affair of the *barqalū*[28] of brazilwood with the Italians (Rūm). The prices of Eastern goods [i.e., spices?] are the same as when you left here.

I hope, God willing, that you will redeem the order of payment when you resume your trading activity, for Mūsā will be leaving soon and you can settle it with him.

I spoke to Al-Baghdādī concerning the camphor-water, and he asked me to buy some at the price of 10 flasks for 8 dinars. As for the mercury, its owner did not want to take it; please let me know your opinion; and as for the *qafār*,[29] if you find someone who is coming (to Fustat), please send them with him.

I send you my best regards. If my master Abū 'Imrān is still there, give him my regards and tell him of my worries. Were it not for them, I would not have neglected writing to him. From now on, he will receive my letters. I have already sent to him with Harūn al-Zajjāj and his son one hundred jars whose price is [. . . . .]. To all of them my best regards.

My trust is in God alone.

---

of an Arabic term may indicate that dealing in this strategic material was illegal except for authorized government representatives. Cf. Goitein, *Mediterranean Society*, I, 60; Goitein, *Letters of Medieval Jewish Traders*, p. 18.

25. Presumably this was cloth produced in Susa, a Tunisian seaport north of Al-Mahdiyya which was the great center of the Tunisian textile industry.

26. The term *farkha* (plural: *afrākh*) referred both to a piece of cloth and to a cloak-like garment. They were regular items of export from Tunisia and Sicily to Egypt.

27. The term *qinṭār* designates a hundredweight, that is, one hundred *raṭl*. Its exact weight could vary greatly, according to which *raṭl* the calculation was based upon. Cf. Hinz, *Islamische Masse und Gewichte*, pp. 24–25. See also n. 37 below.

28. A term, probably of Italian origin, used to designate a package or load smaller in size than a regular bale (*'idl*), cf. Goitein, *Mediterranean Society*, I, 335–36.

29. I have been unable to identify the commodity designated by this word.

III. A letter to Nahray b. Nissīm in Fustat from Yeshū'a b. Ismā'īl in Alexandria.

The letter was written immediately upon Yeshū'a's return to Alexandria from Fustat and is largely concerned with his misadventures with customs authorities in the course of this journey.

It is to be dated to 1070s or 1080s, as Nahray had already achieved the title of ḥaver and the rank of "pre-eminent member of the yeshiva."[30]

The original is in the University Library, Cambridge, Taylor-Schechter Collection, TS 10J 9 folio 21.

> May God lengthen the life of my master, the ḥaver, the pre-eminent member of the yeshiva and its pride and may He preserve your glory, support and well-being. I am writing from Alexandria in a state of health and well-being; praise be to God, lord of the worlds. I long for you, may God in His mercy bring close our meeting in the most favorable and happy of circumstances.
>
> I am unable to describe to you what I experienced after I took leave of you. I returned from Al-Maqs [Port of Cairo] accompanied by five policemen. I was seized by an indescribable fear which left me tongue-tied and very distressed. All of this was on account of the matter which I informed you about, namely, the barqalū of gum arabic (*samgh*) belonging to Ibn Sha'yā.[31] For he [i.e., Ibn Sha'yā] had concluded with the customs authorities the payment of twenty qīrāt and one-quarter of a qīrāt and there remained for me to pay three qīrāt to the *jahbadh*.[32] I had promised the eight dirhams to the Inspector Hasan, may he find no favor with God! I then paid him a new Murābiṭī dinar[33] and one-quarter, from the light coins of the royal mint. After leaving you on the Sabbath, I met Ibn Shay'ā and he told me that the matter of the barqalū was settled at twenty qīrāt and one-quarter. I told him that I had a credit with the inspector of one and a quarter Murābiṭī dinars and that he should take that sum from him and instead pay him the twenty-two qīrāt and eight dirhams. He agreed to do so. As you know, I was to set out on my travels on

30. The title *ḥavēr*—member of the academy—was conferred by the heads of the religious academy (yeshiva) in Jerusalem on individuals in various communities who had outstanding accomplishments in religious learning and communal leadership. Cf. Goitein, *Mediterranean Society*, II, 8.

31. Ibn Sha'yā was an important banker and merchant in Old Cairo.

32. The *jahbadh* was a financial officer of the government who oversaw the technical side of payments to the government; for example, money-changing and accounting.

33. These were gold coins of excellent quality issued by the Almoravids who ruled in Morocco, Algeria, and Spain between 1056 and 1147.

Sunday, and lo, the Inspector Hasan came to the Sinā'a [river port of Old Cairo] having been informed of my departure. He despatched five policemen after me and I was seized by a terror and fright which I am not able to describe. God made it possible for me to extricate myself from him, and I hired transportation to Al-Maqs. But I did not catch up with the boat. I then hired transportation to Shattanawf[34] and I still did not catch it. We reached the ship only after great exertion on Monday night.

I forgot the lock and the medicines in the house. Would my master, may God protect him, please find out from Ibn Sha'yā whether he has already taken the dinar and one-quarter from Ḥasan and let him pay twenty-two qīrāts to him, and no more, since on that day he took a sixth of a dinar from me. Please send me the lock and medicines, since I have need of them.

I have examined the account made at the exchange of *saffayn*,[35] i.e., the account which I told you that Ibn Sha'yā had added up to 150 dinars. However, I found that it came only to 145 dinars of which 50 are Murābiṭī dinars. Three dinars are owed to me. If you have the opportunity, please kindly inform Ja'far of this.

I send you my best regards and greetings to your son Nissīm. I read Rabbi Joseph's letter mentioning that his son was blessed with a male child. May God, the exalted, give him long life. May the well-being of my master increase forever, Amen.

Please intercede with Abraham b. Nusayr regarding the oath which he took to the effect that nobody would give me anything in his name.

IV. A letter to Nahray in Fustat from Yeshū'a in Alexandria. It dates from approximately the same period as the preceding letter. The original is in the collection of the British Museum, Oriental 5546, folio 27.

May God prolong the life of my master the ḥaver, pre-eminent member of the yeshiva and preserve his glory, support and well-being. I am writing to you from Alexandria. Your letter, may God strengthen you, has arrived. In it you mention your well-being, may God, in His mercy, preserve it for you.

You also mention that you have sold two of the cloths and have received five and one-half and one-eighth dinars from this sale and that you will be selling two other cloths; this leaves unsold one cloth

34. Shattanawf was a location on the Nile a short distance to the north of Cairo.

35. This was one of the important centers of business activity in the bazaar of Old Cairo.

of high quality. Of the three high quality cloths and the three of lesser quality (which I have in my possession), I have sold one-half a cloth of lesser quality. There remains (unsold) three of high quality and two and a half cloths of lesser quality. Whoever claims otherwise is either sorely mistaken or is lying. Although textiles are available here in Alexandria in great abundance, there is nothing remaining on the market here from this category (of cloth). If the transactions you mention are already finished and done with, then there is no point to any further discussion. I, however, had hoped that we would be able to keep this shipment together, and transport it from place to place depending upon where the price was better. If the matter is already settled, there is nothing that can be done about it. Perhaps you will realize a higher price for the remaining cloths. As for the loss, I know that your scales are full.

You mentioned that you had already sold all the *zurunbāq*[36] and received its price. If the customers desire to buy more, let them go to Ad-Diryānī and buy the rest from him. Perhaps they can get it from him at the price of seven per unit, since he has to take his commission from that sum. As for the pitch and small amount of lead that is available, it is being withheld by the merchants until God willing, the price is established. For even though more pitch has arrived it is still being withheld. Your cousin has notified me as follows: "I will sell the pitch when it reaches a price of seven and one-half. At present it is not offered for sale."

Of late, Rūmī ships have arrived. Immediately upon their arrival, their merchants were very active. This activity then subsided and they did not show much eagerness except for purchasing indigo at the auction for excessive prices and some brazilwood for 120 dinars per camel load. They then desisted. They do not discriminate between first-class and inferior goods. It appears to be all the same to them and they pay the same price. Similarly with flax; they buy the poor quality for the same price as the excellent variety and are not prepared to pay more for the latter. They are very interested in flax and they say that other Rūm will be arriving.

I hope that you have already collected the three dinars which is the price of the turban. Please look into the sum that my goods have brought in. Perhaps Abū 'Alī can take this sum and buy cowry shells

36. I have been unable to identify the meaning of this word.

with it for me. I was told that they are selling for two and one-half. However, even if the price is two and three-quarters or three for good quality cowry shells, he should buy them to the extent that he is able to. He [i.e., Abū 'Alī] told me that he credited my account with the price of the zurunbāq and that it came to two and one-sixth dinars. Based upon what he says, please add on the entire sum of what my other goods will fetch, and perhaps he [i.e., Abū 'Alī] will acquire cowry shells for the entire sum and carry them to his place. If Ad-Diryānī chances to sell the goods I left with him then Abū 'Alī can use that sum as well for buying cowry shells. If he prefers, he can use only part of the entire sum for this purpose.

I have already informed your cousin of what you told me. Similarly, R. Abraham has accomplished what you mentioned. [..........] We shall complete the matter here with your cousins.

I send you my best regards, and regards as well to R. Nissīm and to all those encompassed by your concern. R. Joseph has not returned, although the people are saying that he will return. May God, the exalted, show favor to them and to us and to "all those who fear Him." Please convey my best regards to his excellency, our teacher the Rabbi, and tell him that I long for his excellency, may God protect him.

As for Aṣ-Ṣayrafī, I did not collect anything from him. If he says: "I paid it," it is like the people who say: "Yes, we will pay it." I did not have the opportunity to go back to him, and the situation remains as I have informed you. I left Ad-Diryānī's account with Al-Kohen Ash-Shāmī so that he would be able to collect the rest of what is due to me from him. He [i.e., Diryānī] drew up my account in a manner which would have required me to deduct an entire dinar from the price of forty dirham weight of goods which he sold for me, but all that is due to him is somewhat less than three-quarters of a dinar. Let him, therefore, pay the balance to you. If he has already given you the account, then let me know. May God, the exalted, allow me to get my due from him. I do not know how the matter will be resolved, because I also left a cloak with him. He said that he has given it to Ibn Al-Muwaydid. The latter swears that he did not give him anything. As far as I am concerned, the latter is more trustworthy. And may peace follow.

As for the pitch, your cousin said that at the moment it is not being sold. Even though a price of 8 and 1/2 is being offered, it is still not being sold to them. Similarly, I left the silk in the provision bag with the person whom you know. There are twenty *ratl*,[37] five or six of which are of that quality. If you can fetch three dinars per ratl, then very good!! Take the bag from the man and withhold the high-quality silk, perhaps, God willing, its price will rise. I am of the opinion that this commodity will go well. I will write to this man so that he will give you the silk, but I believe that if you speak to him a letter will not be necessary. And may peace follow. As for the small amount of goods it might go up, so leave it.

Alexandria—Commercial Suburb of Fustat

These letters are representative of the business letters from the Geniza which passed between Fustat and Alexandria in the second half of the eleventh century. What they reveal most prominently is a close, even intimate, contact between the merchants of the two cities, involving frequent communications and detailed sharing of commercial and other information. Of the three hundred or so documents pertaining to Nahray b. Nissīm's career in the Mediterranean trade during the half-century between 1045 and 1095, fully one-third were communications between Fustat and Alexandria. This is by far the largest category of correspondence within the Nahray corpus and constitutes a rather impressive indication of the importance of this particular geographical-commercial connection. Most of these letters, like those presented above, contain references to numerous other letters between these two cities which have not come down to us. Because of the frequency of contact between the two cities, the completeness of the relevant information transmitted and, above all, because of the nature of the relationship between the Alexandrian and Cairene individuals active in the Mediterranean trade, Alexandria functioned, from a commercial point of view, very much like a slightly distant suburb of Fustat.

Community of Information

The commercial mail service between Alexandria and Cairo in the latter half of the eleventh century was regular and prompt. Several mail couriers—both Muslims and Jews—operated on fixed schedules between the two cities, thus providing an active and frequent service. Letters carried by the regular mail service took from four to six days to travel from one city to a destination in another; there was, as well, a *fayj ṭayyār*, a "flying

37. The *raṭl* was a measure of weight which in Egypt at the time of the Fatimids was equivalent to approximately 450 grams. Cf. Hinz, *Islamische Masse und Gewichte*, p. 29.

courier" who provided an express service, and one special messenger is recorded as having made the round-trip journey between Cairo and Alexandria within seven days.[38] In addition to the commercial mail service, merchants availed themselves of the services of colleagues, friends, and other travelers who regularly journeyed between Cairo and Alexandria to carry letters, news, and goods from one place to the other. So, for example, in the first letter above, Nathan b. Nahray refers to the dispatch of several letters with Baruch, clearly a friend or business associate. In addition, in Nahray's own letter from Fustat, Nahray mentions in several instances letters he has sent with business friends (e.g., Hārūn al-Zajjāj) and inquires of the fate of letters sent to him via colleagues.

It was not only letters which were exchanged frequently. There seems to have been an unending stream of merchants traveling back and forth between Alexandria and Fustat. Plans for travel from one city to another are mentioned in almost every letter. In the four letters presented here, for example, explicit reference is made to the travel of at least ten merchants between the two cities, and one of these letters contains a rather vivid and detailed account of the journey itself. In some cases, travel was so frequent and personal and business interests in both locations so active that merchants permanently resident in one city found it useful, or even necessary, to maintain houses and acquire real property in the other. Nahray b. Nissīm's home was in Fustat, yet in the first letter cited here there is a reference to a request that his cousin in Alexandria oversee some repairs to a house belonging to Nahray in Alexandria. Other letters also contain numerous references to his house in Alexandria and to a warehouse he also owned in that city. Conversely, the third letter reveals that Yeshū'a b. Ismā'īl, whose regular base of operations was in Alexandria, also owned or kept a house in Fustat.

The frequency of personal and epistolary communication created a community of information on a wide range of economic, commercial, and financial matters. This community of information, so clearly reflected in the Geniza letters, was largely responsible for making the commercial distance between Alexandria and Fustat significantly smaller than the geographical distance between the two cities. The information which the correspondents in these letters provided to each other was not limited to discussions of pending transactions or ongoing business affairs in which one or another of the parties had a direct interest. Instead, the letters touched upon everything that was happening in the marketplace and in

38. Goitein, *Mediterranean Society*, I, 285–90.

the town in general and conveyed news of people and events in faraway places. These letters, like modern newspapers and telex systems, provided merchants with the information essential for the business decisions that they were obliged to make.

A rather simple but venerable rule guided the actions of medieval Near Eastern traders: buy low and sell high. To follow this principle successfully and profitably in their daily transactions and investments, merchants required, above all, as much information as possible concerning the factors which could in any way affect either the supply of or the demand for their commodities. And it is precisely this kind of commercial information, bearing directly, indirectly, or even remotely on such market conditions that fills the pages of Geniza business correspondence, most particularly that passing between Fustat and Alexandria. Detailed reports on the arrival and departure of ships, rumors about their progress on the high seas, information concerning their itineraries, cargoes, and passengers are prominent in three of the four letters quoted above. In the principalities of the Islamic Mediterranean, foreign merchants were not restricted to port cities or border areas, but were permitted to travel inland from Alexandria to Fustat or, before 1057, from Al-Mahdiyya on the Tunisian coast inland to Qayrawān. This freedom was not enjoyed in the territories of the Byzantines and others whose commercial policies imposed rigorous restrictions on the movement of foreign traders within their territory. The accessibility of interior cities to foreign and other (overseas) merchants contributed to the prominence of these cities in international trade and made it indispensable for their merchants to be as fully informed as possible about the news from the coast. Thus, in the first letter Nathan b. Nahray reports that he is spending his entire day on the Alexandrian seashore to gather information on ships and shipping to transmit to Fustat. He details the arrival of Spanish, Genoese, and other ships and mentions their passengers and cargo, even though none of the goods is destined for either of the correspondents. In the last letter, Yeshū'a b. Ismā'īl not only apprises his Cairene correspondent of the arrival of the ships but also describes the goods the European merchants are buying up and their erratic and rather peculiar mode of commercial conduct. Inclusion in these four letters of price lists, of information on the availability or scarcity of various commodities, the general state of the market, the level of the Nile ("There is no buying or selling, and no one is spending a single dirham. The eyes of the people are all turned toward the Nile. May God, in His mercy, raise its waters") is of self-evident commercial importance.

"Informal" Business Relations

Of less obvious significance is the space and attention which the writers of these letters devote to describing in a fair degree of detail the activities and business relations of merchants other than those with whom they have any direct dealings. This feature of Geniza business letters is in turn connected with one of the most interesting and original characteristics of commercial association revealed to us by the Geniza documents, namely, that of "informal business cooperation." The nature of and prominence of informal business cooperation in the commercial life of the Islamic Mediterranean of the eleventh century has been described by Goitein in his volume on the economic foundations of Mediterranean society.[39] Essentially, this activity consisted of one merchant entrusting goods or cash to a fellow merchant. The latter was to sell, invest, transport, or otherwise profitably dispose of these items, and all the profit resulting from the transactions accrued to the owner. The person who carried out the instructions received no remuneration whatsoever. The Geniza letters are replete with many instances of such requests, and although such missions often required great expenditures of time and effort, they were invariably fulfilled. The contents of the four letters translated above confirm Goitein's conclusion that "this form of commercial cooperation was the main pattern of international trade in those days."[40] Of all the transactions mentioned in these four letters, only two are explicitly formal business relationships, in this case partnerships between the correspondents. All the other business matters mentioned in the letters fall into the category of informal business cooperation, that is, they entail a variety of business-related activities which the correspondents request and expect of each other, yet which do not hold out any prospect of direct gain for the one who is actually expending time and effort on behalf of his colleague. The effectiveness and prominence of these practices can be explained on several levels. There was, of course, a functional element. Merchants engaged in international trade could in the course of their business careers fully expect to encounter situations that would call for the cooperation and aid of colleagues in distant parts. A merchant, therefore, would presumably be willing to invest much time and effort on behalf of a colleague in the expectation that he could count on reciprocation when the need arose. Yet a closer examination of informal business cooperation—so prevalent

39. Ibid., pp. 164–69.

40. Ibid., p. 165.

in the Geniza commercial correspondence of the eleventh century—reveals that much more than expectations of practical reciprocity were involved. Informal business cooperation was the institutional expression of a system of personal and economic ties and these ties were the sinews that held together the commercial network of the southern Mediterranean during the eleventh and twelfth centuries. The deeper principle that infused informal business cooperation and assured its effective operation was the element of personal guarantee, which often developed out of prior personal, family, or other relationships and resulted in various degrees of personal trust. The relationships which grew out of this personal trust were flexible and open-ended, involving obligations and privileges which were unquantified and unquantifiable. The numerous requests—large and small, personal or business-related—between the writers of these letters are to be understood in this light. In some cases, like that manifested in the letters presented above, the ties were very strong and close. In each of the four letters, information on formal and informal economic arrangements is inextricably intertwined with requests and references of a personal nature.[41]

The point which should be underlined is that the economic relationship between the merchants mentioned in these letters was an extension of their personal relationships. There was no clear line between personal and commercial concerns; they were both located on the same continuum and were part of one undifferentiated relationship. Informal business cooperation between merchants, bolstered by ties of personal trust and mutual responsibility, was not only an efficient method of conducting international trade, but also served as an effective buffer in the face of the numerous uncertainties and difficulties involved in long-distance commerce. The symbiotic commercial relationship which existed between Cairo and Alexandria in the eleventh century was facilitated both by the frequent communications—in person and by letter—between the two cities and by the original and flexible nature of the network of personal and economic ties that existed between the merchants active in these two cities.

41. For a more extensive treatment of informal business cooperation in the Geniza, see, Udovitch, "Formalism and Informalism," pp. 42–56.

9

A Mansion in Fustat: A Twelfth-Century Description of a Domestic Compound in the Ancient Capital of Egypt

S. D. Goitein

Of late, Robert S. Lopez, the undisputed and versatile master of medieval socioeconomic history, has turned his attention to the problems of housing and domestic architecture.[1] Therefore, as a token of my admiration and gratitude, I present here a piece from the Cairo Geniza which contains the most detailed description of a housing compound found thus far in that treasure trove of manuscripts.[2]

The document commands our interest for several reasons. First of all, of course, because of the forty-eight or so details provided about "the large house" (sections B I and II), most, but not all, of which recur in other documents dealing with urban real property. They are explained briefly in the notes to this essay and are discussed in greater detail in the section on domestic architecture in the forthcoming fourth and last volume of my *A Mediterranean Society*.

Two short examples underscore the usefulness of such descriptions. The late Gaston Wiet, certainly one of the most outstanding experts on medieval Egypt, tells us that there was no kitchen in the Cairene house of the Middle Ages. In the house described here there was one, however, and in some houses referred to in Geniza documents there were more than one.[3] In a recent article on the ventilation chimney in Egyptian houses it was assumed

The author wishes to thank the Librarian, University Library, Cambridge, England, for the permission to use the manuscript discussed in this article.

1. See R. Lopez, "L'Architecture civile des villes médiévales: exemples et plans de recherche," *Les constructions civiles d'intérêt public dans les villes d'Europe au Moyen Age et sous l'Ancien Régime et leur financement* (Brussels, 1971), pp. 15–31, 201–07.

2. On the Cairo Geniza see *Encyclopaedia of Islam*, 2d ed., II, 987–89, s.v., and, more detailed, in S. D. Goitein, *A Mediterranean Society: The Jewish Communities of the Arab World as Portrayed in the Documents of the Cairo Geniza* (Berkeley and Los Angeles, 1967–), I, *Economic Foundations* (1967), II, *The Community* (1971).

3. Gaston Wiet, *Cairo, City of Art and Commerce*, (Norman, Okla., 1964), p. 89.

that this protection against the heat was necessary only in houses that lacked an inner court. But here, as in other documents in the Geniza, the *bādahanj*, as this contrivance is called, is found in particular in houses with inner courts.[4]

Second, our document exemplifies that complicated clustering of buildings revealed also by excavations, buildings often held in joint proprietorship, sometimes even held jointly with Muslim or Jewish public bodies. For the convenience of the reader I have sketched the approximate layout of the properties concerned (Figure 9.1).

Finally, the notary's draft translated below betrays the polarity of clannishness and individualism characteristic of the Egyptian society of those days. Members of a family may have lived in adjacent houses, but they tried to keep their property rights carefully separated.

As with most Geniza papers, our document is written in the Arabic language, but Hebrew characters. For the benefit of Arabists and Islamists not familiar with Hebrew, the text has been transcribed into Arabic. I have described the method followed in this transliteration elsewhere.[5]

The language used in this draft is not classical, but "middle" Arabic, common to Muslims, Christians, and Jews.[6]

I would like to remark in advance that a "ruin" (*kharāba* in Arabic) is not necessarily an entirely abandoned building, but rather one that is partially in disrepair. Apartments or storerooms in such a disintegrating house could still be leased, as section B II of the sheet translated here shows.

A Notary's Draft Concerning Three Houses and Two Ruins Forming the Object of a Settlement

University Library, Cambridge, England
Taylor-Schechter Collection
TS K 25, f. 251

The sheet translated here contains the middle part of notes about a complicated settlement between a man, no doubt the Abu 'l-Ṭāhir mentioned in sections B III and IV, and his unmarried sister and his mother.

4. Alexandre Lézine, "La Protection contre la chaleur dans l'architecture musulmane d'Égypte," *Bulletin d'Études Orientales*, *24* (1971), 12.

5. E.g., S. D. Goitein, "Two Eyewitness Reports," *Bulletin of the School of Oriental and African Studies*, *14* (1954), 254. Idem, "The Tribulations of an Overseer," *Arabic and Islamic Studies in Honor of Hamilton A. R. Gibb* (Leiden, 1965), p. 272.

6. On the nature of "middle" Arabic, see J. Blau, *The Emergence and Linguistic Background of Judaeo-Arabic*; *A Study of the Origins of Middle Arabic* (Oxford, 1965). The same author has published a three-volume *Grammar of Christian Arabic* (Louvain, 1966–67).

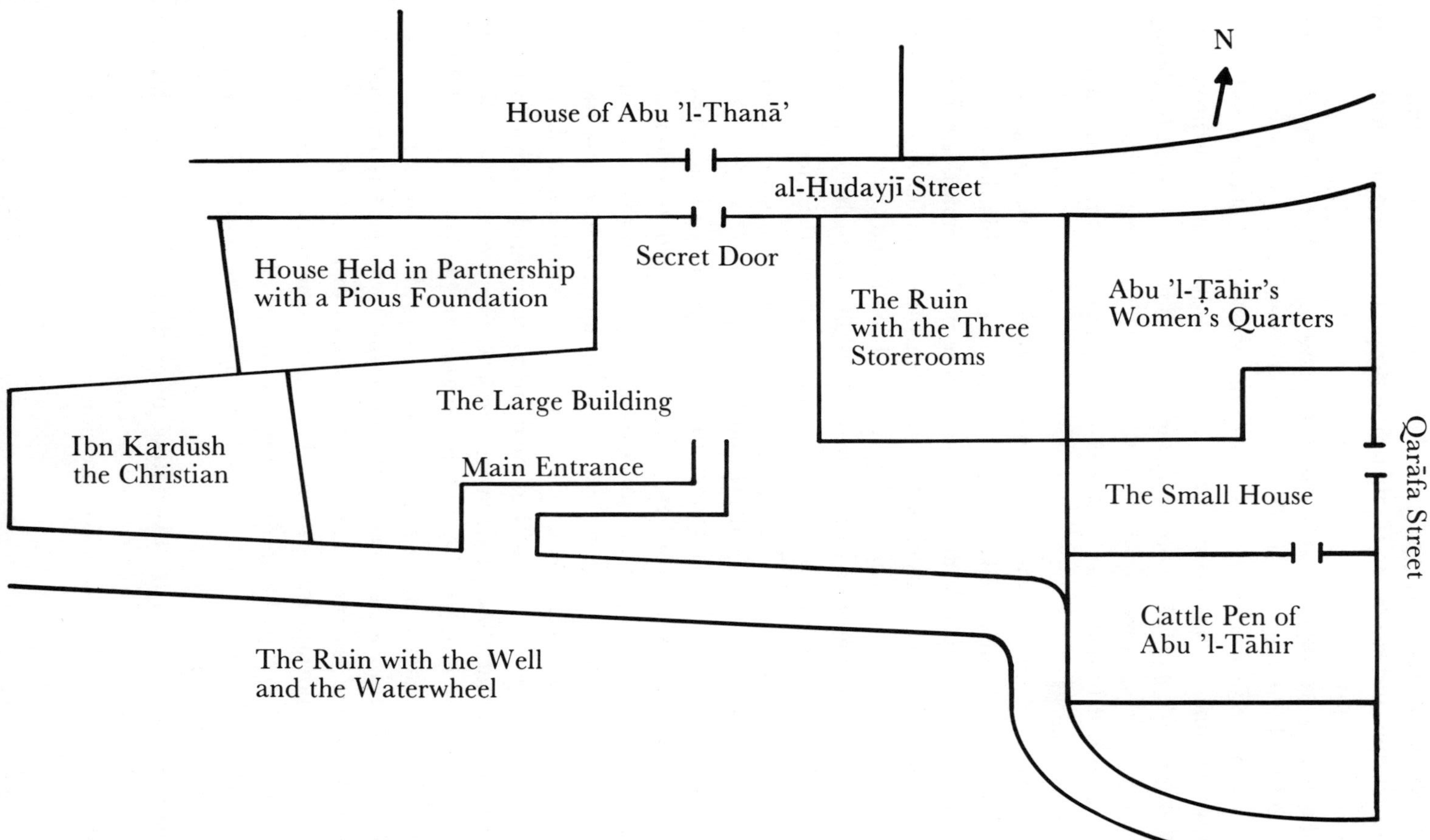

Figure 9.1 Three Houses and Two Ruins ca. A.D. 1190, Fusṭāṭ, Egypt

The first part, which has been lost, must have described the circumstances under which the settlement was reached, that is, why Abu 'l-Ṭāhir ceded to his mother and sister the rights to the properties described in the part that has been preserved.

The text is arranged as follows. On recto, lines 1–12, Abu 'l-Ṭāhir dictated to the notary details about the settlement. Because he had been forced to make several corrections, the notary asked his client whether he had no documents illustrating the case. After a document was produced, the notary made a new beginning on the reverse side, line 1, and after filling that page, he continued on recto on the unused space beginning with line 13. He worked hurriedly and crossed out many words, indicated here by double brackets ⟦ ⟧.

The draft contains the most detailed description of a private home found thus far in the Geniza and perhaps in any other Arabic document from the twelfth century. It is a pity that the third part of the notes, which would have contained a description of the house in the Mamṣūṣa quarter with nine upper floors or apartments, has not yet been found.

The settlement concerns two clusters of buildings which could not have been far away from one another, for both were in the vicinity of two streets, one known as the Old Spinnery and one called *darb al-qarāfa*, or Cemetery Street (see sections B III and V).

In the first and main compound, the family possessed four houses, two ruins, and a cattle pen. Proprietorship was distributed as follows: in one large and one small house, a ruin containing three rooms, and another ruin with a well and a waterwheel the ladies mentioned before owned—or were ceded—a part; a house bordering on the small house belonged to Abu 'l-Ṭāhir; another house was held in partnership by the two ladies with a pious foundation. This latter house is not included in our draft, because it did not form an object of the settlement. Moreover, Abu 'l-Ṭāhir held exclusive ownership of a cattle pen bordering on the small house. Such *zarības* (an Arabic word, which, in the form *zare(e)ba* has entered the English language via the Sudan) were common in Old Cairo. Milk and cheese were important items in the daily diet of the population and some had to be produced within the city itself.

The Ḥudayjī lane, which formed the northern border of the main building of this compound (cf. sections A and B I and II), is mentioned in at least six Geniza documents dating from the middle of the eleventh through the middle of the thirteenth centuries. Thus the neighborhood was presumably partly Jewish in composition.

The second group of buildings consisted of a big house with nine upper floors (or, more likely, nine apartments in an unspecified number of upper floors), in which the ladies had a share, and a house which was known as the property of the grandfather of the brother and the sister who made this settlement. As was common, various branches of the same family lived in adjacent houses.

Since the beginning and the end of the document are missing, no date has been preserved. The references to three persons mentioned in the draft permit us to date it roughly around 1190 (see notes 16 and 36).

A. *Beginning of a draft of a settlement between a man, his sister, and his mother* (recto, ll. 1–12)

Her name is both Sitt al-Rutab and Sitt al-Fakhr.[7] He releases Sitt [al-Rutab] from all claims and concedes to her all which is in her possession, both as her dowry and from other sources. The same applies to his mother, Sitt al-Ni'am.[8] He grants them free disposal (that is, complete proprietorship) of the large house which is known as their domicile.

This house has the following borders:

To the south, the lane which separates it from the ruin[9] and into which its doorway opens.

To the ⟦east⟧ north, the al-Ḥudayjī street, into which another of its doorways opens, as well as ⟦the house . . .⟧ the house held in partnership with the Pious Foundation ⟦and the above-mentioned girl and her mother⟧,[10] of which they possess three-quarters belonging exclusively to them.

To the east, the ruin which belongs to them and the small house.

To the west, the house known as the property of Fakhr al-Dawla

7. Sitt al-Rutab (Lady High Rank), and Sitt al-Fakhr (Lady Glory). These names originally were honorific titles and therefore one person might bear two at a time. Our document speaks about *one* girl only, cf. the words crossed out below (text, l. 4).

8. Sitt al-Ni'am means Lady Grace (i.e., God's grace bestowed on the family through her). Abu 'l-Ṭāhir made no claims against his mother.

9. This is a reference to the ruin with the well and the waterwheel which also belonged to the women and which, in the following, is mentioned as the last of the four items forming the compound (text, l. 8). Before the father of "Lady Glory" died, he legated her real estate as part of her dowry or as a personal gift. In addition, as it was regularly done, her mother, too, made her a gift of some immovables forming her personal property.

10. After having written this down, the notary asked how many shares in the house belonged to the Qōdesh, or Jewish pious foundation, and how many to mother and daughter. Once he had received the exact information, he crossed out what he had written and inserted the relevant details.

Thiqat al-Mulk[11] known as Ibn Kardūsh,[12] and of his partner Abu 'l-Riḍā, son of the chief (physician) Abu 'l-Najm.[13]

The house which is to the east of the large house[14] and which comprises two *qā'as*, or ground floors,[15] as well as an upper floor known as the residence of Munajjā, the son of Abū Sa'd, the druggist,[16] and, finally, the ruin with the well and the waterwheel (also are conceded to be the full property of the two ladies mentioned above).

They also have a share in a property in the Mamṣūṣa[17] quarter, namely, five-eighths of the large house which has a ground floor and nine upper apartments. That house has four borders: The first, to the south, is the house known as ⟦the residence⟧ the property of the elder al-Wajīh,[18] the physician, their grandfather, which is held in partnership with ⟦the h(eirs)⟧ the (Muslim) Ministry of Pious Foundations. The amount of her [*sic*] share is three-quarters, namely, the part of the house known as the residence of Abu-Sḥāq, the son of ⟦al-Marjānī (the dealer in corals)⟧ . . .[19] (discontinued in the middle of the line)

B. *Second draft of a deed on the same settlement*
(verso, ll. 1–27 and recto, ll. 13–29)

In each of the three houses and two ruins described in the document,[20] altogether five places, he[21] has one share out of three and holds possession

11. "The Pride of the State," "The Trustee of the Government." This Christian was either a government official or had some other close connections with the court.

12. "A fat piece of meat clinging to the bone"—a nickname which had become a family name, see S. D. Goitein, "Nicknames as Family Names," *Journal of the American Oriental Society, 90* (1970), 517–24.

13. These names could be borne by either a Christian, a Jew, or a Muslim. Since, however, this man was a partner in a big house of a Christian, it is likely that he belonged to the latter religion. A physician, Abu 'l-Najm (died 1202–03) was one of the many doctors who served Saladin, cf. Ibn Abī 'Uṣaybi'a, *Ṭabaqāt al-Aṭibbā'* (Cairo, 1882), p. 183. It may well be that he is the individual meant here.

14. The writer continues to enumerate the properties which formed the object of the settlement. This house obviously is identical with the small house mentioned before.

15. Two ground floors, that is, two open courts surrounded by buildings, are repeatedly mentioned in the Geniza.

16. "Munajjā, the druggist, son of Abū Sa'd, the druggist," is known from a document dated July 1218, TS 13 J 3, f. 27. The detail about the apartment occupied by Munajjā is given as a means of identification. As we learn in B III, this house had two upper floors and altogether three upper apartments.

17. A large quarter situated to the east of the ancient Roman fortress and containing many Jewish homes, see E. J. Worman, "Notes on the Jews in Fustat," *Jewish Quarterly Review, 18* (1905), 28 ff. It was adjacent to the quarters in which the other houses of that family were situated, see n. 22.

18. "The Eminent," an honorific title. Here again, we see that adjacent houses were owned by members of one family. "Their grandfather" is the grandfather of the brother and sister making the settlement.

19. Houses usually were divided into nominal shares. Here it is stated that the nominal share of the lady coincided with the part occupied by Abu Sḥāq. For him, see n. 36.

20. Namely in the document produced by the brother.

21. Here a hole in the manuscript destroyed about seven letters.

of each, as he claims. All are in Fus(tat) of E(gypt) in the places which will be mentioned hereafter.

I. *Detailed description of the large house* (verso, ll. 3–27)

The large house, which is one of the three main houses mentioned, is described in the document first. It is situated between the two quarters, one known as the Old Spinnery[22] and the other as Mahra,[23] in the alley k(nown) by the name of Ibn Kardūsh, the Christian,[24] the beginning of which alley opens into the way by which one gets to the aforementioned two quarters and to other places.

Description of this house:

It has an arched doorway closed by two dark brown door leaves. Through it one enters a corridor paved with marble in which there are two benches.[25] From the aforementioned corridor one enters a second corridor,[26] through which one comes to a large qāʿa, or ground floor, comprising two reception halls (literally, sitting rooms), facing each other with folding doors fastened on them, whose crossboards and outsides are carved.[27]

One of the two reception halls is longish. Its walls are of marble and it has two passages of carved wood, each of which has a door leading to an adjacent cabinet.[28] The reception hall has on its "front" (i.e. the wall opposite the entrance) a "windcatcher," or ventilation chimney, whose floor and walls are of marble. In front of the ventilation chimney, there is

22. The Old Spinnery was situated in the neighborhood of the Mamṣūṣa quarter, see n. 17. Cf. TS 16.356, l. 30, where a street is described as "leading to the Mamṣūṣa and the Old Spinnery." TS 16.356 (dated 1120) is composed of two fragments, one of which formerly bore the number TS 12.562 and is quoted as such by Worman in "Notes on the Jews in Fustat," p. 34, n. 3.

23. Mahra was the name of an Arab clan, which was settled in Fustat at the time of the Arab conquest, cf. Ibn Duqmāq, *Kitāb al-Intiṣār* (Cairo, 1891) IV, p. 3, l. 16, and p. 14, l. 18, and also Worman, "Notes on the Jews in Fustat," pp. 29, 32. In TS 8 J 5, f. 22 verso, a Jewish woman donates one-quarter of a house which she possessed in the Mahra quarter to the poor (1161).

24. See n. 12.

25. The term used, *maṣṭaba*, does not indicate of which material the benches were made. Most probably they were made of stones or bricks. There, the doorkeeper used to sit, see Martin C. Briggs, "The Saracenic House," *The Burlington Magazine for Connoisseurs*, *38* (1921).

26. Cf. Briggs, "The Saracenic House," p. 234 b: "This passage always has a right-angled turn in its length before it reaches the inner courtyard."

27. Text here (verso, l. 9), as well as in ll. 13, 15 and 18–19: "bi'abwāb muṭwāt murakkaba ʿalayh manqūshat al-jasāra wal-barrāt." The last two words are known to me only from an unpublished document from the year 1285, preserved in the archive of the Karaite community of Cairo. Their translation perforce is guesswork. I take *jasāra* as plural of *jisriyya* in the sense of crossboard as part of a door, cf. *jisr*, crossbeam. See Barthélemy, *Dictionnaire Arabe-Francais* (Paris, 1935), p. 112. and R. Dozy, *Supplément aux dictionnaires Arabes*, I, p. 195a. *Barrāt*, outside, plural of *barrā*, taken as a noun.

I wish to thank D. S. Richards, Oxford, for providing me with a photo of the Karaite manuscript.

28. "Cabinet" is a tentative rendering of *kumm*, literally "sleeve," It occurs frequently to designate an adjunct to a larger room.

a gilded wash basin.[29] The reception hall is encircled by a gilded cornice.[30] On the aforementioned ventilation chimney there are folding doors whose crossboards and outsides are carved. The ceiling of the room is painted with decorations in oil according to the Syrian fashion.

The second reception hall, which faces the first one described before, has folding doors on its entrance and on its front a ventilation chimney with folding doors all of whose crossboards and outsides are carved. The front is of marble in different colors.

The ground floor has two *ṣuffas*, or covered benches,[31] facing one another, with marble walls and ceilings painted in oil.

In the open court of the qāʿa there is a fountain of marble, and the entire court of this qāʿa, both its floor and its walls, are covered with marble. There are also various closets[32] with doors whose crossboards and outsides are of carved wood.

The qāʿa comprises also a kitchen, as well as two loggias[33] which look out on the open court of the ground floor, and each of them one reaches by a staircase of stone.

The floor of the bathroom belonging to the qāʿa is entirely paved with marble and is topped by a copula of carved gypsum. The qāʿa has also a secret door which belongs to it and which opens on the place known as al-Ḥudayjī street. Above the court of this qāʿa there is a gallery of carved gypsum.[34]

A rectangular door belongs to the upper part of this qāʿa, through which one enters a small corridor with a staircase of stone which enables one to reach an upper floor comprising three apartments, adjoining one another. Each of these apartments has a strong ceiling and doors fastened on the closets belonging to it as well as a separate washroom ⟦and four⟧, and other appurtenances and rights.

Above all this there is a roof with a parapet and a wooden railing around the staircase which leads to the upper floor.[35] The house possesses also canalization which belongs exclusively to it and appurtenances and rights.

29. Text: *ṭastiyya*. *Ṭast*, wash basin, occurs in practically all larger lists of trousseaux as an item in the list of copper vessels brought by the bride. However, *ṭastiyya* has not yet been found in the Geniza or elsewhere.

30. "Cornice" translates *'nbd'ryh*, occurring in the same connection also TS 16.356, l. 26 (A.D. 1120). A mere guess.

31. The term "ṣuffa" in the Geniza differs from its modern usage. For the latter see E. W. Lane, *The Modern Egyptians* (London, 1936), p. 12.

32. The term *khizāna* can mean both a cupboard built into the recesses of a wall and a small room.

33. The *mustaraqa*, or loggia, was one of the most common features of the medieval Egyptian townhouse.

34. Text: *maḥḍūr*, which, according to the spelling of those days, is identical with *maḥẓūr*.

35. Thus it seems that the staircase did not end in a door on the roof, but formed there an open circle which was surrounded by a wooden rail. For *darābazīn*, which is Greek *trapezion*, see Dozy, *Supplément*, I, 430 a.

II. *The boundaries of the large house*
(verso, l. 27, and recto, ll. 13–16)

The house is delimited by four borders. First, to the south, the lane from which it is entered and on which its doorway opens. Second, to the north, the house known as that of Abu 'l-Thanā', son of Barakāt, son of 'Ammār, the Jew, the sugar merchant,[36] which is entered from al-Ḥudayjī Lane. Third, to the east, the ruin which belongs to the house. The ruin consists of an open space and three storerooms. Fourth, to the west, the house known as that of Ibn al-Kardūsh and their [*sic*] partners.

III. *Description of the second house*
(recto, ll. 17–21)

Description of the second house. It has two doorways, one, which is approached from the alley which opens on the Qarāfa (Cemetery) Street, and the second, which is approached from the cattle pen belonging to the aforementioned Abu 'l-Ṭāhir.[37] The house is in the quarter mentioned in the document before. It comprises two reception halls and a staircase of stone on which one ascends first to the loggia and then to two floors which are one above the other, the first (the lower) having two apartments, and the second one apartment with the roof bordering on it. The house has also canalization belonging to it exclusively.

IV. *The borders of this house*
(recto, ll. 21–26)

The house is delimited by the following four boundaries. First, to the south, the cattle pen which is in its entirety the property of the aforementioned Abu 'l-Ṭāhir. Second, to the north, the place known as the Women's Qā'a, which also belongs to this Abu 'l-Ṭāhir. Third, to the east, the lane from which the house is entered; fourth, to the west, the rest of the house which belongs to Abu 'l-Ṭāhir and which is known as the Women's Quarters.[38]

36. One Abu 'l-Barakāt, son of 'Ammār, contributed the very considerable sum of seven and a half gold pieces to a public appeal made about 1155, TS Box K 6, f. 149, col. III, l. 15, see *Mediterranean Society*, II, 481–82, sec. 30. This could have been the father of our Abu 'l-Thanā', the *sukkarī*, a term that designated both a manufacturer and a seller of sugar. Abu Sḥāq, the son of Al-Marjānī, whose name was crossed out above, end sec. A, also contributed to that appeal, albeit a small sum, a quarter of a dinar, it seems, TS Box K 6, f. 149, col. IV, l. 4.

37. Abu 'l-Ṭāhir, according to our interpretation, cf. the introduction, was the brother of Lady "High Rank." Details about him were given in the opening section of the draft, which is not preserved.

38. This is the only case known to me from the Geniza of a separate women's apartment in Fusṭāṭ (called *ḥurmiyya*, abbreviated from *al-qā'a al-ḥurmiyya*). Other cases, referring to houses in Alexandria, in TS Arabic Box 30, f. 30^v (dated 1132), and Moses b. Maimon, *Responsa*, ed. J. Blau (Jerusalem, 1957), 1, 2, dated 1194.

V. *Beginning of the description of the third house* (recto, ll. 26–29)

Description of the house which is mentioned in the document as third and as being in the quarter mentioned in it.[39] The house is approached from the alley which opens on the way by which one walks to the Qarāfa Street and el(sewhere). It has a large rectangular doorway from which one enters two qā'as, one of which is . . . The (first) qā'a comprises two reception halls . . . (end of the leaf).

39. Namely, in the Mamṣūṣa quarter, cf. sec. A, n. 17.

Notes Concerning Three Houses and Two Ruins Forming the Object of a Settlement. Arabic Text. TS K 25, f. 251

٠١ الاسم ست الرتب وست الفخر وانه ابرأ ست الرتب من
جميع الدعاوى وسامحها بما حصل لها من

٠٢ (الدار) جهاز وغيره وست النعم والدته وجعل لهم
التصرف في الدار الكبيرة المعروفة بسكنهم في

٠٣ ولها حدود ٤ الحد القبلي ينتهي الى الزقاق الفاصل
بينها وبين الخرابة وفيه يشرع بابها والحد (الشرقي)
البحرى ينتهي

٠٤ الى درب الحديجي وفيه يشرع بابها الآخر (والى الدار
مس) والى الدار شركة القدش*(وللابنة المذكورة وللوالدة)

٠٥ الذى في اياديهم النصف والربع دونه والحد الشرقي
ينتهي الى الخرابة الذى لهم والى الدار الصغيرة
والحد

٠٦ الغربي ينتهي الى الدار المعروفة بفخر الدولة ثقة
الملك المعروف بابن الكردوش وشريكه

٠٧ ابو الرضا بن الريس ابو النجم والدار الذى هي من
شرقي الدار الكبيرة وهي تحتوى على قاعتين وطبقة

٠٨ المعروفة بسكن منجى ابن ابو سعد العطار والخرابة
الذى فيها البير والساقية وما هو لهم

---

* يعني وقف اليهود

٠٩ في سقع الممصوصة وهي النصف والثمن من الدار الكبيرة
ذات قاعة وتسعة طباق ولها

٠١٠ حدود اربعة الحد الاول وهو القبلي ينتهي الى الدار
المعروفة بسكن بملك الشيخ الوجيه الطبيب

٠١١ جدهم الذى هي شركة (الوا) ديوان الاحباس ومبلغ
حصتها النصف والربع المعروفة بسكن ابو سحق

٠١٢ بن (المرجاني)

٠١ ان جميع كل دار من الآدر الـ ٣ والخرابتين له حصة
من الحصص الـ ٣ من المواضع الـ ٥ التي يذكر

٠٢ فيه الذى ذكر ذلك في يده جميع ذلك بفسطاط
مصر بالمواضع (التي) التي تذكر فيه فمن

٠٣ ذلك جميع الدار الكبرى وهي إحدى الآدر الـ ٣ المبدأ
بذكرهم فيه في ما بين الخطين

٠٤ المعروف احدهما بدار الغزل القديمة والآخر بمهرة
داخلة في الخوخة المعروفة

٠٥ بابن الكردوش النصراني الشارع اول هذه الخوخة
على الطريق المسلوك من ذلك الى

٠٦ الخطين المذكورين وغيرهما وصفتها ذات الباب المعقود
حنيه بدرفين سمر يغلقان عليه

٠٧ يدخل منه الى دهليز مرخم الارض وفيه مصطبتان ثم
يدخل من الدهليز المذكور

٠٨ الى دهليز ثاني يتوصل منه الى قاعة كبرى تشتمل
على مجلسين متقابلين كل واحد
٠٩ منهما بابواب مطواة مركبة عليه منقوشة الجسارى
والبرات احدهما طولي
٠١٠ مرخم الجدران وفيه مقطعان خشبية منقوشة كل
منهما بباب يدخل منه الى فرد
٠١١ كم مجاور له وذات الباداهنج في صدره مرخم الارض
والجدران وفي صدر الباداهنج
٠١٢ المذكور طستية مذهبة وذات الانبدارية المذهبة الدايرة
به والباداهنج
٠١٣ المذكور عليه ابواب مطواة منقوش الجسارى والبرات ويعلوه
سقف مدهون شامي
٠١٤ والمجلس الـ ٢ المقابل للمجلس المذكور على بابه ابواب
مطواة وفي صدره باداهنج
٠١٥ بابواب مطواة منقوشة جميع ذلك الجسارى والبرات وصدره
مرخم ملون وذات الصفتين
٠١٦ المتقابلتان المرخمة الجدران وكل واحدة منهما بسقف
مدهون وذات الفسقية
٠١٧ في صحن القاعة المذكورة المرخمة وجميع صحن هذه
القاعة مرخم الارض والجدار

١٨٠ المحيطة به وذات الخزاين المتفرقة بابواب مركبة على
كل واحدة منهما منقوشة الجسارى
١٩٠ والبرات وذات المطبخ برسمها والمسترقتين المطلتين على
صحن قاعتها ويتوصل
٢٠٠ (لكل و) الى كل منهما على سلم معقود بالحجر وارض
المرحاض (الذى) الذى برسم هذه القاعة
٢١٠ مرخم جميعه ويعلوه قبة جبس منقوشة وذات الباب
السر الذى من حقوقها الشارع في
٢٢٠ الموضع المعروف بدرب الحديجي ويعلو صحن هذه
القاعة شرافة جبس منقوشة وذات الباب المربع
٢٣٠ الخالص لعلو هذه القاعة يدخل منه الى دهليز لطيف
فيه سلم معقود بالحجر يتوصل من عليه
٢٤٠ الى طبقة تحوى ٣ منازل متجاورة كل منزل منهم
بسقف وقي وابواب مركبة على الخزاين
٢٥٠ التي من حقوقه ومرحاض برسمه (واربعة) ومرافق
وحقوق ويعلو جميع ذلك سطح محضر (= محظّر) وذات
٢٦٠ الدرابزين الخشب الداير على (سلم هذه) سلم علو
هذه الدار والقنى الخالصة لها والمرافق
٢٧٠ والحقوق ويحيط بها ويجمعه ويشتمل عليها حدود ٤
الحد الاول وهو القبلي ينتهي الى الزقاق

١٣٠ المدخـول منه اليها وفيه يشرع بابها والحد الـ ٢ وهو
البحرى ينتهـي الى دار تعـرف بابو الثـنا

١٤٠ بن بركـات بن عمـار اليهودى السكـرى المدخول اليها
من درب الحديجـي والحد الـ ٣

١٥٠ وهو الشرقي ينتـهي الى الخـربة الذى هي من حقوقها
وصفتـها انها ذات ساحة كشف و ٣

١٦٠ مخازن والحد الـ ٤ وهـو الغربي ينتهي الى دار تعرف
بابن الكـردوش ومن يشركـهم فيها

١٧٠ وصفة الدار الـ ٢ منهـن ذات بابين احدهما يتوصل اليه
من الخـوخة الشارعة

١٨٠ بدرب القرافـة والثاني يتوصل اليه من الزريـبة الجارية
في ملك ابو الطاهـر المذكـور

١٩٠ وهذه الدار بالخط المقدم ذكـره فيه وهي تشتمل على
مجلسين وسلم حجـر يصعد

٢٠٠ من عليه الى مسترقة ثـم الى طبقتين متطابقـتين تحوى
الاولى منزلين والثانيـة

٢١٠ مـنزل واحد وذات السطح قبالته وذات القناة الخلصة
لها ويحيط بها حدود ٤

٢٢٠ الحـد الاول وهو القبلي ينتهي الى الزريـبة الجاريـة
جميعـها في ملك ابو الطاهـر

٢٣ · المذكور والحد الـ ٢ وهو البحرى ينتهي الى الموضع
المعروف بالقاعة الحرمية

٢٤ · الجارية ايضا في ملك ابو الطاهر هذا المذكور والحد
الـ ٣ وهو الشرقي ينتهي الى

٢٥ · الزقاق المذكور المدخول منه اليها والحد الرابع وهو
الغربي ينتهي الى بقية

٢٦ · الدار الجارية في ملك ابو الطاهر المعروفة بالحرمية
وصفة الدار المثلث

٢٧ · بذكرها فيه انها بالخط المذكور فيه يتوصل اليها من
الخوخة الشارعة على الطريق

٢٨ · المسلوك منها الى درب القرافة وهي تشتمل على باب
(كبار) كبير مربع

٢٩ · يدخل منه الى قاعتين احداتهما علو ٠٠ وتشتمل
القاعة على مجلسين

10

Crusader Cities

Joshua Prawer

One of the main achievements of the study of Crusader institutions in the last generation has been the definition of the place of cities in state and society, a recognition of their primordial importance in the state structure and in the social stratification of the Latin establishments in the Near East. The common view, which in this matter as in many others simply applied European notions to the Latin Orient, proved to be misleading. The castle and the countryside, the two dominant features of the early Middle Ages that prevailed well into the central period except in some areas like Italy, did not play the same role in the Latin Near East. Even historians who acknowledged or sensed the importance of the Palestino-Syrian cities, and in the process often exaggerated their economic role, did not realize their importance in fashioning Crusader society.

The new perspective, which describes Crusader society as mainly urban and the Syro-Palestinian cities not only as centers of urban, royal or seigniorial, administration but also as the principal habitat of the Western conquerors and immigrants, opens up new vistas. Monographs on particular cities still remain a desideratum, and this essay does not try to do more than to define problems and outline some of the characteristic features of Crusader cities.[1]

One of the thorniest questions in the study of medieval cities in the West and in the lands of Islam is the problem of their origin. However, in the case of Crusader cities the answer is easy.[2] Students of Crusader cities do

1. For a summary of the position of cities in the Kingdom see J. Prawer, *The Latin Kingdom of Jerusalem: Medieval European Colonialism* (London, 1970), pp. 65–67, 151–53; R. C. Smail, *The Crusaders* (London, 1973), pp. 67–88. M. Benvenisti, *The Crusaders in the Holy Land* (Jerusalem, 1970), pp. 25–207.

2. A very lucid statement of the problem connected with the study of Muslim cities may be found in A. H. Hourani's excellent introduction to *The Islamic City*, ed. A. H. Hourani and S. M. Stern (Oxford, 1970), pp. 1–24. See also I. M. Lapịdus, ed., *Middle Eastern Cities* (Berkely and Los Angeles, 1969); G. E. von Grünebaum, *Islam: Essay in the Nature and Growth of Cultural Tradition* (London, 1955), pp. 141–58. An exhaustive bibliography is furnished by I. M. Lapidus, *Muslim Cities in the Later Middle Ages* (Cambridge, Mass. 1967), pp. 217 ff. The bibliography relating to European cities is overwhelming. The best available summary and bibliography is in the *Cambridge Economic History*, vols. 2, 3.

not have to determine which are *villae novae* or *burgi novi* as opposed to surviving Late Roman cities, and they do not face the Oriental counterpart of the problem: sorting out cities that survived from the Byzantine period and cities that grew up "spontaneously" from cities built by the order of authorities. The Crusaders, during their two hundred years of domination in the Eastern Mediterranean, hardly ever founded an entirely new city. All Crusader cities had long histories predating Western conquest. (The most "recent" city, Ramleh, was founded three hundred years earlier.) The Crusaders had no need to found and build new cities, because from all standpoints—demographic, religious, administrative, or military—the existing cities fully answered their requirements. The Crusader conquest and settlement did not cause overpopulation. As a matter of fact the main weaknesses of Crusader colonization were demographic. The Crusaders remained from beginning to end a minority in the conquered areas. In addition, the Latin religious tradition so closely corresponded to the Byzantine (which continued the early Christian and Jewish traditions) that the existing cities were also adequate as religious centers. Actually one of the problems of Crusader ecclesiastical administration was the excessive number of ecclesiastical centers, a legacy of the Byzantine period.

Economic, administrative, and military needs were also met by existing cities. The disparity between the number of urban agglomerations which thronged the coast and the few in the interior reflected the demographic realities that existed between the end of the Late Roman empire and the Crusader period. Thus the absence of city agglomerations in the Palestinian Negev corresponded to the decline and subsequent disappearance of any but nomadic groupings. Once abandoned, the Negev became an arid area, uninhabited except for small groups clustering around water holes and oases.

Although the Crusaders lived by the sword, military needs did not warrant founding new fortified cities. Whenever needed they built or restored castles, but almost always in places where an ancient site already proclaimed its geopolitical or strategic advantages, and where the availability of water and building material facilitated the task of reconstruction. A famous Crusader proverb—"a castle destroyed is already half-built"—was a self-evident truth.[3]

Although the general rule that the Crusaders did not construct any entirely new cities has no exception, it does have some qualifications. The

3. Eracles, *Recueil des Historiens des Croisades. Historiens Occidentaux* (Paris, 1844), I, 697: "si comme en dist chastel abatuz est demi resez."

first is that during the period of conquest the Crusaders' available manpower was hardly ever sufficient either to settle the whole area of the former city or even to man its defense perimeter. In Jerusalem, for example, the Crusaders were hard pressed to settle even one-quarter of the city; they were equally undermanned in Ramleh, the ancient Arab capital of the southern district of Filastīn, the southern border city of Gaza, or even the port of Jaffa.[4] Excluding Jerusalem, where the former citadel granted some security, the Crusaders in all such cases settled a part of the former area and built a new wall *intra muros*[5] to protect themselves. This obviously cannot be regarded as founding a new city, but it is important to note because it often changed, at least for some period of time, the physical contour of the former Byzantino-Arab city. An interesting example is that of Caesarea on the coast, where recent excavations laid bare the magnificent Crusader fortifications of the middle of the thirteenth century, which no doubt followed the Crusader fortifications of the twelfth century. Unfortunately it is difficult to say if the latter were built over the former Arab fortifications of Qaisārīya or were entirely new. Even more baffling is the discovery of the remains of a strong wall inside the Crusader city, a strong but rustic wall in which the rubble is mixed with a heterogeneous collection of exquisite Herodian and Byzantine columns and capitals. The materials used are the same as those used for the foundation of the houses on the main Crusader street which led from the eastern gate to the port area in the west. It is not too daring to assume that we deal here with an early Crusader settlement, which built an inner wall inside the former Arab fortifications. Yet it can be argued also that this wall was built after the Third Crusade, when the Crusaders regained the city. Caesarea is also important because it exemplifies the shrinkage of the presumably Herodian and certainly the Byzantine city to something like one-tenth of its former area.[6]

The second qualification is that in some cases a Crusader city expanded beyond the perimeter of its Arab predecessor. This happened in the thirteenth century, when the cities of the Crusader rump state on the coast gathered in the Crusader population from the lost interior, and the maritime cities remained the only places which were open to European immigration and to the growing numbers of the nationals of the Italian,

4. For Jerusalem, see J. Prawer, "The Settlement of the Latins in Jerusalem," *Speculum, 24* (1952), 490 ff. For Ramleh, Gaza, and Jaffa, see J. Prawer, "Colonisation activities in the Latin Kingdom of Jerusalem," *Revue belge de philologie et d'histoire, 29* (1951), 1066ff.

5. See, for example, Willelmus Tyrensis, book X, chap. 17. Cf. Prawer, "Colonisation Activities," p. 1078.

6. The report on the archeological excavations of Crusader Caesarea has not yet been published. See J. Prawer, *Histoire du royaume latin de Jérusalem*, 2d ed. (Paris, 1975), II, 344ff.

Provençal, and Catalan communes. Such expansion beyond the former walls is known, for example, in Jaffa, where a *burgus novus*[7] was added to the old city. We also have detailed knowledge about an entire new quarter called Mount Musard in Acre. This suburb began growing near the northern walls of the city even before the end of the twelfth century. At that time it mushroomed beneath the citadel, in the shadow of the formidable walls of the city.[8] This new settlement covered the main roads which earlier led out from the city to the north, and their location is witnessed by the names of the area's piazzas and streets (for example, Ruga Safforia, the street of Sepphoris).[9]

The nearest the Crusaders came to founding new cities was when they erected a castle on an ancient site and a civilian population settled in its shadow. One such case is that of the city of Château Pèlerin ('Athlīth). No extant documents testify to its creation or existence, but archeological excavations have discovered it. Relatively small in area (about 9 hectares) it had its own system of defenses which separated it in the east from the plain and in the west from the magnificent castle. It had its own church (which seems to have never been finished), a marketplace, sties, stables, and cattle sheds. One can assume that in this particular case city life and city occupations were dictated by the requirements of the castle.[10] In Saphet, the new castle, a giant fortification whose garrison and administrative staff counted some 1,500 people, created or rather injected new life into the city of an earlier period. Similar development of small cities around restored castles can be seen in a number of Crusader localities.[11]

Physically, then, the Crusader cities were not new. It is outside the scope of this essay to deal with the problem of continuity between the Late Roman, Arab, and Crusader cities. The problem was studied some fifty

7. For Jaffa, see Auvray, ed., *Regesta Gregorii IX* (Paris, 1890), no. 4013. R. Röhricht, *Regesta Regni Hierosolymitani* (Innsbruck, 1893), no. 1085: "domus in suburbio Joppensi prope portam, qua itur Hierosolyma" (A.D. 1238). A *burgus novus* was established in Nablus in 1168. E. de Rozière, ed., *Cartulaire du Saint Sépulcre* (Paris, 1849), p. 279; R. Rohricht, *Regesta*, no. 444. It is rather strange to find a *burgus novus* in Tyre in 1190, as the city was on a peninsula encompassed by walls. See *Liber iurium Reipublicae Januensis* (Turin, 1853), pp. 358, 406. Yet in 1190 the Genoese quarter in Tyre extended "usque ad murum vetulum, qui fuit antiquitus clausura villae."

8. For Acre, see J. Prawer, "L'Établissement des Coutumes du marché à Saint Jean d'Acre," *Revue historique de droit français et étranger*, *29* (1951), 335–37.

9. Marked in the different versions of the map of Acre probably drawn by Pietro Visconti for Marino Sanudo's *Liber Secretorum Fidelium Crucis*, ed. J. Bongars, *Gesta Dei per Francos* (Hannover, 1611). Cf. J. Prawer, "Historical maps of Acre [Hebrew]," *Eretz Israel*, *2* (1953), 175–85. Cf. map in the photographic reproduction of Sanudo's *Liber*, ed. J. Prawer (Toronto, 1972), pp. xviii–xix. Here also is a color reproduction of one of the famous maps.

10. C. N. Johns, *Guide to 'Athlit* (Jerusalem, 1947), 67ff.

11. Prawer, *Histoire du royaume latin de Jérusalem*, II, 293ff.

years ago in terms of one city, Jerusalem,[12] but new material and especially the newest excavations make a more detailed study essential. For other cities, we are still groping in the dark.

We can thus propose two general conclusions: (1) the perimeter of the Crusader cities almost everywhere remained roughly the same as that which the Crusaders found in the period of conquest (1099–1111); (2) although the Crusaders settled in the beginning relatively small areas or quarters in the conquered cities and hastily built walls inside the old city, usually near the ancient citadel or around the port fortifications, with time and under pressure from a growing population they expanded inside the old walls and the interior walls ceased to be functional. Yet despite the growth of population we find in almost all Crusader cities ruined buildings, vegetable gardens, small orchards, and open spaces. This pattern seems to be a common feature of all Near Eastern cities.[13]

The physical continuity between the Crusader city and its predecessor does not mean that continuity existed in other aspects of city life. Actually, one of the decisive factors which shaped the character of the Crusader cities was the fact that in all of them the shift in domination was accompanied by a wholesale change in population. The Moslem population disappeared either through massacre, expulsion, or voluntary exile. The details are well known. Suffice it to say that even when the Crusader leaders tried to change the ruthless policy of conquest and annihilation, the rank and file of the army opposed the new policy because it deprived them of booty and loot. In one case it was the masses of warriors, in another the Genoese, who ignored a capitulation agreement and insisted on storming a city which was ready to surrender. In still another case, though a capitulation agreement which preserved the life and property of the native inhabitants of Tyre was accepted, the Muslim inhabitants preferred exile to the crushing taxation imposed by the conquerors. Thus almost everywhere large groups were eliminated from the city populations. Yet there were some elements which assured a degree of continuity. The most important of these groups were the Oriental Christians. Some of them were expelled by their Moslem fellow citizens at the approach of the Crusader hosts, some ran away during the turmoil of war, and some were probably massacred during the Crusader conquest. But once the fighting was over the Oriental Christians, Greek Orthodox, Syrians, and Jacobites, to name only the major communities, tried to settle again and regain their former

12. F. M. Abel, *Jérusalem nouvelle*, vol. II (Paris, 1926).

13. Cf. Goitein, "Cairo: An Islamic City in the Light of the Geniza Documents," in Lapidus, *Middle Eastern Cities*, pp. 87 ff. and the remark of A. L. Oppenheim ibid., p. 95.

habitats. At that early period in the history of the Kingdom, they were welcomed by the Crusaders into their virtually empty cities. We know, for example, that in Jerusalem the Oriental Christians, in this case the "Syrians," were transported with their families from Transjordan and settled in the ancient Jewish quarter of the city. This rather exceptional act was the result of royal initiative.[14] In the majority of cases the former Christian inhabitants simply flocked back to their cities. In Ramleh, for example, the former population and even farmers from the countryside settled in the city after the Crusader conquest.[15]

It must have been in the second or third decade of Crusader rule, when the new regime had become more stabilized, that Moslems and Jews also came back and settled in the cities. A sad exception was that of Jerusalem. Crusader legislation barred Moslems and Jews from settling in that city, regarding it sacrilegious that unbelievers should inhabit the place of Christ's passion. With this exception, Moslems and Jews, in addition to the Oriental Christians, became a constitutive element in the population of all Crusader cities.

Another factor which contributed to the continuity of city life was the existence of numerous buildings connected with religion. *Prima facie* this seems rather strange, but in reality it is not. The conquerors, the Latin Crusaders, became overnight the rulers of the ecclesiastical structures of three religions: the mosques of Islam, the churches of Oriental Christians, and the synagogues of Jews and Karaites. Although the Crusaders did not take over all the sanctuaries, all the major mosques and in many cases almost all the mosques in a city became churches.[16] The qiblas were walled up and the altars placed in the eastern part of the buildings. The new churches quickly accumulated "traditions" of their holiness and became integrated into the city's web of the ecclesiastical organization.

This sort of usurpation did not take place, at least not at the same rate, in relation to the Oriental churches, but it is still true that the major sanctuaries in Jerusalem, Bethlehem, and Nazareth became Latin churches, and the previously dominant denominations were forced to take a subordinate place.

14. See Prawer, "The Settlement of the Latins in Jerusalem."

15. Albertus Aquensis, *Liber Christiane Expeditionis*, book V, chap. 42. *Recueil*, *Historiens Occidentaux*, *4* (Paris, 1879), 460.

16. The best known cases are the Dome of the Rock, which became the Templum Domini and al-Aqṣa, which turned into the Templum Salomonis. In Tripoli we find a *regis bafumaria* = royal mosque (bafumaria-mahumaria-mosque) in 1109, *Liber iurium*. p. 18. In Ascalon the mosque called Khidr (the Green), became Sancta Maria Cathara, Röhricht, *Regesta*, no. 356. Cf. J. Prawer, "Ascalon and the County of Ascalon in the Crusader Period [Hebrew]," *Eretz Israel*, *5* (1958), 224ff.

One can assume that Jewish and Karaite prayer places met a fate similar to that of the mosques, but because they were seldom, if ever, magnificent buildings under the rule of Islam, the synagogues probably became simple lodgings, though some might have become churches or chapels. Thus the physical legacy of the cities of the earlier period, as well as the permanency of the sanctuaries and the traditions of the former city population, were important factors in shaping the topography of the Crusader cities despite the tremendous hiatus caused by conquest and its aftermath in the history of the city's population.

As the empty spaces inside the former city walls slowly filled up with immigrants and settlers, the temporary inner walls erected immediately following the conquest became superfluous. The Great Mosques of the cities and the mosques of the quarters became cathedrals, parish churches, and chapels, and as time passed the Crusaders built new churches or restored old sanctuaries.

The earlier physical outline of the city was re-emerging. The fortification pattern of every city was characterized by its major bulwark, the citadel. The citadel of the Arab period, which contained the quarters of the governor and commander, was the civil and military center of the city, and so it remained in the Crusader period. The same buildings continued to have similar functions in almost all Crusader cities. The larger cities were administered by the lord of the city, the *castellanus*, who was the military commander, and the *vicecomes*, the civil governor of the city. The lodgings of the lord of the city were often, but not alwyas, in the citadel. In Jerusalem, for example, the royal palace was in the beginning in the al-Aqṣa mosque and later on in a building of Herodian origin that was adjacent to the citadel. In Acre the lord of the city might have lived in the citadel, but there was a royal palace in the city. Similarly, in Beirut the palace, which was described in glowing colors by the German pilgrim Wilbrand of Oldenburg, was in the citadel.[17] The location of the vicecomes office is rather obscure. It might have been either in the lord's palace or in the citadel. In Jerusalem it was probably in the citadel because the city's customhouse was situated there, though customhouses existed near all the main gates of the city as well.[18]

The Crusaders used the same logic in selecting sites for economic and

17. Wilibrandus de Oldenborg in *Peregrinatores Medii Aevi Quatuor*, ed. J. C. M. Laurent (Leipzig, 1864), pp. 166–67.

18. de Rozière, *Cartulaire du Saint Sépulcre*, no. 45, pp. 83–85. An interesting description of the citadel of Jerusalem is furnished by the Russian abbot Daniel in 1106–07, in *Itinéraires russes en Orient*, ed. B. de Khitrovo (Geneva, 1889), p. 17.

civic installations, namely the marketplaces, baths, and ovens (*furni*), as they did for establishing fortifications and the residences of authorities. It was a matter of expediency to use existing installations. The existing Arab *souks* had catered to a larger clientele than provided by the Crusader cities, at least during the first generation after the conquest and probably for longer. Consequently there was no need for new and costly structures. Naturally pigsties or pig markets were a Crusader innovation, but this simply meant that a former cattle market was adapted for slightly different functions.

The furn of the preceding period also proved to be adequate. Though such an installation is not too complicated to build, the existing furns which dotted the city served the Crusaders' needs well. Still the growth of the population in particular quarters prompted from time to time the building of additional bakeries.[19]

Finally, the Crusader *balnea* (baths) were the Arab *ḥamāmas*. In this case not only was the installation a costly one that required professional builders, but in all cases in which its water supply depended on the ancient aqueducts which brought water into the city from natural sources, the position of the balnea was fixed because building new ones would have meant construction of new supply installations. In other places the balnea were linked to local wells and rainwater reservoirs and as such were in fixed locations. Only when population growth increased demand beyond capacity, which did occur in some thirteenth-century Crusader cities, were new *balnea* erected.

To sum up, visualize a map showing the physical features of the Arab city—the line of walls, the location of citadel and palace, the major mosques and Christian sanctuaries, the marketplaces, baths, and bakeries. If we superimpose on such a plan a map of a Crusader city, we will find an amazing correspondence between the two. However, at the current stage of research, the procedure has to be reversed. We have a rather rich amount of data for the Crusader period, whereas for the earlier period data is scarce and studies almost nonexistent.

Thus we arrive at a rather paradoxical situation. Whereas the main physical features of the Muslim city (we use the expression to mean the city of the preceding period, although we do not believe such cities were created in that period but that most date back at least to the Late Roman period) conditioned the general physiognomy of the Crusader city, its

19. A typical list of furni, twenty-six in all, belonging to the canons of the Holy Sepulcher is furnished in an inventory of the cathedral's possessions, de Rozière, no. 185, pp. 329 ff. The inventory makes a distinction between *furni veteri* and *furni novi*.

population changed in a revolutionary way. And one of the main problems of the study of Crusader cities will thus be to ascertain the profound impact of the old order and the adaptation of the new immigrant population to the pre-existing features of the different localities.

The first clear expression of the new situation is to be found in the long list of privileges accorded to the Italian communes.[20] Four or five items constantly recur in the demands of the Italians. They always request the grant of a *ruga* or *platea* (or both), *funda*, *ecclesia*, furnus, and balneum; that is, a street or square, a place for a market, a church, an oven, and a bath.[21] These are the basic elements of every commual quarter in a Crusader city. The church of the communal quarter would very often be a former *masjid* or *meschita*, as the Crusaders called mosques, though in some cases a new church was needed.

Did the Italians include these features in their demands because such components were essential to the Italian or Mediterranean notion of a self-sufficient quarter or to their image of a city, or did they include them because the Amalfitan and Venetian experience in Byzantium, Egypt, or Syria had already brought the Westerners into contact with the native quarters of the Muslim cities? This is an interesting and debatable point, but for the time being it is hazardous to venture an opinion. One way or another the Italian requests were quite in keeping with the existing physical conditions of the Syro-Palestinian cities.

Whereas the Italian's privileges assume that in the area to be allocated to them they will find all the major features of a quarter, they explicitly demand in some cases a space in which to build their funda, the marketplace, or their *fondaco*, the major economic center of their quarter.[22]

The impact of this seemingly very logical demand can be rightly appreciated if we consider it in terms of the framework of the earlier city. It is here that the major physical differences between the Muslim city and the Crusader city as it developed during the twelfth and thirteenth centuries become apparent. These differences were the result of particular Crusader institutions.

Basically a Muslim city was ruled by one sovereign power. It was of little consequence if it belonged to a larger political entity, caliphate, *jund*

20. A convenient inventory of privileges is listed by J. L. La Monte, *Feudal Monarchy in the Latin Kingdom of Jerusalem, 1100–1291*, (Cambridge, Mass., 1932), app. D, pp. 261–76.

21. See, for example, the agreement with the Genoese in which Philip II Augustus promised to give them: "ecclesiam, fundicum, furnum et balneum atque rugam per quamcumque civitatem in quo videlicet ruga Ianuensis vicecomes maneat cum plena iurisdictione". *Liber iurium*, p. 386.

(military district), or emirate. As far as the population was concerned sovereignty was vested in the local governor, his garrison, and his officials. Inside the walls there was no immunity; no enclave or area which was independent or outside his authority existed. A fortiori no city quarter ever attempted to reach a position of autonomy or autarchy. Consequently the major centers of city life were organized along purely functional lines. The number of bazaars and souks, of ḥamāmas and furni, as well as the location of a mosque in a given quarter roughly corresponded to the needs of the population there. Here and there the establishment of a *waqf* by a private person would furnish the means to build a mosque, which may have exceeded the actual needs of the local population, but this was certainly not the rule. *Madrassas* proliferated according to the rhythm of pietism and benefactors' contributions.

To illustrate the functionality of the Muslim city let us examine the situation in Jerusalem. The ancient forum of the Roman Aelia Capitolina, which still functions as the main grid of the Old City, continued to exist in the Late Roman and Arab periods. As late as the sixth century the Madaba mosaic shows the Roman *cardo* and *decumanus*, a column-flanked main street running from north to south and a forum at the point of intersection with the west-east city artery. We do not know by what stages this area became the medieval and modern bazaar with its three parallel sections, but recent research has proved that specialized bazaars existed at least a generation before the arrival of the Crusaders.[23] Possibly Jerusalem's evolution was similar to that of Damascus where the colonnade and its porticoes were progressively filled with shops and the workplaces of artisans, and this obstruction of the main thoroughfare and open space created the medieval Arab bazaar.

The tripartite bazaar of Jerusalem functioned in the period of the Crusades as a market for fowl, fish, vegetables, spices, and textiles, that is, basically small-volume products with a daily turnover. Additionally there were food stalls and kitchens which catered to the inhabitants and to pilgrims.[24] Obviously this one market was not sufficient for the needs of the

22. For example, Amalric grants the Pisans in Jaffa (A.D. 1157): "plateam . . . ut in ea componant sibi domus et faciant ibidem forum sibi." G. Müller, *Documenti sulle relazioni delle città Toscane coll'Oriente* (Florence, 1879), no. 6., p. 8.

23. The best reproduction and analysis of the famous Madaba mosaic is by M. Avi-Yonah, *The Madaba Mosaic Map* (Jerusalem, 1954), esp. plate 7 and analysis. pp. 50ff. For the Arab period, see J. Richard, "Sur un passage du Pèlerinage de Charlemagne: Le marché de Jérusalem," *Revue belge de philologie et d'histoire*, *43* (1965), 552–55.

24. For example: "Et a seniestre del *Cange*, trouve on une rue toute couverte à vaute qui a non li *Rue des Herbes*. Là vent on tout le fruit de la ville et les herbes et les espesses. Al cief de celle rue a j. liu là où

population, and larger-volume products such as oil and grain actually had their own, large open-air market just across the street from the citadel.[25] The cattle market was in the valley, still in existence today, which divided the Temple Mount from the city. Logically enough, the skinners and tanners were the immediate neighbors of the cattle market. This location facilitated the provision of raw material and solved the problem of drainage for their rather messy occupation.[26]

Similar arrangements can be postulated for any larger urban agglomeration. The specific position in any city was naturally determined by the topography of the site. Thus the skinners and tanners of Jerusalem, as already mentioned, were near the main drainage artery of the city, the valley of Josaphat; in Tyre and in Acre proximity to the port area determined the position of the meat markets and slaughterhouses.[27]

The Crusader conquest had in this regard a far-reaching impact. Under the domination of the Crusaders, the city ceased to be in many cases the administrative and economic entity it had been in the Arab period. The Italian (and to a smaller degree the Provençal and Catalan) communes and, on a different level, the military orders had a decisive impact on city structure. Both had their own quarters inside the main Crusader cities, and "quarter" spelled autonomy, different degrees of sovereignty, and, in the thirteenth century, violent outbreaks which necessitated the erection of new defense lines inside the city. The walled-in city quarters resembled micro-cities within the frame of the city. At least six micro-cities of this type existed in Acre in the middle of the thirteenth century during the "War of the Communes."[28] Obviously such changes were peculiar to those cities in which the communes created autonomous quarters. This phenomenon, however, was confined to the major maritime cities, namely

on vent le poisson; et derrière le *Marchié là où on vent le poisson*, a une grandisme place là ù on vent les oes et les fromages et les poules et les aves" (La Citez de Iherusalem, in *Itinéraires à Jérusalem*, ed. H. Michelant and G. Raynaud [Geneva, 1882], p. 34); "Devant le *Cange*, venant à la *Rue des Herbes*, a une rue c'on apele *Malquisinat*. En celle rue cuisoit on la viande c'on vendoit as pelerins", *La Citez de Iherusalem*, 38. Cf. pp. 155 ff.

25. *Continuateur anonyme de Guillaume de Tyr*, Michelant and Raynaud, *Itinéraires à Jérusalem*, p. 146: "A main senestre de la Tor David avoit une grant place où l'en vendoit blé". The twelfth-century map of Jerusalem (Mss Cambrai) marks opposite the citadel: *Ecclesia Sancti Georgii in funda*. Cf. J. Prawer *Histoire du royaume latin*, I, 227.

26. *Ernoul*, Michelant and Raynaud, *Itinéraires à Jérusalem*, p. 39: "li *Boucerie*, là où l'en vent le car de la vile" (p. 48), "Porte de la Tanerie," The gate of Tanners.

27. The slaughterhouses of Acre were at the edge of the sea or even on the outskirts of the port. Cf. G. Reynaud, ed., *Gestes des Chiprois*, par. 139. A tannery in Laodicea was located near the sea. G. Müller, *Documenti*, nos. 6, 13; p. 6, 16.

28. See Prawer *Histoire du noyaume latin*, II, 359–75.

Acre and Tyre (although Jaffa evidenced some symptoms in the beginning). Jerusalem or the towns of the interior like Nablus or Tiberias, however, remained under the undivided sovereignty of the king or lord of the city. Some changes took place as a result of Crusader policy toward religious minorities, but the main economic establishments neither needed nor experienced any changes. The marketplaces and the bazaars remained at their earlier sites, although, once the Near Eastern seaboard had become part of the new Euro-Levantine trade relations, a quickening of the economic rhythm was discernible.

The creation of the communal quarters broke up the formerly harmonious and functional distribution of the economic establishments of the city. The maps of Acre and Jerusalem drawn up (in all probability by Pietro Visconti) for Marino Sanudo at the end of the thirteenth century make the change visible. Whereas there is continuity in the location of the markets of Arab and Crusader Jerusalem, such continuity is only just discernible in Acre. The economically specialized markets have been replaced. There is even a new vocabulary: ruga Venetorum, ruga Ianuensium, ruga Pisanorum and the like. These autonomous quarters have their own funda and their own fondaci. A variety of independent markets have sprung up with their own market inspectors, their own solid and liquid measures, and their own system of taxation.[29] Functionally defined city markets gave way to a variety of markets dealing often in the same type of merchandise, sometimes catering to a particular clientele but probably also competing with each other. This was one of the results of the privileges granting autonomy to the communes.

The comprehensiveness or specialization of these markets is difficult to ascertain. This was a function of the degree of autarchy which they strove to achieve and the profitability of such enterprises. It is quite possible, for example, that the communal markets did not, at least not always, deal with food provisions, although we find, for example, that even a relatively unimportant commune like that of Marseilles sold wine in its own fondaco, prohibiting the sale of other wine until it sold out its own stock.[30] We can also assume with confidence that the market of the Venetian quarter in

29. The Genoese in Tyre (1190) enjoy: "libertas cantarii, buze et modii et omnium mensurarum in Tyro" (*Liber iurium*, p. 358). An interesting case in Acre is noted by B. Pegolotti: "Grano e orzo e tutti biadi etc. si vendono in Acri a moggio, ed é il moggio del Signore e della ruga di Pisa e della ruga di Vinegia tutto uno con quello delle magione dello Spedale del Tempio." The last words should possibly be read: "dello Spedale e del Tempio" (*La Pratica della mercatura*, ed. A. Evans [Cambridge, Mass, 1936], p. 64, paragraphs 29–31). On the problem of taxation see J. Riley-Smith, *The Feudal Nobility and the Kingdom of Jerusalem, 1174–1277* (London, 1973), p. 71.

30. R. Pernoud, ed., *Les Status municipaux de Marseeille*, (Monacco-Paris, 1949), pp. 29–31.

Tyre handled alimentary products, which came from its own domain in the lordship of Tyre, where the commune held one-third of the countryside.[31]

The main result of the creation of the new markets was the reduction or even disappearance of the central bazaars and their functional specialization. Economic life was altered to fit the new physical framework created by the privileged position of the new quarters. It is thus a remarkable fact that the *funda regis*, the royal market, in Acre is to be found only in one document of several hundred extant for the city, and it is mentioned only once in the one or two narrative texts of the period.[32]

Although the handling of alimentary products in the communal quarters might have varied from commune to commune, one feature, the handling of international commerce, was common to all. The "market of the port," or *catena*, once a royal monopoly, now had new shareholders. Whereas as late as the middle of the twelfth century Baldwin III proclaimed his monopoly in the ports of the kingdom against the claims of his vassals,[33] the reality in the communal quarters was far different. In Acre the "big three", Venice, Genoa, and Pisa, converged on the catena area. Their officials were always present to make sure that their respective nationals enjoyed their full privileges and the merchandise imported or in transit was then handled in the communal funda.[34]

The problems involved in the redistribution of commercial centers were compounded by the system of taxation. Because the taxes on commerce were different in the different markets and their income went into different coffers, there were attempts to monopolize income from given strata of society. There is reason enough to assume that a special royal market in the new suburb of Mount Musard, an area not included in the communal privileges, because the privileges antedated its establishment, became a compulsory market for non-Franks. (There were no communal markets

31. See J. Prawer, "Étude de quelques problèmes agraires et sociaux d'une seigneurie Croisée au XIIIe siècle," *Byzantion, 21* (1952), 5–61.

32. The question of the funda regis in Acre needs more study. The famous tariffs of Acre in Beugnot, ed., *Livre des Assises des Bourgeois, Lois*, vol. II. chaps. 242–43, certainly relate to the royal funda. This is a contention argued by J. Richard, "Colonies marchandes privilegiées et marché seigneurial," *Moyen-Age* (1953), pp. 325–39. The funda is mentioned in a Pisan privilege of 1188. G. Müller, *Documenti*, no. 27; R. Röhricht, *Regesta*, no. 674. The place was near the *cambium*. Marino Sanudo, *Liber Secretorum Fidelium Crucis*, p. 230. Cf. *Gestes des Chiprois* in *Recueil*, *Historiens Armeniens*, p. 805.

33. J. Prawer. "Étude sur le droit des Assises de Jérusalem: Droit de confiscation et droit d'exhéredation," *Revue historique de droit français et étranger* (1961), pp. 520–51; (1962) pp. 29–42.

34. For example, note this statement in the privilege of Conrad of Montferrat to Pisa in Tyre (1187): "pro sui communi ponant homines pro suo velle ad cathenam et fundam et portas civitatis, qui habeant curam de omnibus Pisanis." G. Müller, *Documenti*, n. 24, p. 29.

in Mount Musard.) We even believe that the non-Franks were barred from inhabiting the Old City of Acre.[35] A similar situation existed in Tyre where the lord of the city actually competed with the Venetians to draw to his "two-thirds" of the city Jews and Oriental Christians. He succeeded in his "usurpation" until a vigorous Venetian governor managed to reclaim his rights.[36] One even wonders whether the division between Frankish and Oriental money-changers and textile merchants in Jerusalem was the result of specialization in different kinds of currency only or whether it was, partially at least, the result of different systems of taxation.[37]

A similar change, though certainly less pronounced, was the result of the establishment of the military orders. In Jerusalem and in Acre they possessed entire quarters. Marino Sanudo's map of Acre shows the compounds of the Hospitalers and Templars and they are as large as those of the Italian communes. The compound of the Hospitalers in Jerusalem is of comparable size. We did not find any document explicitly stating that these compounds had their own economic establishments. Yet we hear about weights and measures peculiar to the military orders, and this fact can be explained only if we assume that the compounds had their own marketplaces.[38] However, the sources do not make it clear whether the orders had economic immunity and the rights of jurisdiction over the inhabitants of their own quarters, that is, over those who were not members or affiliates of the order.[39]

Let us now try to envisage the city population, its character, and the way it adopted former institutions or adapted them to suit its needs. The topography of the city in the Arab period conditioned to some degree the diffusion of its population, just as the settlement patterns of ethnic and religious groups influenced the demographic map of the city. The religiously heterogeneous cities (those possessing Christian and Jewish minorities) had concentrations of believers around their respective sanctuaries, but they were not ghettos. Additionally, there was the human factor, the normal urge of minorities to concentrate in given areas in search of community and even security. Thus a Jewish quarter grew up in Jerusalem beneath the al-Aqṣa Mosque in the seventh century, later relocating to the area

35. Prawer, "L'Établíssement des Coutumes," and Richard, "Colonies marchandes."

36. Tafel-Thomas, *Urkunden zur älteren Handels—und Staatsgeschichte der Republik Venedig* (Vienna, 1856), II, 384–85.

37. Textile merchants and money-changers in Jerusalem had special stalls and parts of the market. See Michelant and Raynaud, *Itinéraires à Jérusalem*, pp. 34, 38.

38. See B. Pegolotti, *La Pratica della mercatura;* J. Riley-Smith, *The Feudal Nobility*, p. 71.

39. See J. Riley-Smith, *The Knights of St. John in Jerusalem and Cyprus, c. 1050–1310* (London, 1967).

between the Damascus and Josaphat gates in the northeastern part of the city. The Moslems of Arab Jerusalem (numerically a minority even in the tenth century) settled near the citadel and the Temple area (al-Aqṣa and the Dome of the Rock). The Greek Christians on the eve of the Crusades centered around the Holy Sepulcher, whereas the Armenians kept their Byzantine tradition in the vicinity of the sanctuaries of St. Manes and St. James in the southwestern part of the city. In times of peace and internal security some minority members ventured for economic reasons into other areas, but they did not sever their links with their own quarter. They even regarded it as a privilege to live there. Thus in 1063 the agreement between Constantine IX Monomachos and the Fatimids specified that the Christians would be allowed to concentrate themselves and to live in their own quarter, around the Holy Sepulcher.[40]

It is obvious that the influx of the Westerners brought about a radical change in the structure of the Palestinian city population, although, as already mentioned, physical structure, the presence of Oriental Christians, and the return of the Muslim population preserved some continuity. Judged by Western standards, especially those of northern Europe, the striking feature of this new population is the fact that the cities were not simply the normal and almost exclusive habitat of one strata of society, the "burgesses," who were neither nobles nor members of communes. Instead, members of the two major components of Crusader society lived in cities: nobles and knights as well as "burgesses". In the maritime cities the population also included the nationals of the communes. The sharp line that existed in early twelfth-century Europe between urban agglomerations on the one hand and the manor and countryside on the other did not exist in Palestine and Syria. Consequently, European society's division into three strata—the burgesses, identified with the city (except the castle), the nobility and the villeins and serfs, identified with the country—was far removed from Crusader realities. Nobles and knights usually lived in the city, rubbing elbows with burgesses, and no European settler ever belonged to the class of villeins or serfs. Some Italian and Provençal cities show slightly similar characteristics, but rarely on the same scale. With few exceptions (castles, especially frontier castles, and a very few fortified manor places)[41] the entire Crusader population lived in cities.

This phenomenon had far-reaching consequences. Unlike its counterpart in the contemporary European city or in the Islamic city, the Crusader

40. William of Tyre, book IX, chaps. 17–18 and see above n. 4.

41. A systematic study of the fortified manor houses of the Crusades remains a desideratum. The pioneering work was done by M. Benvenisti, *The Crusaders in the Holy Land* (Jerusalem, 1970), pp. 233ff.

city population did not live according to any common urban law. Instead, each component of the Crusader city population lived within the special framework of their laws and customs. The nobility had a characteristic type of cohesion based on the notions of what constituted fiefs and vassalage, and it followed its own code of laws and customs. The burgesses in the same cities had their own body of legal rules. The Western city population in Crusader cities was thus split into two entities (three, including the nationals of the communes) that differed in their occupations and source of income, in their codes of behavior, and above all in their social and legal institutions.

It is this basic fact that explains why, during the age of communal movements in Europe, the European society transplanted to territory conquered by the Crusaders never created communes in the European sense of the word, not even what is commonly called in France *villes des franchises*. No Crusader city obtained a charter or special privileges. It was a part of a lordship, and almost always the lordship's capital. Thus the Crusader city had no life of its own. The permanent presence of knights and nobles inside the city walls prevented any movement toward autonomy. Consequently the city's administrative institutions were not realy "urban"—they were simply a part of the lordship's machinery of government. The Court of Burgesses was not a body which arose from a movement of burgesses or represented them. It was essentially an administrative and executive body (with a very limited legislative function) through which the lordship dealt with a given segment of the city's population and its particular property, namely the *burgage tenure*. The members of the court, the *jurés*, were the lord's appointees, and the vicecomes was his city governor. It is true that during the two hundred years of its existence the Court of Burgesses tried from time to time to gain some voice in city administration. In some circumstances it may have also had a more representative position, as in the exceptional case when the king requested an oath of fealty from the city because he had reason to doubt its loyalty. Though such an oath might have been given by the *vicomte* for the city, one can speculate that the court may have performed this duty. But this is as far as city representation went. Privileges were granted to the Italian communes, but not to the Latin burgesses as a body.

Although the Crusader cities did not enjoy autonomy, the body of burgesses was not entirely amorphous and different groups sprang up in its midst. These groups, though never institutionalized, contributed their share to city life. The most important was that founded on membership in an ethnic and linguistic group. Though the Crusader establishments were predominantly French in origin and language, the waves of immigration created other ethnic and linguistic nuclei. Immigrants from different regions of Europe and even from different regions of France settled in the neighborhood in which their language or dialect was spoken and in which their customs, brought over from their mother country, were current. In this respect the Frankish population acted according to the same patterns of cohesion as the Italian nationals, the different denominations of Oriental Christians, the Jews, and the Moslems. We do not know whether there were any subdivisions of the Moslem communities in the Crusader cities, but the Jewish community certainly had them. The phenomenon is general. Babylonian and Palestinian Jewish communities had their own synagogues and their own elders in the pre-Crusader period in Syria and Palestine. Similar communities, contemporary with the Crusades, were found elsewhere, for example, in Fusṭāṭ in Egypt. In Moslem Jerusalem a generation after its reconquest by Saladin we find distinct communities of Jews from Ascalon, Jews from France, Jews from North Africa, and Jews from the Egyptian city of Bilbais, each with its own synagogue and elders.[42] We find the same phenomenon again in the middle and in the second half of the thirteenth century in Acre, where European Jews (predominantly French) remain separate from local Jews and from the Jews of neighboring near Eastern countries.

The Crusader population had similar distinctions. Jerusalem in the twelfth century had a Spanish Street, a Street of Lisbon, a Provençal area, and Hungarian and German centers. Acre had, in addition to the great Italian communes, Amalfitans, Provençals, Germans, and Bretons. If such an area did not enjoy any special privileges (the Amalfitans and Provençals had some) than the cohesion resulted from living in the neighborhood alone. This was strengthened by the ecclesiastical parish organization and the hospices which catered predominantly if not exclusively to people from well-defined European regions. It does not seem that among the Franks the simple stage of neighborhood cohesion went beyond the fact of neighborhood. Perhaps some arbitration might have substituted for public authority, but on the whole the jurisdiction was that of state or lordship and common to all the burgesses of the city.

The problem of jurisdiction worked out differently among the non-Franks. The Greeks, the native Syrian Christians, and the Jacobites started out, as "minorities" always do, by maintaining their cohesion as an ethnic, religious, and neighborhood group. We believe that in the beginning of the thirteenth century royal legislation actually relegated non-Franks to the

42. J. Prawer, *Les Juifs dans le royaume Franc de Jérusalem* (forthcoming).

new suburb of Mount Musard in Acre. Their cohesion was strengthened by the important part played by their respective churches in the life of the community. Moreover, in the early history of the kingdom these groups had community heads, the *raicius* or *raīs*, recognized by the public authority as having rights of jurisdiction. One can imagine that the raīses was actually the headman of an ethnic or religious community which lived in a quarter or suburb of a city or village. Later on this autonomous jurisdiction in the cities merged with that of the Court of the Market (*Cour de la fonde*), a Franco-Syrian institution that had judges from both nationalities. The city *rais* probably continued to function, but mixed cases between natives and Franks were handled by the new court. Moreover, the Syrian jurors in the Court of the Market were probably, if the pattern of most medieval institutions was followed, Syrian notables, possibly the former rais of the community. Thus the organization of the Oriental "minorities," preserved more "urban" elements in the cities than the organization of the Western Franks.[43]

Among the Western institutions which one would expect to find among the inhabitants of the Crusader cities are the merchant or craftsmen guilds which are such a salient feature of European city life. Nevertheless, guilds of any type are conspicuous by their absence in the Latin establishments in the East, apparently as the result of two factors. European guilds, whatever their religious antecedents and corporate nature, were everywhere exclusive organizations, designed to keep for their members the monopoly of their trade. Though the guilds certainly contributed to fair business practices, they also controlled prices and ensured that only their members would share the profits of their trade. Moreover, European guild organization was almost always linked with religion and its ceremonial practices. These characteristics explain in a large measure the absence of guilds in Crusader cities. First, the religious heterogeneity of the kingdom rendered exclusivity impossible. Oriental Christians, Moslems, and Jews who practiced the same crafts could obviously not be members of guilds with patron saints and religious and social duties, unless one wishes to credit the Crusaders with a liberalism far in advance of their times.

Perhaps more important was the fact that Palestine was a country of immigrants. There is little doubt that Crusader authorities were conscious of the problem and royal legislation of the first half of the twelfth century

43. J. Riley-Smith, "Some lesser officials in Latin Syria," *The English Historical Review*, vol. *87* (1972); J. Prawer, *The Latin Kingdom of Jerusalem*, pp. 153ff.

actually envisaged the promotion of immigration.[44] The existence of guilds would have been absolutely detrimental to such a policy because by monopolizing access to the exercise of a trade or craft they would discourage immigrants from striking roots in the new land. The system of apprenticeship, with its examinations and slow promotion in the guild hierarchy, militated against the obvious interests of state and lordship, which were to attract Western immigrants. Only in one particular instance do we see in the kingdom something like an examination taken by a member of a profession to enable him to exercise his trade—medical doctors had to take an oath and examination before the bishop of the city. However, this requirement probably had more to do with assuring the salvation of the patients' souls than with healing their bodies.[45]

Another form of association, however, partially compensated for the lack of guilds. In Western Europe this form of association is, generally speaking, older than that of the guilds (unless one believes that medieval guilds were direct descendents of the Roman *scholae*), dating back to Carolingian times. This form is that of a *coniuratio* or *fraternitas*, a voluntary association cemented by an oath, which usually had only social and social welfare functions.

The earliest known fraternitas or *frairie* in the kingdom is that of St. Andrew. It can probably be traced back to the second half of the twelfth century in Jerusalem, though it became famous half a century later in Acre. We do not know its original aims, but in all probability they concerned matters relating to social welfare. Entrance into the frairie required the swearing of an oath, but no special qualifications were needed for admission. The general attitude of lay and religious authorities toward corporate bodies, beginning with Carolingian times, was always that of suspicion. Efforts were generally made to control or supervise such associations. No wonder then that the Fraternity of St. Andrew petitioned and received a royal charter from one of the Baldwins, which was later confirmed by Henry of Champagne (1192–97). With time this type of association began to proliferate.[46] In the second half of the thirteenth century, the frairies flourished. Although we do not know their names, they must have been numerous, as our sources mention them in plural. Although they are usually mentioned in connection with the city of Acre, there is no reason to suppose that they did not spread to other cities. They were strong enough

44. J. Prawer, "La noblesse et le regime féodal du royaume latin de Jérusalem," *Le Moyen—Age*, *65* (1959), 41ff.

45. *Livre des Assises des Bourgeois*, ch. 238. *Lois* II., p. 169.

46. J. Prawer, *Estates, Communities and the Constitution of the Latin Kingdom* (Jerusalem, 1969).

to prompt, for example, the Genoese in Tyre to request a pledge from the lord of the city that no fraternitas should be allowed to settle or receive land near their own communal quarter.[47] The Fraternity of St. Andrew played a major role in the revolutionary movement in Acre, becoming the nucleus of a revolutionary state government. In the second half of the century the Frairies became a power in the state, participating in the meetings of the kingdom's central institution, the Haute Cour, which at that time grew into a Crusader Parliament or États généraux.[48]

Only the social composition of the Fraternity of St. Andrew is known. At first basically a burgess association, the Fraternity of St. Andrew eventually became a mixed body of burgesses and knights. The frairies' growing political power may indicate that others had similarly mixed compositions, but this cannot be documented. Some of the frairies had defined military or humanitarian tasks, like collecting ransom money for the liberation of Christians held by the Moslems as prisoners of war.[49] And one wonders if such associations did not spring up even in the Italian communes.[50]

The impact of the frairies was soon felt among non-Franks, who could perceive that there was strength in unity. Oriental Christians created their own frairies, choosing local saints or sanctuaries as their patrons, for example, the fraternities of Bethlehem and St. George. These native fraternities looked for protectors among the Franks, and in the chaotic conditions in Acre in the thirteenth century powerful Frankish elements provided protection in order to dominate the streets. Thus the Order of St. John and the Templars became the patrons of the fraternities of Bethlehem and St. George.[51] The Frankish and native associations were destroyed by the Moslem conquest of 1291. One has the impression that

47. *Archives de l'Orient latin* II, 227.

48. My study *Estates, Communities and the Constitution of Latin Jerusalem* gave rise to a fruitful discussion. See H. E. Mayer, "On the Beginnings of the Communal Movement in the Holy Land: The Commune of Tyre," *Traditio, 24* (1968), 443–57; H. E. Mayer, "Zwei Kommunen in Akkon?" *Deutsches Archiv f. Erforschung d. Mittelalters, 25* (1970), 434–53; J. Riley-Smith, "The assise sur la ligece and the commune of Acre," *Traditio, 27* (1971), 179–204.

49. J. Riley-Smith, "A Note on Confraternities in the Latin Kingdom," *Bulletin of the Institute of Historical Research, 44* (1971), 301–08.

50. Perhaps the Pisan Societas Vermiliorum, the earliest extant (A.D. 1188), should be regarded as such. G. Müller, *Documenti*, nos. 27–28, pp. 33–34. Some names on the famous maps of Marino Sanudo, like S. Laurentius and S. Romanus, should perhaps be interpreted as references to fraternities.

51. J. Richard, "La Confrérie des Mosserins d'Acre et les marchands de Mossoul au XIIIe siècle," *L'Orient Syrien, 11* (1966), 451–60. In 1264 Philip of Montfort grants the Genoese in Tyre: "quod dominus Tyri non possit dare hoc, quod sibi remaneat de barrigisia . . . communitatibus nec frareriis pro hospitando" (*Archives de l'Orient latin*, II, 227).

at that time they were evolving into political factions along the lines of those in contemporary city-states.

If our main conclusions are correct, then Crusader cities, like Crusader society, had two facets: the heritage of the preceding period—Jewish, Hellenistic, Byzantine, and Moslem—and the European contribution provided by the conquering and colonizing Westerners. To speak of a symbiosis would be incorrect. At best, the Crusader cities represented a juxtaposition of different elements which *nolens volens* were caught in the all-embracing city walls.

When Near Eastern cities become the focus of scholarly investigations, the Crusader cities should not be missed. Although they are more an autonomous episode than a link between the eleventh and fourteenth century in the Near East, their study is most promising. Their physical outlines are far clearer to us than those of their Islamic predecessors and in some cases, Acre and Jerusalem, for example, their existence is evidenced in street grids and wall lines that have remained unchanged to present times.

11

Byzantine Urbanism in the Military Handbooks

John Teall

When (rather more years ago than the present writer or his sometime teacher and present friend would care to proclaim publicly) the completion of a dissertation made of the former an accredited if somewhat surprised Byzantinist, it would have been generous to say that the study of Byzantine cities was in its infancy. During the intervening years, the child has grown so appreciably that most specialists would not hesitate to summarize the course of Byzantine urban development in the following fashion: flourishing in the sixth century, declining in the seventh and eighth, recovering on a different basis after the ninth century.[1] Debate then begins, occasioned in part by a scarcity of sources so critical that Byzantine urban history may never achieve the maturity of which its Western European counterpart may boast. So scant are the data that the historian cannot afford to neglect even the most unlikely class of materials. It is the purpose of the following note to make a *sondage* into one of the less likely and hence neglected genres: that of the strategical treatises or handbooks composed for the use of the Byzantine general in the field.[2]

Reasons for neglect are not difficult to find. The urban historian finds the subject matter of the treatises alien to his purpose. If he examines their textual tradition hastily, many of them seem overly "Byzantine"

1. The first comprehensive survey of Byzantine urban history was that of E. Kirsten, "Die byzantinische Stadt," *Berichte zum 11. Internationalen Byzantinistenkongress, 1958*, vol. I (Munich, 1958), pp. 1–48; a full bibliography up to 1963 is contained in S. Vryonis, "Δημοκρατία and the Guilds in the Eleventh Century," *Dumbarton Oaks Papers, 17* (1963), 287–314. More recently, see: D. Z. Abrahamse, *Hagiographic Sources for Byzantine Cities* (Ann Arbor, Mich., University Microfilms, 1967); D. Claude, *Die byzantinische Stadt im 6. Jahrhundert* (Munich, 1969); S. Vryonis, *The Decline of Medieval Hellenism in Asia Minor* (Berkeley and Los Angeles, 1971), esp. pp. 6–30. Soviet views are given in N. Pigulevskaia et al., "Gorod i derevnia v Vizantii v IV-XII vv.," *Actes du XIIe Congrès International d'Etudes byzantines, 1* (Belgrade, 1963), 1–44, 275–98 (critiques).

2. A survey of the various works in the genre, which all but vanishes after the beginning of the eleventh century because of the advent of mercenary armies, is in A. Dain, "Les stratégistes byzantins," in *Travaux et Mémoires*, ed. Centre de recherche d'histoire et civilisation byantines (1967), II, 317–90.

in that the learned authors or compilers sometimes neglect contemporary practice for *dicta* drawn from the ancients, despite earnest protest that, for example, the passage of time had removed from any serious consideration the tactical value of the chariot or the elephant. But such a negative characterization is far from fair to many of the treatises, and not even the most derivative are totally lacking in value. The successors did not always slavishly copy out the work of their predecessors; at the very least, they translated anachronistic technical terms into a less-specialized idiom which their own age could appreciate. Thus we may learn from them what a later mind had made of the ideas he had found in an earlier mind. In short, the strategists provide a continuing index of intellectual stasis and intellectual change, all the more valuable since the writers interpreted their mandate broadly and viewed military affairs within a larger social context.

An anonymous treatise of the sixth century fully exemplifies this last point.[3] Since warfare is the activity of the "polity" (*πολιτεία*), the author opens his work with an analysis of the civil sector. He views society in terms of the ancient *polis* or *civitas*. For him, the participants essential to the proper functioning of the social order (that is, the flourishing urban culture of the age of Justinian) are teachers, rhetors, lawyers, senators, and merchants of wine, meat, and grain, as well as craftsmen working in metals. Much less central to the author's interests are the priests and peasants, even though he regards the first group as the highest order.[4] If his enumeration of the social orders smells somewhat of the lamp, the rationale he presents of tax assessment, collection, and equalization fully reflects current Late Roman practice and provides a rare—if not unique—explicit statement of the principles supposedly guiding officials charged with the administration of public revenues.[5]

The sixth-century anonymous author, unsurprisingly, lacks direct heirs among the treatises compiled after the seventh century. The world of the later strategists differed profoundly from the nearly classical urbanism of Justinian's day. Peasants and soldiers, not town dwellers, were the pillars of society. Cities were essentially fortresses to be defended by folk who found in their common Christian faith the major prop for their morale.[6]

3. Anonymous, *De re strategica*, in H. Köchly and W. Rüstow, *Griechische Kriegschriftsteller*, III, 2 (Leipzig, 1855), pp. 42–209.

4. Ibid., I, 1; II, 9 (pp. 42–46).

5. Ibid., III, 6–8 (pp. 50–52).

6. See my "Grain Supply of the Byzantine Empire," *Dumbarton Oaks Papers, 13* (1959), 127–29,

In discussing the defense of the city, two of the later strategists—Maurice in the seventh century and Leo in the ninth—provide, when studied together, an excellent example of the techniques used by representatives of the genre as well as evidence to support current revisionist views concerning the supposed military function of the circus factions, the Blues and Greens of the hippodromes. The armed violence employed by the factions in sedition or in outright revolt has traditionally been explained in the following manner. Organized as "demes" (*δῆμοι*) the factions simultaneously served as units of the urban militia and had necessarily to carry weapons as members of the city's fighting force. Recent investigation of the term *δῆμος* has cast doubt upon the identification of deme with faction and upon the military role of either entity. Maurice provides aid and comfort to the revisionists when he notes, in telling the general how to place the city in a posture of defense, that

> If there is a *δῆμος* in the city, it is necessary to mingle them with the soldiers along the stations of the wall. Thereby they will lack the opportunity to pursue revolt and, seeming to be trusted as a guard for the city, they will be ashamed to revolt.

More than two centuries later, Leo copied out the same injuction with the significant substitution of the unambiguous classical term *διχοστασια* or "sedition" for *δῆμος*. Taken together, the texts suggest that cities at least hoped to depend upon. professionals for their defense and that, as a recent critic has concluded, the circus factions were just that and nothing more. "Demos" was a revolutionary group to be distrusted, not an urban militia upon which the general might rely.[7]

The detailed instructions for defending a city found in a treatise of the tenth century, *De obsidione toleranda*, indicate how views of the city and the activities (rather, in this later text, specialties) of its inhabitants had changed since the sixth century. When enemy attacks threatened, cereals were to be taken from the *apothecae* of the merchants and the wealthy and placed in the public granaries. Their distribution was then to be supervised

---

W. Kaegi, "Patterns of Political Activity of the Armies," in *On Military Intervention*, ed. M. Janowitz (Rotterdam, 1971), p. 6. Concerning the religious element see, for example, Maurice, *Strategikon*, proemion; II, 17 (ed. Scheffer, Uppsala, 1664), pp. 1ff, 72; J. Kulakovskii, ed., *Nicephori praecepta militaria*, *Mémoires de l'Acad. impériale des sciences de Saint-Petersbourg*, VIIIe s., Cl. hist-philol., vol. VIII, fasc. 9 (1908), pp. 15, 20 (tenth century); see also the preparations of John Tzimisces for his expedition against the Rus: Leo Diaconus, *Historiae* (Bonn, 1828), p. 128 ff.

7. Maurice, *Strategikon*, X, 3 (ed. Scheffer, p. 246; ed. H. Mihaescu, Bucharest, 1970, p. 254); Leo, *Tactica*, XV, 56 (Migne, *Patrologia graeca*, CVII, col. 901BC). The most recent critique of established doctrine is A. Cameron, "Demes and Factions," *Byzantinische Zeitschrift*, 67 (1974), 74–91.

by the bishop and other leading men in such a fashion that each inhabitant might be assured of a month's supply.[8] The useless must leave the city, a step also advised by Maurice and indeed taken by Emperor Anastasius II when the latter prepared Constantinople for the Arab assault of 717.[9] Private resources were to be used to purchase supplies should public revenues prove inadequate, an expedient that had been forced upon Thessalonica in the seventh century.[10]

The treatise *De obsidione toleranda* is obviously no product of the cabinet, and its anonymous author continues in the same realistic tone when he describes the raw materials he wishes to stockpile together with the craftsmen whose services he deems necessary for the city's survival. The list of raw materials is striking in its range and variety and includes at least one highly significant product introduced into common use since the Late Roman period. In addition to wheat, barley, wine, pulse, oil, cheese, meat, millet, iron, copper, pitch, sulphur, fodder, and chaff, the author further recommends the stockpiling of fibers and fabrics ranging from tow or oakum through flax and kemp to linen and cotton. The last-named product, *βάμβαξ*, *βαμβάκιον* in post-classical Greek, was originally an import from Egypt and during the tenth century was put to military use in the fabrication of a pullover or "duffel" worn by both foot soldiers and cataphracts.[11]

The "useful" folk who remain within the walls include a remarkable range of specialists: armorers to make helmets, shields, and swords; smiths to fashion barbed heads for arrows, spears, and javelins; two different kinds of engineers to attend to siege engines; master builders and ordinary builders to supervise the walls; finally, rope-makers and a mysterious "ladder-climber," possibly the ancestor of the modern steeplejack. It is surprising to learn that the author considered the making of bridles, saddles, and soldiers' boots the responsibility of different specialists and amusing to note that the well-equipped city also boasted of "astronomers" to calculate the movements of wind and water.[12]

8. *De obsidione toleranda*, ed. H. van den Berg (Leyden, 1947), pp. 46ff.

9. For Anastasius's preparations, see Theophanes, *Chronographia* (ed. De Boor), p. 384.

10. *De obsidione toleranda*, secs. 18–20 (ed. van den Berg), ff. pp. 48; on Thessalonica, see the references to the *Miracula Sancti Demetrii* collected in my "Grain Supply," pp. 121ff.

11. The products are enumerated in *De obsidione toleranda*, pp. 48ff.; on the use of cotton by the military, see *Nicephori praecepta* (ed. Kulakovskii), pp. 2, 11, and the *Sylloge Tacticorum*, secs. 38, 4; 39, 1 (ed. A. Dain; Paris, 1938), pp. 59, 61. Earlier, in the ninth century, Leo fails to mention the military use of cotton: *Tactica*, VI, 2, 4, 25 (ed. R. Vari; Budapest, 1917), pp. 99, 102, 115; S. Runciman, "Byzantine Trade and Industry," in *Cambridge Economic History*, ed. M. Postan and E. Rich (1952) II, 92, 94, mentions Egyptian imports but is vague in respect to the appearance of the commodity on Byzantine markets.

12. *De obsidione toleranda*, secs. 10–12 (ed. van den Berg), p. 47. The ladder-climber is a *σκαλοβάτης*, a term about which neither DuCange nor Sophocles is particularly helpful.

One specialist, the καλοφατης or ship's caulker, deserves a closer glance. The word is post-classical, derived apparently from the Arabic root QLF, and its allied verb was eventually to be adopted into Italian (*calafatare*), Provençal (*calafatar*), Catalan (*calfateyar*), French (*calfater*), and German (*kalfatern*).[13] To find the term in a Byzantine treatise of the tenth century is to stumble upon a fascinating microcosmic reflection of early medieval relationships in the Mediterranean world, wherein the exchange of ideas, products, and skills had replaced the shaky political unity of the later Roman Empire.

The discovery, finally, stimulates some broader reflections upon urban development in Byzantium. Seen through the eyes of the strategists, the city had changed from an administrative center in an urban civilization to a fortress defending a rural society. But may it not have gained in the process? Only those cities with a sound economic base survived. And the increasing importance of specialized craftsmen in a leaner and tougher world may explain why urban dwellers turned to their guilds to express political discontent and abandoned demos and the circus faction, the relics of the Roman world.[14]

13. For the etymologies, see Littré, *Dictionnaire de la langue française* (1956), s.v. "calfater."

14. On the growing significance of the guilds, see Vryonis, "Δημοκρατία and the Guilds," pp. 287–314.

The Northern City

12

The Legacies of London: 1259–1330

Harry A. Miskimin

The rich material contained in the wills probated and enrolled in the Court of Husting in London has been available in summary form since Reginald Sharpe prepared his *Calendar of Wills*[1] more than a century ago, and it has often been utilized by those seeking to document city life in the Middle Ages.[2] Despite fairly wide knowledge of this material, two factors justify a more intensive study of the wills of the London property-holding class. On the one hand, Sharpe's *Calendar* provides only a précis, albeit in some cases a quite complete one, of the wills themselves and thus the question of subjectivity in the selection of the information provided remains open. On the other hand, there has been no recent and systematic attempt to extract as much information as possible from the wills themselves in the hope of creating a statistical profile of the property-holding class of medieval London. This essay is a preliminary attempt to study in detail the 1,550 wills enrolled and probated in the Court of Husting between the years 1259 and 1330. Emphasis, however, will be placed primarily upon the period after 1271 when the number of extant wills per decade increases markedly.

Occupations and Numbers

It is difficult to define the social class of those who made wills in medieval London with greater precision than is implicit in the amorphous phrase "property-holding." Any freeman of the city was entitled to make a will,[3] but since the Court of Husting was primarily a court of real estate record, the testators were normally conveying real property by their final act. Indeed, of the 1,550 wills under consideration, only two (Roll 53 Number

1. Reginald R. Sharpe, *Calendar of Wills Proved and Enrolled in the Court of Husting, London,* A.D. *1258–*A.D. *1688* (London: John C. Francis, 1859), Vol. I.

2. See, for example, Sylvia L. Thrupp, *The Merchant Class of Medieval London, 1300–1500* (Ann Arbor: University of Michigan Press, 1962).

3. Sharpe, *Calendar*, I, xxxiii.

94 and Roll 54 Number 48), both from the year 1325, devise chattels alone and no real property. Possession of urban real property rather than absolute wealth is the principle of inclusion in the series. Internal evidence concerning occupation and social status is incomplete, but for the period after 1271, we know the occupations of approximately one-third of the male testators; table 12.1 details this information. The range of economic activity among the testators—seventy-two separate trades—is remarkably broad. Even after discounting members of the upper clergy and the occasional great noble and after noting the obvious absence of the lower class of servants and laborers, the occupational spread seems widely based. The social distance between an alderman, merchant, or knight and a cook, carter, or old-clothes dealer must have been substantial. So diverse, in fact, are the occupations that it seems reasonable to postulate that no special principle of selectivity beyond membership in the middle class was operating to determine which testators chose to specify their professions and which chose to remain silent. If this condition is true, then the 307 occupationally specific wills combined with the 88 ecclesiastical and clerical wills constitute a fair sample of the total male wills. We may therefore reasonably assume that the unknown occupations of the remaining two-thirds of the male testators followed roughly the same pattern as those outlined in table 12.1.

Based on this argument, we may make a cautious demographic speculation. Since the male testators were property-holders, filled responsible positions in London society, and had presumably been admitted to the freedom of the city—a privilege normally attained at the age of twenty-two[4]—we may plausibly assume that the group which the male testators represent was above that age. Since medieval life expectancy was low, a crude death rate of 25 per 1,000 for this group is not an unreasonable hypothesis. This rate would mean that all members of any given cohort would perish within forty years, or put another way, that the members of the group were property-holders between the ages of twenty-two and sixty-two. Some few undoubtedly lived beyond the latter age, but since not all members can be assumed to have entered the cohort at the young age of twenty-two, there is perhaps a crude statistical balance at each end of the age scale. Now if religious and clerics appear with the same frequency in the wills that fail to specify occupation as in those that do, we have as a residual 1,072 wills of adult males engaged in secular occupations over the six decades under consideration.[5] The average number of such wills per

4. Thrupp, *The Merchant Class*, p. 194.

5. This is calculated by taking the total number of wills, 1,515, subtracting 179 female wills, and subtracting three times the 88 wills of known religious and clerics.

Table 12.1

Occupations of Male Testators as Stated in the 307 Wills Listing Occupation, 1271–1330 (Religious and Clerics Excluded)

Occupation	Number	Occupation	Number
Advocate	1	Fustar	1
Alderman	5	Girdler	5
Alum Tawyer	1	Glover	1
Apothecary	3	Goldbeater	4
Armorer	1	Goldsmith	19
Baker	3	Hoodmaker	1
Barber	2	Horsedealer	1
Bater	3	Ironmonger	6
Bater of Cloth	1	Knight	26
Beadmaker	1	Marshall	2
Bowyere	1	Mason	4
Brewer	1	Mercer	6
Burreller	2	Merchant	5
Burser	1	Merchant Tailor	1
Butcher	9	Moneyer	1
Capmaker	2	Nailer	1
Carpenter	10	Ointer	1
Carter	1	Painter	2
Cellerer	1	Pepperer	5
Chaloner	1	Potmaker	1
Chandler	3	Potter	3
Cheesemonger	1	Poulterer	3
Chestmaker	1	Saddler	6
Clothworker	3	Sealmaker	1
Cofferer	2	Sergeant at Queenhithe	1
Cook	2	Skinner	17
Corder	2	Spurmaker	1
Cordwainer	18	Surgeon	2
Cornmerchant	2	Tailor	11
Cutler	7	Tanner	11
Dealer in Old Clothes	1	Tiler	1
Draper	7	Vintner	5
Dyer	4	Woodmonger	1
Enameller	1	Woolmonger	5
Fishmonger	34		—
Fripperer	1	Total	305
Fruiter	2	Earl of Pembroke	1
Furbisher of Armor	3	Lord of Horowell	1

Total Number of Wills, 1271–1330:	1,515
Religious and Clerics	88
Females	179
Males excluding Religious and Clerics	1,248

SOURCE: Hustings Rolls 4–123 to 58–113.

year is thus 17.9, and if we apply our crude death rate of 25 per 1,000 to this figure, we emerge with an estimate of the population of property-holding, secular testators of 716.[6] The mathematical reasoning that led to this conclusion is admittedly somewhat tenuous, but our figure of 716 becomes quite persuasive when it is compared with the 784 persons listed as members of the London liveried companies in 1501.[7] At that time, the city had recovered from the depopulation of the plague years but had not yet entered upon the remarkable expansion of the sixteenth century so the figures should have been roughly comparable. If our 716 testators averaged a wife and two children, their family group would rise to 2,864 or just under 10 percent of the standard estimate of the population of London at the end of the thirteenth century.

Food Supply

Occupational status and a rough estimate of total numbers are important identifying attributes of the will-making class of medieval London. To these we may add another—the capacity of members of this class to insulate themselves from disaster. Although there is a gentle upward trend—nearly linear from 1271 to 1320—the total number of wills per decade remains remarkably stable from period to period.

Table 12.2

Number of Wills per Decade, 1259–1330

Years	*Wills*
1259–1270	35
1271–1280	169
1281–1290	222
1291–1300	243
1301–1310	278
1311–1320	311
1321–1330	292

Source: Hustings Rolls 2–17 to 58–113.

The absence of any violent fluctuations in the number of wills, particularly during the critical years of desperate famine from 1315 to 1317, suggests that the will-making class of medieval London led comfortable lives,

6. 17.9/25 × 1000 = 716.

7. Thrupp, *The Merchant Class*, pp. 45–47. According to Thrupp the figure of 784 is somewhat understated.

largely free from nutritional hardships. Later, in mid-century, when the enemy was plague, wealth was impotent to protect its possessors and the number of wills enrolled soared as rich and poor joined hands in the dance of death, but pan-European famine does not appear to have affected our property-holders. In the decade 1311–20, 311 wills were probated. If the distribution were perfectly even from year to year, we would expect 93.3 deaths to occur during the three famine years; the actual number is 95.

How may we account for this apparent lack of susceptibility to famine? London was, of course, an important trading center and a port which even in the fourteenth century had access to much of the European world; imported grain was indeed significant. Edward II sought and received some grain from Normandy and Gascony and more from the less affected lands of Sicily[8] and it is likely that such grain increased England's and London's resistance to famine. Even so, however, the Flemish city of Ypres, which as a result of its world-famous cloth industry was more important than London in international commerce, suffered heavily from famine and lost at least a tenth of its population to starvation between 1315 and 1317.[9] Unqualified comparison between the statistics from Ypres, which refer to the total population, and those from London, which refer only to the affluent middle class, is unwise, but the figures do suggest that urban wealth was the significant defense against pan-European famine. It was not simply London's role as a trading center and port that protected the testators, but wealth; unfortunately, there are no aggregate figures that permit us to know how less affluent Londoners fared.

However, we may compare, although somewhat crudely, the survival rates of wealthy Londoners with those of the richer elements in England's agrarian sector. Postan's and Titow's study of heriot payments on the manors of the bishops of Winchester traces the relationship between these death duties and grain prices from 1245 to 1350.[10] Although a few substantial tenants paid money heriots, it is argued that money heriots were paid in general by those too poor to be liable for animal payments and thus that the type of payment constitutes a rough demarcation between rich and poor. During much of the century studied, there was a positive correlation between grain prices and the number of money heriots, but little

8. H. S. Lucas, "The Great European Famine of 1315, 1316 and 1317," (*Speculum*, 1930) reprinted in *Essays in Economic History* ed. E. M. Carus-Wilson, (New York: St. Martin's Press, 1966), II, 69.

9. Lucas, "Famine," p. 67.

10. M. M. Postan and J. Titow, "Heriots and Prices on Winchester Manors," with a statistical appendix by J. Longden, *The Economic History Review*, *11* (1959), 392–417.

evidence of any influence of grain prices upon the quantity of animal payments. In most years, then, the affluent tenants appear to have been immune to scarcity and to have possessed adequate reserves to carry them through a lean harvest or a few bad years. In 1315–17, the years of the great famine, however, the number of animal heriots rose precipitously as even the more substantial tenants succumbed.[11] Middle-class farmers died of malnutrition during a period in which there is no evidence of an increasing death rate among their middle-class counterparts in London. Wealth alone, in the absence of an adequate distribution mechanism, does not appear to have protected its possessors from famine.

Heavy dependence on cereal diets obviously increases the danger of hunger when crops fail. Inspection of table 12.1, the list of the occupations of London's property-holding class, suggests a further reason for their relative security in periods of great dearth. The largest single occupational category is fishmonger with thirty-four representatives or 11.1 percent of the occupationally specific wills. Leather-workers—bursars, cordwainers, girdlers, glovers, saddlers, skinners, and tanners—total fifty-nine souls or 19.3 percent of the total and the nine butchers constitute a further 2.9 percent. All, of course, were involved in trades that brought edible animals to London, since their raw material was normally driven to the city on the hoof. Cheesemongers, fruiters, and poulterers together number six or 2 percent of the total. In all, the combined participants in these trades that provided food other than grain mounts to 108 or 35.4 percent of our total of occupationally specific wills. Proximity to the sea and involvement in the world's commerce gave our testators access to distant grain. Wealth gave them the means to pay very high famine prices for such grain as could be had domestically or from abroad. Heavy personal participation in the trade in fish and edible animal products gave them alternatives to grain when crops failed. Indeed, it is worth noting that later in the century, when plague greatly increased the number of animal heriots, the London market was flooded with meat as landlords sought to convert their newly acquired wealth into cash. Taken together, wealth, access to world markets, and the presence of foods other than grain are sufficient to explain the immunity of our testators to famine.

11. Ibid., p. 407, table I, p. 417. The correlation between high grain prices and increased numbers of animal heriots is firm, but it leaves open the inexplicable question of why a peasant would die before eating the animal which subsequently served as payment for the death duty. Pure speculation would suggest that prolonged malnutrition and the resultant increase in susceptibility to disease rather than actual starvation accounted for the rise in the death rate as peasants sought to preserve seed corn and capital animals for the future.

Demographic Profile

In addition to information concerning occupation and survival rates over time, the Hustings wills contain considerable material of demographic interest, although the abbreviated testamentary formulae make it somewhat difficult to extract immediately useful figures. The wills invariably give the name of the testator and almost always, if he is male and married, the name of his wife. Since the wife's dower right to a life term in one-third of the estate was protected by law, one can assume with some confidence that few wives were overlooked in the probate records. In a few cases, an omitted wife appears before the court to demand her dower portion and thus makes her presence known on the formal record. Children too were protected by law and could normally expect to receive at least another third of the estate, but there is more variation in their appearance in the wills. Fifty-two of the 1,515 wills enrolled between 1271 and 1330 mention "my children" as legatees but do not specifically name or enumerate them; a number of the wills make provision for "my unborn child" or "my child if my wife should be pregnant." While the latter phrase perhaps expresses the irrepressible hope of mankind, even on the deathbed, the use of the nonspecific phrase "my children" has, I believe, a darker side. No hard evidence can be marshaled to justify the hypothesis, but context suggests that the unnamed children were often simply very young and that high infant mortality rates precluded an itemized property division among children who were unlikely to survive to maturity. The fact that a number of wills contain references to more than one child with the same forename as the father-testator confirms this view; a father interested in perpetuating his name was well advised to give it to more than one of his fragile young heirs. The results of an initial probe into the demographic content of the wills appears in table 12.3.

Further refinement is, of course, necessary to eliminate some of the distortions still present in table 12.3 as a result of the possible inclusion of an unknown number of unspecified religious and clerics whose presence would create a downward bias on the number of surviving heirs, but it is useful to inspect the table in its present form. That women legally could and, in fact, did hold real property is attested to by the 179 female decedents whose appearance in the rolls establishes their ability to devise real property. On the other hand, their relatively small number, only 12.5 percent of the total number of testators, suggests that female property-holding was not common and it stands in contrast to the large number of surviving widows who inherited real estate from their deceased spouses. The disparity in the

Table 12.3

Family Structure of Testators by Decade, 1271–1330
(Known Religious and Clerics Excluded)

Decade	*Number of Wills*	*Number of Female Testators*		*Number of Male Testators*	*Number of Surviving Widows*	*Widows as % of Males*	*Number of Sons of Male Testators*		*Number of Daughters of Male Testators*	
		#	%				#	*Average*	#	*Average*
1271–1280	160	17	10.6%	143	80	55.9%	104	.72	103	.72
1281–1290	207	18	8.7%	189	100	52.9%	114	.60	108	.57
1291–1300	226	26	11.5%	200	127	63.5%	116	.58	119	.60
1301–1310	260	36	13.8%	224	144	64.0%	173	.77	141	.63
1311–1320	297	44	14.8%	253	169	66.8%	196	.77	161	.64
1321–1330	277	38	13.7%	239	147	61.5%	168	.70	162	.68
1271–1330	1,427	179	12.5%	1,248	767	61.4%	871	.70	794	.64

Source: Hustings Rolls 4–123 to 58–113.

Note: The number of wills mentioning, but not explicitly naming, children are as follows: 1271–80, 5; 1281–90, 10; 1291–1300, 7; 1301–10, 14; 1311–20, 10; 1321–30, 6.

size of the two categories is a consequence of the custom of London that prohibited a husband from leaving his wife more than a life estate in real property. In most cases, the property which a widow enjoyed during the remainder of her life had already been delegated to others by her deceased husband, contingent only upon his wife's death.[12] Women could, however, inherit real property from their fathers and they could, if they so wished, purchase such property with their own money or with money left to them by their husbands, but the figures indicate that the practice was not common.

Custom and the laws related to property-holding may account for the paucity of testatrices, but they do not explain the high proportion of surviving widows. Unfortunately the wills are silent in regard to the precise ages of testators and heirs so the crucial information concerning the age disparity between husbands and wives is lost. In some instances, property is left to surviving grandchildren, which at least establishes a minimum possible age for the will-maker; in others, property is devised to children of a former marriage, thus revealing a second and perhaps much younger wife. The evidence is too frail to support strong generalizations concerning female survival rates or age at marriage, but in a period when the risk of

12. Sharpe, *Calendar*, I, xxxviii.

death in childbirth was extraordinarily high, the appearance of significant numbers of widows tends to confirm the widely held opinion that men married rather late in their life cycle. Even this modest hypothesis must be taken cautiously, however, since there is no way to adjust our results to measure or exclude the possible bias from substantial numbers of second marriages.

Much stronger conclusions may be drawn from the figures relating to the lineal heirs of our testators. Adding the 88 identified religious and clerics to the 1,248 other male testators, we have a total of 1,336 males who leave at death 1,665 male and female offspring. This averages to 1.24 children and .65 male children per male testator; it is clear that the upper-middle-class population of London at this time was far from maintaining a sufficient rate of reproduction to replace itself. Even when the figures are considered without the inclusion of religious and clerics, the average number of sons per male testator increases only to .698 during our sixty-year period; the rise to 1.33 children of both sexes is also minimal. The upper middle class of London was, of necessity, compelled to replenish its numbers from the outside, thereby permitting considerable upward mobility, assuring an active real estate market, and preventing coalescence into a rigidly aristocratic bloc. We might expect that six or seven new families would be added to the group each year.[13]

The statistics given above reflect the replacement rate for the class as a whole, but they understate the rate for those families most likely to reproduce by including an unknown number of clerics, bachelors, and other types less apt to produce offspring. It is possible to restructure our sample, however, and observe only those segments to whom we would accord the highest probability of successful reproduction. By looking only at the records of those male testators survived by their widows, we exclude at a stroke all men in the higher religious orders, all bachelors, and most misogynists. Problems of impotence and sterility remain, but they are perhaps likely to be less among those men known to have married. Furthermore, the survival of the widow may indicate relative youth at the time of her marriage and thus a greater chance for conception and childbirth. The statistics for this group appear in table 12.4.

It is immediately apparent from the table that the average number of children surviving at the deaths of testators who predecease their wives is

13. If our assumption of a crude death rate of 25 per 1,000 is correct and if the size of the class of property-holding testators was in fact 716, a survival rate of .65 sons per male testator would result in the admission of 6.265 new emtrants per year. (.35 × .025 × 716 = 6.265) The population would turn over completely in 114 years.

Table 12.4

Offspring of Male Testators with Surviving Widows
By Decade, 1271–1330

Decade	*Number of Testators with Surviving Widows*	*Sons of Testators with Surviving Widows*		*Daughters of Testators with Surviving Widows*	
		Total	*Average/Male Testator*	*Total*	*Average/Male Testator*
1271–1280	80	73	.91	81	1.01
1281–1290	100	79	.79	63	.63
1291–1300	127	96	.76	92	.72
1301–1310	144	124	.87	83	.58
1311–1320	169	170	1.00	139	.82
1321–1330	147	133	.90	118	.80
1271–1330	767	675	.88	576	.75

SOURCE: Hustings Rolls 4–123 to 58–113.

much higher than that evident in the less refined evidence in table 12.3. The overall figure of .88 sons per male testator with surviving widow is significantly greater than our crude figure of .65 sons per male testator without regard to family structure. This is not surprising, of course, since our purpose here was to exclude the unmarried, but even under the most favorable conditions, the survival rate of sons is still well below the number needed to replace our new and smaller class of testators. Even among this presumably most prolific group, the statistics sustain our earlier conclusion regarding the impact of insufficient replacement rates on upward social mobility. Sylvia Thrupp has considered similar evidence.[14] Using a sample of ninety-nine wills, she has found an average of 1.3 sons per merchant during the 1288–1317 period, a figure considerably greater than ours. The disparity is not readily explicable, but it may perhaps be a consequence of the greater affluence of her selected testators, of whom almost a third were aldermen and thus presumably wealthier on average than the members of our larger and more inclusive group. The possibility that, even within the upper middle class of London, relative wealth affected survival is not without interest, but since our figures are based on the total corpus of Hustings wills, it seems likely that the lower replacement rate is a more accurate reflection of the actualities of medieval London than that derived from Thrupp's more limited sample. The lower rate is consistent with the

14. Thrupp, *The Merchant Class*, Table 13, p. 200.

evidence from other medieval cities which shows that internal population growth was invariably too small to maintain the urban community.

It is interesting to contrast the progenitive experience of the female will-makers with that of the males who predeceased their spouses. The statistics for this group appear as table 12.5. Initially the most striking

Table 12.5

Offspring of Testatrices
By Decade, 1271–1330

Decade	*Number of Testatrices*	*Identified as Widows*		*Sons of Testatrices*		*Daughters of Testatrices*	
		#	%	*Total*	*Average/Female*	*Total*	*Average/Female*
1271–1280	17	6	35%	9	.53	9	.53
1281–1290	18	5	28%	4	.22	6	.33
1291–1300	26	7	27%	6	.23	10	.38
1301–1310	36	22	61%	15	.42	18	.50
1311–1320	44	22	50%	29	.66	22	.50
1321–1330	38	19	50%	17	.47	10	.26
1271–1330	179	81	45%	80	.45	75	.42

SOURCE: Hustings Rolls 4–123 to 58–113.

fact that emerges from the table is the small number of children per testatrix; the average is far lower than that for males survived by widows and indeed even than that for the general population, including clergy. This paucity would seem to result from the joint influence of property laws which made property-holding more likely for unmarried daughters than for wives and from the fact that less than half of the females can be positively known to have married. Failure to specify widowhood in the wills, however, does not in itself establish either an unmarried state or celibacy; 61 of the 155 children in table 12.5 are the heirs of women whose testaments do not mention marital status. Surely more widows are present among the testatrices than the internal evidence of the wills reveals, and we are thus prevented from making a simple proportional adjustment to explain the relatively low number of children per testatrix. Illegitimate children were, of course, born, and they could inherit real property, but there are only two clear cases in our collection and only one among the testatrices.[15] The

15. Roll 51–13 (July 25, 1322) Will of Alice de Mondene mentions John de Mondene, son, and Peter de Mondene, the testatrix's brother.

other case occurs in the will—incidentally one of the very few in French rather than Latin—of one John de Ashford, who divided his property among his two living mistresses and his parallel families of one son and two daughters by each mistress.[16]

The sex ratios of the heirs in tables 12.3, 12.4, and 12.5 vary considerably, both among themselves and by comparison with the biological ratio of male to female births. The ratios of male to female offspring are shown in table 12.6. Since our testators could not enter the cohort of will-makers

Table 12.6

Sex Ratios among the Heirs by Category of Testator, 1271–1330

	Males	*Females*	*Ratio*
Biological ratio of male to female births			1.05[a]
Ratio of male to female heirs in wills of males, table 12.3	871	794	1.097
Ratio of male to female heirs in wills of males survived by spouse, table 12.4	675	576	1.172
Ratio of male to female heirs in wills of females, table 12.5	80	75	1.067

Source: Hustings Rolls 4–123 to 58–113.
[a] A. J. Coale, "The History of Human Population," *Scientific American, 231* (1974), 43.

until they had reached maturity, they enjoyed the higher life expectancy of those who had survived the difficult childhood years and were thus likely to live at least until their late forties or fifties. As a result, the heirs may be presumed to have lived long enough for their own experience to cause substantial divergence from the biological ratio between the sexes at birth. Furthermore, since death in childbirth was a major threat, it is not surprising to discover that the statistics reveal a sex ratio increasingly favorable to males. This does not account, however, for the significant difference between the sex ratios for the heirs of men survived by spouses (1.172) and that for the heirs of females (1.067). Some interesting speculations have recently appeared that suggest that infanticide may have been practiced earlier in the Middle Ages to eliminate economically less useful daughters,[17] but before infanticide can be accepted as a cause for the superabundance of

16. Roll 57–161 (January 13, 1330) Each family inherits real property, sums of money apparently chosen so as to equalize disparities in the value of the real estate, and perhaps not surprisingly, two complete beds. Roll 7–21 (November 18, 1275) leaves one mark rent to a bastard daughter.

17. E. R. Coleman, "Medieval Marriage Characteristics: A Neglected Factor in the History of Medieval Serfdom," *The Journal of Interdisciplinary History, 2* (1971) 205–19.

male offspring among the London heirs, one would have to explain why the sex ratios diverge so markedly among the subgroups of the London middle class. More detailed research in individual family records would be necessary to document it, but the following hypothesis might well account for much of the disparity between the sex ratios in tables 12.4 and 12.5. As will become apparent shortly, males survived by their spouses leave considerably more property than do female will-makers. If relative affluence led to richer dower portions for the daughters of such males, we might well presume that these women were more readily marriageable and thus that more were exposed and exposed earlier in their lives to the dangers of childbirth. This in turn would have lowered their survival rate in relation to their brothers and thus have raised the male to female sex ratio beyond that for the offspring of the less wealthy testatrices. While it is admittedly speculative, this hypothesis fits the evidence and provides a more humane explanation than infanticide; until further research is undertaken, it remains plausible.

The Wealth of Londoners

Thus far we have concentrated primarily on the indirect information contained in the wills, but it is well to recall that their purpose was to convey property and to turn our attention now to wealth and the investment patterns of the upper middle class of medieval London. Although the Court of Husting served mainly as a court of real estate record, numerous other forms of property appear in the testaments. Few complete inventories survive, but much personal property was devised by will; a complete list is not practicable here since the goods so disposed of are too diverse for effective classification or statistical treatment. They include: silver and gold flatware, plate, and cups; a few books, mostly in the hands of clerics; substantial quantities of clothing, sometimes obviously of foreign origin; bedding; mazer cups; brewing and other utensils; pots; pans; chests; and the unspecified contents of rooms and wardrobes. Although the multiplicity of types and qualities defies summary treatment of such personal goods, one standard item, money, appears in a sufficient number of wills to merit separate consideration. Money gifts are summarized in table 12.7.

To merit inclusion in table 12.7, a cash bequest must have appeared in a testament in such manner as to indicate that it was to have been paid from money actually on hand at the testator's death. Numerous other wills specify that gifts of money be paid from the proceeds of the sale of some piece of real estate, that property be sold and fractional shares be used to purchase rents for various charities, or that similar receipts be divided among certain

Table 12.7

Gifts of Money by Decade, 1259–1330

Decade	*Number of Wills*	*Number with Cash Legacies*	*Number with Cash to London Bridge Only*	*Wills with Cash Legacies Other than to London Bridge*		*Average Cash Legacy (in £)*	
				#	*% of Total*	*Average*	*Excluding London Bridge Only*
1259–1270	35	0	0	0	0	0	0
1271–1280	169	3	0	3	1.8%	61.1	61.1
1281–1290	222	2	0	2	.9%	26.7	26.7
1291–1300	243	13	4	9	3.7%	35.9	51.8
1301–1310	278	103	70	33	11.8%	12.3	35.9
1311–1320	311	64	26	38	12.2%	24.4	40.1
1321–1330	292	37	4	33	11.3%	94.2	105.5

SOURCE: Hustings Rolls 2–17 to 58–113.

heirs. Such gifts are excluded here since their inclusion would result in the double counting of property considered separately in table 12.8 and since the major purpose of table 12.7 is to measure the monetary liquidity of the upper middle class of medieval London.

Cash bequests may be divided into two broad categories: those sums, often substantial, that are left to close relatives and those, usually more modest, grants that devolve upon various charities, religious houses, the poor of London, the purchase of candles, the saying of masses, or the great conduit. Gifts to London Bridge lie in the latter category, but they are here considered separately both because of their substantial number and because they reveal a certain reasoned circumspection in Londoners' civic pride and sense of community. During the early years of the reign of Edward I, the revenues of London Bridge were paid to Eleanor, the queen mother, and she appears to have diverted them to her own purposes at the expense of bridge maintenance.[18] During this period, the wills record no gifts to the bridge. In 1281, the city apparently regained control of the revenues and a royal patent was obtained authorizing the solicitation of funds; steep tolls of a farthing per man and a penny per horseman were charged for each crossing. However, these efforts to fund reconstruction were too late; five arches collapsed from ice damage in the winter of 1282–83.[19] Allowing for some lag between the time when the need for and the final use of funds

18. Gordon Home, *Old London Bridge* (New York: Dodd, Mead and Co., 1931), p. 63.
19. *Ibid.*, pp. 63–65.

became certain and the time when those aware of the problems died, the wills seem to reflect a collective civic effort to endow the bridge. Beginning in the 1290s, wills mentioning the bridge are recorded, and in the following decade, almost 80 percent of the testaments provide funds for the bridge.[20] By 1315, the bridge revenues were secure enough so that the emergency tolls were ended.[21] Not surprisingly, bequests to the bridge decline sharply thereafter. The bourgeoisie of London had responded to civic need when it arose, but they were shrewd enough to retrench quickly once the crisis had been met.

Astute though Londoners may have been in choosing their charities, one cannot but wonder at the immense sums of cash which many appear to have possessed at the time of their deaths. The fact that few left cash in the early years probably reflects a change in testamentary custom, but after 1300, close to an eighth of the decedents devise substantial sums of money. Excluding those wills which leave cash only to London Bridge, the average cash bequest amounts to £59.5. Purchasing power comparisons across long periods remain extremely tentative, but some estimate of the value of these legacies may be obtained by converting them into modern wage equivalents. In the 1300–30 period, a building craftsman in southern England could expect to earn from three to four pence a day while a common building laborer would earn about half that wage.[22] At these rates, the average money legacy during the first decades of the fourteenth century would have purchased either 4,080 days of skilled labor or 8,160 days of manual labor. Using a modern wage rate of $8.00 an hour for an eight-hour day, the present equivalent labor purchasing power would be represented by a sum of $261,000 for skilled labor. At $2.50, just above the United States minimum wage, the average medieval cash legacy would still be the equivalent of $163,000. During the nonfamine years of the early fourteenth century, the price of wheat averaged about six shillings per quarter of eight bushels,[23] and if one converts to wheat, rather than wage, equivalents, the sums are very considerably reduced. Disregarding controversies concerning the size of the bushel and using a recent price from the rapidly fluctuating modern marketplace of $4.00 a bushel, the average medieval cash legacy would have purchased as much wheat as $6,400. The

20. Seventy wills leave cash only to London Bridge, but ten more mention the bridge among other cash legacies.

21. Home, *Old London Bridge*, pp. 75–76.

22. E. M. Phelps Brown and Sheila Hopkins, "Seven Centuries of Building Wages," *Economica* (1955), reprinted in *Essays in Economic History*, II, 168–78, table I.

23. J. E. Thorold Rogers, *A History of Agriculture and Prices in England* (Oxford: Clarendon Press, 1866), I, 228–30.

disparity between the wage and wheat equivalents is not as disturbing as it looks, since it really measures the results of the Industrial Revolution and of the massive application of fossil energy in the modern production of food and goods. A medieval laborer had to work for six days to earn a bushel of wheat, whereas our least skilled laborers work less than two hours to accomplish the same task. The correct modern equivalent of the average cash legacy is elusive, but it is surely greater than the wheat and less than the wage conversions suggest; let us settle for something in between and suggest a sum of say $50,000 as a fair guess.[24]

Such conversions of values across centuries are at best approximations, but they do enable us to sense that £59.5 was a very substantial sum of money in the early fourteenth century. The fact that such vast sums appear to have been in the possession of a number of testators at the time of their deaths immediately leads to questions regarding the investment alternatives available to, and perceived to be sound by, the upper middle class of medieval London. Table 12.8 is an attempt to analyze the real estate holdings of our will-makers.

Perhaps the most problematical issue raised by table 12.8 is the definition of "property." The wills are not specific with regard to the size or value of various properties; the most recurrent phrases used to describe holdings are "my tenement with all its equipment and buildings constructed thereon" or "my shop with solar above." Needless to say, the range of values that might be concealed in such amorphous terms could be vast, but since we are here interested in the nature of Londoners' investment habits rather than in absolute levels of wealth, much may be learned simply from the number of separate investments. A second difficulty arises from the practice of dividing holdings among the heirs. When a holding is left under the formula "my tenement," it is counted only once, but if that tenement consisted of say two shops with solar above, a capital house, and a garden,

24. One may compare the £59.5 average to the internal evidence of the prices of London houses. The following are housing prices mentioned in the wills: Roll 6–66 (October 18, 1274), one house to be sold for £100; Roll 11–48 (July 20, 1280), houses to be sold for more than 65 marks or £43.3; Roll 15–42 (April 25, 1285), houses to be sold for 100 marks or £66.6; Roll 18–46 (October 28, 1288), brother to buy houses for 60 marks or £40; Roll 21–61 (June 1, 1292), tenement to be sold for more than £40; Roll 24–83 (October 28, 1295), tenement to be sold for 100 marks or £66.6; Roll 28–57 (July 20, 1299), houses to be sold for £50; Roll 29–54 (July 20, 1300), tenement worth £90; Roll 40–100 (May 21, 1313), shop to be sold for 50 marks or £33.3; Roll 43–74 (February 22, 1315), tenements to be sold for 70 marks or £46.6; Roll 44–26 (October 18, 1315), tenement left in return for 24 marks or £16. Roll 45–126 (February 2, 1317), tenement to be sold for 60 marks or £40, two shops to be sold for 40 marks or £26.6, houses and a piece of land to be sold for 40 marks or £26.6. When one considers the fact that these properties were located in central London, our estimate of a $50,000 equivalent for £59.5 does not seem unreasonable.

Table 12.8

Property-Holdings of Testators by Decade, 1271–1330

Decade	*Number of Males*[a]	*Number of Properties Held by Males Greater than*[b]	*Average Number of Properties per Male Greater than*	*Number of Females*[a]	*Number of Properties Held by Females Greater than*[b]	*Average Number of Properties per Female Greater than*	*Median Number of Properties per Female Greater than*
1271–1280	117	613	5.2	16	42	2.6[c]	1.0
1281–1290	150	630	4.2	14	41	2.9[d]	2.0
1291–1300	168	658	3.9	24	70	2.9	1.0
1301–1310	217	774	3.6	35	80	2.3	2.0
1311–1320	228	788	3.5	44	150	3.4	3.0
1321–1330	208	691	3.3	35	71	2.0	1.0
1271–1330	1,088	4,154	3.82	168	454	2.70	

SOURCE: Hustings Rolls 4–123 to 58–113

[a] Where property is left as "all my tenements" the will is excluded.

[b] Where property is itemized and then a phrase such as "my other houses and properties in London" is used only the itemized properties are counted but the will is marked "greater than"; the result is that the figures given understate the actual holdings in many cases.

[c] In the period 1271–80, one woman holds sixteen properties and distorts the average.

[d] In the period 1281–90, one woman holds eleven properties.

the value would be understated in comparison with another will which devised the shops, the house, and the garden separately. Where sufficient information exists in the will, I have reduced fractional shares of a single property to unity and counted it as a single holding, but in many cases this is not possible. The same practice has been followed in the numerous cases in which rents against a property are left to one heir while the property itself is left to another. Many difficulties remain, but the process of property enumeration has been followed consistently throughout so that while the precise definition of "property" remains elusive, the quantities themselves may be considered broadly comparable. One may, as a result, accord reasonable confidence to secular trends in property holding or to numerical comparison of property-holding between the sexes.

On the latter count, the figures are strong enough, I believe, to sustain our earlier statement that testatrices owned less property than male testators. The average number of properties held by males is 42 percent greater than the average for females and the size of both groups is large enough so that the comparison is both significant and valid despite difficulties in defining property. The median number of properties held by testatrices in three of the six decades considered was one. Thus the statement that the daughters of widows made less attractive marriage partners, at least in so far as materialistic concerns affected the hearts of London swains, appears confirmed.

Multiple real estate investments per testator clearly indicate that London property was considered a sound investment. Indeed, beyond normal investment in the capital stock of the testators' trades and two or three ships which may also be treated as capital stock, there seem to have been very few alternatives to investment in real estate. In the entire body of wills, there are only five which refer to credit instruments or written documents of any kind and every one of these is clearly associated with real property.[25] The contrast with Italian commercial practice in the same period is striking; the comparable class of an Italian city state would have devised quantities of credit instruments, commenda contracts, and various other forms of commercial credit employed to diversify risks and to maximize returns. The total absence of such documents from the London wills may also

25. Roll 39–157 (May 6, 1311) leaves "all deeds and charters." Roll 40–25 (October 28, 1311) leaves "all deeds and writings touching said tenement." Roll 56–85 (May 29, 1328) leaves "100 marks which Gilbert Poignam, chancellor of the king owes me for lands and tenements and £200 which Roger de Bosenham owes me." Roll 58–44 (May 1, 1330) leaves "£30 which they owe me for a house they bought." Roll 58–107 (November 1, 1330) instructs "my executor to hold the covenant between me and William de Aleg for £46 and if he is deficient in any payment the executors to sell the tenement with shops in which he lives."

account for the substantial sums of cash in the possession of the decedents. Over the period from 1270 to 1330, there is a decade by decade decrease in the average number of real estate holdings per male testator. As the average falls from 5.2 to 3.3 properties, particularly after 1291, the portion of the wills specifying cash legacies rises sharply. After 1300, the amount of cash per legacy moves sharply upward as well. Such figures imply that capital was not needed for investment in the decedents' business ventures and perhaps also that the slow rate of population growth of the early fourteenth century had limited the potential for investment in London property. Given the backward state of commercial credit in medieval England and the north of Europe generally, there may simply have been no alternative to the holding of large sums of cash.

A Composite Testator

By way of conclusion, the reader will perhaps pardon a speculative attempt to create a composite portrait of a typical testator. While no such person existed, of course, the exercise may still be illuminating. The hypothetical will-maker would have been a male, probably in his late forties or fifties, who had worked during his life either in a branch of the leather trades, or as a fishmonger, or as a goldsmith, in that order of likelihood. He could feel satisfied that his larder was sufficiently extensive to tide him over all but the worst disruptions of the domestic harvest and that he could supplement his stock of food from abroad if real famine struck. Despite material comfort, however, it is likely that he would already have suffered personal loss through the death of at least one of his children and perhaps that of his first wife in childbirth. Through a combination of inheritance and his own earnings, he would have acquired enough real property in London to allow him to live above the average standard of life from his rents alone, and he might even have found that he had somewhat more money than he needed for his own consumption or could soundly invest. Under these conditions, it is not likely that he would have resented the custom of London that dictated that a third of his wealth go to charity at his death. Secure in this world, he found it important to make preparation for the life to come.

13

Industrial Protectionism in Medieval Flanders: Urban or National?

John H. Munro

If protectionism, along with bullionism, constituted the heart of early-modern mercantilism, its true significance can be understood only in terms of its medieval foundations. With some nascent manifestations evident as early as the twelfth century, its truly definitive formation took place during the fourteenth and fifteenth centuries, especially in response to the disruptive, contractionary forces of that era's "great depression." Unlike bullionism, almost always a princely or national obsession, protectionism was born and long remained chiefly urban, so that much of what is called mercantilist policy for a later era is simply urban government and urban guild regulation "writ large," on the national scale.

Although the earliest examples of urban protectionism are to be found in the rapidly developing Italian city-states, which acquired powers unmatched elsewhere in Europe, the towns of Flanders did not lag far behind in implementing this policy. Indeed, because these towns had evolved in such peculiar circumstances that they were neither subservient to the princely authority nor completely independent, the county of Flanders was one of the first larger-scale principalities to have a "municipal policy superimposed on a state basis."[1] The most striking form of that urban policy was a continuously applied, statewide prohibition against imports of English woolen cloths, from at least the mid-fourteenth to the mid-sixteenth centuries.

In Flanders, this state protectionism did not, however, lose its essentially urban character and result in the subordination of the original municipal interests, as Heckscher argues happened later in many West European

1. For this concept, cf. Eli Heckscher, *Mercantilism*, 2 vols. (rev. ed. by E. F. Söderlund, London, 1955), I, 131–32.

mercantilist countries. For, from the early fourteenth to the sixteenth centuries, the three chief towns of Bruges, Ghent, and Ypres also pursued a complementary protectionist policy that was a typical expression of medieval particularism. They attempted to restrict rural cloth-making, especially to prevent the village draperies from imitating their own luxury products. But only Ypres persisted in maintaining this latter policy to the bitter end, to the late sixteenth century. Despite periodic support from the prince, Ypres never succeeded in enforcing a prohibition on rural cloth-making with any of the effectiveness of Flanders's general ban against the much more dangerous external threat.[2]

Flanders's precocious mercantilism was primarily the result of an urban economic structure that, while not unique, was certainly unusual for its very considerable dependence on the one industry of woolen textiles. This industry in turn became very dependent on foreign trade from the twelfth century, for both markets and raw materials. Indispensable for the luxury draperies especially were English wools, the most abundant in Europe and, until they were surpassed by Spanish merino wools in the sixteenth century, the finest as well.[3] For almost two centuries those conditions of economic dependence seem to have been fully justified. Wool supplies usually remained cheap, and the Flemish and neighboring Artesian cloth industries successfully dominated virtually all European markets, to produce an urban growth and prosperity unmatched anywhere but in Italy.

Then, from the late thirteenth century, the Flemish and Artesian draperies suffered three debilitating blows that led to their slow but irredeemable decay and ultimate ruin. The first was the development of foreign competition, especially in the lucrative field of luxury woolens: from the neighboring towns of Brabant, then from Italy, Holland, and finally and most strongly from England. Such competition became quite intolerable when, in the early to mid-fourteenth century, the second blow struck: a secular economic decline or a series of depressions that seriously contracted markets everywhere in Europe. The combined forces of almost incessant warfare, famines, and pestilence, the drastic depopulations, the

2. The best study, for the period up to 1384, is David Nicholas, *Town and Countryside: Social, Economic, and Political Tensions in Fourteenth-Century Flanders* (Bruges, 1971), pp. 76–116, 203–21. For the fifteenth century, see Henri De Sagher, ed., *Recueil de documents relatifs à l'histoire de l'industrie drapière en Flandre: IIme partie, le sud-ouest de la Flandre depuis l'époque bourguignonne*, 3 vols. (Brussels, 1951–66), I, 1–24, 29–54, 63–64, 71–77, 97–98; II, 23–24; III, 93–94, 102, 141–42.

3. Peter Bowden, *The Wool Trade in Tudor and Stuart England* (London, 1962), pp. 25–37; Julia de L. Mann, *The Cloth Industry in the West of England from 1640 to 1880* (Oxford, 1971), pp. xvi, 257–59, 266–67. See n. 36 below.

disruptions of established trade routes, chronic insecurity, and perhaps a more highly skewed income distribution seem to have damaged particularly the cheaper-line textile industries of the Low Countries. Producing coarse and light fabrics known as sayes, biffes, fauderts, serges, and tiretaines, chiefly for export to the populous Mediterranean regions, their profitability had depended upon concentrated bulk sales, with low unit production, transport, and marketing costs. When these commercial conditions changed so drastically, this branch of the Flemish textile industry, as an urban export industry, evidently found it impossible to compete with the surviving southern European producers, who were much closer to the main markets. Thus the Flemish textile industry responded by concentrating upon luxury cloth production, which was economically more viable at a lower volume of sales and higher unit costs. Such specialization was apparently also one in which the Flemish had long enjoyed a comparative advantage. But a relative shift to luxury manufacturing at the same time made the Flemish industry all the more dependent upon fine English wools.[4]

England was quick to take advantage of that increased dependence in the 1330s by inflicting upon the Flemish the third and most serious blow: a sharp increase in the duties on wool exports. As table 13.1 indicates, these specific duties, varying from 40s. to 50s. or more a sack in the late fourteenth and fifteenth centuries, inflated the average of wool export prices by about 45 percent. From 1363, that tax burden was passed almost fully onto the foreign buyers by the Crown's establishment of the Calais Staple Company as the exclusive seller of English wool to northern Europe.[5] Those onerous wool export duties also provide the critical reason why the English cloth trade competition then became such a threat to all other luxury cloth producers. For English clothiers, and they alone, could purchase these same fine wools tax-free, while their cloth exports were subject to just a minimal duty of 1s.2d. apiece after 1347, no more than 3 percent of the average value. The Crown, to be sure, had levied an additional "poundage" tax of 5 percent on cloth exports

4. John H. Munro, *Wool, Cloth, and Gold: The Struggle for Bullion in Anglo-Burgundian Trade, 1340–1478* (Brussels and Toronto, 1973), pp. 1–9; Herman Van der Wee, "Structural Changes and Specialization in the Industry of the Southern Netherlands, 1100–1600," *Economic History Review*, 2d ser., *28* (1975), 205–11; Alain Derville, "Les Draperies flamandes et artésiennes vers 1250–1350: Quelques considerations critiques et problèmatiques," *Revue du Nord*, *54* (1972), 353–70; Harry Miskimin, *The Economy of Early Renaissance Europe, 1300–1460* (Englewood Cliffs, N.J., 1969), pp. 86–105, 134–44; David Herlihy, *Medieval and Renaissance Pistoia* (New Haven, 1967), pp. 55–120, 180–212.

5. Munro, *Wool, Cloth, and Gold*, pp. 36–41; Eileen Power, *The Wool Trade in English Medieval History* (London, 1941), pp. 86–103.

in 1373, but only non-Hanseatic aliens were required to pay it after 1410.[6] The English cloth industry had two other if less decisive advantages over its competitors: a largely rural organization, which offered a much cheaper labor force and freedom from guild restrictions; and the adoption of water-powered fulling, the basic process in cloth-finishing.[7] But since luxury quality depended fundamentally on the use of specific amounts of English wools, and since such wools could account for two-thirds of predyeing production costs, as table 13.2 demonstrates, no amount of conceivable technological change by the Flemish draperies could possibly have overcome the cost disadvantage imposed by the English export taxes.

Contemporaneous political and constitutional changes in Flanders, however, at least permitted the drapery towns there to make an organized response to this English challenge. From the 1270s, partly as a manifestation of their growing difficulties, the Flemish drapery towns had been beset with intermittent strife between the guilds of weavers and fullers—associations of industrial-entrepreneurs, artisans, and journeymen, *not* proletarians—and the textile merchants. Although the so-called merchant patricians never possessed the monopolistic organization described by Pirenne, their command over raw materials, credit, cloth-marketing, and the offices of urban government evidently permitted them to exploit the drapery artisans to some degree. Opposed by a curious alliance of the count and the guilds known as the Clauwaerts, the urban "patriciates" or Léliaerts sought support from the count's overlord, the king of France. In 1302, their rule was abruptly terminated by the bloody Matines de Bruges and the Battle of Courtrai, in which the guild militias inflicted an incredible defeat on the pride of the French cavalry.

Although the Clauwaert party lost the subsequent battles, was forced to cede the Walloon drapery towns of Lille, Douai, and Béthune to France, and had to pay the French enormous indemnities, the Flemish guilds nevertheless managed to salvage some significant gains. First, they were given a permanent and often dominant share of the aldermanic seats in the urban governments. The mercantile and landed élite, now known as the *poorters* (bourgeoisie, privileged citizens), continued to exercise a significant influence, but retained only a minority of the seats. They also

6. N. S. B. Gras, *The Early English Customs System* (Cambridge, Mass., 1918), pp. 66, 72–73, 81–83; Public Record Office, King's Remembrancer Exchequer (Customs) E. 122/40/30, 51/27 (Ipswich, 1410–11). Hanse merchants paid only 1 s. 0 d. but other aliens paid 2 s. 9 d. on standard broadcloths of 24 yards by 7 quarters, "without grain."

7. Cf. Edward Miller, "The Fortunes of the Early English Textile Industry in the Thirteenth Century," *Economic History Review*, 2d ser., *18* (1965), 64–82.

suffered a loss of economic power as Italian and especially German merchants gained increasing control over the Flemish cloth trade. Second, the French and civil wars had so weakened the count's powers that he was forced to accept the claim of Ghent, Ypres, and Bruges to be his virtual co-equal in governing Flanders as the Three Members (*drie leden* or *gemeen land*).[8] Subsequently the drapery towns revolted against their count three times, usually under the weavers' leadership: in 1323–28, 1338–49, and 1379–85. Fortunately for the count, however, internecine strife among the guilds and then among the towns permitted him to crush each of these revolts. Despite these defeats and an industrial decline that was certainly exacerbated by such disruptions, at least some of the cloth guilds always retained their aldermanic seats, and the weavers were never excluded for long.[9] Even after the establishment of the powerful Burgundian ducal regime in Flanders in 1384, the Three Members continued to share fully in governing the county. Perhaps, as many argue, the Burgundian dukes did gradually curb their powers, especially by adding the rural Franc de Bruges (Brugse Vrij) as their own fourth Member.[10] But Burgundian policies also encouraged the Four Members to submerge their particularist differences to a greater extent and to act as a more cohesive unit in order to counterbalance ducal power.

Certainly on the issue of the English cloth trade the Three (then Four) Members, the drapery guilds, and the prince were always in harmony, at least until the late fifteenth century. But precisely when a countywide ban on that trade was first imposed cannot be ascertained. No such ban, in any event, may be inferred from the three earliest recorded restrictions on the cloth trade: a 1285 *keure* or ordinance of the Bruges Lakenhalle permitting only the town's citizens to sell cloth there; a 1291 keure of the

8. Henri Pirenne, *Histoire de Belgique*, 4 vols. (new illustrated ed. by Franz Schauwers and Jacques Paquet, Brussels, 1956; editions nos. 1 to 5 in 7 vols., 1902–32), I, 225–56, 287–94; Hans Van Werveke, *Gand: Esquisse d'histoire sociale* (Brussels, 1946), pp. 29–52; Nicholas, *Town and Countryside*, pp. 11–13; 152–72, 178–79, and his "Economic Reorganization and Social Change in Fourteenth-Century Flanders," *Past and Present*, no. 70 (1976), pp. 3–29; Raymond Van Uytven and Willem Blockmans, "Constitutions and Their Application in the Netherlands during the Middle Ages," *Revue belge de philologie et d'histoire*, *47* (1969), 400, 412–17.

9. Nicholas, *Town and Countryside*, pp. 12–13, 152–72, 203; Van Werveke, *Gand*, pp. 51–69; Pirenne, *Belgique*, I, 297–326, 339–40, 352–62; Victor Fris, "Les Origines de la réforme constitutionelle de Gand de 1360–1369," *Bulletin de la société d'histoire et d'archéologie de Gand*, *9* (1909), 427–59; Willem Blockmans, I. De Meyer et al., *Studiën betreffende de sociale strukturen te Brugge, Kortrijk, en Gent in de 14e en 15e eeuw*, 3 vols. (Heule, 1971–72).

10. Walter Prevenier, "Realité et histoire: Le Quatrième Membre de Flandre," *Revue du Nord*, *43* (1961), 5–14; Richard Vaughan, *Philip the Bold: The Formation of the Burgundian State* (London, 1962), pp. 138–39, 173–87.

Ypres cloth merchants' guild allowing the import of "foreign" cloths made in the style of Ypres only during the free-fair times; and Count Guy de Dampierre's Great Charter of 1297 to Ghent, which merely denied noncitizens the right to sell there any cloths fulled elsewhere.[11] Then on August 23, 1302, just six weeks after the Battle of Courtrai, the count forbade anyone to bring into Ghent any cloths that had not been woven or fulled within the town. That ban was reconfirmed by succeeding counts and Ghent civic governments using the more generalized term "foreign cloths."[12] Though this prohibition would obviously include English woolens, its chief target was probably cloths produced by the rural draperies.

The earliest known document that may just possibly refer to a ban on English cloth in particular is an entry in the Bruges municipal accounts of 1306–07 recording the confiscation of "seven cloths belonging to an Englishman from Bristol."[13] If these cloths are not indisputably English, those of another similar confiscation recorded in the Bruges accounts of 1346–47 most certainly are.[14] Unfortunately neither of these accounts specifies the reason for the confiscation. But it seems unlikely that the explanation can simply be the narrow particularist opposition to all cloths made outside the urban jurisdiction, as in the Ghent decrees. For Bruges, as one of Flanders's five free-fairs and especially as the official, exclusive staple for the textile trades, dealt in cloths from all over the Low Countries and adjacent regions. Furthermore, for the twice-yearly garbing of its officials throughout the fourteenth and fifteenth centuries, the Bruges government purchased woolens from all the various Flemish drapery towns, even from those hated rural and small-town industries known as the *nouvelles draperies*, and occasionally also from the towns of Brabant, Holland, Hainaut, and northern France—but never from England.[15]

11. Georges Espinas and Henri Pirenne, eds., *Recueil de documents relatifs à l'histoire de l'industrie drapière en Flandre : Ire partie, des origines à l'époque bourguignonne*, 4 vols. (Brussels, 1906–20), I, 460, no. 143:19 (1285); III, 499, no. 764:56 (1291); II, 393, no. 406:149 (1297).

12. Espinas and Pirenne, *Recueil*, II, 399–400, no. 412 (1302); 404–08, no. 417 (1314, 1325, 1485); 423, no. 424:1 (1337); 472, no. 439 (1349); 479–80, no. 451:3 (1353); 492–94, nos. 461–62 (1360); 546, 500:2 (1376).

13. Or possibly Boston ("Briston"). Louis Gilliodts-Van Severen, ed., *Cartulaire de l'ancienne estaple de Bruges*, 6 vols. (Bruges, 1904–08), I, 115, no. 154. Several historians have referred to a "cloth ban" at Bruges in 1307. But the true date of the document they had cited is June 1359, as Gilliodts-Van Severen noted in *Estaple de Bruges*, I, 224, no. 303. See n. 19 and n. 52 below.

14. Louis Gilliodts-Van Severen, ed., *Inventaire des chartes et documents des archives de la ville de Bruges*, 6 vols. (Bruges, 1871–76), V, 154, no. 917. Cf. Pirenne, *Belgique*, I, 352–53, 367 (n. 65).

15. Gilliodts-Van Severen, *Archives de Bruges*, III, 358–60, no. 815 (charter of 1313), 427–34, no. 867

The first concrete proof of a general Flemish ban against English woolen cloths, possibly in force for some time, is found in the Flemish-Hanse treaty negotiations of 1358–60. In May 1358, after the Flemish had arbitrarily increased commercial taxes and refused to indemnify Hanse merchants for piracy damages, the Hanseatic League had collectively imposed a total embargo on Flemish trade. That August, in a list of complaints placed before the Lübeck Diet, some Hanse merchants charged that Bruges officials had been seizing English cloth from their ships docked at the outport of Sluis on the Zwin, even though they were merely shipping the cloths elsewhere, without ever intending to sell any in Flanders. Another condemned the confiscation of English cloths from a Hanse *kogge* shipwrecked near Bruges.[16] Similar complaints may have been simmering for years. But it is perhaps significant to note that English cloth exports first became impressive only during these very years, averaging about 10,000 pieces annually from 1357 to 1360.[17] Evidently the English cloth trade was benefiting at last from that differential in export duties. At the same time, it was probably also gaining new customers in the Baltic and Germany as a result of the Hanseatic embargo against Flanders.

Certainly the Hanseatic League, as the dominant force in northern trade, had become by far the most important dealers in Flemish cloth;[18] and by June 1359 the Three Members had become so desperately anxious to secure the return of the Hanse that they finally capitulated on most of their demands, including the English cloth issue. Thus article 19 of the Flemish draft charter offered the Hanse merchants the right to bring English cloths to Sluis, but only on condition that such cloths "remain bound within the bales that they were packed in, without being unpacked or placed on sale, and that they then be re-exported from the Zwin by sea . . . even though this will be greatly harmful to the drapery of Bruges."[19] When Count Louis de Mäle formally confirmed the treaty with the Hanseatic League on July 30, 1360, so ending the crippling embargo,

(1400). See cloth purchases in the Bruges municipal accounts in: Stadsarchief te Brugge, Stadsrekeningen, 1302/03–1495/96.

16. Karl Koppmann, ed., *Die Recesse und andere Akten der Hansetäge von 1256 bis 1430*, 8 vols. (1st ser. of *Hanserecesse*, Leipzig, 1870–97), III, 226, no. 238:18; 234, no. 240:5:10.

17. E. M. Carus-Wilson and Olive Coleman, *England's Export Trade, 1275–1547* (Oxford, 1963), tables in pp. 75–77, graph on p. 138.

18. Hektor Ammann, "Deutschland und die Tuchindustrie nordwest-europas im Mittelalter," *Hansisches Geschichtsblätter, 72* (1954), 1–61; Hans Van Werveke, "Die Stellung des hansischen Kaufmans dem flandrischen Tuchproduzenten gegenüber," in his *Miscellanea Medievalia* (Ghent, 1968), pp. 123–30.

19. Konstantin Höhlbaum, ed., *Hansisches Urkundenbuch*, 11 vols. (Halle and Leipzig, 1876–1939), III, 201, no. 430; 221, no. 452. Gilliodts-Van Severen, *Estaple de Bruges*, I, 224, no. 303.

the transit-shipping privilege had been more sensibly constructed to allow Hanse merchants to bring English cloth to any Flemish port, to transfer it if necessary to another ship, and to transport it elsewhere either by land or by sea, while paying the count's tolls.[20] In that formulation the privilege made more explicit what was implicit by virtue of Bruges's staple rights: that a general ban on English cloth applied to the whole of Flanders. The penalties then applicable for evading the Flemish ban are not known. But a Bruges keure, issued some time afterward and subsequently reconfirmed in the fifteenth and sixteenth centuries as part of the staple law, imposed fines of £50 *parisis* (= £4. 3 s. 4 d. *groot*)—an artisan's wage for about nine months—for each and every English cloth seized, "without prejudice to the privilege of the Easterlings."[21]

In its revised form, the Hanse transit-shipping privilege was also granted to two towns which, though not then members of the League, were important commercial auxiliaries: Kampen on the Zuider Zee in 1361, and Nürnberg in 1362.[22] Thereafter, until the sixteenth century or later, this privilege remained quite unchanged. When the Hanseatic League imposed another embargo against Flanders from mid-1388 to December 1392, the Hanse evidently tried to have this transit-shipping privilege further liberalized. The Four Members and the duke, however, adamantly refused to amend it, even though they finally agreed to pay an enormous indemnity of £11,100 groot and to meet virtually every other Hanse stipulation for ending that ruinous blockade.[23]

Only one other mercantile power, Genoa, appears to have succeeded in extorting a similar transit-shipping privilege from Flanders, but it applied for only a brief period at the turn of the century. In the 1390s the Flemish economy was suffering a severe depression as a result of the dislocations of the devastating civil war of 1379–85, the four-year Hanse embargo, the duke's rigorous hard-money policy, unchecked North Sea piracies fostered by the Anglo-French war, and a general exodus of foreign

20. Höhlbaum, *Hansisches Urkundenbuch*, III, 261–62, no. 497:34 (Flemish); 247, no. 495:24 (Latin); cf. Gilliodts-Van Severen, *Archives de Bruges*, II, 51–53, no. 532; Philippe Dollinger, *La Hanse, XIIe–XVIIe siècles* (Paris, 1964), pp. 85–91, 305–12.

21. J. Gailliard, *De Ambachten en neringe van Brugge*, 2 vols. (Bruges, 1854), II, 35, no. 7; Gilliodts-Van Severen, *Archives de Bruges*, VI, 12 (1470): Gilliodts-Van Severen, *Estaple de Bruges*, II, 554–55, no. 1515:2 (1522). Wages were estimated from data in Herman Van der Wee, *Growth of the Antwerp Market and the European Economy, Fourteenth to Sixteenth Centuries*, 3 vols. (The Hague, 1963), I, 38–50, 345, 457–58, 540.

22. Gilliodts-Van Severen, *Archives de Bruges*, II, 77–82, no. 542:28 (May 1361); Gilliodts-Van Severen *Estaple de Bruges*, I, 249, no. 319:34 (January 1362 n.s.)

23. Koppmann, *Recesse, 1256–1430*, IV, 26–27, no. 34:4 (Oct. 1391); 23–24, no. 30; 29–37, no. 38; Gilliodts-Van Severen, *Estaple de Bruges*, I, 370, no. 441; 374–76, nos. 445–46; 382–83, nos. 456–57; Gilliodts-Van Severen, *Archives de Bruges*, II, 229, no. 735; Dollinger, *La Hanse*, pp. 91–103.

merchants.[24] The return of the highly important Genoese, who had shifted their staple in northern trade to England, proved especially difficult to secure. Finally, in December 1395, the Four Members agreed to pay the Genoese a heavy indemnity of £4,500 groot and to grant them a generous new concession: the right to re-export their own English cloths, but only by sea from Sluis, without unloading them, only by "special authorization," and on payment of a 2 percent toll. In return, the Genoese were to agree for the ten years following to staple all their merchandise at Bruges first, before trading with England. According to the proclamation issued by Duke Philip and Doge Antoniotto Adorno, the treaty and the staple were to take effect on Easter (April 22) 1397.[25] But the Genoese merchants stayed put in England, perhaps because some treaty provisions had not yet been met. Whatever the reason, the records of the Four Members' *parlamenten* show that from March 1397 to July 1398 they conferred at least thirteen times to find some way of securing Genoese agreement to re-establish their Bruges staple.[26] Shortly afterward, the Genoese apparently did return. If they were then granted the privilege of re-exporting English cloth, it must have been very narrowly interpreted, for in the next few years there are several recorded instances of fines imposed upon Genose merchants or sailors for having English cloths on board their ships at Sluis.[27]

An incident of 1405 suggests that the Genoese privilege, if it was in fact ever granted, was indeed a very restricted one. Some Genoese merchants informed the Sluis water bailiff that, in retaliation against recent unredressed acts of English piracy, they were terminating their trade with England, but that they could repatriate their assets only in the form of English cloth. Therefore, "because of the prohibition against bringing English cloths to Sluis by all except the Francs Allemans [the Hanse]," they requested special permission to ship those cloths via Sluis to Genoa, without unloading them, but paying a tax of 6s.6d. groot per bale. The water bailiff then sought the advice of the chancellor of Flanders, who finally did grant the Genoese such a license—but only on condition that they swear never to return to England. Two more licenses for shipping

24. Vaughan, *Philip the Bold*, pp. 168–73, 180–82; Van der Wee, *Antwerp Market*, II, 14–18; Munro, *Wool, Cloth, and Gold*, pp. 46–63.

25. Gilliodts-Van Severen, *Estaple de Bruges*, I, 391–93, no. 469; 397–98, no. 472; cf. Jules Finot, *Etude historique sur les relations commerciales entre la Flandre et la republique de Gênes au moyen âge* (Paris, 1906), pp. 52–53 (with some inaccuracies).

26. Walter Prevenier, ed., *Handelingen van de leden en van de staten van Vlaanderen, 1384–1405* (Brussels, 1959), pp. 135, no. 373; 141–44, nos. 385, 387–92, 394–96; 152, no. 410; 155–56, no. 416.

27. Finot, *Gênes*, pp. 64, 66. In 1402, 1403, and 1406.

English cloths were sold to the Genoese in 1407, perhaps in connection with this incident.[28] But after that date, the tenth anniversary of the treaty, there is no further record of any such Genoese dealings in English cloth in Flanders.

Surprisingly, even the English once had the audacity to request, in the late fourteenth century, a similar if very limited transit-shipping privilege for their cloths. They certainly had good grounds for doing so then in view of the provisions of the Anglo-Flemish commercial treaty of 1359, and of all their subsequent trade treaties, that guaranteed them full freedom "to import and sell all manner of merchandise."[29] The English, however, seem to have resigned themselves at a very early date to the exclusion of their cloth from Flanders. Thus in 1364, for example, Edward III issued various licenses to ship cloths "to places beyond the seas towards the east and north, Flanders excepted."[30] What the English were not prepared to accept without challenge was the arbitrary confiscation of those cloths entering Flemish jurisdiction only by accident. During the Anglo-Flemish trade negotiations of July 1378, the English demanded the return of their woolens seized from two ships that had been forced into Sluis by storms. The Flemish delayed a response on that issue until May 1379, when Count Louis and the Three Members together formally announced that, "pursuant to the customary laws long in force in Flanders, the said cloths are forfeit to the count." The Flemish ambassadors nevertheless offered the hope that, if the English complied with all their demands and made full restitution for all damages, Count Louis might restore the cloths.[31] An account of confiscated English cloths prepared by the Bruges bailiff in May 1379, however, suggests that they had already met with another fate.[32]

A decade later, in the treaty negotiations of April 1389, the English once again raised the cloth trade issue. When the Flemish stated that, as before, "all English goods may freely enter Flanders, except cloths,"

28. Finot, *Gênes*, pp. 65–66. Cf. Wilfred Brulez, "Engels laken in Vlaanderen in de 14e en 15e eeuw," *Handelingen van het genootschap "Société d'Emulation" te Brugge, 108* (1971), 10–11. Finot's reference to "import licenses" is surely a misreading of "re-export licenses."

29. Emile Varenbergh, *Histoire des relations diplomatiques entre le comté de Flandre et l'Angeleterre au moyen âge* (Brussels, 1874), pp. 447–54, doc. no. 8; Gilliodts-Van Severen, *Estaple de Bruges*, I, 226–32, no. 304 (1359); 263–66, no. 342 (1370); 268, no. 347 (1371).

30. *Calendar of Patent Rolls* (*Edward III*), *1361–64*, pp. 495, 500, 517.

31. Roger Degryse, "De Vlaamse westvaart en de Engelse represailles omstreeks 1378," *Handelingen der maatschappij voor geschiedenis en oudheidkunde te Gent*, new ser., *27* (1973), 225–26, nos. II: 26–27; 232–33, no. IV:6.

32. Gilliodts-Van Severen, *Estaple de Bruges*, I, 291, no. 375.

the English sarcastically retorted that this stance hardly accorded with their own interpretation of "équalité." Without disputing that point, the Flemish ambassadors nevertheless stated that, if English cloths were to enter Flanders, "it would mean the destruction of our country." Recognizing reality, the English were actually more concerned with obtaining guarantees that their woolens would not be confiscated from any ship forced into Flemish ports by storms or pirates. They also requested safe passage for their cloths bound for Prussia or Bordeaux, provided that they were kept strictly on board bound in bales.[33] That the Flemish were unwilling even to respond to these reasonable demands is still surprising in view of their political and economic straits in the 1380s. With their economy ravaged by the recent civil war and the current Hanseatic embargo, the Flemish, in Walter Prevenier's view, "were ready to make all the concessions that the English could imagine" for a treaty that would guarantee them neutrality in the Anglo-French war and a secure supply of English wool.[34] They were even willing to dismantle their fortresses of Gravelines and Sluis—but not their ban on English cloth. Perhaps the English would have better appreciated Flanders's tenacious defense of that policy had they paid proper attention to the fact that, on the very eve of the negotiations, Ypres had enacted a strong ordinance against not only the import but the wearing or handling of English cloth in any form, on pain of confiscation and a fine of £10.[35]

Thirty years later, in the Westminster Parliament of 1420, just when Henry V and Duke Philip the Good of Burgundy had contracted a formal alliance to conquer France, the English seemingly made one final protest against Flanders's cloth ban. A Commons petitioner complained that, in flagrant violation of a "long-standing" agreement with Flanders not to contest the cloth ban so long as the Flemish used English wools exclusively, Duke Philip was permitting the sale of Scottish and Spanish wools, even though "the said cloth ordinance is still being enforced in Flanders." The next year, after Henry V had replied in some bewilderment that he would "serche" for such an agreement, some petitioners boldly demanded that Henry make a new treaty with Philip and the Four Members obligat-

33. Prevenier, *Handelingen*, pp. 28–29, no. 74; 434, no. II:16. Cf. confiscations of English cloths from a ship wrecked kogge in 1387, in Gilliodts-Van Severen, *Archives de Bruges*, III, 95–96, no. 686; Gilliodts-Van Severen, *Estaple de Bruges*, I, 351, no. 413.

34. Walter Prevenier, "Les Perturbations dans les relations commerciales anglo-flamandes entre 1379 et 1407," *Economies et sociétés au moyen âge: Mélanges offerts à Edouard Perroy* (Paris, 1973), pp. 486–97. Cf. also Vaughan, *Philip the Bold*, pp. 47–51.

35. Espinas and Pirenne, *Recueil*, III, 532, no. 770:10 (March 20, 1389. The conference began on April 1.)

ing them either to ban entirely the sale of Scottish and Spanish wools in Flanders, or else permit the unhindered sale of English cloths there, "as in Brabant, Holland, and Zealand." Undoubtedly, as accompanying complaints about the "great drop" in wool sales and wool prices suggest, some or all of these petitioners were Calais Staplers rather than cloth merchants. If, in fact, some of the Flemish nouvelles draperies were already substituting Spanish for English wools in counterfeiting fine woolens, the Staplers evidently hoped that, in this crucial time of war, such threats to open up the cloth trade would coerce the Flemish into granting them exclusive control over wool sales. But the Flemish did not yet see any compelling reason to choose between the Scylla of a Stapler monopoly and the Charybdis of the English cloth-trade competition. No such treaty was negotiated.[36]

The Flemish, however, were not totally, inflexibly hostile to the textile trades of the British Isles. Not all wool-based fabrics were excluded. For the object of the Flemish ban, after all, was to protect the chiefly urban luxury draperies, not the chiefly rural sayetteries or *draperies légères*. The cheap, coarse, light fabrics known as worsteds or serges hardly posed a threat to the Flemish luxury cloth producers. The luxury cloths were, in contrast, woolens properly speaking, made from very fine, short-stapled wools.[37] Dyed and dressed, they had a texture, and often a price, as table 13.3 shows, rivaling those of silks. Nor did the Flemish have much to fear from a wide variety of other low-priced, mixed woolen-worsted or inferior cloths that also appear, if much less often than the regular broadcloths, in the English customs accounts: panni bastardi, russets, "cottons," coverlets, friezes, streits, dozens, Welsh and Irish cloths. The higher-priced woolen kerseys, however, seem to have been a borderline case in Flemish eyes. How considerably cheaper than the fine English or Flemish broadcloths a number of such textiles were is also demonstrated by tables 13.3 and 13.5, which further indicate the significant price advantage that English short-broadcloths enjoyed in the mid-fifteenth century—even over products of the nouvelles draperies.

At least some of these inexpensive English textiles were evidently exempt from the Flemish cloth ban from its very beginning. Certainly their import received legal sanction from the Flemish-Hanse treaty of

36. *Rotuli Parliamentorum*, IV, 126: no. 16 (8 Hen. V); 146–47: no. 28 (9 Hen. V). Cf. also Richard Vaughan, *Philip the Good: The Apogee of Burgundy* (London, 1970), pp. 3–6. On Spanish and Scottish wools, see Munro, *Wool, Cloth, and Gold*, pp. 1–5, 8, 152–54, 183–84.

37. Emile Coornaert, *Un Centre industriel d'autrefois: La Draperie-sayetterie d'Hondschoote, XIVe–XVIIIe siècle* (Paris, 1930), pp. 1–22, 189–254; Herbert Heaton, *The Yorkshire Woollen and Worsted Industries* (2d ed., Oxford, 1965), pp. 259–63; Bowden, *Wool Trade*, pp. 1–76; Guy De Poerck, *La Draperie médiévale en Flandre et en Artois: Technique et terminologie*, 3 vols. (Bruges, 1951). Cf. n. 36 above and n. 38 below.

July 1360, which specified that the port tax on English and Irish worsteds (*zarken* = serges) was to remain unchanged.[38] Their continued import is verified by a decree that Duke Philip the Bold issued in February 1400 to resolve a dispute between Bruges and Sluis over these textiles. While basically confirming Bruges's historic staple and drapery privileges, he granted Sluis one minor concession: the right to dye English worsteds (*sayes Dengleterre*), Scottish cloths, and other such cheap imported textiles, but only for domestic sale, not for re-export. Furthermore, the dyers of Sluis were permitted to buy such textiles and *draps manteaulx d'Irelande* only at Bruges. If any Flemish merchant purchased them abroad, he was required to take them directly to their "true staple" at Bruges. Finally, Sluis merchants were permitted to sell such dyed textiles only at retail in Sluis.[39]

Duke Philip's concession concerning Scottish cloths, or his lack of specificity about them, may have made the Four Members apprehensive, for they met later at Bruges, in March 1405, to discuss a possible ban on Scottish cloths.[40] According to an account of the Sluis bailiff recording confiscations of Scottish cloths in 1424, the Four Members and Duke Philip had finally enacted such a prohibition on August 4, 1423.[41] Shortly afterward, in a charter granted to the Scottish merchants on December 6, 1427, Duke Philip modified or defined the ban more precisely. While the sale or exchange of Scottish woolens in Flanders was indeed strictly forbidden, Scottish merchants were free to import their cloths in order to have them dyed, under inspection, provided that they were immediately re-exported.[42] Accounts of the Sluis bailiff for the following year record more confiscations of Scottish cloths and fines levied; but subsequent accounts make no further mention of them.[43]

Much later the Flemish agreed to exempt a number of textiles from the ban on Scottish cloths. First, in April 1441, after the Scottish merchants had deserted Bruges for Middelburg in Zealand over a tax dispute, the

38. Höhlbaum, *Hansisches Urkundenbuch*, III, 265, no. 497:5. For other references to such worsted imports, see ibid., III, 571; and Koppmann, *Recesse, 1256–1430*, II, 362, no. 306:6, 369, no. 331:3. On definitions, cf. Public Record Office, Lord Treasurer's Remembrancer Exchequer (Customs) E. 356/9. m. 35 (1366–67): "285 sargos vocatos pannos de Worstede, . . . 1,760 pannos de Worstede vocatos sargos."

39. Gilliodts-Van Severen, *Archives de Bruges*, III, 427–34, no. 867; 358–60, no. 815 (1313 charter); 534–50, no. 906 (1407).

40. Prevenier, *Handelingen*, pp. 360–61, no. 735; Brulez, "Engels laken," pp. 13–15.

41. Algemeen Rijksarchief van Belgie (hereafter cited as A.R.A.), Rekenkamer, no. 13,926, f. 5ʳ: account of January 10 to May 8, 1424.

42. Louis Gilliodts-Van Severen, ed., *Cartulaire de l'ancien grand tonlieu de Bruges*, 6 vols. (Bruges, 1904–08), V, 65, no. 2669.

43. A.R.A., Rek., no. 13,926: accounts of May–September 1425, f. 5ʳ; January–May 1428, f. 4ʳ; May–September 1428, f. 6ʳ; no. 32,481, f. 21ʳ (1426–27).

Four Members and Philip granted the Scots a new treaty that permitted them inter alia to sell in Flanders a narrow cloth of five quarter-ells called *scotbreede* (also *stocbrede*), evidently a cheap, coarse fabric.[44] Then judicial decisions of the Bruges magistrates in May 1461 and August 1465 removed all restrictions on the sale of small, narrow Scottish *ghewreven* (scoured) cloths; gray and white kerseys of 3.5 quarter-ells; *mantellakens* (cloak cloths); cloths of Ireland, Berwick-on-Tweed, and "Espierche." Articles in both Bruges's staple charter and the Flemish-Scottish treaty, revised by Duke Charles in March and April 1470, formally confirmed the right to sell all these textiles in Flanders.[45] Officials of the Bruges Lakenhalle tried to limit this right shortly thereafter by ordering the tailors' guild not to use or to retail any of these textiles, but their decree was quashed by the Council of Flanders in November 1475.[46] Finally, in October 1497, when Archduke Philip the Fair was imposing his own, short-lived protectionist policy on the Low Countries, public outrage forced him to exempt from a general ban on foreign wool-based garments these very same Scottish and Irish textiles "of little value . . . by which the poor and miserable folk are principally clothed."[47]

None of these or other edicts refers specifically, to be sure, to the similarly coarse and cheap English worsteds or woolen stuffs. But there was no real need to do so, since there is no known decree revoking the provisions of the 1360 Flemish-Hanse treaty or the Bruges-Sluis staple ordinance of 1400 that specifically sanctioned the sale of English worsteds at Bruges. Furthermore, in the early fifteenth century, the Sluis bailiff's court convicted, fined, and even imprisoned several persons for handling English "cloths," not on the grounds of evading the cloth ban but of violating Bruges's staple rights as specifically defined in that 1400 ordinance. Possibly the bailiff chose the latter law as grounds for prosecution because its penalties were the more severe. But in virtually every instance the English textiles, imported from nearby Middelburg in Zealand, were materials for stockings, hose, or breeches—hardly luxury fabrics. In one

44. Gilliodts-Van Severen, *Tonlieu de Bruges*, V, 69, no. 2676. The treaty was reconfirmed in 1448: Gilliodts-Van Severen, *Archives de Bruges*, V, 299–302, no. 1050.

45. Gilliodts-Van Severen, *Estaple de Bruges*, II, 108, no. 1033 (1461); 133, no. 1067 (1465); Gilliodts-van Severen, *Archives de Bruges*, VI, 12, no. 1107 (March 1470); 33–43, no. 1111 (April 1470).

46. I. L. A. Diegerick, ed., *Inventaire analytique et chronologique des chartes et documents appartenant aux archives de la ville d'Ypres*, 5 vols. (Bruges, 1853–60), IV, 20, no. 1049. Cf. Brulez, "Engels laken," p. 14, who cites a different source for this incident, indicating that Bruges had appealed this decision to the Grote Raad of Mechelen.

47. Gilliodts-Van Severen, *Archives de Bruges*, VI, 481–82, no. 1305 (ban of October 20, 1497); Gilliodts-Van Severen, *Estaples de Bruges*, II, 314, no. 1302 (exemption of November 17, 1497); Diegerick, *Archives d'Ypres*, IV, 271, no. 1323. The general ban was rescinded in May 1499 (see n. 81).

case of 1405, the offender's fine was subsequently reduced because he was a "povre homme" and the offending cloths were "bien rudes et de petite valeur;" in another, of 1424, the confiscated cloth was valued at just 25 percent of the average price of short broadcloths then exported from Southampton.[48] Much later, in 1485, a Tournai merchant's purchase from Londoners of 18 English *ossettes*, a worsted fabric, with instructions to deliver them at Bruges, would indicate that such textiles continued to be exempt from the Flemish ban.[49] As a final example, two English merchants contested the seizure of their cloths at Bruges in 1520 on the grounds that they were not the prohibited broadcloths (*lakens*) but *karsayen* and stocbreeden. The Bruges magistrates, pending an examination of the textiles, apparently accepted their defense in principle.[50] English kerseys, though narrow, fairly coarse, and generally cheap were nevertheless woolens, not worsteds. Certainly they had been confiscated at Bruges on earlier occasions, and perhaps had been exempted from the cloth ban only in recent times.[51]

To define, limit, and explain the evolution of the Flemish cloth-ban policy is a far easier task than to prove that it was effectively enforced. To be published elsewhere, as a sample of actual or supposed violations of the bans, is a chronological listing of fifty prosecutions, fines, and cloth confiscations (1307–1534). No such list, however, will likely ever convince those who believe, as a canon of free-trade doctrines, that no import ban can possibly succeed. To them, all apprehended smugglers are merely the careless exceptions. No one, to be sure, would seriously deny that some English cloths escaped the net, though even my critic Wilfrid Brulez has not yet shown that any actually succeeded in doing so.[52] The true test of enforcement of any ban, however, is really whether there is a continuously

48. A.R.A., Rek., no. 13,925: bailiff's account of May–September 1405, f. 3^v (excerpt in Gilliodts-Van Severen, *Estaple de Bruges*, I, 443, no. 532), and no. 13,926: account of May–September 1424, f. 3^r (cloth of 18 ells worth 9 s. 0 d. groot); P.R.O., K.R. E.122/141/4 (Southampton customs account, 1424–25).

49. Gilliodts-Van Severen, *Estaple de Bruges*, II, 251, no. 1222; *New English Dictionary*, VII, 222. Brulez, "Engels laken," p. 13, mistakenly identifies this textile.

50. Louis Gilliodts-Van Severen, ed., *Coûtume de la ville de Bruges*, 2 vols. (Bruges, 1875), II, 404.

51. For the confiscation of English kerseys from Hanse merchants at Sluis in 1431, see Gilliodts-Van Severen, *Estaple de Bruges*, I, 574, no. 705. Cf. definitions in *Calendar of Fine Rolls* (*Henry VII*), *1485–1509*, pp. 17–21 (September 1485); *Statutes of the Realm*, IV: 1, 136–37 (5–6 Ed. VI c. 6 pt. 1); and table 13.3 above.

52. "Engels laken," pp. 5–25. After closely examining all of his sources, in many instances the original documents as well as the précis or secondary sources that he cited, I can find no substantiated evidence of any successful evasion of the cloth ban in Flanders. Although some of his sources may possibly suggest smuggling, many of his sources and interpretations of documents are, in my view, erroneous. A more appropriate place than a festschrift, however, to respond to his arguments, and to other opposing or inaccurate views on the cloth bans, would be a separate article that I intend to publish shortly under the tentative title of "English Cloth and Cloth Bans in the Medieval Low Countries: Myths and Realities."

certain risk of confiscation and serious economic loss that outweighs any reasonable prospect of gain and that is sufficient therefore to discourage any significant trade in the prohibited good, especially if alternative markets exist.

Some of the best proof that the Three, then Four Members of Flanders unceasingly sought to enforce their ban may be found in the records of Hanseatic violations, supposed or real, of their privilege to transport English cloths via Flanders for sale elsewhere. The Flemish themselves generally always honored the Hanseatic privilege—except for suspensions during the four great Anglo-Burgundian trade wars of 1434–39, 1447–52, 1464–67, and 1494–95.[53] But they also always placed the strictest possible interpretation on it: more akin to the Three Members's original, harsh draft article of 1359 than to the actual article of the 1360 treaty. Thus from at least the 1370s and on into the fifteenth century there are several recorded instances of cloth confiscations from Hanse merchants on board their ships, at Sluis or Bruges, or in transit across Flanders, on the grounds that their English cloths were unpacked. In at least two of these cases (1387, 1443) the Bruges government was forced to indemnify the victimized Hanse merchants, though in the latter case only after fifteen years, in fulfilling the treaty obligations to end yet another Hanse embargo (1458). In two other cases (1431, 1437) Hanse merchants contended, successfully in the first, that certain English cloths confiscated by Flemish officials belonged to them and not to other merchants, as the officials had maintained. In the remaining cases, Hanseatic shippers and merchants were fined and had their cloths confiscated for variously "importing," or "having in their possession" English cloths. But they are never specifically accused in these documents of having sold them.[54]

In 1468, the Cologne Hanse complained that their transit-shipping privilege for the English cloth trade was not being properly respected.[55] Some events of the 1470s seem to bear this charge out in part. First, in a

53. For the first three bans, see Munro, *Wool, Cloth, and Gold*, pp. 104–08 (esp. n. 41), 134–44, 163–66; for the last, see Georg Schanz, ed., *Englische Handelspolitik gegen Ende des Mittelalters*, 2 vols. (Leipzig, 1881), II, *Urkunden und Beilagen*, 191–93, no. 5 (April 1494). The clearest restatement of the privilege is in a cloth confiscation at Sluis in 1431: "pour ce que tous draps d'Engleterre sont baniz du pays de Flandres, excepté que les marchans dudit Alemaigne les peuent amener oudit Flandres en fardeaux et ramener hors sans les y despacquier ou vendre et non autrement" (Gilliodts-Van Severen, *Estaple de Bruges*, I, 574, no. 705).

54. Koppmann, *Recesse*, 1256–1430, III, 409–10, no. 404:25 (1370); II, 413, no. 343:13; 422, no. 344:10; 437, no. 345:7; 445, no. 346:9 (May–June 1387); Gilliodts-Van Severen, *Archives de Bruges*, V, 431, no. 1087 (1443, 1457–58); Walther Stein, ed., *Hansisches Urkundenbuch*, VIII (Leipzig, 1899), 471, no. 756:a:7 (1458); Gilliodts-Van Severen, *Estaples de Bruges*, I, 577, no. 711 (1431–32); A.R.A., Rek., no. 13,926, f. 3^v (account of 1436–38). Cf. Brulez, "Engels laken," pp. 9–11, 16; and n. 52 above.

55. Stein, *Hansisches Urkundenbuch*, IX, 402, no. 537:11:3; Brulez, "Engels laken," p. 9^n.

case heard before the Grote Raad or high court of Mechelen in November 1470, two Hanse merchants cited the transit-shipping privilege as their defense in contesting a recent confiscation of nine bales of English cloths at Sluis. They further testified that they had not purchased the cloths, but had received them as security for a loan granted to a Danziger privateer, who had acquired them by plundering an English ship. The procurator-general of Flanders retorted that the Hanse privilege was no longer valid because the Hansards had forfeited all rights by repeated "abuses" in frequently "importing" English cloths, because Duke Charles had never reconfirmed it, and because the existing ban on English cloth had expressly abolished all exceptions. In its verdict, the Grote Raad rejected all the procurator-general's arguments and then expressly reaffirmed the Hanse transit-shipping privilege. Finally it returned the stolen cloths to their rightful English owners![56] Shortly after, in 1471–72, when Cologne was temporarily suspended from the League, its merchants were forced to request special licenses to continue shipping English cloths through Flanders. After much difficulty, they finally obtained ducal licenses; but even so, overzealous Flemish officials still confiscated some of their cloths.[57] Finally, in June 1477, the Council of Flanders revoked the confiscation of English cloths from some Hanse merchants at Bruges and overturned their conviction by agreeing with their contention that they were shipping the cloths in transit, not trying to import them into Flanders.[58]

These Flemish suspicions, a veritable obsession, that the Hanse were deviously misusing their transit-shipping privilege to market English cloths in Flanders have not been proved in either the courts of law or of history. Nevertheless, the history of these incidents is very important for demonstrating how rigorously, tenaciously, and continuously the Flemish sought to enforce their cloth ban during these two centuries. For surely no one can suppose that the Flemish would have so persecuted their very best customers, while only indifferently or capriciously enforcing the ban against other merchants. Indeed, had the Hanse, with their vast markets, their shipping and mercantile services, gone over entirely to the English

56. Brulez, "Engels laken," pp. 18–20 (citing proceedings of the Grote Raad van Mechelen in the Algemeen Rijksarchief. His interpretation, however, differs from mine.)

57. H. J. Smit, ed., *Bronnen tot de geschiedenis van den handel met Engeland, Schotland, en Ierland*, 1150–1485, 1st ser., 2 vols. (The Hague, 1928), II, 1061, no. 1661; Bruno Kuske, ed., *Quellen zur Geschichte des Kölner Handels und Verkehrs im Mittelalter*, 2 vols. (Bonn, 1917–23), II, 289, no. 577; 293, no. 585; Stein, *Hansisches Urkundenbuch*, X, 100–01, no. 106; Goswin von der Ropp, ed., *Hanserecesse, 1431–1476*, 2nd ser., 7 vols. (Leipzig, 1876–92), VI, 409, no. 437; Dollinger, *La Hanse*, pp. 375–81.

58. Stein, *Hansisches Urkundenbuch*, X, 374–76, no. 562; cf. Brulez, "Engels laken," pp. 9–10.

cloth trade at the outset, they would have quickly doomed the Flemish draperies. Nor, on the other hand, is it logical to suppose that the Hanse or other foreign merchants would risk trading in English cloths in Flanders, when the costs of confiscation and fines for *each* piece could amount to more than a skilled artisan's annual income, and when they could buy or sell English cloths so easily in adjacent regions of the Low Countries.

Indeed the quite astounding growth of the English cloth trade to Holland, Zealand, and Brabant again affords proof that the Flemish enforced their ban effectively enough to compel the English to seek alternative outlets. For initially these provinces were far less promising cloth markets than Flanders, which remained the hub of northern trade and finance until the late fifteenth century. English cloth was particularly welcomed by those shipping and commercial towns that had no cloth industry of their own to protect: first, beginning in the 1350s, by the Zealand towns of Zierikzee and Middelburg; and then especially by Antwerp, at least after Flanders returned this town to Brabant in 1406. The very next year, those London merchants trading at Antwerp were given a royal charter to organize themselves as the famous Company of Merchants Adventurers, which would come to dominate the entire English cloth trade.[59] By at least 1406, moreover, Leyden, Holland's chief cloth producer, had reacted vigorously to this new threat by banning any import or sale of English cloths within its jurisdiction and forbidding its citizens to handle those cloths anywhere.[60]

Then, after the Anglo-Burgundian Treaty of Troyes of May 1420, English cloth imports grew so large and so rapidly that the drapery towns of Holland and Brabant began clamoring for the same general protection that the Flemish towns had so long enjoyed. In 1426 and 1427, they met together several times at Mechelen to discuss ways of banning English cloths from their lands.[61] The next year, on July 25, 1428, Duke Philip the Good issued just such a general prohibition for the counties of Holland, Zealand, and Friesland. Only one month later, his cousin and protégé Duke Philip of St. Pol issued the same ban on English cloth for the duchy of Brabant.[62] Since Philip the Good's acquisition of Holland and Zealand,

59. N. J. M. Kerling, *Commercial Relations of Holland and Zealand with England from the Late 13th Century to the Close of the Middle Ages* (Leyden, 1954), pp. 73–76; Van der Wee, *Antwerp Market*, II, 1–28; Oskar De Smedt, *De Engelse natie te Antwerpen in der XVIe eeuw*, 2 vols. (Antwerp, 1950), I, 62–64.

60. Nicolaas Posthumus, ed., *Bronnen tot de geschiedenis van de Leidsche textielnijverheid, 1333–1795*, 6 vols. (The Hague, 1910–22), I, 59, no. 58. Leyden's ban was reissued in May 1446 (213–14, no. 166) and January 1459 (360, no. 312).

61. Posthumus, *Leidsche textielnijverheid*, I, 116–18, no. 102. See table 4 for English cloth exports.

62. Frans Van Mieris, ed., *Groot charterboek der graven van Holland en van Zeeland*, 4 vols. (Leyden, 1754–56),

ratified only on July 3 by the Treaty of Delft, had depended on the support of the Dutch towns, perhaps they had exacted the cloth bans as their price for that support.[63] But Philip showed little interest in enforcing the Dutch ban. Nor did he strive to enforce the ban in Brabant, after he inherited that neighboring duchy in August 1430. On the contrary, he soon succumbed to the furious protests from the Middelburg and Antwerp merchants, the Cologne Hanse, and the English government by allowing the two cloth bans to lapse, shortly before March 1431.[64]

In the view of most historians, however, once Duke Philip had effectively acquired the better part of the Low Countries and set about to unify them into a cohesive Burgundian "state," he again took up the banner of protectionism by totally prohibiting English cloths from all the Burgundian Low Countries on June 19, 1434. According to these same authorities, the duke's "reissues" of this cloth ban in 1439, 1447, and 1464, and Maximilian's ban of 1494 demonstrate the ultimate futility of this policy.[65] Since I have already written at length on these later cloth bans and Anglo-Burgundian commercial relations in general, there is no need to repeat that complex history here.[66] The viewpoint just outlined, however, is so misleading, in my opinion, and so pervasive, especially because it has Pirenne's imprimatur, that my chief conclusions and some additional research must be summarized in order to place Flemish protectionism in its proper perspective.

First, Duke Philip the Good did not himself intend any of his three general cloth bans of 1434–39, 1447–52, and 1464–67 to serve as permanent instruments of protectionism, even if many drapers undoubtedly

IV, 923–24; Smit, *Bronnen, 1150–1485*, I, 627, no. 1012; Stadsarchief te Leuven, Chartes, no. 1358; also no. 1235, ff. 69^{v}–70^{v} (August 25, 1428).

63. Munro, *Wool, Cloth, and Gold*, pp. 7–9, 67–70; Vaughan, *Philip the Good*, pp. 31–50.

64. W. S. Unger, ed., *Bronnen tot de geschiedenis van Middelburg*, 3 vols. (The Hague, 1923–31), II, 303, no. 217; Smit, *Bronnen, 1150–1485*, II, 625, no. 1012; 635, no. 1024; Koppmann, *Recesse, 1236–1430*, VIII, 365–66, no. 558; Kuske, *Kölner Handels*, I, 270, no. 791; 276, no. 800; *Calendar of Patent Rolls* (*Henry VI*), *1429–36*, p. 26; E. R. Daenell, *Die Blütezeit der deutschen Hanse*, 2 vols. (Berlin, 1905), I, 389.

65. Pirenne, *Belgique*, I, 352–53, 467–69; and Henri Pirenne "Une Crise industrielle au XVI siècle: La Draperie urbaine et la 'nouvelle draperie' en Flandre," in *Histoire économique de l'occident mediéval*, ed. E. Coornaert (Paris, 1951), pp. 624–26 (also cf. pp. 356–57); Schanz, *Englische Handelspolitik*, I, 441–43; De Smedt, *Engelse natie*, I, 48–49; Kerling, *Commercial Relations*, pp. 80–90; M. R. Thielmans, *Bourgogne et Angleterre: Relations politiques et économiques, 1435–1467* (Brussels, 1966), pp. 60–61, 209; Wilfred Brulez, "Bruges and Antwerp in the Fifteenth and Sixteenth Centuries: An Antithesis?" *Acta Historiae Neerlandicae, 6* (1973), 15–16.

66. "Bruges and the Abortive Staple in English Cloth," *Revue belge de philologie et d'histoire, 44* (1966), 1137–59; "The Costs of Anglo-Burgundian Inter-dependence," *Rev. belge de philologie et d'histoire, 46* (1968), 1228–38; "An Economic Aspect of the Collapse of the Anglo-Burgundian Alliance, 1428–1442," *English Historical Review, 85* (1970), 225–44; *Wool, Cloth, and Gold*, chaps. 3–6.

hoped that they would be retained for this purpose. Instead, the duke, the Four Members, and the Dutch and Brabantine town assemblies explicitly stated that the bans were retaliatory weapons designed to force the English to revoke or at least to moderate some draconian regulations imposed on the wool trade from 1429, known as the Calais Staple Bullion and Partition Ordinances. In the Burgundian view, these laws, strengthened in 1433 and restored partially in 1445 and 1463, threatened both to cripple their drapery industries and to drain their lands of precious metals by steeply increasing wool prices, forbidding the use of credit, and requiring full payment in bullion and English coin alone.

Second, the Burgundian bans themselves and the English reaction to them provide further evidence for the continuous enforcement of the Flemish cloth ban. In each of Philip's and Maximilian's general edicts, an article permitted all foreign merchants a forty-day period of grace to dispose of their English cloths, "affin qu'ilz n'ayent cause de prétendre excusacion ou ignorance de ceste nostre presente ordonnance," in all of the Burgundian Low Countries, "reservé en nostre pays de Flandres, où lesdiz draps et fillez d'Angleterre ont esté bannis et deffenduz anciennement."[67] Then, after the bans of 1447 and 1464, the English Parliament threatened to prohibit all imports from the Burgundian Low Countries unless Duke Philip freely restored the English cloth trade to all its former markets, in Holland, Zealand, and Brabant especially. But Flanders is never once mentioned in these ultimatums, nor in the accompanying royal letters, even though one document meticulously lists the thirteen principalities held by the duke that had to be reopened to the English cloth trade.[68]

Third, except for some minor concessions gained from the English in 1452 and 1467, Philip the Good's cloth-ban policy itself was a failure. Indeed, after the first ban Philip also suffered a humiliating defeat in the Anglo-Burgundian war of 1436–39, and that war was only terminated by a trade treaty of September 1439 that granted the English very generous commercial privileges. Shortly afterward, on December 1, the Four

67. L. P. Gachard, ed., *Collection de documents inédits concernant l'histoire de Belgique*, 3 vols. (Brussels, 1833–35), II, 180–81, no. 19 (1464); Charles Piot, ed., *Inventaire des chartes de la ville de Léau* (Brussels, 1879), 26–28, no. 8 (1434: Flemish text); Raimond Van Marle, ed., *Le Comté de Hollande sous Philippe le Bon* (The Hague, 1908); pp. xcviii–cx, no. 37 (1447, misdated 1446); Schanz, *Englische Handelspolitik*, II, 191–93, no. 5 (April 1494: partial text in French); 193–94, no. 6 (January 1495); Diegerick, *Archives d'Ypres*, IV, 233–34, no. 1278 (April 1494: complete in modern French).

68. N. H. Nicolas, ed., *Proceedings and Ordinances of the Privy Council of England*, 6 vols. (London, 1834–37), VI, 69–73 (March 1449), 76–85 (July 1449); *Rotuli Parliamentorum*, V, 150: no. 20 (1449), 201: no. 57

Members had Philip formally reaffirm the standing Flemish cloth ban, evidently for fear that the treaty's "freedom of trade" provisions would open Flanders to an influx of English cloth.[69]

While the repeated failures of the general Burgundian bans have to be attributed to a complex combination of political, military, and economic factors, a very prominent reason, as in the collapse of the two 1428 bans, was the bitterly trenchant opposition encountered in Holland, Zealand, and Brabant. Too many people in too many towns there had become dependent on the English cloth trade in some form: in importing and transshipping, in cloth dyeing and finishing, in tailoring, in wholesaling, and in re-exporting. Too much of the entrepôt trade of the Brabant Fairs of Antwerp and Bergen-op-Zoom, attracting merchants from all over Europe, was being based on those cloths. The cloth guilds and drapery towns of Holland and Brabant, on the other hand, simply lacked the economic paramountcy, the cohesive organization, and the political power of their Flemish counterparts.[70] Finally, it should be remembered that in Flanders local officials policed a traditionally sanctioned domestic policy. In the recently acquired Burgundian provinces, however, the policing was done by ducal officials, who were generally considered to be foreign gendarmes. Indeed they were not always tactful. Though forays of Burgundian troops may have succeeded in confiscating many English cloths, they also ensured the public rejection of ducal policy in these lands.[71]

The ultimate failure of Philip the Good's cloth-ban policy was a cruel blow to the urban draperies of the Burgundian Low Countries. If the duke's concern had been primarily bullionist, certainly the drapery towns everywhere had had a strong protectionist interest in these general cloth bans. They evidently hoped that even if the bans failed to force a revocation of the Calais Staple ordinances, then at least the prohibition could be maintained to exclude English cloth permanently from all the Low Countries. But when the English finally did renounce the Calais ordinances

---

(1450), 565–66: no. 53 (1465); *Statutes of the Realm*, II, 345–46 (27 Hen. VI c. 1, 1449); 353–54 (28 Hen. VI c. 1, 1450); 411–13 (4 Ed. IV c. 5, 1465).

69. Gilliodts-Van Severen, *Archives de Bruges*, V, 189–90, no. 1015; Munro, *Wool, Cloth, and Gold*, pp. 117–20.

70. Van der Wee, *Antwerp Market*, II, 26–55, 70; De Smedt, *Engelse natie*, I, 62–65; Kerling, *Commercial Relations*, pp. 76–83, 170–71; Van Uytven and Blockmans, "Constitutions," pp. 403–09. Individual towns, such as Leyden and Mechelen, however, maintained their own bans against English cloth. Cf. n. 60 above and Thielemans, *Bourgogne et Angleterre*, pp. 205–06.

71. Munro, *Wool, Cloth, and Gold*, pp. 109, 115–16 (1436); 136 (1447–49); 146 (1452); 165 (1465). Kerling, *Commercial Relations*, pp. 76–77.

in the 1470s, in return for Burgundian aid in restoring Edward IV to his throne, the half-century of damages could not be undone.[72] As tables 13.4 and 13.5 indicate, the output of most of the Burgundian draperies plummeted catastrophically from the late 1420s, while English cloth exports rapidly expanded, evidently gaining an insuperable price advantage in overseas markets. Then, from the mid-1440s to the mid-1460s, the English cloth trade itself suffered a sharp setback from an unusually severe cyclical depression in northern Europe. But thereafter the English cloth trade quickly recovered, then soared higher than ever before to become an irresistible force, sweeping almost all before it by 1500. Even in 1487, a merchant likened English cloth imports into Brabant and Holland to an *inundacioni maris immensi*.[73] With competition in the luxury woolens market all but destroyed, it is hardly surprising to note from table 13.5 that, by the early sixteenth century, average English cloth prices were rising faster than the Flemish cloth prices, though still remaining well below the latter.

The nature of the English cloth-trade victory helps to explain in retrospect the rationale of the Burgundian drapery towns, the Flemish as much as the Dutch and Brabantine, in promoting and not merely supporting their duke's cloth-ban policy. First, even without forbidden Flanders, the Low Countries offered one of the largest and wealthiest markets in Europe. Second, as Herman Van der Wee has argued, the Brabant Fairs gave the English cloth trade the opportunity for the decisive breakthrough it required: a direct link to the large Rhenish, South German, and central European markets. From the 1450s, those fairs became even more important for the English cloth-merchants when political conflicts led to their exclusion from Gascony, the Baltic, and Scandinavia; and especially when the fairs' rapid growth permitted Antwerp finally to displace Bruges as the capital of northern trade. A third and equally compelling reason for the cloth ban was to deny the English cloth trade access to the technical expertise of the Dutch and Brabantine drapery towns in those dyeing and finishing processes that truly determined luxury quality. Once the English were free to utilize both the industrial and mercantile expertise of the Low Countries they were able to rob the Burgundian draperies of their chief comparative advantage.[74]

72. Munro, *Wool, Cloth, and Gold*, pp. 175–78, 181–85. Even in January 1451, Duke Philip's Brabant councillors had advised him that "non obstant les deffenses faites et publiéz sur lesdiz draps d'Engleterre, le fait de la drapperie es bonnes villes pardeça n'est en riens amendé" (A.R.A., Rekenkamer, no. 17, f. 72^{v}).

73. Dietrich Schäfer, ed., *Hanserecesse, 1477–1530*, 3rd ser., 9 vols. (Leipzig, 1881–1913), III, 105 (also cited in Pirenne, "Crise industrielle," p. 625).

74. J. A. Van Houtte, "La Genèse du grand marché international d'Anvers à la fin du moyen âge,"

At the same time, it may well be that market demand in the new, early modern European economy was less favorable than before to the most luxurious, costly type of woolens, which now had to face stronger competition from Italian silks as well. In view of all the circumstances, even apart from those of the English victory, the traditional urban draperies might have been better advised at this time to switch to various cheaper-line textiles. The sixteenth-century successes first of such nouvelles draperies as Armentières and Neuve-Eglise (Nieuwkerke), manufacturing lower-priced imitations of traditional woolens from Spanish wools especially, and then of the cheap, worsted-type sayetteries of Hondschoote, Arras, and Lille offer support for such a contention.[75] But the very guild structure and urban regulation that were necessary to ensure standards of luxury quality, which indeed had helped sustain the traditional Flemish draperies from the early fourteenth century, now prevented the required industrial transformation in the chief towns. The obdurate adherence to a protectionism that had lost most of its raison d'être, except for preserving the domestic Flemish market, now proved self-defeating for Flanders as a whole by channelling the victorious English cloth trade into adjacent towns of the Low Countries. Antwerp especially grew steadily richer from both the development of ancillary industries and a European-wide entrepôt commerce that this trade fostered.

In Bruges, however, not all the guilds had been blind to the true significance of this radical change in the towns' fortunes. The dyers, cloth-finishers, and merchants had evidently broken ranks with the weavers as early as the 1480s. In April 1489 the Bruges magistrates ruled that the "free trade" provisions of the recent Anglo-Flemish treaty gave the English the legal right to import their own cloths. Some may then have done so.[76] The following February Bruges also agreed in principle to a Spanish request for the right to ship English cloths purchased at Antwerp via Sluis and promised to seek formal approval from the archduke.[77] But

---

Revue belge de philologie et d'histoire, 19 (1940), 87–126; Van der Wee, *Antwerp Market*, II, 51, 70, 73–142; De Smedt, *Engelse natie*, II, 353–55; G. Asaert, "Handel in kleurstoffen op de Antwerpse markt tijdens de XVe eeuw," *Bijdragen en mededelingen betreffende de geschiedenis der Nederlanden, 88* (1973), 377–402; Munro, "Bruges," pp. 1143–44, 1147–59.

75. Cf. Coornaert, *Hondschoote*, pp. 10–41, 236–54, 335–42, and his "Draperies rurales, draperies urbaines: L'Evolution de l'industrie flamande au moyen âge et au XVIe siècle," *Revue belge de philologie et d'histoire, 28* (1950), 59–96; Pirenne, "Crise industrielle," pp. 621–42; and n. 84 below.

76. Gilliodts-Van Severen, *Archives de Bruges*, VI, 316–31, no. 1234 (treaty of April 3, 1489); Gilliodts-Van Severen, *Estaple de Bruges*, II, 266–68, no. 1250 (judicial decree of April 6); 265, no. 1248; 274, no. 1255 (possible English cloth imports, 1489–90).

77. Louis Gilliodts-Van Severen, ed., *Cartulaire de l'ancien consulat d'Espagne à Bruges*, 2 vols. (Bruges, 1901), I, *1280 à 1550*, 145 (February 5, 1490).

any transit-shipping, let alone a regular cloth trade, became impossible with the blockade of Bruges during the Flemish revolt of 1489–92. Once peace had been restored, Bruges on its own energetically sought from the English an agreement to staple English cloths there, only to be thwarted by an Anglo-Hapsburg conflict that culminated in Archduke Maximilian's cloth-trade ban of April 1494.[78] English cloth imports were again permitted in September 1495, but only after being stapled at Bergen-op-Zoom and only for wholesale trade, finishing, and re-export. Flanders was explicitly excluded from even this limited trade at the behest of the Four Members, who, with other drapery towns, had evidently succeeded temporarily in reimposing a protectionist policy for all the Low Countries.[79] By this time the Spanish merchants, after having twice more requested those transit rights for English cloth, had given up that vain quest.[80] Finally, when the Anglo-Hapsburg treaty of May 1499 forced the Low Countries to restore the former free trade in English cloth, it also reaffirmed the traditional Flemish cloth ban.[81]

Then in October 1501, in another seeming volte-face, Archduke Philip the Fair decreed that Bruges was now to be the official staple for English cloth. The provisions, however, were most restrictive. English cloths were to be imported there only for re-export, without even being dyed or finished, as the cloth-finishers had earlier requested. This emasculated decree was ignored by all, and Flanders returned to its former rigid protectionism.[82] Thirty years later, in October 1531, after the Bruges government had tried to establish various new textile trades, often with large subsidies, it revived the English cloth staple proposal. Again Bruges

78. Schanz, *Englische Handelspolitik*, II, 191–93, no. 5; 193–94, no. 6; Gilliodts-Van Severen, *Estaple de Bruges*, II, 294, no. 1281; Munro, "Bruges," pp. 1150–53. In January 1494, Ghent, Ypres, Lille, and Menen apparently appealed to Archduke Philip to nullify Bruges's cloth-staple proposal and, possibly, to reinstate the general cloth ban in the Low Countries. Cf. Willem Blockmans, ed., *Handelingen van de leden en van de staten van Vlaanderen* (*5 januari 1477–26 september 1506*), 2 vols. (Brussels, 1973–76), II, 669–70, nos. 452–53.

79. See A.R.A., Rek., no. 49,851, ff. 1^{v}–2^{v}; and nos. 49,850–55 and 23,250–51 for English cloth imports via the Bergen-op-Zoom toll. That Flemish exclusion was reaffirmed in August 1497 when Archduke Philip promised to abolish the toll on English cloth. (Later, however, it was only reduced.) Gilliodts-Van Severen, *Estaple de Bruges*, II, 312, no. 1300.

80. Gilliodts-Van Severen, *Consulat d'Espagne*, I, 165 (September 1493), 173 (September 1494), 186–89 (treaty of August 1497).

81. Thomas Rymer, ed., *Foedera, conventiones, literae, et acta publica*, 12 vols. (2d ed., London, 1709–12), XII, 713–20 (especially p. 716).

82. Octave Delepierre, ed., *Précis analytique des documents des archives de la Flandre occidentale à Bruges*, 2 vols. (Bruges, 1840–43), I: 3, 5–15; Gilliodts-Van Severen, *Consulat d'Espagne*, I, 199–203. For examples of confiscations of English cloths in 1520 and 1522, see n. 50 above and Gilliodts-Van Severen, *Estaple de Bruges*, II, 554–55, no. 1515.

was thwarted by the rest of the Four Members.[83] By this time, however, princely support for the cloth ban had clearly evaporated. The following February, Marie of Hungary, sister of Emperor Charles V and governess of the Low Countries, instructed her ambassadors that, "if the English complain about edicts banning their cloths, you are to reply that the towns have the power to enact such laws for their own regulative administration [*pollice*], and that they do so without the sanction and seal of His Majesty."[84] Then, in August 1540, Charles V submitted the cloth-staple proposal once more to the Four Members. Ghent and Ypres remained adamantly opposed, but this time the Franc de Bruges lent its support to enable the emperor finally to grant Bruges, for at least three years, the long sought re-export staple in English cloths. Furthermore, this decree expressly permitted the dyeing and finishing of such cloths, though certainly not for domestic sale.[85] The protectionist opposition does not seem to have accepted this decree with good grace. Just a month later, at Bruges's urgent request, Charles V issued another ordinance sternly forbidding Flemish officials from interfering with the legal transport of English cloths into and out of the Bruges staple.[86] Although the staple ordinance was extended for another three years in August 1543, there is no evidence to indicate that this finishing trade in English cloth was any more successful than Bruges's various hot-house new draperies.[87] Certainly it did nothing to deflect the English cloth trade from Antwerp, at the very time when both the city and the trade were approaching their apogee. Bruges had thus escaped from the collective will of the Four Members and the dominance of the urban drapery guilds a century too late.

83. Gilliodts-Van Severen, *Estaple de Bruges*, II, 617, no. 1376; 679–80, no. 1637.

84. Schanz, *Englische Handelspolitik*, II, 262, no. 32 (February 27, 1532).

85. M. J. Lameere and H. Simont, eds., *Recueil des ordonnances des Pays Bas, deuxième sér.: 1506–1700*, 7 vols. (Brussels, 1893–1960), IV, *1537 à 1543*, 222–24 (Flemish text); Gilliodts-Van Severen, *Estaple de Bruges*, II, 689, no. 1644; 691–94, no. 1647 (August 1540: French text).

86. Gilliodts-Van Severen, *Estaple de Bruges*, II, 694–95, no. 1647 (September 10, 1540). The Ghent aldermen in particular may have been angered by Charles V's letter to them defending his approval of the Bruges cloth staple, especially by his statement that "les drapiers de nostre pays et conté de Flandres n'y sauroyent avoir prejudice n'y interest meismes en recepvrant prouffit pour la generalle et estroicte deffense de l'usaige et portaige des draps d'Angleterre." He did promise, however, to reconsider his edict should the cloth staple prove harmful to the Flemish draperies. Schanz, *Englische Handelspolitik*, II, 277, no. 37 (August 10, 1540).

87. Gilliodts-Van Severen, *Estaple de Bruges*, II, 695, no. 1647 (August 10, 1543, with a schedule of rates for dyeing and finishing). Cf. J. A. Van Houtte, *Bruges: Essai d'histoire urbaine* (Brussels, 1967), pp. 88–92, 101–04. The one significant exception was the sayetterie established there in 1545. See n. 75 above.

Table 13.1

Decennial Averages of Domestic Prices of Medium- to High-Quality English Wools, and of Denizen and Alien Wool Export Duties, in Pounds Sterling, 1320–29 to 1490–99

Decade by Michaelmas Years	*Average Annual Domestic Prices of Selected Wools, in Pounds Sterling per Sack Weight* [a]	*Indices of Decennial Average Wool Prices. Average of 1400–24 = 100*	*Decennial Averages of Denizen Wool Export Duties in Shillings per Sack* [b]	*Denizen Wool Export Duties as a Percentage of Average Wool Prices*	*Decennial Averages of Alien Wool Export Duties in Shillings per Sack* [c]	*Alien Wool Export Duties as a Percentage of Average Wool Prices*
1320–29	7.451	134.7	10.9	7.3	14.2	9.6
1330–39	5.219	94.4	17.0	16.3	24.3	23.3
1340–49	4.785	86.5	47.3	49.4	55.7	58.2
1350–59	4.702	86.4	49.2	52.3	52.6	55.9
1360–69	6.022	108.9	42.5	35.3	45.8	38.0
1370–79	7.733	139.8	50.3	32.5	53.7	34.7
1380–89	5.756	104.1	49.8	43.3	53.3	46.3
1390–99	5.067	91.6	49.4	48.8	53.7	53.0
1400–09	5.814	105.1	50.6	43.5	60.6	52.1
1410–19	5.443	98.4	50.0	45.9	63.0	57.9
1420–29	4.998	90.4	42.9	42.9	59.6	59.7
1430–39	5.548	100.3	40.0	36.1	58.8	53.0
1440–49	5.384	97.4	40.0	37.2	63.3	58.8
1450–59	4.302	77.8	45.5	52.9	89.0	103.4
1460–69	5.150	93.1	45.4	44.1	94.7	92.0
1470–79	5.571[d]	100.7	40.6	36.4	78.6	70.5
1480–89	7.957[e]	143.9	40.0	25.1	76.7	48.2
1490–99	5.525[f]	99.9	40.0	36.2	76.7	69.4

Table 13.1 (*continued*)

SOURCES: T. H. Lloyd, *The Movement of Wool Prices in Medieval England* (Cambridge, 1973), pp. 40–44, cols. 3–5, 10–13; *Calendar of the Fine Rolls*, IV (*1327–1337*) to XXI (*1471–1485*); *Rotuli Parliamentorum*, II to V; F. R. Barnes, "The Taxation of Wool, 1327–1348," in *Finance and Trade under Edward III*, ed. G. Unwin (London, 1918), pp. 137–77; N.S.B. Gras, *The Early English Customs System* (Cambridge, Mass., 1918), pp. 76–80; E. M. Carus-Wilson and Olive Coleman, eds., *England's Export Trade, 1275–1547* (Oxford, 1963), pp. 194–96.

[a] Unweighted average price of wools from Hampshire (Winchester manors), Wiltshire and Berkshire Downs, Berkshire, Worcestershire, Cotswolds, Chilterns, Northeast Oxfordshire, and North Buckinghamshire. 1 sack = 26 stones = 52 cloves = 364 lb.

[b] Denizen wool export duties: the fixed customs of 6 s. 8 d. per sack plus variable subsidies.

[c] Alien wool export duties: the fixed customs of 10 s. 0 d. per sack plus variable subsidies.

[d] Average of prices of 1470, 1471, and 1478 only.

[e] Average of prices of 1480, 1481, 1482, 1484, and 1485 only.

[f] Average of prices of 1492, 1493, 1494, 1496, 1497, and 1499 only.

Table 13.2

Costs of Manufacturing Fine Black Cloths at Leuven, from English Staple Wools, in Pounds Groot Flemish, in 1434 and 1442

Cost of Manufacturing Fine Black Woolen Cloths, 30 ells long[a]	*November 1434* *Pounds Groot Flemish*	*Percentage of Prefinishing Costs*	*Percentage of Total Costs*	*November 1442* *Pounds Groot Flemish*	*Percentage of Prefinishing Costs*	*Percentage of Total Costs*
Cost of the wool	3.094[b]	76.2%	62.5%	2.288[d]	68.8%	55.1%
Other manufacturing costs before finishing	0.967[c]	23.8%	19.5%	1.039	31.2%	25.0%
Subtotal of prefinishing costs of production	4.061[c]	100.0%	82.0%	3.327	100.0%	80.1%
Dyeing and dressing	0.892[c]		18.0%	0.825		19.9%
Total cost of production	4.953		100.0%	4.152		100.0%
Total manufacturing costs exclusive of wool	1.859		37.5%	1.864		44.9%

Source: Stadsarchief te Leuven, Stadsrekeningen 1434–35 and 1442–43, nos. 5058, f. 34^{r} and 5072, f. 40^{v}–41^{r}. A reference to the latter is given in Raymond Van Uytven, *Stadsfinanciën en stadsekonomie te Leuven van de XIIde tot het einde der XVIde eeuw* (Brussels, 1961), p. 343.

[a] 30 ells by 9 quarter-ells wide = 20.850 meters by 1.564 meters [32.609 square meters] = 22.802 yards by 1.710 yards [38.991 square yards]. These were first-quality woolens purchased annually for the municipal rentmeesters and aldermen.

[b] From 1 sarplar of unspecified English wools, purchased at the Calais Staple, containing 5 *waghen* [= 2.5 sacks] and 32 *nagelen* [nails, cloves] = 2.856 sacks Flemish weight = 480.915 kg. = 1060.23 lb. avoirdupois = 2.913 sacks English weight. The wool was purchased for 237.16 rijnsguldens, which, at 68⅔ groot Brabant each, were worth £67.854 groot Brabant = £48.992 groot Flemish [since £1.000 groot Flemish = £1.385 groot Brabant]. Thus one sack of wool English weight was worth £16.818 groot Flemish. From the 2.913 sacks were manufactured 15.833 cloths, or 5.435 cloths per sack. Hence each cloth required 66.97 lb. wool, less waste wools.

[c] Only total manufacturing costs, exclusive of wool, were given. Finishing costs were estimated as 18 percent of total costs by taking the average proportion of total costs accounted for by the dyeing and dressing of such cloths at Leuven in 1415, 1417, 1442, and 1444–47. That proportion corresponds closely to the average cost of finishing second-quality cloths of English wools at Leuven from 1435 to 1444: 17.2 percent of total costs.

[d] From 2 sarplars of English Lindsey wools, purchased at Calais, containing 10 waghen and 21 nagelen = 5.233 sacks Flemish weight = 881.17 kg. = 1942.65 lb. av. = 5.337 sacks English weight. The wools were purchased for 173.6875 English gold nobles = 472.81 rijnsguldens, which, at 54 d groot Brabant each, were worth £106.382 groot Brabant = £70.921 groot Flemish [since £1.000 groot Flemish = £1.500 groot Brabant] = £57.896 sterling. Thus one sack of English weight was worth £13.289 groot Flemish or £10.848 sterling. From the 5.337 sacks were manufactured 31 cloths, or 5.809 cloths per sack. Hence each cloth required 62.67 lb. wool, less waste wools.

Table 13.3

Comparative Textile Prices

PART I. *The Purchase of Textiles for the Royal Wardrobe of Henry VI, Michaelmas 1438–Michaelmas 1439*

Textile Type	*Price of the Piece in Pounds Sterling*	*Value of 24 Yards in Pounds Sterling*	*Value of the Yard in Shillings*	*Percentage of the Mean Value of Short Dyed Broadcloths*
A. *English Woolens and Worsteds*				
1. *Cloths Dyed in Grain*: 30 yds by 7 quarters				
a) *Scarlets*				
highest price	28.500	22.800	19.00s	896
mean of 5.808 cloths	18.035	14.428	12.02s	567
lowest price	14.125	11.300	9.42s	444
b) *Violet, Murrey, and Sanguine Cloths*				
highest price	17.250	13.800	11.50s	542
mean of 3.967 cloths	15.210	12.168	10.14s	478
lowest price	12.000	9.600	8.00s	377
2. *Long Dyed Broadcloths*: 30 yds by 7 quarters				
highest price	14.000	11.200	9.33s	440
mean of 24.183 cloths	7.462	5.969	4.97s	235
lowest price	6.000	4.800	4.00s	189
3. *Short Dyed Broadcloths*: 24 yds by 7 quarters				
highest price	4.000	4.000	3.33s	157
mean of 31.354 cloths	2.545	2.545	2.12s	100
lowest price	1.400	1.400	1.17s	55

Table 13.3 (*continued*)

Textile Type	*Price of the Piece in Pounds Sterling*	*Value of 24 Yards in Pounds Sterling*	*Value of the Yard in Shillings*	*Percentage of the Mean Value of Short Dyed Broadcloths*
4. *Ray Cloths (panni radiati)*: 24 yds by 7 qtrs				
highest price	2.400	2.400	2.00s	94
mean of 10.510 cloths	2.281	2.281	1.90s	90
lowest price	2.200	2.200	1.83s	86
5. *Kerseys Dyed*: 18 yards by 4¼ quarters				
highest price	2.700	3.600	3.00s	141
mean of 3.598 cloths	1.345	1.793	1.49s	70
lowest price	0.750	1.000	0.83s	39
6. *Straits and Kendale Dozens*: 12 yards by 4 quarters				
highest price	0.600	1.200	1.00s	47
mean of 10.625 cloths	0.329	0.658	0.55s	26
lowest price	0.150	0.300	0.25s	12
7. *Worsteds*				
"large" worsteds[a]	1.750			
"medium" worsteds[b]	0.900			
"small" worsted[c]	0.550			
worsted[d]	[0.437]	0.350	0.29s	14
B. *Silk Fabrics*				
1. *Velvets*: 8 yards				
highest price	9.333	28.000	23.33s	1100
mean of 23.703 cloths	6.037	18.112	15.09s	712
lowest price	5.000	15.000	12.50s	589

Table 13.3 (*continued*)

2. *Damask*: 6 yards				
red damask	3.625	14.500	12.08s	570
white damask	3.600	14.400	12.00s	566
3. *Satin*: 8 yards				
purple satin	3.600	10.800	9.00s	424
plain satin	3.500	10.500	8.75s	413
C. *Tartaryn (Tartarium, Cloth of Tars)*: 10 yds				
highest price	1.167	2.800	2.33s	110
mean of 17.325 cloths	1.094	2.626	2.19s	103
lowest price	1.000	2.400	2.00s	94
D. *Linens*				
1. *Linens of Reims*				
highest price		3.600	3.00s	141
mean of 122.5 yards		3.411	2.84s	134
lowest price		3.000	2.50s	118
2. *Linens of Champagne*				
highest price		2.400	2.00s	94
mean of 124.5 yards		2.223	1.85s	87
lowest price		2.000	1.67s	79
3. *Linens of Holland*				
highest price		3.100	2.58s	122
mean of 107.5 yards		2.912	2.43s	144
lowest price		2.800	2.33s	110
4. *Linens of Flanders*				
highest price		1.900	1.58s	75
mean of 104.0 yards		1.206	1.01s	47

Table 13.3 (*continued*)

Textile Type	*Price of the Piece in Pounds Sterling*	*Value of 24 Yards in Pounds Sterling*	*Value of the Yard in Shillings*	*Percentage of the Mean Value of Short Dyed Broadcloths*
lowest price		0.650	0.54s	26
5. *Linens of Brabant*				
highest price		0.700	0.58s	28
mean of 163.5 yards		0.632	0.53s	25
lowest price		0.500	0.42s	20

SOURCE: Public Record Office, King's Remembrancer Exchequer, Wardrobe Accounts, E. 101/409/2, ff. 6^r–11^v.

[a] Possibly worsted "beddes de le pluis grande assise," officially measuring 14 yards by 4 yards [= 56 square yards].

[b] Possibly worsted "beddes de la mene assise," officially measuring 12 yards by 3 yards [= 36 square yards].

[c] Possibly worsted "beddes de la pluis petit assise," officially measuring 10 yards by 2.5 yards [= 25 square yards].

[d] Possibly roll worsteds, officially measuring 30 yards by 0.5 yard [= 15 square yards]; but possibly monk's cloth [12 yards by 2.5 yards = 30 square yards], or chanon cloths [6 yards by 2 yards = 12 square yards]; or double worsteds [10 yards by 2.5 yards = 25 square yards], or half-doubles [6 yards by 2.5 yards = 15 square yards]. The prices were given in yards only, for this particular worsted. These dimensions should be compared to those of the short broadcloth of assize: 24 yards long by 7 quarter-yards wide = 42 square yards [1 yard of the cloth assize = 37 inches.] The descriptions and dimensions of these textiles have been taken from Statutes 20 Henrici c. 10 (1441–42) and 7 Edwardi IV c. 1 (1467) in *Statutes of the Realm*, II, 322–23, 419–20.

Table 13.3 (*continued*)

PART II. *The Purchases of Domestic Woolen Cloths by Municipal Governments of Flanders and Brabant for the Garbing of Their Officials on Ceremonial Occasions, 1438–1443*

Town of Manufacture and Type	*Year*	*Length in Ells*[a]	*Price of the Piece in Pounds Groot Flemish*	*Value in Pounds Sterling*[b]	*Value of 24 Yards in Pounds Sterling*	*Value of a Yard in Shillings*	*Percentage of Mean Value of English Dyed Short Broadcloths*
A. *Traditional Urban Draperies*							
1. *Ypres (Ieper)*							
scarlet	1440	35	12.567	11.384	10.480	8.73s	412
black broadcloth	1439	35	7.000	6.341	5.838	4.86s	229
black smallcloth	1439	30½	3.050	2.763	2.919	2.43s	115
2. *Bruges*							
scarlet	1441	33	11.000	9.964	9.729	8.10s	382
black broadcloth	1439	33	8.000	7.247	7.076	5.90s	278
3. *Ghent*							
dickedinnen	1439	30	7.000	6.341	6.811	5.68s	268
strijpte laken (ray)	1439	30	5.600	5.073	5.449	4.54s	214
small dickedinnen	1439	?	3.000	2.717			
4. *Mechelen*							
long blue	1438	30	7.275	6.590	7.191	5.99s	283
blue	1440	30	5.923	5.365	5.854	4.88s	230
short red	1440	24	1.667	1.510	2.060	1.72s	81
5. *Leuven*							
1st quality	1442[c]	30	4.152	3.761	4.069	3.39s	160
2d quality	1439[d]	30	3.230	2.926	3.165	2.64s	124
3d quality	1439[c]	30	2.646	2.397	2.593	2.16s	94

Table 13.3 (*continued*)

Sources: For Ypres (Ieper), Algemeen Rijksarchief van België, Rekenkamer, no. 38,663, f. 35^{v}; for Bruges, A.R.A., Rek., no. 32,492, f. 18^{r}, and Stadsarchief te Brugge, Stadsrekeningen 1440–41, f. 25^{v}; for Ghent, Stadsarchief te Gent, Stadsrekeningen 400:15(5), f. 218^{v}; for Mechelen (Malines), Stadsarchief te Mechelen, Stadsrekeningen I:113, f. 201^{r-v}; I: 115, f. 118^{v}; for Leuven (Louvain), Stadsarchief te Leuven, no. 5067, f. 41^{v}; no. 5072, f. 40^{v}.

[a] The various ells had the following lengths:

(i) Ell of Flanders = 0.700 meter = 27.559 inches = 0.745 yard of the English cloth assize of 37 inches.

(ii) Ell of Brabant (Leuven) = 0.695 meter = 27.362 inches = 0.740 yard of the English cloth assize.

(iii) Ell of Mechelen = 0.689 meter = 27.126 inches = 0.733 yard of the English cloth assize.

[b] Prices in pounds groot Flemish and Brabant were converted into pounds sterling according to the relative silver contents of the moneys-of-account. From October 1433 to August 1464, the ratios were £1.500 groot Brabant = £1.000 groot Flemish = £0.90583 sterling; and thus £1.000 sterling = £1.104 groot Flemish = £1.656 groot Brabant.

[c] Leuven cloths made from English wools of the best quality, purchased for the rentmeesters and aldermen.

[d] Leuven cloths made from English wools of lesser quality, purchased for the middle-rank civic officials.

[e] Leuven cloths made from domestic or non-English wools, purchased for the lower rank civic officials.

Town of Manufacture and Type	*Year*	*Length in Ells*[a]	*Price of the Piece in Pounds Groot Flemish*	*Value in Pounds Sterling*[b]	*Value of 24 Yards in Pounds Sterling*	*Value of a Yard in Shillings*	*Percentage of Mean Value of English Dyed Short Broadcloths*
B. *Nouvelles Draperies*							
1. *Wervik*							
dark green	1439[c]	27	3.900	3.533	4.216	3.51s	166
green	1442[d]	20	3.083	2.792	4.498	3.75s	177
fine black	1446[e]	20	5.750	5.209	8.392	6.99s	330
2. *Kortrijk (Courtrai)*							
red	1438[d]	30	3.500	3.170	3.405	2.84s	134
fine black	1441	20	3.083	2.793	4.500	3.75s	177

Table 13.3 (*continued*)

3. *Menen*							
fine black broadcloth	1440[e]	30	6.000	5.435	5.837	4.86s	214
perse	1443	30	4.600	4.167	4.476	3.73s	164
4. *Nieuwkerke (Neuve-Eglise)*							
medley cloth	1439[c]	30	2.125	1.925	2.068	1.72s	81
5. *Hesdin*							
green	1439[c]	30	3.000	2.717	2.918	2.43s	115
6. *Niepkerke*							
red	1440[c]	30	2.125	1.925	2.068	1.72s	81
perse	1440[c]	30	2.750	2.491	2.675	2.23s	105
7. *Roeselare*							
red	1443[c]	30	2.500	2.265	2.433	2.03s	96
8. *Diest*							
green	1443[c]	30	2.687	2.434	2.614	2.18s	103

SOURCES: For Wervik (Wervicq), A.R.A., Rekenkamer, no. 32,492 f. 44^{v} (1439), and Rijksarchief van West-Vlaanderen te Brugge, Stadsrekeningen van het Vrije, no. 176, f. 39^{v} (1442), and A.R.A., Rek., no. 42,558, f. 43^{r} (1446); for Kortrijk (Courtrai), A.R.A., Rek., no. 42,555, f. 44^{r} (1441), and Rijksarchief van West-Vlaanderen, Stadsrekeningen van het Vrije, no. 172, f. 39^{v} (1438); for Menen, A.R.A., Rek., no. 42,554, f. 43^{v} (1440), and no. 32,495, f. 25^{r} (1443); for Nieuwkerke (Neuve-Eglise), A.R.A., Rek., no. 32,492, f. 44^{r}; for Hesdin, A.R.A., Rek., no. 32,492, f. 44^{r}; for Niepkerke, A.R.A., Rek., no. 32,493, f. 19^{r}; for Roeselare (Roulers), A.R.A., Rek., no. 32,495, f. 25^{r}; for Diest, A.R.A., Rek., no. 32,495, f. 25^{r}.

[a] The ell of Flanders = 0.700 meter = 27.559 inches

[b] £1.000 sterling = £1.104 groot Flemish = £1.656 groot Brabant

[c] Cloths purchased for the lesser officials, chiefly *sergianten*, of the Bruges civic government.

[d] Cloths purchased for the lesser officials, chiefly messengers, of the government of the Vrije van Brugge (Franc de Bruges).

[e] Cloths purchased for the aldermen of the Vrije.

Table 13.4

Indices of English Cloth and Wool Exports, and of the Drapery Production of Ypres, Ghent, Mechelen, and Leuven, in Decennial Averages, 1400–09 to 1510–19 (Average of 1400–24 = base 100)

Decade	*English Cloth Exports from All Ports* [a]	*English Wool Sack Exports to Calais* [b]	*Ypres: Number of Drapers' Stalls Rented Annually* [c]	*Ypres: Total Sales of the Drapery Tax Farms* [d]	*Ghent: Sales of the Drapery Tax Farms* [e]	*Mechelen: Total Sales of the Drapery Tax Farms* [f]	*Leuven: Total Sales of the Drapery Tax Farms* [g]
1400–09	99.7	98.0	93.5	101.6	86.2	94.9	126.7
1410–19	91.3	100.5	102.4	100.1	105.9	95.1	96.8
1420–29	126.3	102.3	88.8	97.1	118.3	122.1	44.4
1430–39	135.8	41.2	60.5	76.2	81.3	75.4	26.2
1440–49	172.4	62.7	39.1	65.1	62.6	62.1	16.6
1450–59	121.4	57.7	20.5	56.8	37.4	50.7	13.2
1460–69	107.1	50.9	15.0	36.2	20.8	55.7	11.0
1470–79	131.0	59.6	14.9	28.9	34.8	73.9	12.9
1480–89	168.1	58.3	3.6	31.5	14.7	85.4	26.3
1490–99	188.5	58.2	0.0	43.8	3.5	77.0	29.7
1500–09	261.1	49.1	n.a.	n.a.	6.9	80.2	n.a.
1510–19	280.5	54.3	n.a.	n.a.	4.5	67.7	n.a.

[a] English cloth. The base 100 = 30,849 broadcloths of assize, measuring 24 yards by 7 quarters, with three kerseys and four "dozens" counted as 1 broadcloth. Calculated from unprocessed data in E. M. Carus-Wilson and Olive Coleman, *England's Export Trade, 1275–1547* (Oxford, 1963), pp. 87–115. (See note d of Table 13.5.)

[b] English wool. The base 100 = 13,029.72 wool sacks, each weighing 364 lb. The statistics include all wool exports from all ports by "denizens," who were required to ship the wools directly to the Calais Staple for sale. Alien exports, rarely more than 10 percent of the total, were chiefly by Italians, who had the privilege of shipping wool free of the Staple, directly by sea to the Mediterranean. Calculated from *England's Export Trade*, pp. 55–72.

[c] Ypres drapers' stalls. The base 100 = 443.38 stalls of drapers, *upzetters* (finisher-drapers), and dyers rented in both the *ghemijnghede* and *blaeuwe* cloth-halls. Calculated from the annual municipal accounts of Ypres in the Algemeen Rijksarchief van België, Rekenkamer, nos. 38,635–722 (1408–1500).

[d] Ypres drapery tax farms. The base 100 = £298.969 parisis = £24.914 groot Flemish. It is the sum of the laken (cloth production), wulle (wool purchase), snijden (retail cloth

Table 13.4 (*continued*)

sales), and the blaeuwvaerwers (blue-dyers) *accijnzen* or excise-taxes, which were farmed annually by public auction. Calculated from the source cited in c above.

[e] Ghent drapery tax farms. The base 100 = £89.270 parisis = £7.439 groot Flemish. It is the sum of the ramen (tentering of cloths for finishing) and huusgeld (cloth hall) accijnzen or excise taxes, farmed annually by public auction. Calculated from the municipal accounts of Ghent in the Stadsarchief te Gent, Stadsrekeningen 1400–1520, Reeks 400: 11–38.

[f] Mechelen drapery tax farms. The base 100 = £318.996 oude groot and [nieuw] groot. It is the sum of the wede (blue woad), wolle (wool purchase), rocghewande (weaving) and ghereeden ghewande (cloth finishing) accijnzen or excise taxes, farmed annually by public auction or collected directly by the town government. The pound oude groot was a gold-based money of account until 1428, when it became a silver-based money of account, tied directly to the current Flemish groot or penny. During the often severe silver debasements from 1466 to 1496, it was subject to considerable inflation. Calculated from the municipal accounts of Mechelen (Malines) in the Stadsarchief te Mechelen, Stadsrekeningen 1400–1520, nos. 76–194, and A.R.A., Rekenkamer, nos. 41,219–72.

[g] Leuven drapery tax farms. The base 100 = 2121.342 rijnsguldens (Rhenish florins). It is the sum of the laken (cloth production), wolle (wool purchase), weet (blue-dyers' woad), zieden (red-dyers' dyestuffs), 6d gelde (sales tax), and uutvaert (export tax) accijnzen or excise taxes, again farmed annually by public auction. The rijnsgulden was a gold-based money of account until 1460, when it became a silver-based money of account, tied directly to the current Flemish silver groot. Calculated from the municipal accounts of Leuven (Louvain) in the Stadsarchief te Leuven, Stadsrekeningen 1400–1500, nos. 5006–124.

Table 13.5

Prices and Price-Relatives of Fine Dickedinnen Cloths of Ghent, and of English Short Broadcloths, as Exported from London and Southampton, in Decennial Averages, 1400–09 to 1510–19 (Average of 1400–24 = base 100)

Decade	*Ghent Dickedinnen Cloths, First Quality*		*Weighted Price Index of a Basket of Consumables*[b]	*Ghent Dickedinnen Cloths, First Quality*		*Short English Broadcloths (Usually Dyed)*	
	Prices in Pounds Groot Flemish[a]	*Price-Relatives*		*Values in Pounds Sterling*[c]	*Price-Relatives*	*Values in Pounds Sterling*[d]	*Price-Relatives*
1400–09	5.921	99.8	91.8	5.643	89.7	1.667	88.6
1410–19	5.864	98.9	102.6	6.969	110.8	n.a.	n.a.
1420–29	6.073	102.4	111.9	5.754	91.5	2.001	106.3
1430–39	7.058	119.0	117.7	6.235	99.1	2.655	141.1
1440–49	7.845	132.3	105.4	7.108	113.0	2.494	132.5
1450–59	7.326	123.5	99.3	6.637	105.5	2.052	109.0
1460–69	8.050	135.7	94.0	7.819	124.3	2.017	107.2
1470–79	8.759	147.7	105.6	7.854	124.9	2.131	113.2
1480–89	12.621	212.8	172.7	7.334	116.6	2.845	151.2
1490–99	15.450	260.5	127.1	10.436	165.9	2.683	142.6
1500–09	14.500	244.5	121.1	9.976	158.6	2.910	154.6
1510–19	13.110	221.0	143.4	9.020	143.4	3.219	171.0

SOURCES: For Ghent cloth prices, Stadsarchief te Gent, Stadsrekeningen 1400–1519, Reeks 400:1–43; for English cloth prices from the port of London, Public Record Office, King's Remembrancer Exchequer, Particulars Accounts: Customs, E.122/76/13, 74/11, 77/11, 77/4, 73/23, 73/25, 194/14–18, 78/7, 79/5, 81/1–2, 83/2, and Lord Treasurer's Remembrancer, Enrolled Customs, E. 356/19–24; and for English cloth prices from the port of Southampton, P.R.O., K.R. Exchequer, Customs, E. 122/139/4, 139/7–8, 141/4, 141/21–22, 209/1, 141/25, 140/62, 141/29, 141/31, 141/33, 141/35–36, 209/8, 141/38, 142/1, 142/3, 142/8, 142/10, 143/1, 142/11–12, 209/2, and L.T.R. Enrolled Customs, E. 356/19–24. The weighted price index was calculated from prices given in Herman Van der Wee, *Growth of the Antwerp Market and the European Economy, 14th to 16th Centuries*, 3 vols. (The Hague, 1963), I, 175–77, 190–92, 195–97, 200–02, 204–07, 279–81, 283–85, 211–14, 218–21, 230–32, 296–98, 239–41, 250–52, 246–48, 270–71, 273–76.

Table 13.5 (*continued*)

[a] Dyed and dressed Ghent dickedinnen woolens (excluding scarlets or *scaerlakens*), purchased annually to garb the 39 aldermen and judges on ceremonial occasions. The cloths normally measured 30 ells by 10 quarters = 21.0 meters by 1.75 meters = 36.75 square meters = 43.953 square yards.

[b] The index is composed of the price-relatives of 17 commodities sold in the Antwerp-Lier-Mechelen-Brussels region. It has been weighted to correspond to the well-known "composite unit of consumables" index constructed by Phelps Brown and Hopkins as follows: farinaceous 20 percent; meat, eggs, and fish 25 percent; butter and cheese 12.5 percent; beer and wine 22.5 percent; fuel and light 7.5 percent; coarse woolens and linen textiles 12.5 percent.

[c] The Ghent cloth prices for each year were converted into pounds sterling by ratios derived from the relative silver contents in the two moneys of account.

[d] English *panni curti sine grano*, but usually dyed at least in the wool, often in the piece, measuring 24 yards of the cloth assize [37-inch yard] by 7 quarter-yards = 22.556 meters by 1.645 meters = 37.103 square meters = 42.00 cloth-assize square yards = 44.366 standard square yards. Cloth exports by individual merchants were recorded in the customs accounts in terms of such cloths of assize and of extra yards, and were taxed by quantity; cloth exports by aliens were also taxed by value, for the subsidy of poundage. The poundage accounts are unfortunately not continuous and, in some periods, exist only for scattered years. The decennial averages were computed by taking the arithmetic mean of the evaluations of total exports from both London and Southampton in each decade. The means are thus influenced by the number of accounts that have survived per decade, and by the volume of exports registered in those surviving accounts.

14

The Costs and Profits of War: The Anglo-French Conflict of 1294–1303

Joseph R. Strayer

From 1214, the year that saw the final victories of Philip Augustus, to 1294, neither England nor France had engaged in a major European war. Wales was a constant problem for the English, but the fighting there involved relatively few men. Henry III's fumbling attempts to regain some of the old Plantagenet domains in France were brushed aside by the French with very little effort. Crusades were a more serious matter for the French government, but the Church bore much of the expense, and volunteers, who made up a large part of the army, paid their own way as far as they could. It was an ominous sign that the brief and futile Crusade against Aragon in 1285 cost almost as much (according to French accountants) as St. Louis's six-year campaign in the Levant,[1] but no one in the 1290s realized the significance of these figures. In the long run, the Church again had carried most of the burden, and while in 1294 there were still debts outstanding from the Aragon campaign,[2] they were not large enough to affect French policy.

During the eighty years of relative peace significant changes had taken place in political and military organization. On the one hand, central governments had increased their revenues and their power. They could spend more because they could ask more from their subjects. On the other hand, feudal service, which had never been capable of providing an adequate army, had become almost useless.[3] Thus there was a temptation

1. J. R. Strayer, *Medieval Statecraft and the Perspectives of History* (Princeton, 1971), p. 114; *Recueil des historiens des Gaules et de la France* (Paris, 1738–) XXI, 515–16 (hereafter cited as *H. F.*).

2. Strayer, *Statecraft*, p. 120.

3. Even in England, where rules about knightly service had been particularly strict, little actual service could be obtained by a feudal summons. See John E. Morris, *The Welsh Wars of Edward I* (Oxford, 1901), chap. 3, and especially pp. 43–49. It was even worse when the summons was for service overseas;

to raise bigger armies and to keep them in the field for longer periods than before, because the state could demand and pay for military service, unhindered by feudal restrictions on time and place. But it is doubtful if anyone realized how expensive it would be to give up feudal service and have a salaried army.

The "war of Aquitaine" (the French term), or the "Gascon War" (English style) was one of those wars that accomplish nothing and should never have occurred. There was bound to be friction as long as the king of England held a large part of southwest France—clashes between the mariners of Bayonne and of Normandy, appeals to the French Parlement from Edward's officials in Aquitaine, unsolved boundary disputes. But the friction had not been unendurable in the decades before the war, and it was not unendurable in the decade that followed the war, even though the peace settlement removed none of the major irritants. The young Philip the Fair was taking a very high line in the 1290s, asserting his right to be final and supreme judge over all parts of France,[4] but Edward was perfectly ready to concede this supremacy. He agreed early in 1294 to surrender officials guilty of misconduct and to allow a token occupation of the duchy until Philip was satisfied. Philip instead pronounced the confiscation of Aquitaine and sent in a large army to enforce the order. Edward made one serious effort to push back the French in 1295–96, when this failed he was content to hold Bayonne and a few other strong points.

That Edward, deeply involved in Wales and in Scotland, did not want a war with France is evident. Judging by his subsequent behavior, Philip very rapidly concluded that he did not want a serious war with England. In that case, why did he start the war? Fawtier, who knew the documents of the reign better than any other scholar, admitted that he could not answer the question.[5] Philip may have feared an alliance between his

---

ever since John's day English vassals had denied that they owed service abroad. Charles Bémont, *Rôles Gascons*, III (1290–1307), (Paris, 1906), nos. 3372, 3416, 3419. Edward's summonses for service in Gascony in 1294 had little effect. Michael Prestwich, *War, Politics and Finance under Edward I* (Totowa, N. J., 1972), pp. 72–76, English lords would serve in Scotland and Wales without pay if the king were present, but everyone who served in Aquitaine was paid. As for France, Philip the Fair never relied on unpaid feudal service. It is true that a summons put some pressure on a vassal to serve for wages, but late thirteenth century armies included many men who were not vassals.

4. Georges Digard, *Philippe le Bel et le Saint Siège de 1285 à 1304* (Paris, 1936), II, 249, "nullum et nullius judicis territorium . . . intra fines regni nostri exemptum a nostra jurisdictione recognoscimus." (c. 1289).

5. R. Fawtier, *L'Europe occidentale de 1270 à 1380* (Paris, 1940), p. 324. F. M. Powicke, *The Thirteenth Century* (Oxford, 1953), pp. 644–48, tends to agree with Fawtier. Bémont, *Rôles Gascons*, pp. cxxiv, gives a factual rather than interpretative account of the origins and progress of the war.

unruly vassal Guy of Flanders and Edward, but mistreating Edward was scarcely the best way of preventing such an alliance. Philip's brother Charles of Valois was always eager for glory and lands; he might have pressed for war in the hopes that he could get something out of it. But Philip had a very poor opinion of Charles's political sagacity. He had just liquidated Charles's claim to the throne of Aragon, and he gave Charles little military assistance in his later attempts to gain new lands and new titles. It seems unlikely that Charles had much influence on the decision.

About all that can be said is that Philip was still young, that even a cautious and patient man (which Philip was) may have sudden fits of impatience, and that Philip may have judged that a sudden coup against his most powerful vassal would end all opposition within the realm. It appears that Philip miscalculated his chances for a quick and spectacular success and that as soon as he realized that this miscalculation was interfering with a much more difficult and important project—the reduction of Flanders to obedience—he was ready to cut his losses. A truce was arranged in October 1297, a preliminary peace in 1298, and a final peace, returning Aquitaine to Edward, in 1303.

From a purely military point of view, the war of Aquitaine hardly deserves notice. Given Edward's state of mind, and the state of mind Philip soon reached, it is easy to understand why there were no major battles, no prolonged sieges, very few deaths in combat, and relatively little devastation of the countryside. From the point of view of finance, however the war is instructive. Philip, after all, had to have a sizable army to occupy the duchy, even if the army met little resistance. He had to maintain large garrisons in the towns and castles of the occupied area even after the truce of 1297. He had to build a fleet to menace English ports and English communications. Edward, even if he had not wanted war, had to make some effort to defend his possessions and to retain a foothold in parts of the duchy. As a result, this war which was no war cost as much as or more than many of the English campaigns in Scotland or the French campaigns in Flanders.[6] As we shall see, the greatest expense was the pay of soldiers, and soldiers who did not fight were no cheaper than those who did. In fact, they were more expensive, because their ranks were not reduced by casualties and desertion. In Scotland, Edward at times lost 80 percent of his army,[7] which was hard on the generals but a relief to the

6. Prestwich, *War, Politics and Finance*, p. 171, says that this was the most expensive of Edward's wars. Fawtier remarks: "L'on est d'ailleurs surpris de l'immensité des préparitifs, et de la faible ampleur des opérations militaires" (*L'Europe occidentale*, p. 318).

7. Prestwich, *War, Politics and Finance*, pp. 95–96.

Treasury. In Aquitaine few men were hurt; pay was fairly regular; and desertion was no problem. Thus expenses built up, and the costs of this useless war helped bring about a constitutional crisis in England in 1297, and the great conflict over taxation of the clergy that began with *Clericis laicos* in 1296.

It is easier to analyze military costs in a static situation, such as that in Aquitaine in 1294–1303, than in a war of movement, where the number of troops swings back and forth erratically. It is also easier to keep books, which may be why we have such remarkably good records from both the French and the English sides. For France we have one overall estimate made in 1295–96 that purports to give the amount of money available for the war[8] and a large number of partial accounts.[9] For England we have a summary (very likely not quite complete) of expenses for the period 1294–99, that is, for the years in which the greatest costs were incurred.[10] It is curious, but understandable, that the French estimate of what *could* be spent and the English summary of what *was* spent are very close together—about 1,735,000 l.t.[11] and about £360,000,[12] (or 1,440,000 l.t.). After all, action and reaction should be equal if no movement results. It is also

8. Frantz Funck-Brentano, "Document pour servir à l'histoire des relations de la France et l'Allemagne sous le règne de Phillippe le Bel," *Revue Historique, 39* (1889), 326–48.

9. These partial accounts are for the most part collected in Robert Fawtier, ed., *Comptes royaux, 1285–1314*, 3 vols. (Paris, 1953–56) (hereafter cited as *C.R.*), II, under the heading "Guerre d'Aquitaine," but the accounts of the seneschals in *C.R.*, I contain some useful material, and there is an account of the expenses of an expedition of the count of Artois in 1296 in *C.R.*, III, nos. 30105–30287. Robert Mignon's list of accounts for the war (*Inventaire d'anciens comptes royaux*, dressé par Robert Mignon, publié par C. V. Langlois, Paris, 1889) begins with no. 2263 and runs through no. 2489.

10. This is P.R.O. E 372/160 (Pipe Roll 8 Edward II) no. 41. The most interesting parts were published by Bémont, pp. cxli–cxlii, and clxvii–clxviii. I should like to thank Professor Richard Kaeuper of the University of Rochester for sending me photostats of this roll. Some very useful accounts were published by Bémont, *Rôles Gascons*, pp. cl–clxxv. Prestwich, *War, Politics and Finance*, pp. 76, 93, 120–21, 172, 209, gives references to other accounts.

11. Funck-Brentano, "Document," pp. 333–34. The actual total of what was believed to be available was 2,125,200 l.t. I subtracted the 200,000 l.t. in the treasury, most of which would already have been committed, and most of the 215,000 l.t. expected from the Jews, since there is no evidence that they were paying at this rate in 1295–96. R. Fawtier, *Comptes du Trésor* (Paris, 1930), p. 14, shows only about 15,000 l.t. received from Jews of Normandy, Paris, and the north of France in 1296. Fawtier, *L'Europe occidentale*, p. 318, estimates the total sum available at 1,734,000 l.t. However, the unknown author of the "Document" gave no estimate for taxes on Languedoc, nor for any taxes after 1295, and expected only 60,000 l.t. from depreciating the currency. Not all this money could be spent on the war in Aquitaine, since Flanders was becoming a problem by 1295, but a very rough guess would be that the war cost the French at least 2,000,000 l.t.

12. For England, P.R.O., E 372/160 (Bémont, *Rôles Gascons*, p. clxix) gives a total of £359,000. Adding in other expenses, Prestwich, *War, Politics and Finance*, p. 172, estimates the total cost at £400,000, and Powicke, *The Thirteenth Century*, p. 650, at £405,000.

The official rate of exchange was one pound sterling for four pounds Tours. Actually the purchasing power of sterling was higher than this ratio indicates; on the other hand, the commercial exchange rate sometimes went lower (though it was higher toward the end of the war). Wages remained constant in

instructive to compare these figures with the normal annual revenue of each king. Borrelli de Serres estimated French income in the period just before the war at 450,000 l.p. a year, that is, 562,500 l.t.[13] Edward at the same time was receiving something less than £30,000 a year[14] (120,000 l.t.) and should have been much harder pressed than Philip. But Edward's financial system was much more flexible than that of his rival. For example, he could double his income simply by manipulating customs dues,[15] while Philip was never able to get more than a few thousand pounds from this source.[16] Edward's internal administrative expenses were much lower than those of Philip; in England, unpaid local notables did work which in France was performed by a host of paid officials. A single French province such as the *sénéchaussée* of Beaucaire-Nîmes had almost as many royal judges as all of England, and the salaries were about the same.[17] Thus, once war had started, Edward and Philip were operating on about the same level. Ordinary income could not cover military expenses; extraordinary sources of revenue had to be found.

England found these sources in heavy levies on the clergy (50 percent of their income in 1294, 10 percent thereafter), annual taxes on personal property, increased customs dues (as mentioned above) and some borrowing.[18] In France the clergy paid a 10 percent income tax in 1295

---

both armies, however, so the overall figures do permit meaningful comparisons. Since English wages were lower than French, £400,000 would support about the same war effort as 2,000,000 l.t.

13. Borrelli de Serres, *Recherches sur divers services publics* (Paris 1885–1909), II, 489, and appendix, table II. I have deducted 200,000 l.p. from Borrelli's figure of 650,000 l.p. because the tenth levied on the clergy, while it yielded about 210,000 l.p. a year, was not an guaranteed source of royal income. It was not granted every year; until 1294 much of it went to pay the costs of the Crusade against Aragon, and it could be abruptly suspended by the pope, as it was in 1296. Note that the ratio of Paris to Tours money was 4 to 5.

14. Prestwich, *War, Politics and Finance*, p. 178.

15. Prestwich, *War, Politics and Finance*, pp. 196–97. Edward also frightened the clergy into giving half their income in 1294; Prestwich estimates this at £101,000 to £105,000 (p. 186).

16. Strayer, *Statecraft*, pp. 232–37.

17. J. R. Strayer, *Les Gens de justice du Languedoc* (Toulouse, 1971), pp. 54–91. There were fourteen judges in this district about 1295 (pp. 28–29), salaries of 80 l.t. to 160 l.t. were not uncommon. According to Francis Palgrave, *Parliamentary Writs* (London, 1827), I, 382, there were twenty judges for the central and circuit courts of England in 1278. Only the two chief justices drew 60 marks (40 l.st.) a year, and two central court judges and seven circuit court judges were paid 40 marks (about 28 l.st.) a year, which gives in money of Tours a range of 112 l. to 160 l.

18. Prestwich, *War, Politics and Finance*, pp. 178–99, 209. Aside from his very complicated dealings with the Riccardi and other Italian bankers, which may not have produced much in the way of new funds, though they did relieve the government of old debts, Edward borrowed £45,763 from a group in Bayonne and about £4,400 from other men in Gascony, see Bémont, *Rôles Gascons*, pp. clxxi–clxxii.. For Edward and the Lombards, R. W. Kaeuper, *Bankers to the Crown* (Princeton, N. J., 1973), pp. 216–27, is excellent. In his article on "The Frescobaldi and the English Crown," *Studies in Medieval and Renaissance History, 10* (1973), 47–50, Kaeuper shows that the Italians lent Edward £28,966 between 1294 and 1298. See also Prestwich, *War, Politics and Finance*, pp. 208–10.

and 1296, and 20 percent in 1297 and 1298. Because there was no tradition of general taxation in France as there was in England, there was a good deal of experimenting with property taxes and sales taxes. Rates were low—1 percent and 2 percent on property, a penny in the pound ($\frac{1}{240}$) on sales—and many communities bought off taxes (especially sales taxes) with lump sum payments or changed property taxes into hearth taxes.[19] Respectable sums were raised; the author of the memorandum on war finance estimated the value of the 1 percent property tax at 315,000 l.t. and Paris bought off the sales tax for 100,000 l.t., to be paid in eight yearly installments.[20] But this was not enough. The government had to borrow heavily from the Italian bankers at the fairs of Champagne and even more heavily from "rich burgers."[21] Very soon after the loans were received deliberate inflation of the currency began, largely by overvaluing the *gros tournois*, the standard coin used in business.[22] The peak of inflation did not come until after the truce of 1297, but even in the first year of "weak money" the government was supposed to make 60,000 l.t. by minting overvalued coins, and actually took in a little over 101,000 l.t.[23]

These facts are well known; the only reason for rehearsing them is to make the point that in each kingdom the war of Aquitaine was paid for largely by the more productive elements of the community. The clergy were not entrepreneurs, but they were good estate-managers in most of England and in many parts of France. The English property tax was usually a heavier burden on urban than on rural taxpayers. In 1294 the urban rate was $\frac{1}{6}$ of the assessment, and the rural rate $\frac{1}{10}$; in 1295, $\frac{1}{7}$ and $\frac{1}{11}$; in 1296, $\frac{1}{8}$ and $\frac{1}{12}$; in 1297, $\frac{1}{9}$ on both. The French sales tax could be collected (or compounded for) only in the towns, and the towns also paid property taxes (or hearth taxes). Increased customs dues (mostly on wool) certainly affected large and enterprising landlords in England, since they were the

19. For additions to French income during the 1290s see J. R. Strayer and C. H. Taylor, *Studies in Early French Taxation* (Cambridge, Mass., 1939), pp. 17–19, 25–31, 45–54.

20. Ibid., pp. 12, 47; Funck-Brentano, "Document," p. 334.

21. According to Funck-Brentano, "Document," pp. 333–34, 200,000 l.t. was raised in the fairs and about 630,000 l.t. from burgers and royal officials. Mignon, *Inventaire*, nos. 1105–170 gives details for most French provinces. Languedoc is omitted in this section, but there is some material on loans in Languedoc in nos. 2109–112. Many men preferred to give money outright rather than to make a risky loan, e.g., no. 1159 states that 5,661 l.t. in loans and 44,910 l.t. in gifts were collected in Poitou and Saintonge. On the other hand, no. 1132 states that in the *bailliage* of Sens loans came to 25,139 l.t. and gifts to only 1,547 l.t.

22. Borrelli de Serres, *Les Variations monétaires sous Philippe le Bel* (Chalon-sur-Saône, 1902), pp. 320–24 and appendix B (reprint of a 1902 article in *La Gazette Numismatique*).

23. Funck-Brentano, "Document," p. 334. According to Fawtier, *Comptes du Trésor*, p. lvi, and pp. 12–13, actual receipts from *monetagium* at All Saints 1296 were 101,435 l.t.

most important raisers of sheep, and the custom dues also put a burden on commerce. Large loans which were never repaid or were repaid only long after they were due hurt many businessmen. For example, it was in the years of the Gascon war that the Riccardi were driven into bankruptcy.[24] Inflation certainly caused more problems for merchants, bankers, and landlords than it did for peasants who owed fixed rents.

In England bankers and merchants who lent money to the Crown and who received deferred payments or no payments at all were probably harder hit than any other group. Landlords who raised sheep were hurt by a 25 percent drop in wool prices, from 2 s. a clove or better in the prewar period to 1 s. 6 d. or 1 s. 5 d. in the period 1294–96,[25] a drop probably caused by the increase in export dues. Annual taxes, which were a novelty in England, were a burden on the possessing classes and were increasingly resented. The yield of the personal property tax was £81,833 in 1294 and only £34,419 in 1297.[26] The rate of taxation did decrease during those years, but not enough to account for an over 50 percent drop. The fact that nobles and gentlemen who served in the army were officially or unofficially excused from paying taxes[27] accounts for some of the decline. It is also true that the tax assessors were unpaid local notables, and they may not have wanted to push their neighbors too hard when the levy was repeated year after year. The very poor were exempt from taxation and those just above the poverty level paid only a few pennies a year.[28] Both groups may have increased in size during a period of declining prosperity. Merchants, artisans, and middle-level landholders received fewer exemptions than other classes and probably paid more than their share of the taxes.

The French urban classes were clearly heavily burdened. The 200,000 l.t. borrowed in the fairs of Champagne and the 65,000 l.t. squeezed out of the Lombards came from bankers, mostly foreign bankers. The 630,000 l.t. borrowed from Frenchmen (or given to avoid a forced loan) must have come largely from businessmen, though royal officials also contributed. The sales tax, or lump sum payments in lieu of a sales tax, yielded more than 100,000 l.t., perhaps as much as 150,000 l.t. The 215,000 l.t. expected from the Jews may not have been paid in full; as far as it was paid it represented a tax on business operations. There is no way of telling how

24. Kaeuper, *Bankers to the Crown*, pp. 216–27; Prestwich, *War, Politics and Finance*, pp. 207–08.

25. J. Thorold Rogers, *A History of Agriculture and Prices in England* (Oxford, 1866), I, 386–87.

26. J. F. Willard, *Parliamentary Taxes on Personal Property* (Cambridge, Mass., 1934), pp. 343–44.

27. Willard, *Parliamentary Taxes*, pp. 111–12. Prestwich thinks that the burden of rural taxation fell largely on villeins and free tenants; *War, Politics and Finance*, p. 192.

28. Willard, *Parliamentary Taxes*, pp. 87–88.

much the urban areas contributed to the 1 percent and 2 percent property taxes, but an estimate of 100,000 l.t. is probably too low. Thus the urban and mercantile population would have contributed about 1,325,000 l.t. during the active period of war in Aquitaine. Not all this money was spent on the conflict in the southwest; Flanders was a problem after 1297, and the support or at least the neutrality of German princes had to be purchased. It is also true that towns could reduce the burden of taxation by offering lump sums to royal officials, although they gained less by such deals than the nobles who were pacified by grants up to 50 percent of the taxes paid by their subjects. But even if we reduce the figure of 1,325,000 l.t. by a third, it still appears that bankers, merchants, and artisans paid about half of the costs of the war of Aquitaine.[29]

Who received the money that was collected by the two governments? Most of it was spent in paying the wages of soldiers. This is easy to demonstrate from the English records, which show that £192,574 were spent directly on wages. In addition, almost £30,000 went to various Gascons for hiring soldiers and garrisoning fortified places both during the actual fighting and in the period of truce, and another £30,000 as pensions to those whose lands had been occupied by the French. Presumably most of these men had fought for Edward, so the pensions could be considered a supplement to wages. Pay of sailors came to £16,869. Another entry lists £26,667 spent before November 1294. Most of this money must have been used to raise troops and to strengthen garrisons. If total English expenses were £400,000, then as much as 75 percent of the sum (£296,000) could have been spent on wages and bonuses for soldiers and sailors.[30] Even if some of the payments to the Gascons were not connected with military operations, wages would account for at least 65 percent of the total.

For France the figures are not so complete, but they point the same way. In the *sénéchaussée* of Toulouse alone Jean l'Archévêque, a high royal official, spent 50,844 l.t. on wages for campaigns in 1295–96.[31] In the same phase of the war (April–July 1296) the count of Artois spent 75,538 l.t., almost all of it for wages.[32] Mignon's list of the accounts rendered for war expenses in the 1290s duplicates some items, omits others, and is not always very explicit about the way money was spent. Nevertheless, it is certain

29. Most of the figures in this paragraph come from Funck-Brentano, "Document," pp. 333–34. See also Strayer and Taylor, *Studies in Early French Taxation*, pp. 11–13, 18, 19–21, and pp. 47–53 for taxes shared with nobles.

30. P.R.O., E 372/160, m. 41 (published in part by Bémont, *Rôles Gascons*, pp. cxli, clxvii) and summarized by Prestwich, *War, Politics and Finance*, p. 171.

31. *C.R.*, II, nos. 26364–776.

32. *C.R.*, III, nos. 30105–287.

that at least 1,255,927 l.t. was accounted for and that of this at least 719,818 l.t. went for wages.[33] The proportion is really higher than it seems, because many entries simply give lump sums—64,670 l.t. for the fleet, for example[34] —and it is impossible to decide how much should have been listed as wages. A brief flurry at the very end of the war, caused by a rising in Bordeaux in 1302, gives us a chance to test our conclusion in a specific case. Of 124,397 l.t. spent in regaining control of Bordeaux, 72,433 l.t. went for wages,[35] almost exactly the same proportion that we found for the war as a whole.

Bordeaux also gives an example of how expensive a small force could be. In 1299 (as in 1302) there was unrest in the city, and the garrison had to be increased. At least 452 men were added—4 bannerets, 23 knights, 154 fully equipped and 33 less well equipped squires, and 168 foot soldiers. The cost of such a force was almost 90 l.t. a day.[36] This particular group served only 15 days, but if they had been with the count of Artois in his campaign of 1295 they would have cost about 9,000 l.t., since he was in the field 104 days. If they had been on permanent garrison duty, as some men were, they would have received 32,000 l.t. for a full year of service. And there were many such units in the duchy during ten years of war, occupation, and negotiation.

Wage scales varied in the two armies. The French were the best paid—bannerets received 1 l.t., knights 10s., squires with good horses, 7 s. 6 d., squires with inferior horses 5 s.t., and foot soldiers 1 s.t. Next came the English—bannerets 4 s. ster., knights 2 s. ster., squires and men-at-arms 1 s. ster., bowmen 2 d. ster. Worst paid were Gascons and Spaniards in English service—bannerets 16 s. *chipotenses*, knights 8 s. chip., squires 6 s. chip., and crossbowmen 1 s. chip. (chipotenses or chapotenses were coins of Bordeaux; 5 d. chip. = 1 d. st. or 4 d.t.).[37] If wc accept official exchange rates these discrepancies are hard to understand. Why should

33. Mignon, *Inventaire*, nos. 2337–344, 2352–374. Some, but not all of these accounts are summarized in nos. 2436–454 under the heading "Debita que debentur per fines compotorum guerre Vasconie."

34. Mignon, *Inventaire*, no. 2481.

35. Mignon, *Inventaire*, nos. 2430–435.

36. *C.R.*, II, nos. 25489–507. F. Maillard, ed., *Comptes royaux*, 1314–1328 (Paris, 1961), II, no. 15714. In the Bordeaux revolt of 1302, a company of two knights and forty-three squires cost 312 l. 10 s.t. for twenty days.

37. For English and Gascon wages see P.R.O., E 372/60, m. 41; Bémont, *Rôles Gascons*, p. cxli, and Prestwich, *War, Politics and Finance*, pp. 93, 160. For France, the rates are given or implied in many accounts, for example, *C.R.*, II, nos. 25489–507, 26800–815. The cross-rate for chipotenses–turonenses is given in *C.R.*, II, 17660, and in J. Viard, *Journaux du Trésor de Philippe IV le Bel* (Paris, 1940), nos. 3415, 4073. The last example is the easiest to work out: 1,700 l. chip = 1,360 l.t. Note that some knights serving Robert of Artois got 15 s.t. a day and some knights of Gui of St. Pol 12 s. 6 d.t. J. Petit, *Essai de restitution des plus anciens mémoriaux de la chambre des comptes* (Paris, 1899), pp. 176–77.

English knights and squires get less than Frenchmen but more than Gascons? Why did Gascon knights and squires, who could have served with the French, take the equivalent of 6 s. 2 d.t. or 4 s. 9 d.t. instead of 10 s.t. or 5 s.t.? The case of the Gascon crossbowmen makes a little more sense, as Prestwich points out.[38] They were armed with a more expensive weapon than the longbow and so were paid more than English bowmen, though still a little less than French crossbowmen.

About all that can be said is that these were traditional rates of pay, that official exchange rates did not reflect real purchasing power (especially for the English), and that the average soldier, even the average knight, was not very good at arithmetic. If an English knight thought that sterling was really worth five times tournois he may have been right, and in that case he was paid as well as a French knight. If the Gascons thought Bordeaux money was as good as Tours money, then they were saved the difficult process of dividing by five to see how their wages compared with those of the French or the English. In fact, one wonders if English clerks in the field went through the difficult process of converting chipotenses to sterling or tournois. In the end the English did save some money on wages, but during the war it is probable that most people assumed a rough equivalence.

For the upper classes the wage rates were high, at least in comparison to their other sources of income. In England a man with £20 a year was supposed to be able to assume the burdens of knighthood;[39] 200 days of service at 2 s. st. a day would produce the sum in much less than a year. In France many of the lesser nobility had incomes of less than 100 l.t. a year; 90 days of garrison duty at 10 s.t. a day would increase their incomes by 50 percent or more. Even those knights and squires who served for 30 days or less (and such men were numerous on the French side) must have found payments of 5 to 15 l.t. very welcome in a period of inflation.

Commanders of companies and larger units could have done even better, since they were paid lump sums for the men they enlisted and had many opportunities to pad their payrolls. But if the surviving accounts are at all accurate there was not much cheating in the war of Aquitaine. This was the first of the wars in which large numbers of soldiers were paid, and, as in the case of any other new institution, it took the nobility some time to learn how to cut corners. When the earl of Lincoln furnished 60 men-at-arms for £1,000 a year, and Edmund of Cornwall provided 150 men for £2,000, the king of England was getting a bargain. If they served 360 days at the

38. Prestwich, *War, Politics and Finance*, p. 93.
39. Stubbs, *Select Charters* (1921 ed.), pp. 448–49.

accepted rate of 1 s. st. a day, 60 men-at-arms should have cost £1,080, and 150 men should have cost £2,700. Nor does it seem that the count of Artois could have made much profit out of his campaign of 1296, though with household expenses of 8,762 l.t. for 108 days he was clearly living in a style befitting his rank.[40] It is a little more difficult to understand why the count of Foix was owed 48,000 l.t. for service in Gascony; he took part in the campaigns of 1295 and 1296 but the size of his contingent is not given. Edward I was seeking his support and the count may have demanded excessive payments to stay on the French side. The fact that he was never paid in full may show that there were doubts about his claims, but relations between count and king were usually strained, and there were many other reasons for holding back money owed to him.[41]

On the whole, mounted men profited from the war (if they lived through it). Foot soldiers were not so fortunate. Skilled workmen in England could make at least 2 d. st. a day and usually more.[42] In France 1 s.t. a day was almost the minimum wage for all sorts of occupations, and many craftsmen were paid 18 d.t.[43] In both countries daily wages below these levels were given only to boys, women, carpenters' and masons' helpers, and other unskilled or partially trained workers. In France the lowest grades of royal officials—watchmen, jailers, forest guards, and porters—might receive only 6 to 8 d.t. a day, but many of these men could increase their income by receiving fees, free lodging, and other perquisites.[44]

40. See Prestwich, *War, Politics and Finance*, p. 76, for the English earls; *C.R.*, III, no. 30286 for the count of Artois.

41. *Histoire de Languedoc* (rev. ed., Toulouse, 1885), IX, 183, 193, 200; X, cols. 338–339 (hereafter cited as *H.L.*). According to J. Petit, *Essai de restitution*, p. 177, the count got 10,000 l. par. "pour sa terre garder." Roger-Bernard of Foix was also viscount of Béarn, and hence a vassal of Edward. For Edward's attempts to gain the count's support see Bémont, *Rôles Gascons*, no. 2936 and *H.L.*, IX, 184.

42. Rogers, *History of Agriculture and Prices*, I, 281–84. In the 1290s thatchers made 2 d. to 3 d. st. a day; carpenters, tilers, and plasterers, 2 d. to 4 d. Helpers often got only ½ or ¾ d., occasionally 1 d., rarely 1½ d. H. M. Colvin, *The History of the King's Works* (London, 1963), II, 1030–031, gives a higher range—masons 4 to 6 d., smiths 5 d., carpenters 5 or 6 d., common laborers (ditchdiggers, hod carriers) 1½ d. But these men were working on Edward's castles in Wales where labor was scarce. Carpenters who worked on the king's galleys in 1294 got 3 d. a day and their helpers 1½ d.; see articles listed in note 52.

43. The best examples come from the accounts in Toulouse in 1294; *C.R.*, I, nos. 9758–771. Ditchdiggers (117 in all) were paid 6 d.t. a day, carpenters 16 or 18 d.t., a roofer 18 d.t., carpenters' helpers 8 d.t. *C.R.*, I, nos. 11608, 11629, states that in 1299 in Toulouse a mortar-mixer got 9 d.t. and a roofer's helper 6 d.t. On the whole, French wages, at the official rate of exchange, averaged a little higher than English wages.

44. *C.R.*, I, nos. 7304, 7453. In Poitou, in 1293–94, seventeen forest guards and porters received 8 d.t. a day. According to nos. 7644 and 7848, in Saintonge such men got 6 d. or 8 d.t., and nos. 8215 and 8707 state that nine guards in Auvergne received 6 d. or 8 d.t. a day. According to A. Hellot, *Baillis de Caux* (Paris, 1895), guards of a fishpond in Caux were paid 8 d. par. (10 d.t.), but sergeants and forest guards at Maulévrier got only 4 d. par. (5 d.t.), pp. 171–72.

Thus the foot soldiers must have come from the poorest elements of the population; they were the only ones who had anything to gain by serving in the army. This conclusion fits well with what we know about recruiting methods; usually a district was simply ordered to provide a certain number of men. The easiest way out would be to send the most useless members of the community; they would never be missed and could not resist.

After wages, the next most expensive item was payment for horses lost by mounted soldiers. Each mounted man provided his own horse or horses (often one to ride and one to carry baggage), but if a horse died or broke down it had to be replaced by the government. It is interesting to note that the English spent £25,616 on horses and only £17,923 on their principal group of foot soldiers.[45] It is not surprising, however; a good horse cost more than the year's wages of an infantryman. At 1 s.t. a day, the man would earn about 18 l.t. a year. An ordinary packhorse could be had for less—say 5 to 10 l.t.—but a horse that could carry a man in armor would cost 25 to 100 l.t.[46] We have no summary of French payments for horses, but judging by the frequent entries in the accounts they must have spent about as much as the English on this item.

Equipment was not much of a burden to either treasury. Mounted men were supposed to provide their own weapons and armor; fortunately for them this material was durable since it was relatively expensive. There are some French accounts which give prices of armor, probably purchased for men-at-arms and the poorer nobles, perhaps as replacements for damaged pieces. The price of new equipment was deducted from the wages of the nobles, a practice that would have sharply reduced their profits if they had to buy much armor. Thus a bassinet with a noseguard cost 6 l.t., a simple bassinet 1 to 4 l.t. A mail shirt could go as high as 6 l.t., though there were many at 2 to 3 l.t. Swords were surprisingly cheap, 10 s.t., 16 s.t., 21 s. 6 d.t. A saddle for a knight was 25 to 28 s. One entry gives 200 l.t. as the cost of a horse and "armatura."[47] At least in theory, however, all this cost the government little or nothing.

Foot soldiers were given their equipment, but it was of inferior quality

45. P.R.O., E 372/160; Bémont, (*Rôles Gascons*, p. clxxiv, horses were valued at 25 l.t. to 100 l.t. (4 at 80 l.t.)

46. See note 45 for horses for the Anglo-Gascon army. For the French, see *C.R.*, II, nos. 26183, 26199, 26267, 26275, 26276, 26360 list packhorses at 4 to 10 l.t.; nos. 26094, 26100, 26101, 26102, 26104, 26151, 26264, 26271, 26273 list combat horses at 30 to 100 l.t.

47. *C.R.*, II, nos. 26044, 26047, 26048, 26050, 26056, 26063, 26065, 26067, 26172, 26182, 26217, 26241, 26245–246. *C.R.*, II, no. 25386, states that 5,498 l.t. were deducted from wages of those who needed armor in 1296.

and added little to overall expense. We have two very interesting accounts of arms purchased for foot soldiers in Toulouse in 1295.[48] Standard equipment was a quilted tunic, a bassinet (probably leather, since they cost much less than the iron ones mentioned above), a gorget, a crossbow, and a belt and quiver. The first order, for defensive arms for 1,000 men, was filled fairly quickly and probably at standard prices. The average cost of a tunic was 17 s. 4 d.t. All the bassinets were 5 s.t. apiece, and all the gorgets 1 s. 9 d. each. Crossbows were not included. The second order was for 2,000 bassinets, gorgets, and crossbows. It could not be completely filled, and there was more variation in prices. Gorgets were a little more expensive (up to 2 s. 3 d. or 2 s. 4 d.) while bassinets were cheaper, (2 s. 6 d. to 4 s. 8 d.). But the greatest variations were in the price of crossbows; the cheapest were 3 s. 4 d. and the most expensive 15 s.[49] Crossbows with two stirrups naturally were more expensive (11 to 15 s.) than crossbows with one stirrup, but some of the one-stirrup bows cost 14 s. and a great many were 8 or 10 s. apiece. Quality differences and increasing scarcity probably caused these variations in price. The average cost for the 1,431 crossbows that were bought was 7 s. 3½ d. Thus a foot soldier could be equipped with tunic, bassinet, gorget, crossbow, and such trimmings as belt and quiver, for about 34 s.t. Equipment for 1,000 men would have cost 1,700 l.t. For a company that served a little more than two months equipment would cost 6 d. per day per man.

These figures may be compared with those for English infantry sent to Gascony in 1295. Tunics were 3 s. st. (12 s.t.) The men also had knives and swords. Equipment and expenses (whatever the latter were), came to 5 s. 1 d. st. per man (20 s. 4 d.t.).[50] This is less than the French average, but the difference would be largely made up by the cost of a crossbow. English foot soldiers were supposed to provide their own bows.[51]

Both England and France spent considerable sums of money in hiring and building ships, but the financial records for the navies are very imperfect. Edward was worried about a possible French invasion, and he seems to have been especially concerned by the fact that the French had leased or were building galleys. He ordered the construction of thirty galleys

48. *C.R.*, II, nos. 25075–303. These documents were discussed by Philippe Wolff in his article "Achats d'armes pour Philippe le Bel dans la région Toulousaine," *Annales du Midi*, *61* (1948–49), 84–91. For similar prices in Bruges see n. 63 below.

49. Prices are confused by the fact that some dealers charged a flat price per bow, no matter what type, see, for example, *C.R.*, II, no. 25168, which lists forty bows, twenty-seven with one stirrup, thirteen with two, "una cum alia computata. 14 s." Cf. no. 25165. Both these dealers came from Montpellier.

50. Prestwich, *War, Politics and Finance*, p. 101.

51. Ibid., p. 105.

in November 1294; the vessels were completed in 1295. We have accounts for seven of these; the costs run from £116 for a small galley built at Lyme to £304 for a very large galley built at London.[52] The average price was £230, which may be a little low, since larger vessels should have formed the bulk of the fleet. On the other hand, not all the galleys ordered were built. A rough estimate would be that Edward spent about £6,900 on the fleet.

The king also ordered the strengthening of 210 ships so that they could carry horses, and also have fighting decks.[53] There is no way of estimating how much this work cost, if it were done at all. On the whole Edward relied largely on hiring or impressing merchant ships for short periods. This was not very expensive. The account for the Gascon war lists only £16,869 as payments to mariners, and other wages given by Prestwich include so many non-Gascon items that it is doubtful that the total amount spent on shipping to Gascony was much above £25,000.[54]

Philip made a serious effort to distract the English by threatening an invasion. In 1294 he ordered twenty galleys from Marseilles and an unspecified number from Genoa.[55] The number of Provençal galleys was soon increased to thirty; they were to serve the king at a cost of 360 l.t. per month per galley. This figure included food and wages for the crew, but not arms and weapons.[56] If Philip employed the thirty galleys for four months it would have cost him 43,200 l.t. or £10,800, plus the cost of arms. Edward's galleys cost him £6,900; pay for 120 men a galley at the English rate of 3 d. st. a day would have come to £5,400 if he had thirty galleys for four months. Again the cost of arms would be an additional expense. Thus Philip's galleys were cheaper for a short campaign, but over several years would have been more expensive.

Philip also hired twelve Spanish and Portuguese ships, and leased or impressed some hundreds of those of his own subjects (chiefly Normans). We can make a fairly good estimate of the size of his fleet through a curious

52. See Robert J. Whitwell and Charles Johnson, "The Newcastle Galley," *Archaeologia Aeliana*, 4th ser., *2* (1926), 145, for the cost of five galleys; Charles Johnson, "London Shipbuilding, 1295," *The Antiquaries Journal*, *7* (1927), pp. 424–30, for the cost of the two London galleys; and R. C. Anderson, "English Galleys in 1295," *The Mariner's Mirror*, *14* (1928), 222–233.

53. Bémont, *Rôles Gascons*, pp. cxlv-cxlvi, and nos. 3281–288.

54. Prestwich, *War, Politics and Finance*, p. 141, gives £12,852 for sailors' wages in 1295 (but this includes an attack on Anglesey). He gives £18,278 in 1296 for naval expenditures and prisoners taken in Scotland, and of this £1,519 went to fifty ships of the Cinque Ports sailing to Gascony. In 1297 £5587 went for sailors' wages, but only forty-four ships went to Gascony, while the main fleet went to Flanders.

55. Mignon, *Inventaire*, no. 2329.

56. Ch. Jourdain, "Mémoire sur les commencements de la marine militaire sous Philippe le Bel," *Mémoires de l'Académie des Inscriptions et Belles-Lettres*, *30* (1881), 406.

document that lists the ships and galleys to which wine was sent early in 1296.[57] There were 206 ships and about 50 galleys (there are some duplications in the latter group). Edward certainly had reason to worry about an invasion, though in the end the French force accomplished little.

As with the armies, the biggest expense for navies was wages, and relatively little money was spent on building and repairing ships. A rough idea of relative costs can be worked out from a memorandum sent to Philip in 1295 by Benedetto Zaccharia, the famous Genoese admiral.[58] He proposed a raid on England by sixteen ships and four galleys. The vessels were to carry 400 knights, 400 men-at-arms, and 4,800 armed mariners. The latter were to be paid 40 s.t. a month, although Benedetto admitted that they might be hired for 35 s.t. But he thought that he could get better men for 40 s. and that if they had higher pay they would grumble less about very simple food (bread, beans, and peas), which would cost only 15 s.t. per man per month.[59] He recommended a four-month campaign. Wages for mariners would be 38,400 l.t. and food 14,600 l.t. But arms were to cost only 3,000 l.t. and repairing, caulking, and refitting the ships, only 5,000 l.t.

By some curious chance, surviving accounts deal mainly with manning and provisioning the ships and rarely mention work on the ships themselves. Thus we know that over 1,600 mariners were sent from Provence and Genoa, presumably to man the galleys in Normandy,[60] but nothing is said about the size or cost of the galleys. We know that Benedetto Zaccharia was serving Philip by 1296 at very high wages—2 l. par. a day, a life pension of 200 l.t. a year, and 12,000 l.t. for certain special contracts—and that he commanded some galleys in 1297,[61] but we do not know if the 12,000 l.t. included a payment for providing the galleys. We know how much the wine cost that was distributed to ships and galleys at Rouen, but we have only one fragmentary account of work done on galleys at

57. *C.R.*, II, nos. 24719–734, 24827–858, 24905–941, 24736–825. Jourdain, "Mémoire," knew this document, pp. 397–99, he agrees with me about the number of ships and is fairly certain that there were only fifty galleys—I think there may have been a few more. Some of them were surely Provençal or Italian, see *C.R.*, II, nos. 24729, 24821, 24823, 24857, 24921–923.

58. E. Boutaric, "Notices et extraits de documents inédits relatifs à l'histoire de France sous Philippe le Bel," *Notices et Extraits*, *20*, pt. 2 (1861), 112–19.

59. Boutaric, "Notices et extraits," p. 116. Note that sailors were more expensive than soldiers. French foot soldiers would have received only 30 s.t. a month. Note also that, as usual, French wages were higher than English. E 372/160 m. 41. English sailors were paid 3 d.st. or 12 d.t. a day. French sailors paid 40 s.t. a month would receive 16 d.t. a day.

60. Mignon, *Inventaire*, nos. 2316–318, 2320, 2322, 2323, 2326–328, 2329, 2331, 2333.

61. Ibid., no. 2325; *C.R.*, II, no. 24676; J. Viard, *Journaux du Trésor de Philippe le Bel*, nos. 345, 938, 996, 1237, 2478, 2525, 2994, 3259.

Rouen and this is for the period from All Saints, 1297, to Pentecost, 1298, when both England and France were relaxing their naval preparations. During this period there were never more than sixty men and women employed in the shipyard at any one time and one week the total sank as low as eleven. The total wage bill was only 428 l.t.[62] There was a fleet in the Gironde protecting the approaches to Bordeaux, but the 23,141 l.t. spent on it in 1296 was largely, if not entirely, for wages.[63] The only useful entry dealing with shipbuilding and repairs comes from Bruges, where 27,737 l.t. was spent in 1295, largely to repair and strengthen ships.[64] Bruges was not the chief center of French shipbuilding. Much more must have been spent in Normandy, but it is impossible to determine how much more.

Considerable amounts of money were spent on victualing, especially when large numbers of men were to be transported by sea. Thus the peak of expenses for food and drink for both countries came in 1295–96, when Edward was sending a large army to Gascony and Philip was trying to provision his invasion fleet. Theoretically, soldiers and sailors were supposed to feed themselves, buying supplies with their wages, but this was not always possible, especially on a sea voyage. Living off the country was another possibility, but both sides were trying to conciliate the inhabitants of Aquitaine and little plundering took place in the duchy. At the very least, both Edward and Philip had to accumulate stocks that their troops could buy, and on many occasions they had to give them away, as Philip did at Rouen in 1296.[65] This could be fairly expensive. If 653 tuns of wine were given ships in 1296 and the average price per tun was 6 l. par., then the cost, not including carrying charges, would have been 3,918 l.p. or about 4,887 l.t.[66] The entries for bread, grain, peas, and bacon are fragmentary, and prices are not always given, but these supplies must have cost as much as the wine.

We have figures for grain purchased by Edward, but they must be

62. *C.R.*, II, nos. 24640–669.

63. Mignon, *Inventaire*, no. 2311.

64. *C.R.*, II, nos. 25416–434. According to nos. 25387–415, arms and armor cost 20,342 l.t. Some of this was heavy metal, but prices for ordinary equipment were close to those in Toulouse in the same year. Crossbows (with all the fittings) were a little over 6 s.t. each; bassinets, 6 s. 10 d.; and tunics (côtes gamboisiees), 11 s. 5 d.

65. *C.R.*, II, nos. 24717–890, 24905–942.

66. *C.R.*, II, no. 24942, gives the total amount of wine given to the ships. Nos. 24947–953 give prices for wine bought in Paris the same year for about 7 l. 10 s. a tun. Wine bought in 1295 was cheaper. Nos. 24502–532 list 282 tuns at an average price of 5 l. 10 s. (par.?) a tun; nos. 24535–24549 list poorer quality wine at 4 l. 10 s.

used with caution. When he was provisioning the expedition sent to Gascony in 1296 he ordered 13,500 quarters of wheat and 13,000 quarters of oats. At prevailing prices, this would have cost about £6,190 for wheat and £2,600 for oats. After the harvest of 1296, when prices had dropped, he ordered 33,800 quarters of wheat and 20,400 quarters of oats. If he collected it all, which is doubtful, the cost would have been £8,168 for wheat and £2,380 for oats. This, of course, was neither all net outlay, since many payments were postponed, nor all net loss, since some of it was certainly sold to troops. But it was a large operation. Next year (1297) grain expenditures for Gascony were much lower, 6,470 quarters of wheat and 10,452 quarters of oats or £2,049 for wheat and £1,500 for oats.[67]

Garrisons also had to be supplied when they were cut off from surrounding areas. Much of the English grain, especially in 1297, went to the garrisons of Bayonne, Bourg, and Blaye.[68] The French accounts list two large payments in 1295, one of 43,064 l.t. for "garnisionibus . . . pro exercitu Vasconie" and another of 32,075 l.t. for "munitionibus Fronciaci et aliarum villarum."[69] It is very likely that most of this money was spent on food and wine, but "garnisiones" can mean simply the pay of troops and "munitiones" can include weapons.[70] Where supplies were easily available the government bought only small amounts at a time. For example, provisioning La Rochelle in 1294 cost about 360 l.t., and buying grain and pork for the garrison of Carcassonne in 1302–03 cost 819 l.t.[71]

Overall, the pay of troops certainly was far more expensive than their sustenance. At best, governments supplied only minimum amounts of food for their soldiers and sailors, such as the 6 d.t. a day allowed for sailors. In 1299 hostages from Bordeaux, who were prominent men, were granted 1 s.t. a day for food.[72] A little later, in 1303, captive Flemish

67. Prestwich, *War, Politics and Finance*, pp. 120–21, D. L. Farmer, "Some Grain Price Movements in Thirteenth Century England," *The Economic History Review*, 2d ser., *2* (1957), 212, for prices. Since Farmer's prices are by harvest years I have used his figure for 1295 (9 s. 2¾ d. for wheat and 3 s. ½ d. for oats) for the order early in 1296, and the 1296 figure (4 s. 10 d. for wheat and 2 s. 4 d. for oats) for the second order. In 1297 Farmer gives 6 s. 4 d. for wheat and 2 s. 10½ d. for oats.

68. P.R.O., E 372/160, m. 41 "freta navium diversa victualia de Anglia portantium in Vasconia usque Baionam . . . et de ibidem per vices usque Burgum et Blaviam." Bémont, *Rôles Gascons*, pp. cliv–clvi, gives some useful documents on supplying these garrisons.

69. Mignon, *Inventaire*, nos. 2264, 2283.

70. *C.R.*, I, nos. 12816ff., "garnisiones" in Carcassonne in 1302–03 are all expenses for wages; according to no. 13864, the same thing is true of Beaucaire. But, in Mignon, *Inventaire*, nos. 2265–289, "garnisiones" are all food for the navy. In *C.R.*, I, nos. 13017–020, "munitiones" in Carcassonne in 1302–03 include a large number of expensive crossbows.

71. *C.R.*, I, nos. 7712–728 (wheat cost 140 l.; beans, bacon, salt, spices, oil, wine, 110 l.), for La Rochelle; nos. 13017–019, for Carcassonne.

72. *C.R.*, I, nos. 12028–029.

knights were given 2 s. par. a day for food, and squires 6 d. par.[73] Thus even if all expenses for food and drink had been paid for by the government, which surely was not the case, the additional cost would have averaged out at less than 20 percent of wages.

Granting that the figures for purchases of arms and of food are very incomplete, it still seems unlikely that enough was spent to cause a boom in either the armaments industry or in agriculture. Only rarely were purchases so concentrated that they might have encouraged increases in production. Thus the orders for clothing and weapons sent to Toulouse in 1295 were divided among many suppliers (twenty-nine for tunics, twenty-two for bassinets, thirty-three for crossbows), and the biggest single payment was 168 l.t.[74] Moreover, the order for crossbows was not entirely filled, even though the king's agents went as far as Carcassonne, Béziers, and Montpellier in search of weapons.[75] Demand had not increased production.

Jean l'Archévêque had much the same experience when he was buying armor for the nobles of Toulouse in 1295. He had to go all over his province to acquire equipment, and some of it was certainly secondhand. Thus a notary supplied five sets of shoulder guards and a money-changer provided shoulder guards and a horse.[76] No one was making enough arms and armor to fill a very modest order.[77] Yet 1295 was the year in which the English were making a serious effort to recover Aquitaine and Philip was trying hard to prepare his invasion fleet. The equipment for foot soldiers bought in Toulouse was sent to Paris and Rouen,[78] almost certainly for the fleet, which suggests that manufacturing towns nearer the Channel were not producing large quantities of armaments. And if production were low in 1295, it must have been even lower as the tempo of the war lessened.

The one exception was the town of Bruges, which filled a large order (16,607 l.t.) for armor and weapons in 1295–96 without much difficulty.[79]

73. *C.R.*, I, nos. 4516, 4517.

74. See Wolff, "Achats d'armes pour Philippe le Bel," pp. 87, 88.

75. *C.R.*, II, nos. 25155–218.

76. *C.R.*, II, nos. 26091–093, 26096–098.

77. Jean's account is in *C.R.*, II, nos. 26044ff. As the heading shows, he spent 10,176 l.t., much of it on horses. If a horse and armor cost 200 l.t. (see n. 47 above) then Jean had only enough for fifty mounted men. Of course, he was not buying complete equipment but simply making up deficiencies. But many of the nobles received equipment that cost 20 to 70 l.t. so that the total force could have been only a few hundred men.

78. *C.R.*, II, nos. 25105, 25304–305.

79. *C.R.*, II, nos. 25387–407. The total for this account was 20,342 l.t., but I deducted 3735 l.t. for money spent on ships' stores.

But Bruges was a large and prosperous manufacturing town, and it was not really part of the French economic sphere. In fact, money spent in Bruges was apt to depress rather than stimulate business in northern French towns.

In England the rule that the individual or the community provided equipment seems to have been adhered to throughout the war.[80] Edward did pay for some heavy artillery,[81] but the cost of other equipment was fairly evenly spread throughout the country. No great center of war industry can have existed in England.

As for the building and refitting of ships, the same pattern of dispersion of activity seems to hold true. In France there should have been a concentration of shipyard workers in Rouen, Harfleur, and the ports at the mouth of the Seine, but if they were there they do not appear in the records. The one list of king's ships that we possess shows them scattered in twenty-one ports from St. Malo and Cherbourg to Dieppe and "Flanders." Presumably there were shipwrights in each port.[82] The galleys were concentrated in Rouen and Harfleur, but many, if not most of them had been built in Provence or Genoa[83] and required only maintenance work. It may be purely accidental, but it is curious that the one large account for work on ships that has survived comes from Bruges, just as the one large account for arms does.[84] On the whole, it would seem that French shipbuilding was not greatly stimulated by the war.

In England, the same conclusion seems to be true. Orders for galleys were carefully distributed throughout the country, one to a port in most cases, two to London.[85] When the king leased or requisitioned ships, he drew on many ports, though Yarmouth and the Cinque Ports usually had the largest contingents.[86] Demands for service from the king probably did no more than fill the decline in trade caused by the war. There was no reason for a boom in English shipbuilding.

On the whole, government purchases did not raise prices of agricultural

80. Prestwich, *War, Politics and Finance*, pp. 105–06.

81. Bémont, *Rôles Gascons*, pp. cxli (and E 372/160 m. 41). But this was only a part of some miscellaneous expenses which totaled £13,778, so the artillery cannot have been very costly.

82. This is the list mentioned in n. 57.

83. See n. 57 above. If there were only fifty galleys at Rouen and Harfleur and if over thirty of them came from the Mediterranean, there would not have been a massive shipbuilding effort in the ports of the Seine, though it would have been greater than that in any English district.

84. *C.R.*, II, nos. 25416–434. This account was for 27,737 l.t., but over half of this was spent on wages, guarding the port, and "damages" to shipmasters.

85. See the articles cited in n. 52 above.

86. Prestwich, *War, Politics and Finance*, pp. 140–41.

products or increase the profits of landlords and peasants. In the first place, royal estates produced large quantities of cereals (especially in southern France) which could be sent directly to the armed forces, thus decreasing demand in the open market. Except in emergencies, such as the provisioning of expeditionary forces in 1295, grain buying was spread out fairly evenly; not much was bought in one place at one time. Finally, royal officials could always commandeer supplies (the English right of "prise"). Even if they promised a fair price, delays in payment reduced the real value of the producer's income.[87]

The picture for England is fairly clear. Thorold Rogers's fragmentary data and the more refined tables of D. L. Farmer both show actual decline in grain prices during the war.[88] There had been a rising trend just before the war; it culminated in 1295 with wheat at 9 s. $2\frac{3}{4}$ a quarter and oats at 3 s. Heavy purchases by the Crown in that year may have contributed to the increase, but the king was still buying large quantities of grain in 1296 when wheat dropped to 4 s. 10 d. and oats to 2 s. 4 d. There was a recovery in 1297 (wheat 6 s. 4 d., oats 2 s. $10\frac{1}{2}$ d.) and then a steady decline to the 1303 low of 3 s. $7\frac{3}{4}$ d. for wheat and 1 s. 8 d. for oats. It is easy to agree with Prestwich's conclusion that no one was getting rich from sales of grain.[89]

For France the problem is more difficult. There are few precise figures, and those that do exist are not always comparable. There were wide differences in the measures used in different parts of the country, and after 1297 serious inflation of the currency must have had some effect on prices.

In 1296, when provisioning the fleet should have put pressure on prices, a large amount of wheat was sold in Andely, some at 17 s. 3 d.t. a *setier* and some at 18 s. 9 d.t. a setier.[90] This marks an increase over the 12 to 15 s. a setier which was the official rate for wheat in this region in the 1260s, but prices had been rising in France as in England during the latter part of the century, and the official value assigned to grain in estimating income from farms was at times below the market rate.[91] Much more striking

87. Prestwich, *War, Politics and Finance*, pp. 130, 135.

88. Rogers, *History of Agriculture and Prices*, I, 39–53; Farmer, "Some Grain Price Movements," p. 212.

89. Prestwich, *War, Politics and Finance*, pp. 135, 287.

90. *C.R.*, II, nos. 24601–602. The measure of Andely was slightly smaller than that of Rouen (98 *muids*, 11 *mines* = 95 muids 7 setiers, 1 mine, and 1 bushel) but this difference is not enough to affect the price per setier.

91. J. R. Strayer, *The Royal Domain in the Bailliage of Rouen* (Princeton, 1936), p. 25. Wheat in Rouen in 1261 was 12 s. a setier; west of the Seine, it was 14 or 15 s. For rents in grain taken above the official price, see ibid., pp. 58–59, wheat valued at 10 s. a *setier* taken for 12 s., barley at 6 s. taken for 8 s., and oats at 2 s. taken for 3 s. and, pp. 121–22, wheat valued at 13 s. 4 d.t. raised to 14 s.t.

are wheat prices in Paris, Senlis, and Ham (in Vermandois) in 1298–99.[92] When they are adjusted for differences in measures and for the 4 to 5 exchange rate between Paris and Tours money, we find that a setier, Rouen measure, would have cost from 21 s. 8 d.t. to 25 s.t. By this time money was overvalued by about a fourth,[93] however, so that if we allow for inflation we would come back to the 17 s. to 18 s. range of 1296. And by 1304, even though inflation was worse, both the market price and the price in terms of prewar money had dropped. There were extensive purchases of wheat in and around Tours in 1303–04; the price range was 9 s.t. to 10 s. a setier. After converting the Tours setier to the Rouen setier, the price is 16 s. 8 d.t. to 18 s.t. a setier.[94] By this time the currency was even more overvalued,[95] so that in terms of prewar money the cost of a setier would have been 9 s.t. at most. Just as in England, real prices had dropped by the end of the war. And just as in England, there was a recovery after the end of the war; in 1308–11 grain in the region of Gisors was valued at 10 s. par. or 12 s. 6 d.t. a setier.[96] If we assume that this district used Paris measure as well as Paris money, then a setier, Rouen measure, would have been worth 16 s. 8 d.t. This fits fairly well with an entry for Menneval in 1310 where the setier was 15 s.t.[97] On the other hand, wheat at Ecouis in 1308 was 20 s.t. a setier,[98] and in 1312 it went as high as 20 s. 8 d. a setier in the viscounty of Auge.[99] Peace and the restoration of good money had raised real prices above those of the war period.

92. *C.R.*, I, no. 374 (Paris and Senlis, 1298), nos. 1418–419 (Paris, 1299), no. 1925 (Ham, 1299). All of these have been adjusted to Rouen measure, because I have more data on Rouen prices than on any other region. The equivalences are given in J. Petit, *Essai de restitution*, p. 143. 16 setiers Paris = 12 setiers Rouen; 20 setiers Ham = 4 setiers, 6 mines, 3 bushels Paris. There are some less reliable entries for wheat from Melun, the Amiens region, and Senlis in 1298, less reliable because it is not certain what measure was used. Wheat from Melun seems to have been valued at 16 s. 8 d.t. to 17 s. 6 d.t. a setier; from Senlis, at 15 s. 8 d.t. to 17 s. 8 d.t. a setier; from Amiens, at about 17 s.t. See J. Viard, *Les Journaux du Trésor de Philippe IV le Bel*, nos. 1567, 1568, 921, 124. All figures have been converted to Rouen measure and Tours money.

93. Borrelli de Serres, *Variations monétaires*, pp. 324, 326. In 1299 the gros tournois, originally valued at 12 d.t., was taken by the French treasury at 16½ d.t. and by the count of Flanders at 16 d.t.

94. *C.R.*, II, nos. 27134–149, 27150, 27161, 27163, 27166. According to Petit, *Essai de restitution*, p. 142, 1 muid Tours = 8 setiers, 1 mine, 1 bushel Paris.

95. Borrelli de Serres, *Variations monétaires*, pp. 329–30, states that by 1304 the gros tournois was at 26 d.t. (instead of 12 d.t.) and other coins were even more overvalued.

96. J. Favier, *Cartulaire d'Enguerran de Marigny* (Paris, 1965), pp. 34, 53, 61, 124.

97. A.N., JJ 47, f. 64 v, no. 98.

98. Favier, *Cartulaire*, pp. 102, 103. This was Andely measure, almost the same as Rouen measure.

99. *C.R.*, II, nos. 17391, 17424. No. 17400 would put the *setier* at 30 s.t., but it is in the same district as the first two and there must be an error. Probably 20 s. was for the whole year and not for two of three terms. Strayer, *Royal Domain*, p. 202, a setier of wheat from the same farm was valued at 16 s.t. in 1261.

I have not tried to list price changes in the Midi, although there are many mentions of grain prices in

The war of Aquitaine transferred money from merchants, artisans, and producers of commercial crops (such as wool) to a few great lords, many middling and petty nobles, and some thousands of poor commoners. Very few of these people were in a position to invest their earnings in any productive enterprise. Most of them must have used their wages to maintain or slightly improve their level of living; that is, the money was spent on such consumption goods as food and clothing. A very large percentage of both armies came from the poorer parts of southwestern France and (for the English forces) northern Spain. Army pay doubtless relieved the poverty of these areas a little but it did not increase their productivity. The process is most clearly illustrated by the English accounts. About 200,000 £. st. was paid directly to Gascon and Spanish supporters of Edward I. English soldiers must have spent a considerable part of their wages in Aquitaine rather than in England, perhaps as much as 10,000 £. st. The horses bought to replace those lost must have been bought largely from Gascons and Spaniards—this would add another 25,000 £. st. The garrisons during the period of truce cost 30,690 £. st.; again most of this money must have been spent in Gascony.[100] Thus something like £265,000 was transferred from England to Gascony—more than the £257,000 raised by personal property taxes in England from 1294 to 1301. England was pouring huge sums of money into Gascony—and getting nothing in return.

France was in a somewhat better position, because the money spent on the war remained within the country and some of it flowed back into the central and northern provinces. But even for France there was a heavy shift of income from prosperous regions to the sub-Pyrenean counties and the petty lords of Languedoc and the Massif Central. In France as in England there were clear signs of financial exhaustion by the early 1300s. The yield of English taxes went down, and in France general taxes practically ceased for twelve years. Both countries found it difficult to pay for wars that they really wanted to win—the English conquest of

---

the seneschals' accounts of 1293–94 and 1299. This is because I could find no sure basis for comparison. But it may be worth noting that in the Toulouse area the setier of wheat was 6 s. 4 d.t. in 1294 and from the same farm 7 s. 3 d. in 1299. A setier from another region in the same year was valued at 9 s.t. The *quarton*, the most common measure used in Toulouse, was valued at 18 s.t. and at 24 s.t. in 1294, and regularly at 40 s.t. in 1299. Allowing for inflation, this would still mean a significant rise for the quarton and no increase at all for the setier. I cannot reconcile these figures. The data may be found in *C.R.*, I, nos. 9220, 11296, 12064 for the setier and nos. 9226, 9246, 11205, 11253, 12062 for the quarton. (1 s. tol. = 2 s. tur.)

100. P.R.O., E 372/160 m. 41; Prestwich, *War, Politics and Finance*, p. 171.

Scotland and the French conquest of Flanders—because they wasted so much on a war they had not desired.

Prestwich has pointed out that the Welsh and Scottish wars of Edward I enriched a few border families, such as the Percies and the Cliffords, but did not enhance the fortunes of the propertied classes in the settled part of the realm.[101] Mallet has shown that the Italian wars of the fourteenth and fifteenth centuries transferred wealth from the great commercial and banking centers of Florence and Venice to poorer towns, such as Urbino, because many of the leaders of the condottieri came from the poorer regions of Italy.[102] These examples suggest that the new type of warfare that begain the 1290s had similar economic consequences throughout western Europe.

These economic consequences of war certainly contributed to the great European depression of the later Middle Ages. There were other causes—overpopulation in some areas, inability to increase significantly the production of raw materials or manufactured goods, lack of new markets—but the costs of war may have been the determining factor. A certain equilibrium might have been, and indeed was achieved from time to time, but it was constantly upset by war expenditures. War transferred wealth from the productive to the nonproductive sector, from the savers to the wasters, from the innovators to the traditionalists. And it may be that the invention of gunpowder and cannon, which created a military-industrial complex, was one of the first steps out of the depression because it began to funnel war costs back into industry.

101. Prestwich, *War, Politics and Finance*, p. 284.

102. Michael Mallet, *Mercenaries and Their Masters—Warfare in Renaissance Italy* (Totowa, N.J., 1974), p. 228. D. Waley, "The Army of the Florentine Republic from the Twelfth to the Fourteenth Century," in *Florentine Studies*, ed. N. Rubenstein (London, 1968), pp. 92–93. By the end of the thirteenth century Florence was recruiting a considerable part of its cavalry from the poorer, mountainous areas of central Italy.

15

Wrocław Citizens as Rural Landholders

Richard C. Hoffmann

Urban dwellers' investment in rural lordships was a protean phenomenon of the later Middle Ages. Around Metz wealthy *patriciens* had begun to buy up landed properties as early as the twelfth century, but they expanded their rural interests in response to social unrest, economic instability, and weakening of commercial markets beginning in the late thirteenth century. By enclosing fields for pasture or vineyards and by restructuring arable into efficient large farms, they helped to spread an urban commercial orientation in the countryside.[1] Especially in the wake of the troubles of the fourteenth century, land seemed a secure investment for what had become surplus capital, whether it was managed for market production by leading families of Pistoia or yielded a stable *rentier* income to those of Ypres, Bruges, and Ghent.[2] But a landed estate offered more than mere economic diversification. For those townsmen who continued to accept traditional values, it was a first step toward an elevation of status and ultimate upward mobility into the traditional noble or gentry elite.

Portions of this study were presented in somewhat different form at the Eighty-sixth Annual Meeting of the American Historical Association, New York, 1971. The comments of David Herlihy aided subsequent revisions. So, too, did those of students in my undergraduate seminar on the late medieval economy at York University, 1974–75. In this study modern Polish place names are used for all settlements which still exist. Settlements which disappeared during or after the Middle Ages are given the reconstructed names found in Józef Domański, *Nazwy Miejscowe Dzisiejszego Wrocławia i Dawnego Okregu Wrocławskiego* (Warszawa, 1967). Reconstructed names are enclosed in asterisks (i.e. *Bienkowice*). Personal names are given in a standard English form where such exists (i.e. Peter), but where more appropriate or necessary, a standardized medieval form is used (i.e. Hans, Lenart, Poppo). Orthographic convention was not characteristic of late medieval Silesian writers.

1. Jean Schneider, *La ville de Metz aux XIIIe et XIVe siècles* (Nancy, 1950), pp. 394–426.

2. David Herlihy, *Medieval and Renaissance Pistoia: The Social History of an Italian Town, 1200–1430* (New Haven, 1967), pp. 120–79, 192–97; David M. Nicholas, "Town and Countryside: Social and Economic Tensions in Fourteenth-Century Flanders," *Comparative Studies in Society and History, 10* (1968), 473–84, and *Town and Countryside: Social, Economic, and Political Tensions in Fourteenth-Century Flanders* (Bruges, 1971), pp. 267–330.

Wealthy and powerful Flemish bourgeois avidly emulated their poorer but more prestigious noble neighbors and saw in their own acquisitions of land a means for attaining the leisurely life inherent in their ambitions. For London merchants, too, land ownership provided security and status, a means not of disrupting traditional relationships, but of joining in them.[3] The acquisition of rural lordships by city people is, therefore, no evidence for significant changes in landlord practices or attitudes or for accelerated diffusion of the commercial revolution into the countryside.[4] Instead each individual case partakes of that variety and local contingency so characteristic of medieval urban history.

In east-central Europe the chief city of Silesia, Wrocław (German Breslau), achieved in the later Middle Ages local autonomy and considerable power over its immediate hinterland, the duchy of Wrocław.[5] At the same time members of the city's ruling families acquired extensive estates in the countryside. In a massive study of the Wrocław *Patriziat* Gerhard Pfeiffer gave great attention to this, the most widely documented of their economic activities. He reached two complementary conclusions: between the early fourteenth and the mid-sixteenth century the urban magnates uninterruptedly expanded their rural holdings in the duchy and, especially from the fifteenth century, their "capitalist" attitudes and motivations impelled significant innovations in property management and agricultural practice.[6] Because Pfeiffer's has become the standard

3. Nicholas, *Town and Countryside*, 250–66; Sylvia L. Thrupp, *The Merchant Class of Medieval London, 1300–1500* (Ann Arbor, 1948), pp. 118–30. Herlihy, *Pistoia*, 192–97, notes the traditional paternalism of urban landlords toward their peasant tenants, while several further examples of the desire for security and status on the part of late medieval townsmen who purchased country estates appear in Jacques Heers, *L'Occident aux XIVe et XVe siècles: Aspects économiques et sociaux* (2d ed. rev., Paris, 1966), pp. 226–27.

4. E. J. Hobsbawm spoke of another period, but his conclusion applies to the later Middle Ages as well: "The mere existence of urban investment in agriculture or urban influence over the countryside, therefore, did not imply the creation of rural capitalism" ("The Crisis of the Seventeenth Century," *Past and Present*, *5* (1954), as reprinted in *Crisis in Europe, 1560–1660: Essays from Past and Present*, ed. Trevor Aston [London, 1965], p. 24).

5. For a detailed discussion see Richard C. Hoffmann, "Towards a City-State in East-Central Europe: Control of Local Government in the Late Medieval Duchy of Wrocław," *Societas: A Review of Social History*, *5* (1975), 173–99. In brief, hereditary subdivision and fraternal warfare within the old Piast ducal line reduced the area ruled by dukes in Wrocław in the early fourteenth century to about half that of Rhode Island. Simultaneously, Silesia gradually slid out of the traditional Polish orbit and into that of Bohemia. Under the terms of an inheritance agreement, the death of the last Wrocław Piast, Henry VI, in 1335 brought the city and duchy into the direct rule of John of Luxemburg, King of Bohemia. Although the province remained part of the Bohemian crown until the eighteenth century, the hereditary duchies like Wrocław were governed for the king by appointed captains, initially indigenous or Czech noblemen, but increasingly (and from the early fifteenth century to 1636 almost exclusively), the Wrocław Rat itself. The city and its citizens dominated, too, other levels of the duchy's administrative and judicial institutions.

6. Gerhard Pfeiffer, *Das Breslauer Patriziat im Mittelalter* (Breslau, 1929), notably pp. 206–22, 317–18.

work, his interpretation of citizen landlordship has served to explain the disappearance of some rural settlements and certain aspects of the sovereigns' progressive loss of fiscal rights,[7] although some recent Polish scholarship also sees in the quantitative growth of townsman properties an increasing congruence between the interests of noble and citizen "feudal lords."[8] Though advanced without additional evidence, this last assertion conflicts with Pfeiffer's view of urban attitudes. In addition, earlier work by Heinrich Wendt contains unsubstantiated suggestions that the half-century of rural anarchy after the Hussite invasions of the 1420s may have interrupted the steady increase in the proportion of holdings in townsmen hands.[9] With such remarks in mind, closer examination of Pfeiffer's evidence and reasoning raises doubts as to the sufficiency of his demonstration.

Pfeiffer used simple but potentially biased techniques. He first acquired all available information about members of all lineages ever represented on the city council and assembled these data into family histories. Grouped according to family origin, these histories are then discussed under three chronological headings which derive from Wrocław's internal political history. Pfeiffer made, however, no attempt to count citizen landholdings at any time or to assess possible rates of change over time. His conclusion that these properties equaled or exceeded those of the nobility in the fourteenth and fifteenth centuries is based solely upon the numerous recorded instances of townsmen buying land from noblemen.[10] Pfeiffer offers similar reasoning from exemplary evidence to support the qualitative assertion that, because townsmen behaved differently toward landed

7. Karl Eistert, "Die Wüstungen Bartuschowitz und Sdanowitz bei Alt Schlesing (früher Alt Schliesa), Kreis Breslau," *Zeitschrift des Vereins für Geschichte Schlesiens, 77* (1943), 138; Jozef J. Menzel, *Jura ducalia: die mittelalterlichen Grundlagen der Dominialverfassung in Schlesien* (Würzburg, 1964), p. 155. Rudolf Stein, *Der Rat und die Ratsgeschlechter des alten Breslau* (Würzburg, 1963), is, in the main, merely a popularization of Pfeiffer.

8. Karol Maleczyński in Wacław Długoborski, Józef Gierowski, and Karol Maleczyński, *Dzieje Wrocławia do roku 1807* (Wrocław, 1958), p. 265; Roman Heck in *Historia Śląska*, ed. Karol Maleczyński, I, *Do roku 1763*, pt. 2, *Od polowy XIV do trzeciej ćwierci XVI w.* (Wroclaw, 1961), p. 56.

9. Heinrich Wendt, "Breslaus Streben nach Landbesitz im 16. Jahrhundert," *Zeitschrift des Vereins für Geschichte Schlesiens, 32* (1898), 215–16, is followed by August Kraemer, *Die wechselnde wirtschaftliche und politische Bedeutung des Landbesitzes der Stadt Breslau* (Breslau, 1927), p. 34, whose argument is equally unsupported. For a full examination of the duchy's rural difficulties, see Richard C. Hoffmann, "Warfare, Weather, and a Rural Economy: The Duchy of Wroclaw in the Mid-Fifteenth Century," *Viator: Medieval and Renaissance Studies, 4* (1973), 273–305.

10. Pfeiffer, *Patriziat*, esp. pp. 204–06. In fairness, Pfeiffer admits that he knows little about the size of the nobility's share. He is most impressed, however, by the contrast between the indubitably extensive citizen holdings of the late Middle Ages and the twenty nonurban properties held by citizens in the eighteenth century.

property than did older landlord groups, nobles or churchmen, they must have possessed different attitudes toward it. Rapid turnover of their holdings and the reputed absence of enduring and personal involvement with their tenants supposedly manifest their speculative concern to maximize short-run gains.[11] Conversely, capital improvements, construction of water mills, excavation of fish ponds, operation of good-sized herds, and even a move toward increased direct exploitation of demesnes for large-scale cereal production indicate the advanced and rationalized economic thinking which Wrocław's citizens brought to the late medieval countryside.[12] Pfeiffer's examples are accurate. Anecdotal references do show citizens purchasing properties, dealing in them at an amazing rate of turnover, and making various profitable improvements. But the reality of such incidents alone cannot suffice to confirm assertions as to the relative proportion of such lordships or as to the existence of a difference in kind between their owners' behavior and that of other landlords.

Even a cursory look at activities of "traditional" landlord groups demonstrates the inadequacy of anecdotal answers to what are comparative questions. For example, by about 1400 a townsman named Nicholas Owras had bought up almost all of Wróbłowice. He was succeeded in this lordship by Lenart Reichart and, in the 1440s, Conrad Steinkeller, both fellow citizens. But by 1425 the noble Franz Schellendorf had acquired the demesne once held by Reichart; it remained in Schellendorf hands until 1450. Meanwhile lordship over (and rents from) the peasant tenants who occupied most of the local arable had passed in 1446 from Conrad Steinkeller's heirs to Peter von Falkenhain, member of an ancient and durable knightly lineage. Not until the ambitious Wrocław merchant and politician Hans Popplaw bought it in 1531 did Wróbłowice return to citizen control.[13] Similar instances of noble acquisition of former citizen holdings are not at all uncommon. After a century of townsman ownership the village of Damianowice fell to the noble Seidlitz clan from

11. Ibid., pp. 317–18.

12. Ibid., esp. pp. 207–22, 317.

13. Repertorium Frobenianum. Repertorium investiturarum in praediis ducatus Wratislaviensis, quae in libris ejusdem cancellarie continentur" (hereafter cited as RF). 5 vols., Archiwum Państwowe we Wroclawiu, Archiwum miasta Wroclawia (hereafter cited as APW, A.m.), C 24, 1–5, I, 133–39; II, 826; "Registrum omnium bonorum sive villarum et allodiorum in districtibus Wratislaviensi, Noviforensi et Awrassensi super pecunia Burnegelt anno etc. XXV" (henceforth RB), APW, A.m., C 20, f. 13ʳ; Heilige Geist: Zinsbuch (1430–37), APW, A.m., Q 28, "Inhaltsverzeichniss der ausserurkundlichen Papiere des Jesuiter-Collegium zu Breslau (1352–1788)," APW, Rep. 135, B 72, sec. VII, pt. III, no. 11. On the Popplaw family see Ludwig Petry, *Die Popplau: Eine schlesische Kaufmannsfamilie des 15. und 16. Jahrhunderts* (Breslau, 1935).

1446 to 1542, while at Kobierzyce the mid-fifteenth century rule of Conrad Schellendorf, Hans Löbil, and Christina Reibnitz intervened between that of citizens in the fourteenth and sixteenth centuries.[14] Nor were townsmen the only ones involved in high-speed property transactions. Of the twenty-eight officially recorded conveyances concerning lands of the rather small village of Krajków from 1350 to 1399 (better than one every two years), only one participant was a citizen.[15] When George Busswoin bought the demesne at Cesarzowice near Środa from Hans and Christoph Schellendorf in November 1496, and sold it back to them less than four years later (neither price is known), he behaved no differently than did the Wrocław citizens whose similar actions are seen as evidence of real estate speculation.[16]

Improvement of their landed estates was not an activity unfamiliar to traditional landlords, whether nobles or churchmen. Ecclesiastical promotion of the more productive institutional arrangements called German law is a commonplace of east-central European history. More concretely, noble landlords often pursued long-term policies of property consolidation. Poppo von Haugwitz bought most of the land in Bagno from Jesco of "Symeanowicz" and from his wife's cousins, Bernard and Kedelo of "Baruth" in 1337 and the next year purchased a variety of ducal rights from Conrad von Borsnitz. Then he waited until 1365 to complete control of the village by acquiring the share of Bartholomew of "Wesenburg."[17] Between 1427 and 1429 Hans Radak, in six separate transactions, bought into and then bought up all of Zakrzyce, while it took George Kreiselwitz nine purchases over thirty-eight years (1479–1517) to do the same in Cesarzowice.[18] When it came to capital investment, even Pfeiffer's own listing of five instances in which "rücksichtslos kaufmännisch" ("ruthlessly commercial") landlords flooded peasant fields to create fish ponds for their own profit includes among the participants two members of the oldest nobility, Hans Swenkenfeld and Landisloth

14. RF, I, 76^{v}–79^{r}, 462–66, for the two cases mentioned. At Sadowice, Ratyn, and Sośnica, too, noble owners replaced townsmen in the fifteenth century (RF, III, 265–69, 2069–081, 2409–425).

15. RF, I, 487–88.

16. Ibid., IV, 3039–059.

17. Colmar Grünhagen et al., eds., *Regesten zur schlesischen Geschichte*, 6 vols. in 8 (Breslau, 1875–1925), nos. 5819, 5988, and 6031 (hereafter cited as *Reg.*); RF, I, 239–40.

18. *RF*, III, 270–77; IV, 3039–059. Between 1369 and 1398 Henry Zweibrodt and his brothers, none of whom ever claimed to be citizens, created the extensive property thereafter called "Zweibrodt" (now Zabrodzie) by purchase and merger of the since-disappeared *Bienkowice*, *Łagów*, and *Cesarzowice* (RF, I, 147–54; IV, 3077–083). Acquiring ducal jurisdictional and fiscal rights over one's property, an act of townsmen and nobles alike, was, from the landlords' perspective, but another step in the consolidation process. See the separate but similar descriptions in Menzel, *Jura ducalia*, pp. 145–52, 155–57.

Schellendorf.[19] Churchmen, too, often spent their funds to maintain and improve their herds and buildings.[20] Thus the similarity of other landlords' behavior to that which Pfeiffer adduces for Wrocław citizens suggests that piling up examples cannot resolve the issues. The mere presence of citizen lordships cannot establish changes in their quantitative importance or any peculiar qualities which they may have brought to this new role. In this situation assessment of the significance of townsmen's rural properties requires an explicitly comparative and quantitative approach. Data from the Wrocław duchy permit such an analysis of both the numerical and operational features of citizen landownership. In addition, by lending meaning to still other aspects of citizen behavior, the analysis will indicate that such holdings brought little novelty to the countryside because the townsmen conceived of them more as a secure means of rising within the traditional social order than of breaking with it.

When John of Luxemburg arranged for the governance of his newly inherited Wrocław duchy in 1336, he introduced from his Bohemian kingdom a requirement that conveyances of properties held as fiefs from the sovereign be recorded in official registers. Thus each time a landlord sold, pawned, made a gift of, or sold annuities on a holding, the transaction achieved legal force through a charter issued in the duchy's highest court, the iudicium curiae or Hofgericht. These charters were copied into an official Landbuch. The Landbücher, in turn, served as both an administrative tool and a legal record if the transaction were disputed or the original lost. By the mid-sixteenth century these totaled more than thirty chronological volumes with, after 1367, separate series for permanent transactions,

19. See Pfeiffer, *Patriziat*, p. 213, although he omits mention of other ponds constructed at Cesarzowice under the Schellendorf and the Kreiselwitz about 1500. On the general importance, profitability, and sophistication of pisciculture in sixteenth-century Silesia, see Aleksander Nyrek, *Gospodarka rybna na Górnym Śląsku od połowy XVI do połowy XIX wieku* (Wrocław, 1966). Other noble landowners constructed a mill to grind woad (*waytmole*) at Jakubowice before 1400. See Gertrude Dyhernfurth, *Ein schlesisches Dorf und Rittergut. Geschichte und sozial Verfassung* (Leipzig, 1906), pp. 25–26.

20. One of the praiseworthy acts for which the canons regular of St. Mary on the Sand Islet at Wrocław remembered Abbot John of Prague (1375–86) was his construction of good buildings on their demesne farms at Gajowice and Tyniec Mały. See *Chronica abbatum Beatae Mariae virginis in Arenae*, ed. Gustav A. H. Stenzel (Breslau, 1839), p. 207. According to *Reg.*, no. 1275, the cathedral chapter's demesne at Polanowice contained 200 sheep, 4 cows, 22 swine, 12 oxen, and 2 draft cows in 1267 (*Reg.*, no. 1275), while that at *Siedlec* included over 100 sheep when a canon leased it to some townsmen in 1358. See "Auszüge aus dem verlorenen Breslauer Stadtbuch Hirsuta Hilla, 1328–1360," APW, A.m., G 3, ff. 10^{r}–10^{v}. A full range of managerial activities, including improvements, herds, and cereal production with wage and forced labor, may also be found in the accounts kept by the Holy Spirit Hospital for its demesne farms at Trestno and Wysoka. See "Heilige Geist: Zinsbuch," f. 26^{v} and passim.

repurchasable pawns and rents, and marriage settlements.[21] Only in the 1560s did the secretary of the duchy reorganize even the records of permanent transactions, the so-called "libri perpetuorum" whose eight volumes then contained some 10,000 entries, into an easily consulted topographic-alphabetical register, the "Repertorium Frobenianum," in which for each settlement all pertinent charters were summarized in chronological order.[22] The complete set of original Landbücher was available to Pfeiffer, but he used only information about his leading townsmen; since 1945 all have been lost. Only the "Repertorium Frobenianum" survives. Its virtually complete listing of permanent conveyances of landed property from the accession of the Luxemburgs to the mid-sixteenth century permits, however, reconstruction of the sequence of lordships in most of the duchy's settlements. These, in turn, can be verified by comparison with all other information about each place, primarily but not exclusively fiscal surveys and tax accounts from 1353, 1425, and 1443, and a register of landowners' privileges compiled in 1548. Ecclesiastical landlords, the bishop, abbeys, convents, and hospitals, kept their own cartularies and also appear in many of the fiscal texts. Thus the property conveyances and other supporting documents enable creation of lordship series (some with gaps, true) for each of the 384 rural settlements known for the Wrocław duchy before 1540.[23] For identification and linkage of individuals and lineages one must rely heavily on Pfeiffer, but most individuals bore surnames and the conveyancing charters themselves usually distinguished the status of the participants and often mentioned relevant family connections.[24]

21. The conveyancing and registration system is fully described in Pfeiffer, *Patriziat*, 197–200, with several examples of regular official and private reference to it in the fourteenth and fifteenth centuries. The fullest description of the records themselves remains, however, Georg Bobertag, "Die Gerichte und Gerichtsbücher des Fürstenthums Breslau," *Zeitschrift des Vereins für Geschichte Schlesiens, 7* (1866), 102–75.

22. RF. The compiler's difficulty with some fourteenth-century name forms does, however, require some care in its use.

23. The reference to 384 rural settlements counts all identifiable places up to 1540. Places documented only thereafter are invariably new and later, not medieval, settlements. Of course not all of the 384 places existed at the same time. About a dozen sites of early medieval habitation disappeared during the course of the twelfth and thirteenth centuries and more vanished during the later Middle Ages. At the same time, some villages were founded only during or even after the thirteenth century. Tables 15.1 and 15.2 relate the samples used to both the gross total, 384, and to estimates of the places actually inhabited at the times investigated.

24. Examples of the collation and linkage techniques used to establish lordship series may be found in Richard C. Hoffmann, "Nazwy i miejscowości: trzy studia z historii średniowiecznej okręgu wrocławskiego," *Śląski Kwartalnik Historyczny Sobótka, 29* (1974), 1–25, where sequences of buyers and sellers serve

The assembled lordship series permit measurement of the quantitative importance of citizen landholding at any time in the later Middle Ages. The technique adopted was comparative statics, the calculation and comparison of townsmen's shares in rural properties at specific dates. The particular five years here compared (1300, 1353, 1425, 1480, and

---

to distinguish among settlements with virtually identical names. For another example, considerably briefer than most, here are summary translations of the entries for Kazimierzów (then called Nidenchen) in RF, II, 810–14, beginning after a break between 1375 and 1388 during which Peter Beyer apparently obtained the property from the last known holder, Nicholas Dobrischow, schulz of Ludów Śląski:

May 20, 1388—Peter Beyer, citizen of Wrocław, cedes to Paul Werber, schulz at Żurawina, the property Nidenchen.

December 18, 1406—Paul Werber, schulz at Żurawina, cedes to Steffan Kindelswirth, his stepson, all of his property in Nidenchin. (RF erroneously dates this entry to 1466, but its appearance at this point in the sequence and the presence of Beneš of Chustník as captain (who served 1400–03 and 1404–08) makes 1406 the most likely correct date.)

March 28, 1408—The same Paul Werber, the "old schulz" at Żurawina, repeats his cession of all his property at Nidenchin to his same stepson, Steffan Kindelswirth.

April 7, 1434—Caspar, son of Steffan Kindelswirth, schulz at Żurawina, cedes to Peter Stronchen, citizen of Wrocław, all of his properties in Nidenchin.

January 23, 1447—Peter Stronchen, citizen of Wrocław, cedes to Wenceslas Reichel, citizen of Wrocław, his property and demesne at Nidenchin.

April 27, 1448—Hans Bank, citizen of Wrocław. (During the later fifteenth century the RF entries are often restricted to names and dates alone or even, as immediately below, just a name. Comparison with surviving copies of original charters indicates that the names are those of purchasers and the dates those at which they acquired the property from the individual who precedes them in the list.)

undated—Steffan Bank [citizen of Wrocław, son of Hans (Pfeiffer, *Patriziat*, p. 322)].

April 1, 1471—Wenceslas Bank [citizen of Wrocław, brother of Steffan].

November 9, 1476—Corroborative reference in a letter from the Wrocław city council to King Mathias Corvinus reporting the kidnapping of Wenceslas Bank from his property at Neidenchen by a band of brigands who held him in a Czech castle for ransom. See Berthold Kronthal and Heinrich Wendt, eds., *Politische Correspondenz Breslaus im Zeitalter des Königs Matthias Corvinus*, 2 vols. (Breslau, 1893–94), I, 202–03.

undated—Steffan Bank [see entry above].

April 22, 1482—Michael Spiegler, son-in-law of Steffan Bank [also called Joppener, citizen of Wrocław (Pfeiffer, *Patriziat*, p. 281)].

August 20, 1491—Christina Spiegler [née Bank, wife of Michael] cedes to Nicholas and Hans, brothers Seidlitz [an old noble family], her demesne Nidenchin with hereditary rights as a knightly fief.

September 28, 1528—Sebastian Seidlitz cedes to Nicholas Uthmann "the Younger," citizen of Wrocław, the property Nidenchin.

October 1, 1566—Lucas Uthmann.

To summarize the lordship series for this small demesne farm, the relatively short tenure of the townsman, Peter Beyer, gave way in 1388 to that of the schulzen from Żurawina, wealthy village headmen who sold out in 1434 to another townsman, Peter Stronchen, who was in fact, their own lord in Żurawina (RF, IV, 2632–640). From 1434 to 1491 citizen families controlled the property, chiefly the Bank, who acquired it in 1448 and simply passed it on to a relative by marriage in 1482. Noble lordship under the Seidlitz then lasted from 1491 to 1528 before another town family, the Uthmann, returned.

1530) were selected equally on methodological grounds and for their substantive relevance to a larger study of the economic history of the Wrocław duchy.[25] In brief, most lie within periods of relatively rich surviving records of conveyances and coincide with especially full supporting texts that helped with other inquiries as well.[26] Of equal importance, each date approximates a culminating or turning point in the late medieval history of the region. In central Silesia, the end of the thirteenth century marked the close of the first and most extensive phase of the shift from Polish rural institutions to the so-called German law and also the emergence of Wrocław as a politically active urban community. By about 1350 the Wrocław region had weathered certain difficulties of the previous generation and approached a good degree of prosperity under the orderly government of Charles IV, while 1425 marks the final years of internal peace before the Hussite invasions ushered in a half-century of turmoil. The results of that political and economic crisis are reflected in conditions of about 1480. In the following fifty years of reconstruction, then, Silesia imperceptibly abandoned its medieval past. The profiles of Wrocław citizen landholding set forth in table 15.1 thus partake of the fullest available documentation and approximate periods with long-term significance for the larger economic history of the city and the region.

Table 15.1 provides not only indicators of the relative importance of citizen landlordships, but also information to help judge the adequacy of the samples used. The first four rows show that, after the comparatively incomplete sample for 1300, places for which lordship information has been compiled always total more than three-quarters of all rural settlements then known to exist and more than two-thirds of those ever known in the

25. This investigation is initially and partially attempted in Richard C. Hoffmann, "Studies in the Rural Economy of the Duchy of Wrocław, 1200–1530" (Ph. D. diss., Yale University, 1970) and is in preparation as "Men, Structures, and Trends in an East-Central European Countryside: The Duchy of Wrocław in the Later Middle Ages."

26. For 1300–05, the *Liber fundationis episcopatus Wratislaviensis*, ed. Hermann Markgraf and J. W. Schulte (Breslau, 1889), is an episcopal income register which includes considerable information about villages where the bishop had only tithe incomes. The 1353 *Registrum villarum, allodiorum et jurium ducatus Wratislaviensis et districtus Nampslaviensis* (henceforth cited as *Reg. vill.*) ed. Gustav A. H. Stenzel as "Das Landbuch des Fürstenthums Breslau," *Ubersicht der Arbeiten und Veränderungen der schlesischen Gesellschaft für vaterländischen Cultur im Jahre 1842* (Breslau, 1843), pp. 48–141, is an elaborate fiscal register of nearly every settlement in the duchy. From 1425 there is RB, the returns for the *burnegelt* tax, and complementary, if slightly earlier, records for church properties omitted therein: Wilhelm Schulte, ed., "Quellen zur Geschichte der Besitzverhältnisse des Bistums Breslau," in his *Studien zur schlesischen Kirchengeschichte* (Breslau, 1907), pp. 210–25, and Herbert Ludat, ed., *Das Lebuser Stiftsregister von 1405: Studien zu den Sozial- und Wirtschaftsverhältnissen in mittleren Oderraum zu Beginn des 15. Jahrhunderts* (Wiesbaden, 1965), pp. 36–38. For 1480 and 1530 such good-sized survey-type documents are lacking.

Table 15.1

The Quantitative Importance of Citizen Landlordship: Comparative Statics, 1300–1530

	1300	*1353*	*1425*	*1480*	*1530*
1. Rural settlements documented	234	354	362	345	340
2. Rural settlements with known lordship	163	317	291	266	278
Known lordship sample as % of					
3. Rural settlements documented to 1540 (row 2/384 × 100)	41%	83%	76%	69%	72%
4. Rural settlements documented in the sample year (row 2/ row 1 × 100)	70%	89%	80%	77%	82%
5. Rural settlements with citizen lordships	27	88	101	77	107
6. Rural settlements with citizen lordships as % of settlements with known lordship (row 5/ row 2 × 100)	16%	28%	35%	29%	38%
7. Rural settlements with citizen lordships as % of settlements documented in the sample year (row 5/row 1 × 100)	12%	25%	28%	22%	31%
8. Rural holdings[a] with known lordship	207	579	411	328	348
9. Citizen holdings	28	147	118	87	124
10. Citizen holdings as % of holdings with known lordship (row 9/row 8 × 100)	14%	25%	29%	27%	35%

[a] Table and text distinguish between counts of settlements where at least one owner is known or at least one lord was a citizen (row 2 and rows 5–7) and counts of holdings (rows 8–10). The term "holding" refers to the property of an individual (or corporation) in a settlement. If a place thus contained the property of more than one lord, it counts as more than one holding. Tabulation of "rural settlements with citizen landlords" measures the spread of these owners across the duchy's sites of habitation and, since the latter are a known number (row 1), can be compared with a total "population" (in the statistical sense). Counts of holdings presumably give a better sense of the townsmen's share of all lordships, but, because the existence of a lordship or holding is confirmed only if the landlord is known, rows 8–10 cannot be compared with the whole duchy, only with the known lordship sample.

duchy to 1540.[27] The rest of the table offers two complementary measures of the citizen's rural properties, the places in which members of this group held land (rows 5–7) and the separate holdings of individuals (rows 8–10). Transforming the raw data to percentages of the known lordship sample, all settlements then occupied, and all holdings of known lordship provides

27. The sample for 1300 is admittedly incomplete and biased in favor of ecclesiastical holdings. Of the 163 places in the sample, 101 (62 percent) had church holdings. By comparison, the considerably larger samples from 1353 and 1425 show only 123 and 124 sites with church lordships respectively (38 percent and 42 percent of all places) despite pervasive evidence that neither the number nor the identity of church holdings had changed very much. Even the places added to the ecclesiastical holdings list during the fourteenth century were, in the main, small properties which, when they enter the documentary record, were not new acquisitions but already in church hands. Ecclesiastical lordships were overwhelmingly creations of the twelfth and thirteenth centuries; later changes in their proportion of the known lordship samples are an unfortunate creation of the fluctuating total representation of known lay owners.

a control for changes in sample size. The different values in rows 6 and 7 also suggest upper and lower bounds for that measure. In each year examined the three percentages show a welcome consistency: the share of townsman holdings (row 10) never exceeds limits set by the two estimators of the proportion of places in which they held (rows 6 and 7); all trends are in the same direction for each interval. The sample for 1300, however, is most valuable for its absolute figures. No official registers were then maintained, but the late Piast dukes did confirm conveyances by issuing charters for those who wished them, principally churchmen and citizens. The low totals for citizens in 1300 thus provide a fairly good indicator of their small but detectable role as landlords then.[28] Thereafter the townsmen's share, however measured, increased quite rapidly to 1353 but more slowly from 1353 to 1425. Then, contrary to Pfeiffer's assertion but in accord with Wendt's speculation, it declined during the difficulties of the mid-fifteenth century before again rising from 1480 to 1530. Long-term expansion of citizen lordships is not to be denied, but the peak involvement in perhaps a third of the duchy's settlements of the early fifteenth century was not maintained in the years that followed. The instances of nobles replacing citizen landowners during the mid-fifteenth century are in that sense more typical of contemporary trends than those which have been used to infer the contrary. Only in the early years of the sixteenth century did Wrocław citizens again expand their share of the rural lordships toward a new maximum.

Estimates of the quantitative importance of citizen landlords establish a necessary precondition for an attempt to detect their qualitative impact on the countryside. Certainly the share of lordships attained by, and even that maintained through, the fifteenth century offered adequate potential for significant influence, but such influence could be realized only to the extent that townsmen behaved differently from other owners with regard to their holdings. But a lack of extant account books and like records from citizen properties prevents attaining the ideal level of comparison of rent rates, profits, investment, or production and marketing decisions.[29] The

28. It is unlikely in the extreme that citizen lordships were severely underrepresented in the 1300 (or in any other) sample. Almost all places which enter the documentary record between 1300 and 1353 do so only before or at the very moment the first members of this group acquired them. The nobility's consistently lower concern for obtaining written proof of their ownership, which is manifested by their more frequent appearance in fiscal texts alone and not conveyances, makes it likely that all estimates of the citizen share tend to be closer to maxima than to minima.

29. Only one fragment of a citizen's account book contains information relevant to rural property management. "Preise, Einnahmen, Ausgaben," APW, Rękopisy Klose, Kl 49 (Kl 48), ff. 2^r–3^v, is a copy made by the eighteenth-century antiquarian, Samuel B. Klose, of excerpts from Michael Bank's records of grain received from his rural holdings and sold in the city in 1421 and 1426.

anecdotes discussed above can demonstrate little, even though their similarity fails to support an argument for significant distinctions. Another tactic must be employed.

A more feasible and broadly relevant test for peculiarities in the management of citizen properties is to compare them with the estates of other landlords in terms of the relative importance of the two distinct arrangements used in the duchy, the direct exploitation demesne and the fixed rent peasant tenancy. Did townsmen allocate resources between operations on their own account and those of tenant farmers any differently than did churchmen or nobles? For this inquiry surviving documents will serve because demesne and rental uses meant variation in the incidence of certain taxes and tithes. Thus fiscal surveys and the accounts of tithe recipients normally distinguished between *mansi censuales* and *allodia*, while conveyance charters likewise labeled holdings according to these categories. Careful collation of the transaction series with fiscal and other, more incidental, records thus permits identification of these land-use types in all rural settlements and in most items in the known lordship samples. Any given holding can therefore be classed at a particular time as tenancies,

Table 15.2

Landlord Groups and Managerial Arrangements: Comparative Statics, 1300–1530

	1300	*1353*	*1425*	*1480*	*1530*
1. Rural settlements documented	234	354	362	345	340
2. % independent demesnes	44%	45%	33%	30%	29%
3. % tenant villages with demesne	34%	32%	35%	38%	39%
4. % tenant villages only	22%	23%	32%	32%	32%
5. Rural settlements with known lordship	163	317	291	266	278
Church corporations					
6. Holdings	104	125	125	114	119
7. % demesne land only	53%	47%	27%	22%	20%
8. % with tenancies and demesne	19%	17%	25%	28%	30%
9. % tenancies only	28%	36%	48%	50%	50%
Citizens of Wrocław					
10. Holdings	29	147	118	87	124
11. % demesne land only	78%	51%	21%	22%	25%
12. % with tenancies and demesne	11%	19%	36%	53%	45%
13. % tenancies only	11%	30%	43%	25%	33%
Nobility					
14. Holdings	48	226	118	87	74
15. % demesne land only	41%	38%	41%	34%	33%
16. % with tenancies and demesne	41%	44%	39%	54%	55%
17. % tenancies only	18%	18%	20%	12%	12%

demesne, or tenancies with demesne.[30] The combined distributions for the duchy and each important landlord group in the five sample years used previously are given in table 15.2.

The managerial arrangements favored by various landlord groups must be examined against the general trend throughout the duchy. As shown in rows 2–4 of the table, which cover all settlements in the duchy, land resources were, between 1300 and 1425, transferred from demesne farms to peasant tenants. Whereas in 1300 there were direct exploitations in 78 percent of the documented settlements, in 1425 the percentage was 68 percent. Tenancies meanwhile increased in frequency from a presence in 56 percent of settlements to 67 percent.[31] The clearest shift is the drop in independent demesnes (not attached to a tenant village) from almost half

30. Useful discussions of the terminological distinctions employed in texts from the twelfth through the sixteenth century are Pfeiffer, *Patriziat*, pp. 207–10; Wacław Korta, *Rozwój wielkiej własności feudalnej na Śląsku do połowy XIII wieku* (Wrocław, 1964), pp. 94–115; Anna Rutkowska-Płachcińska, "W sprawie charakteru rezerwy pańskiej w okresie gospodarki czynszowej," *Przegląd Historyczny*, *48* (1957), 411–35; Roman Heck, "Uwagi o gospodarce folwarcznej na Śląsku w okresie odrodzenia," *Śląski Kwartalnik Historyczny Sobótka*, *11* (1956), 170–75.

As an example of the use of fiscal surveys and conveyance registers to reconstruct the discrete changes in the land use types present in a given settlement, Wierzbice appears in the earliest texts of the 1320s and 1330s with a demesne of 8–10 *mansi* and the rest of the land let out to tenants (*Reg.*, nos. 4312, 5657, 5900, 6174, 6209, 6316). But then the 1353 fiscal survey records no demesne and in fourteen sale charters dating from 1354 to 1414 as well as the tax return of 1425, only tenant land is mentioned (despite a high probability that all lordships are known; see *Reg. vill.*, no. 5; RF, IV, 2942–957; RB, f. 5^v). Only in another tax roll of 1443 does a new reference to $2\frac{1}{2}$ mansi in demesne occur, to be conveyed in turn in several charters from the later fifteenth and early sixteenth centuries. See "Districtus Wratislaviensis liber de mansis comparatus sub anno 1443 per religiosum validum et strennuum ac honestos viros dominos, magistrum s. Mathiae, Mulich Haugwitz militem, Wenceslaum Reichil consulem et Henricum Jenkwitz collectores pecuniae ejusdem," APW, Rękopisy Klose, Kl 132 (Kl 128), f. 15; RF, IV, 2957–958. The convention adopted was to date each change to the first evidence of a previously undocumented arrangement. Thus Wierzbice was a tenant village with demesne from its first documentation in 1324 until 1353, a simple tenant village from 1353 to 1443, and a village with demesne again from that date until after 1530. An identical procedure served to classify each lord's holding in the village. Thus Franz Dompnig, citizen of Wrocław, the sole lord of Wierzbice in 1425, held tenancies occupied by rent-paying peasants, but Sebastian and Paul Monaw, citizens and unseparated joint holders in 1530, possessed tenancies with demesne.

31. These percentages come from adding row 2 and row 3 to get the percentage of places with any demesne and rows 3 and 4 to get those with any tenancies. Note further that rows 1–4 deal with *all settlements*, not just the known lordship samples and not with holdings (here employed to mean the property of each individual lord in each separate place where he owned some). The first portion of the table thus describes a population (all settlements) against which the samples, both partial in coverage and using slightly different units, can be compared. Recognize that a *settlement* with both tenancies and demesne will, if two different lords hold them, appear in the lower portion of the table as two *holdings*, one under demesne land only, the other under tenancies only. But because the total number of holdings remains unknown, no population distribution for them can be calculated. The three groups here compared possessed from 86 percent to 91 percent of the holdings with known lordship at the dates examined and hence all but monopolized landownership in the duchy.

to a bare third of the settlements while there was a rise in those with tenants only from a fifth to nearly a third.[32] But after 1425 the earlier trend all but disappeared. The proportion of places without demesne ceased to grow and, under conditions of considerable aggregate stability in rural institutions, the only arrangement to increase its frequency of occurrence from 1425 to 1530 was the village with demesne where landlords retained a portion of the land under their own direct control.

The duchy-wide distributions and trends were, however, only the aggregate result of disparate arrangements on properties of the three chief landowning groups, none of which replicated the overall pattern. The two supposedly traditional orders, ecclesiastics and nobles, behaved quite differently from each other. The former, consistently favoring tenant farming, until 1425 strongly shifted land out of demesne and thereafter maintained the highest proportion of holdings with no demesne at all. Only a minimal number of direct exploitations served to meet their clerical owners' consumption needs.[33] Possessing few properties with both tenants and demesne, the churchmen also made little attempt to adjust their managerial arrangements to the changing conditions of the fifteenth century. Noble landlords reversed this pattern. While in general, they tended to retain their demesnes, the prime characteristic of their property management was a firm commitment to the "classic manor," an estate where tenants and a demesne farm coexisted on the same holding. After 1425 this tendency became still more marked; noble landlords were in the forefront of the new trend that was hinted at in the evidence for the duchy as a whole. Thus the two older landholding elites emphasized different forms of property exploitation, followed different lines of development, and set the trend at different times. They shared, however, a loyalty to their individual tendencies over time, never truly reversing the direction

32. Even the figures for 1300 may record a point well beyond the start of this transformation, for one aspect of the thirteenth century spread of German law in the duchy was as a means for conversion from landlord-run to tenant-run farming. Günther Dessmann, *Geschichte der schlesische Agrarverfassung* (Strassburg, 1904), pp. 14–18; Richard Koebner, "Locatio. Zur Begriffssprache und Geschichte der deutschen Kolonisation," *Zeitschrift des Vereins für Geschichte Schlesiens, 63* (1929), 1–32; Zdzisław Kaczmarczyk and Michał Sczaniecki, "Kolonizacja na prawie niemieckim w Polsce a rozwój renty feudalnej," *Czasopismo Prawno-Historyczny, 3* (1951), 59–86; Karol Malecyński in *Historia Śląska*, I, pt. 1, *Do połowy XIV w.* (Wrocław, 1960), 393–426. I have summarized the chronology of the German law movement in the Wrocław duchy in an introductory section of Hoffmann, "Warfare, Weather, and a Rural Economy," pp. 277–78.

33. Annual accounts for the Holy Spirit Hospital's demesne farms at Wysoka and Trestno in the 1430s record considerable grain and livestock production but no market sales ("Heilige Geist: Zinsbuch," f. 26^{v} and passim).

of their development or changing the fundamental structures of their landed estates taken as a whole.

Citizens of Wrocław never pioneered a unique trend nor ordered their properties in as extreme a fashion as either other landlord group. They did, however, diverge from the pattern of structural continuity by modifying the aggregate arrangement of their holdings in the mid-fifteenth century. Up to 1425 the townsmen converted demesne to tenant farms even more rapidly than did the churchmen, thus following the trend to rentier lordship which the ecclesiastics had pioneered. But after 1425 the urban landlords abandoned their thrust toward purely absentee and fixed-rent incomes. Although they resembled the church corporations in possessing more holdings without demesne than without tenants, in 1480 and 1530 the townsmen also began to conform to the old noble pattern of having more mixed holdings than either pure form. Pfeiffer's assertion that townsmen landlords played a different role in the fifteenth century is, therefore, a half-truth. Its application is limited to the perspective from which he saw it, that of citizen behavior alone. In the countryside, however, emphasis on the mixed property of demesne farm and tenancies was no entrepreneurial innovation, for noble landlords had, since at least the early fourteenth century (to go only as far back as the statistics here presented), maintained the very arrangements only later adopted by townsmen. This statement is not intended to disparage the townsmen's perceptivity, however. The course newly followed by Wrocław citizens was not unsuited to the relative depopulation and land surplus created by the disorders of the fifteenth century. It coincided with the slow shift of east-central European agriculture from the peasant autonomy and rentier lordship of the German law movement toward the "second serfdom" on direct exploitation demesnes typical of the early modern period. But, as an older pattern long preserved by noble landlords, it was no more a citizen innovation than had been their fourteenth-century imitation of the clerics who promoted rental tenancy.

This attempt to elucidate the scale and significance of landlordships held by citizens of Wrocław has concentrated upon the quantitative and comparative levels of analysis necessarily implict in the questions themselves. The most complete body of data available indicates the absence of a unilinear trend in the growth of those lordships and instead a close coincidence between the expansion of townsmen's rural holdings and the relative political stability and rural order of the fourteenth century and the period after 1480. In the troubled mid-fifteenth century a noticeable hiatus interrupted this movement. Security seems an important consideration to citizens who contemplated rural investments.[34] Comparison of the managerial arrangements employed by various landlord groups further manifested no significant innovations or consistent peculiarities in the way Wrocław landlords exploited their estates. Even when the townsmen changed their approach, their emulation of existing practices and older classes is difficult to reconcile with assertions of their notably "capitalist" behavior and motivation. Quantified techniques have yielded generalized conclusions on certain specific issues. The numbers, however, mean less in themselves than they do as guideposts toward more likely interpretations of scattered but more human evidence and, on a larger scale, of urban life in late medieval Wrocław.

Within the interpretative limits thus imposed by quantitative comparisons, certain further anecdotes encourage more realistic assessment of the significance of the Wrocław magnates' rural holdings. As their choice of managerial arrangements suggests, citizen landlords operated within traditional norms for that role. When Nicholas Rempel left the city during a political dispute, official messengers found him on his estate at Ratyń, supervising his laborers and presiding while the headman conducted a village court.[35] The active Heinz Dompnig, too, partisan for Corvinus on the Rat, irregular royal appointee as its chairman and hence functional captain of the duchy, a noted wheeler-dealer of the 1480s, spent considerable time on his demesne at Brzezina.[36] Others engaged with apparent gusto in less wholesome aspects of country life, like violence and brigandage. In 1458 Heinz and Christoff Skopp, Jan Bleicher, and a servant were outlawed for their murder in the Skopp lordship of Domasław of a man named Jaxe

34. Members of the Popplaw family first acquired rural property by inheritance in 1456 but, after lengthy court battles, sold it off in 1463 and re-entered the land market only in the calmer years after 1480. When their early sixteenth-century commercial account book permits detailed knowledge of their business affairs it turns out that major land purchases followed immediately after difficulties and decisions to withdraw large sums of capital from trade. Hans Popplaw liquidated the family firm in 1516 and then bought Karczyce, Jarząbkowice, Zakrzyce, and a quarter share in Bielany. In 1522 he pulled out of his silent partnership with his Hornig relatives and obtained *Gurse*, Lenartowice, Wały, and *Butschau* (Petry, *Popplau*, pp. 28, 148–49).

35. Cited from the messengers' reports by Hermann Markgraf, "Aus Breslau's unruhigen Zeiten, 1418–1426," *Zeitschrift des Vereins für Geschichte Schlesiens, 15* (1880–81), 74. The point is not Rempel's voluntary exile, although that, too, scarcely fits the stereotype of a convinced city politician or a man who saw rural property as only an income source, but the apparent ease with which he fit into the lord's role.

36. See his letter to the city's chamberlain, Kronthal and Wendt, *Politische Correspondenz . . . Corvinus*, II, 68. Note, too, that Wenceslas Bank was kidnapped from his demesne at Kazimierzów (Ibid., I, 202–03; see n. 24 above). On the career of Heinz Dompnig see Hermann Markgraf, "Heinz Dompnig, der Breslauer Hauptmann †1491," *Zeitschrift des Vereins für Geschichte Schlesiens, 20* (1886), 157–96.

Rot. Although Pfeiffer would have it that Heinz thereby and with an earlier robbery of a Wrocław merchants' caravan "plac[ed] himself outside the bounds of the civic order,"[37] his actions differed little from some reported of other contemporary citizen landlords.[38] Nor did all townsmen simply hold rural properties for short-term gains. The successive lordships of the Thiele, Merboth, and Hornig families over Wojtkowice in the late fourteenth and most of the fifteenth century each ended not with the initial purchaser selling out, but only when a later generation had to divide its holdings among several heirs, in the Merboth case, only daughters.[39] Four generations of Dompnigs had property in Wojkowice from 1347 to 1445. After Agnes Haunold inherited one share of that village between 1441 and 1443, it then passed successively to her husband, Valentine, her son, Hans, who acquired the rest of the place, and it was sold only by her grandson, Achatius, in 1507. The new lord, Paul Hornig, then began at least three generations during which his lineage ruled Wojkowice; the heirs of his son George still retained it in 1558.[40] Hans Rothe began a still more durable family lordship when he bought into Wilczków in 1375. It remained a Rothe property through the entire fifteenth century and by the 1530s the last member of the clan to sit on the Wrocław city council, another Hans, was calling himself "Rothe zu Wiltschaw." He died, still possessed of the village, in 1542, but the family, who had by then withdrawn from city life and joined the nobility, lasted until 1617.[41]

The specific case of the Rothe and the general conformity of Wrocław citizen landlords to economic and social norms established by older rural elites imply that a central significance of townsman lordships lay in their enduring value as instruments for ascent and assimilation into traditionally and continuously more prestigious social orders. Before the mid-fourteenth

37. ". . . sich ausserhalb der Schranken bęrgerlicher Ordnung stellt" (Pfeiffer, *Patriziat*, pp. 266–67). The Rot murder is reported in August Meitzen, ed., *Urkunden schlesischer Dörfer. Zur Geschichte der ländlichen Verhältnisse und der Flureinteilung insbesondere* (Breslau, 1863), pp. 64–65.

38. In 1440 Dietrich Dompnig, scion of an old and well-off city lineage, went out to Cieszyce where he pulled down Thomas Leuen's house, seized his money and movables, and dragged the man behind his horse until the victim nearly died. The city council reduced Dompnig's punishment to a fine of 360 marks in view of his "youth." See O. Stobbe, "Mitteilungen aus Breslauer Signaturbüchern," *Zeitschrift des Vereins für Geschichte Schlesiens*, *8* (1867), 446. About 1460 a knight, Ulrich Bredel, accused Melchior Ungerathen, another citizen, of using his property at Gniechowice as a base for horse thievery. See Georg Steinhausen, ed., *Deutsche Privatbriefe des Mittelalters*, 2 vols. (Berlin, 1899–1907), I, 369.

39. RF, IV, 2898–911.

40. RF, II, 866–75, and IV, 2898–911; Pfeiffer, *Patriziat*, p. 296.

41. RF, IV, 2928–930; Meitzen, *Urkunden schlesischer Dörfer*, pp. 83–85; Pfeiffer, *Patriziat*, pp. 184–85; Hans J. von Witzendorff-Rehdiger, "Der ritterliche Adel und der Stadtadel in Schlesien," *Jahrbuch der Schlesischen Friedrich-Wilhelms-Universität zu Breslau*, *6* (1961), 208. The Hornig lords of Wojkowice also achieved noble rank in the mid-sixteenth century.

century John Reste, a Wrocław merchant and landowner whose father, Conrad, had acquired citizenship in 1261 and been an active politician at the turn of the century, employed the title *miles* but remained on the city council. His son, also John and also a miles, inherited the country property and withdrew from urban life to perpetuate a noble lineage.[42] More sharply defined social distinctions by the early fifteenth century created a market for royal letters of nobility and grants of arms to ambitious and wealthy townsmen. Among the Wrocław citizen families who so invested their capital in the first third of the century were the Mühlschreiber, Ungerathen, Merboth, Beda, and Stolz, the latter two progenitors of the later noble lineages of von Biedau and Stolz von Simsdorf respectively.[43] As one final example, consider the history of the Sauermann clan. The founder, Sebald, came to Wrocław from a small Upper Franconian center and took citizenship in 1466. In thirty years his commercial success had also gained him lordship over Wierzbica, Jaksonów, and Krzyżowice. The continued prosperity of his descendants brought the family into the nobility as first Freiherren and, in 1840, counts Sauerma, and all the time they maintained their hold on Wierzbica and Jaksonów. Sebald's nephew, Conrad, got himself expelled from the Wrocław city council in 1515 for owning too much property outside the duchy, notably the castle at Jelcz. His son, George (1492–1527), pursued the career of a knightly humanist. Later generations, their landed estate made secure by creation of a family trust in 1569, became the noble lineage of counts Saurma-Jeltsch.[44] For all of these families rural lordships served as a necessary (if not sufficient) tool for social ascent out of the citizen class and out of the urban into the noble elite.

42. Colmar Grünhagen, "Die Herren von Reste. Ein Beitrag zur Geschichte des Breslauer Patriziats im 14. Jahrh.," *Zeitschrift des Vereins für Geschichte Schlesiens, 7* (1866), 36–38, 53–54. The other line, that of Gisco, remained more active in the city, acquired fewer rural properties, and ended with the entry of both Gisco's sons into holy orders. Pfeiffer, *Patriziat*, pp. 79–81, emphasizes the earlier, more strictly urban, generations and then asserts that those who withdrew from the city are irrelevant to his concerns.

43. Witzendorff-Rehdiger, "Ritterliche Adel und Stadtadel," pp. 207–08. The six families listed possessed twenty-four rural properties in the duchy in 1425. A century later still, urban magnates built houses in the high Renaissance style, supplanted the clergy as the chief artistic and architectural patrons of the region, and even staged tournaments for prideful display of their sons. See Stanisław Tync, "Z życia patrycjatu wrocławskiego w dobie renesansu," *Słaski Kwartalnik Historyczny Sobótka, 8* (1953), 72–73.

44. Pfeiffer, *Patriziat*, pp. 240–41, and Gustav Bauch, "Ritter Georg Sauermann, der erste adelige Vorfahr der Grafen Saurma-Jeltsch," *Zeitschrift des Vereins für Geschichte Schlesiens, 19* (1885), 145–81. Like the story of the Sauermann clan is that of the Popplau. Early fifteenth century migrants from Legnica to Wrocław, they became wealthy in the cloth trade from the west to Silesia and Poland. Even in the second generation, Hans Popplau, a younger son, who, after university training, had worked for a time as the family firm's factor in Kraków, became the famous knightly traveler of the 1480s and 1490s (see

The acquisition and use of landed property and rural lordships by citizens of Wrocław, though intimately connected to the wealth and territorial power of the city in the later Middle Ages,[45] cannot otherwise be linked to intended social revolution or economic transformations in the countryside. Urban magnates like the Sauermann, Hornig, and Rothe epitomize the traditionalism of an urban elite whose ultimate goals—familial upward mobility, withdrawal from urban economic and political activities, and a stable income from prestigious rural properties—neither transcended nor transgressed existing socioeconomic structures. Failure of as wealthy, influential, and autonomous a center as Wrocław to create a self-sufficient value system signifies the limits of urbanism in late medieval east-central Europe.

---

the article by Paul Pfotenhauer in *Allgemeine deutsche Biographie* XXVI (Leipzig, 1888), 428–31). His stay-at-home brothers, cousins, and nephews meanwhile developed an extensive consolidated estate in the north of the Środa district some 20 kilometers from Wrocław. The ultimate heir, another Hans, lived as a manorial lord at Stabłowice, gave up his Wrocław citizenship in 1509, liquidated the textile company to buy more land in 1516, and closed out his last mercantile investments for still more land in 1522. But before Hans's death in 1537 his daughter eloped with a merchant from Zittau. Resultant disputes over the rich inheritance dissipated the family's wealth. Heavily in debt, the last Popplau did not survive the sixteenth century. (Petry, *Popplau*, pp. 97–135, 142–52.) Other old magnate families and even some recently risen from artisan origins, the Beckenschläger, Mühlschreiber, and Hoppe, for example, succeeded in their sixteenth century moves from the city to the landed aristocracy (Tync, "Życia patrycjatu," pp. 99–100).

45. Hoffmann, "Towards a City-State."

16

The Earliest Scandinavian Towns

Sidney Cohen

The medieval Scandinavian town was a small, densely populated area which was also an administrative district. It possessed historic and cultural traditions, had a distinctive marketplace with specialized commerce and industry, and was governed by laws. Unlike towns elsewhere in Europe, the medieval Scandinavian town often developed without walls. Moreover, Scandinavian towns had diverse origins. Not every town had its beginning as a market center at the confluence of streams or at a crossroads. Some towns were on inlets of the sea, others on lakes, and still others were in the interior. A number of towns developed without the efforts of missionaries or bishops, or without the benefit of the royal power. Some arose in the vicinity of fortresses and others acquired their fortresses because of their importance as towns. In short, no Scandinavian town provides an ideal example to fit a theory of town origins like that proposed by Henri Pirenne.

The problem of determining town origins is well known. For Scandinavia, the problem is compounded by difficulties of interpretation and by an almost total lack of written sources before the late eleventh century. Archeology and numismatics are the primary fields in which the study of Scandinavian urban origins are pursued. The resulting emphasis upon material culture has brought the scholarly predilections of those fields to the area of urban history.

The study of early medieval Scandinavia has been strongly influenced in the past generation by socialist political theory. The principal argument of Aksel Christensen and others is that the Church played relatively little role in the development of the Scandinavian monarchies before the twelfth century.[1] The medieval state was the work of the powerful kings, who

1. A. E. Christensen, *Vikingetidens Danmark: Paa Oldhistorisk Baggrund* (Copenhagen, 1969). Cf. Christensen's article: "Denmark between the Viking Age and the Time of the Valdemars," *Mediaeval Scandinavia, 1* (1968), 28–50.

possessed considerable military and lawmaking authority. This theory has been applied to the problem of town origins. In this case, the Church—in the form of missions or patronage by bishops—is said to have had an insignificant impact on the rise of towns. The king is claimed to be the principal owner and organizer in the earliest towns. Even the merchants and the commercial activity of the town are subordinate in importance to the entrepreneurship of the king.[2]

A second major theory of town origins is that the Frisians and other foreign merchants were the dominant factor in the economic life of early medieval Scandinavia. They are said to have founded the first towns and paved the way for the later control of Scandinavian commerce by the Hansa.

The earliest Scandinavian towns were the market-centers Hedeby in Denmark (now in Germany), Birka in Sweden, and perhaps Kaupang in Norway. Birka and Hedeby are studied more than other sites because impressive archeological discoveries have been made there. The towns are also mentioned in an early written source, the *Vita Anscharii* of Rimbert, which was composed after 865.

In 822, Ebbo, archbishop of Reims, received from Louis the Pious and Pope Paschal I the missionary command to contact the Danes of the Sli (Schlei) fjord region, with the assistance of the bishops of Bremen and Cambrai. Some heathen were baptized and some preaching was done, but no community was established. In 826, after the baptism of the Danish chieftain Harald Klak at Louis's court, Anscharius, or Ansgar, a monk of Saxon Corvey, or New Corbie, a foundation established after 822 by the abbot of Corbie in Picardy, undertook a second royal mission. Ansgar, together with a companion, Aubert, embarked from the Frisian emporium Dorstad for Denmark, arriving at a place called Sliestorp. Ansgar was not successful in establishing a community here, and he returned to the empire. In 829, after the visit of some Swedes to the court of the emperor, Ansgar made another journey northward to the Swedish emporium Birka.

The location of Ansgar's Sliestorp is one of the major questions of Viking archeology and the early history of Scandinavian towns, although a consensus on the problem has been reached. Alfred the Great, in an appendage to his translation of Orosius's *Historia adversum paganos*, described the northern countries, and a place *aet haethum* (at the heaths) at approxi-

2. See H. Schledermann, "Stad," *Kulturhistorisk Leksikon for nordisk Middelalder* (1971), XVI, cols. 557–61. Cf. R. Blomquist, "Stadsbebyggelse och stadsplan," XVI, cols. 611–30.

mately the same location as Sliestorp at the neck of the Jutland peninsula. Sliestorp may be the modern town of Schleswig or a site nearby that is now in ruins but was a thriving settlement in the ninth century. There may have been two towns or one town with two names. The English writer Aethelweard (late tenth century) noted that the place was called Sleswic by the Saxons and Haithabu by the Danes. No one has found any ninth century ruins under Schleswig. It is likely that the town was moved to its present site in the eleventh century (after 1050) from the ruins now called Haithabu (Danish: Hedeby). Since the identification of a "black-earth zone" (a rich soil with evidence of human occupation) at this site in the late nineteenth century, no one has doubted that Hedeby is the settlement mentioned in the Carolingian and English sources.

Hedeby was located on the natural route for merchants traversing the Jutland peninsula. From the North Sea one entered the Ejder River (Eịdora), the traditional boundary of King Godfred's Denmark,[3] and thereafter journeyed by way of its north fork (called the Trene) to a rise of ground in the rather swampy soil, a place called Hollingsted. Here the Trene headed almost due north. A branch of the river, called Rejde AA (stream), which was not navigable, went eastward from this point to the vicinity of an ancient track known as the Haervejen (military road). Portage was necessary from Hollingsted to a shallow southerly arm of the Sli fjord (a distance of ten miles), now known as the Haddeby Noor. The market town of Hedeby was situated on the west bank of this water-course. There is some doubt that Hedeby was a town by Maitland's definition, because we have no knowledge that it was a legal entity. There is strong evidence, however, that Hedeby was a permanent settlement and not a seasonal fairgrounds.

The evidence is archeological. Millstones imported from France in a half-finished state were completed at Hedeby and exported throughout Scandinavia. The Hedeby excavations have produced a significant quantity of locally made textiles, as well as the tools for their manufacture. The local textiles are found with imported stuffs such as cloth interwoven with gold thread and mohair yarn. There is also evidence of a leather-goods industry. Products such as textiles and millstones are not likely to have been made seasonally for visitors, but are substantial testimony to a strong native market and a permanent settlement.

Other commercial activity ascertained at Hedeby includes the import of glass from the Rhineland and its transshipment to Gotland and the

3. The theory that all of modern Denmark was unified in the ninth century is unprovable.

Mälar district of Sweden (Birka); the manufacture of jewelry based on Frankish models; the making of Frankish-style swords; the importation and imitation of pottery; and the distribution of wine.

Local production included the forging of iron; the casting of bronze; work with tin and lead; the making of glass; and, in association with the native jewelry industry, manufacture of glass beads and the carving of walrus ivory.

A traffic in raw materials must have been an important factor in town life. Metals, especially iron ore; amber and bone (for combs, spoons, and pins); soapstone for bowls; fur and hides, especially walrus and seal skins for ship's ropes; and perhaps lumber, were among the most widely imported bulk goods. On the other hand, foodstuffs, such as dried fish, probably were not among the major commodities traded at Hedeby in this period.

Traffic in slaves was a significant by-product of Viking activity. The most important commerce of Hedeby may have been the slave trade. The slaves were war captives and Slavs as well as Scandinavians. Hedeby's position at the edge of the Wendish lands made it one of the most important slave markets. Rimbert, Ansgar's successor in the Scandinavian mission, bought slaves at Hedeby about 870. The *annales regum francorum* (808) note that the Danish king Godfred destroyed the Wendish emporium Reric and transferred its merchants to Sliestorp (Hedeby). One may suppose that these merchants included Arabs and Jews engaged in the slave trade. The Arab merchant al-Tartuschi (from Spain) was a visitor at Hedeby about 950.

As reported by Ibn Jakub, al-Tartuschi described Hedeby as a rather wretched place where the people growled like dogs. But the site may have been selected because it had several freshwater streams, including the Hedeby baek (brook), which emptied into the Haddeby Noor. Hedeby began as two (or possibly three) villages, each with its own cemetery, although the largest settlement lay at the noor's edge and immediately north of the Hedeby brook. The villages were at first unwalled, but by the late ninth century a semicircular earthwork of turf and sand, perhaps faced with timber, protected the whole site. The wall was about two-thirds of a mile long, and enclosed approximately sixty acres. On the north side of the town, it extended out into the waters of the noor as a mole for about 480 feet. The original height of the earth-work may have been no more than a few feet, though this was apparently raised in the tenth century to about thirty feet. Three main entrances interrupted the rampart's course and there may have been other breaks in the wall. The wall probably designated a trading quarter for merchants and was at first more symbolic than useful. It was strengthened in the tenth century when Hedeby was attacked by pirates.[4]

To the north of the town was a fortress (tilflugtsborg) in which there are no traces of habitation. It is upon this earthwork that the population must have depended for safety from attack, rather than the semicircular rampart.

In the eastern part of the main settlement area immediately north of the brook were some substantial houses (the largest upward of fifty feet in length) and to the west of these there were rather more humble ones. Some of the houses were stave-built, that is, they were made of tree trunks cut vertically into planks which were stuck in the ground (later, in a sill), joined to one another by the tongue-in-groove method, with the curved side facing outward. A small number of houses were frame-built with wattle-and-daub (mud and thatch) filling the spaces between the posts. The more westerly houses, which are thought to have belonged to poorer residents, are usually smaller and often have sunken floors. We may assume that there were also many tents and temporary structures in the area to accommodate seasonal visitors.

The town was unplanned. A timber roadway meandered haphazardly through the settlement from north to south, and one may suppose that there was a constant traffic on the beach and in the vicinity of the brook. The houses' gable ends generally faced the one main street. Outhouses and wells (the latter admired by al-Tartuschi) were to the rear. The general impression is of a teeming, lively center thronged with visitors in the summer, quieter in winter. Hedeby flourished for several hundred years, but in the late tenth century, its fortunes waned. The town was destroyed by fire, perhaps set by the Norwegian Harald Haardraade, about 1050.

Ansgar arrived at Birka, the northern terminus of the Frisian-Frankish trade routes to the Baltic, in the spring of 830. The settlement was located on an island (Björkö means Birch Island) in Lake Mälar not far (eighteen miles) from present-day Stockholm. Ansgar was attracted to Birka because Christians traveled there—the *Vita Anscharii* specifically mentions (Byzantine) Greeks—and because the king there, Björn, or his "prefect" (*praefectus regi*) was favorably disposed to the Franks. The prefect presided over a *placitum* or "thing" (folk-moot) and apparently gave the missionary official protection.

The *Vita Anscharii* supports an oft-made claim that Sweden in the ninth

4. There is runic evidence that the Swedes invaded the Jutland peninsula in the tenth century. There is a discussion of the problem in Gwyn Jones, *A History of the Vikings* (Oxford, 1968), pp. 111–13.

century was a unified state under the leadership of a single family. The *Vita* at least implies that the Swedish king was the entrepreneur who encouraged the Frankish trade and thus was responsible for the growth of the town. The existence of the *placitum* suggests that Birka's commerce was not seasonal. Grave finds of ice-skates, ice picks, and spiked shoes are positive evidence that Birka was not a seasonal settlement.

The commercial life of Birka is well documented by archeology. About two thousand graves are associated with the site, of which more than eleven hundred have been excavated. While most of the grave goods display native workmanship, there are many imported wares, including pottery and glass, woolens, silks, and massive quantities of silver. Coins are an important part of this inventory, and provide significant clues to the character and variety of Birka's far-flung connections.

The Birka graves have yielded 131 coins of Islamic origin, 17 Western European coins, 38 Scandinavian coins, and 3 Byzantine coins. Islamic coins minted in the period after 800 outnumber coins from before that date by more than two to one. However, only one Islamic coin from the latter part of the tenth century has been found.

The Scandinavian issues are typologically related coins and bracteates which appear to be locally produced copies of Carolingian coins minted at Dorstad. Such coins are also numerous at Hedeby, and constitute the "Hedeby-Birka series." They may have been minted at Hedeby and carried north by travelers or they may have originated at Birka.

Frequently, the inscriptions on the local issues are retrograde or are victims of the moneyer's artistic imagination. In one example, the letters TAT of Dorstat (Dorstad) have become the wall-posts and doorway of a house. Scholars have raised several questions concerning the Hedeby-Birka issues. Were they a true coinage or did they have to be weighed individually or in groups? Did they have religious significance? Were they used by locals or visitors? Did they have currency beyond Scandinavia? Were they merely ornamental?

It is likely that the Birka coins were weighed in groups and could be ornamental. This seems evident from the large hoards of hacksilver—chopped, mangled, twisted lumps, wires, and bars of silver; silver jewelry; and bits of coins—which accompany entire coins in the graves. Scales for weighing the silver have been found with some of these hoards. Moreover, most of the whole coins have been found in graves belonging to women. Thirty-six of the thirty-eight Scandinavian coins are in this category, as are two of the three Byzantine coins found, the greatest part of the Western European coins, and a majority of the Islamic coins. Unless the women at

Birka held the purse strings, the coins they possessed were almost certainly ornamental.

Sawyer suggests that Birka was wealthy because merchants returning home with Arab silver wanted to spend it at Birka on products to be used locally, not exported.[5] According to this argument, when the merchants ran out of silver, Birka disappeared. This most contrived argument would explain the relative paucity of other types of grave goods, even though Sawyer admits that hides and furs, woolen cloth, timber, wax, salt, and other biodegradable commodities as well as slaves would not leave any appreciable archeological record. We do know that there were both ordinary inhabitants (*populi*) and merchants (*negociatores*) at Birka, and they bartered for weapons, pottery, glass, jewelry, clothing, and food. Some of these commodities were locally produced, and others imported. It is not likely that the sole acquisitive impulse of the populi was directed toward amassing silver, and it is dangerous to predicate the existence of the town on the availability of this single commodity. Moreover, while the Arab silver may have run out, the Anglo-Saxon silver was rather abundant. Sawyer is correct in noting that the disappearance of Arab silver in the late tenth century is an event contemporary with the decline of Birka. There are alternative reasons, however, including the development of the commerce of Gotland; the shifting of channels in the Mälar lake; and the rise of the town of Sigtuna, closer to the royal seat of Uppsala.

The most important information that the archeological evidence provides is that Birka's commerce was oriented toward the east, toward Russia and the Abassid Caliphate. While it was a terminus of western trade, Birka was a principal starting point for those vast territories explored and exploited by the Swedish Vikings called Rus.

Birka lay on a sloping sandy shore at the north end of Birch Island, close by two coves where ships could be sheltered. The black-earth zone and other evidences of habitation cover about twenty-nine acres, or half the space occupied at Hedeby. Only about one-thirtieth of the black-earth zone has been excavated (exclusive of the graves) and that excavation took place between 1871 and 1895. Our knowledge of the ground plan of Birka is therefore most incomplete.

The walls of a fort on a hill (about one hundred feet high) are connected to the remains of an embankment of stone and earth which curves around part of the black-earth zone. The land immediately adjoining the walls appears not to have been inhabited, possibly as a preventive measure

5. P. Sawyer, *The Age of the Vikings* (2d ed., London, 1971), pp. 184–85.

against fires. The low wall was built over a series of graves, of which one can be dated by coin evidence to after 925. Thus Birka, like the first settlements at Hedeby, originally had no walls.

While the remains of streets have yet to be uncovered, and we are virtually without knowledge of any sort of ground plan, it is possible to study the arrangements of the harbors. In addition to the two natural harbors and the oaken logs along the beach which presumably were piles for jetties and docks, an artificial harbor survives. It apparently allowed ships to enter a tunnel-like gate and anchor in a square artificial basin at least ten feet deep. This harbor, now called Salviksgropen, reminds one of the harbor of Jomsborg, described in the thirteenth century *Saga of the Jomsvikings*. The legendary harbor was enclosed by walls and was entered by an iron gate surmounted by a watchtower.

The Birka excavations show us primarily that the town flourished for about one hundred fifty years as the principal commercial emporium of central Sweden. The town served a local market but was dependent for luxuries on the western, and more importantly, the Oriental trade. It is likely that local events and conditions in the Mälar region led to Birka's eventual disappearance.

The Anglo-Norman historian Ordericus Vitalis, writing in the twelfth century, named six cities in Norway, of which one was Kaupang. By this designation he meant Nidaros (Trondhjem) on the northwest coast of Norway, the burial place and cult center of St. Olaf. The name Kaupang means "market" (related to English "cheap," cf. Cheapside) and survives today in numerous Scandinavian place-names, particularly as the second element "-köping" in Swedish city-names. Thus it is impossible to identify positively the site Kaupang in the Vestfold district of southern Norway with the marketplace Sciringes-heal described by Alfred the Great as a commercial stopover on the trip to Hedeby. But Norway must also have its earliest town, and this is the identification now usually made.

Two cemeteries at the site have yielded a fair quantity of grave goods, though one of the cemeteries, which is primarily a cremation field, is much poorer than the other. Typical ninth-century goods are found, especially Anglo-Irish ceramic wares. The black-earth zone has comparable materials. Evidence of a soapstone bowl industry and of goods imported from the British Isles demonstrate Kaupang's extensive connections.

It is not yet possible to comment on Kaupang's ground plan, since it has not been found, though the site has been investigated annually since 1956, and has been known for over one hundred years. There are no traces of fortifications, and with the exception of a paved embankment, remains of docks, and some traces of houses close by the beach, little structural evidence has survived. Kaupang was probably a harbor with a seasonal fairgrounds. There may be no trace of a town because none ever existed.

One of the best known Scandinavian towns which had its roots in the Viking Age, yet survived into the Middle Ages,[6] is Sigtuna in Sweden. There is substantial archeological, numismatic, and runological evidence from Sigtuna, and the modern town preserves the original plan. Sigtuna lies northwest and approximately halfway between Stockholm and Uppsala (which cities are about forty-five miles apart) on one of the northerly arms of the great Mälar lake. Sigtuna appears to have developed at the end of the tenth century to fill the void left by the decline of Birka. Sigtuna's rise refutes Sawyer's argument that Birka disappeared when Arab silver vanished from Swedish commerce. Why would Sigtuna have emerged when it had as little silver as Birka? Obviously, a silver shortage is not involved. If Sigtuna had a better harbor, it could have developed for this reason alone.

A number of scholars have suggested that Sigtuna was founded as a countercultural center (*motpol*) to the great heathen temple of Uppsala, since the earliest historical evidence of the town, coins, are Christian issues bearing the legends "In nomine Dei" and "Si Dei" (Si[gtuna] Dei).[7] It must be cautioned, however, that none of these coins has been found at Sigtuna itself.[8] The coins were minted for the Swedish convert-king Olaf Skotkonung by an Anglo-Saxon moneyer after English prototypes. They may be compared to rare coins with a Christian cross minted for the Danish king Svend Forkbeard (c. 985–1014), which were probably never circulated. Thus the coins are not evidence that Sigtuna was founded as a Christian city, but only that a Christian Swedish king may have planned to use it as a base for his operations.

The runic evidence is more convincing, though somewhat later in date. Uppland, the district in which Sigtuna is located, is the richest province of Sweden in terms of the number of surviving rune stones. (Over half of all the rune stones in Sweden are found in Uppland.) It is not surprising that more than thirty partial or complete inscriptions have been found at Sigtuna. A number of memorial inscriptions bear the legend "God Help

6. See E. Floderus, *Sigtuna, Sveriges äldsta medeltidsstad* (Stockholm, 1941).

7. A runic inscription preserves the spelling "Sihtunum." Floderus, *Sigtuna*, p. 46.

8. Floderus, *Sigtuna*, p. 34.

His Soul" or a close variant. These inscriptions are stylistically dated to the second half of the eleventh century, a time when, according to Adam of Bremen,[9] the heathen temple still flourished at Uppsala.

The archeological inventory of Sigtuna, its "subterranean archive,"[10] is similar to those of Birka and Hedeby. There are a number of Anglo-Saxon and (German) imperial coins; glass beads; silver and gold jewelry (including a magnificent gold necklace); a rather significant quantity of bone objects such as combs, pins, and spoons; bronze harness, belt buckles, pins, and sword chapes (the metal piece at the end of the scabbard which keeps the sword from making a hole in it); and a rather crude pottery. There are fewer imported goods evident at Sigtuna, undoubtedly because of Christian burial practices and the absence of a major heathen cemetery. (The largest cemetery has twenty graves.)

The plan of the original Sigtuna survives to this day. The town had a single long street running about six hundred yards along the shore of the lake but not directly at the shoreline. Smaller lanes crossed the main street and descended to the beach. South of the street were the tents and storehouses of the merchants and seamen whose ships were moored at docks along the beach. Above (north of) the main street there were several substantial houses and workshops. Beyond the house plots, abutting on a rise of ground, churches were built by the various merchant groups and guilds which began to flourish at Sigtuna during the course of the twelfth century. The various merchant quarters (trade zones) were probably located nearby. It is worth noting that the churches do not appear to have played any significant role in determining Sigtuna's ground plan or any part in the development of the town's prosperity.

Lund in Scania, part of Denmark until 1660, is an early Scandinavian town which did not have a harbor and is worth studying for that reason. Moreover, the town was planned. It grew up near the Three Barrows (Tre Högars) Market in the vicinity of the place where the Scanian folk-moots were regularly held. The town was established by Canute the Great (ruled 1016–35) in the winter of 1019–20. An old track on some high ground between two branches of a brook became the basis of the town plan.[11] Canute built a residence here and laid out plots of ground for merchants and craftsmen. It is likely that his plan was modeled on those of the Anglo-Saxon boroughs. Canute sought to have an administra-

9. Adam of Bremen, *Gesta Hammaburgensis Ecclesiae Pontificum*, IV, 26.

10. Floderus, *Sigtuna*, p. 52.

11. Blomquist, "Stadsbebyggelse," col. 614.

tive center to secure his power in Scania. He built a town, not a Trelleborg.[12]

According to the Swedish scholar Ragnar Blomquist, the Church does not appear to have been of major importance in the early development of the town.[13] After Lund became the archepiscopal see of the Scandinavian Church in 1103,[14] however, the Church became all-important. By 1300, there were twenty-seven churches, including eight monastic foundations and the impressive Romanesque cathedral—this in a town with no more than 5,000 population!

Like most of the other towns of Scandinavia, Lund began as an unwalled town. It remained so until 1134, when the political stability of Denmark was destroyed by civil war, and fortification became necessary. The town seems to have retained Canute's plan, however, with a principal street, Torget, running northeast-southwest to the cathedral, and with a number of cross streets leading from this principal street to trackways and other towns in the vicinity.

The earliest Scandinavian towns had similar origins. They developed as unwalled harbors frequented by farmer-merchants and traders, whose goods attracted merchants from overseas. Cottage industries were established which finished the raw materials produced in the district or imported from outside. Inhabitants crowded the site, perhaps only seasonally at first, and then built docks, jetties, houses, trackways, fences, outhouses, and wells. They raised food at the townsite itself, they partitioned the town, and they argued frequently over their individual rights. The cemeteries became crowded. Some kind of protection for persons and goods, some kind of public order, became necessary. How did it develop and who was responsible?

I will venture to hypothesize that the ancient Germanic tradition of hospitality described first by Tacitus (*Germania*, chap. 21) may have led to the creation of free-trade zones within the generalized limits of the town with each group of merchants or craftsmen, divided either by origin or preference, responsible for policing its own members and building its own facilities. We need not suppose that there were formal guilds.

My argument will be opposed by the apologists for royal entrepreneurship. Christensen has argued that historians who believe that the royal power in Denmark underwent a slow development are captives of late

12. See H. Arbman, "Aggersborg," *Reallexikon der germanischen Altertumskunde*, I, 1, pp. 95–96. Cf. S. L. Cohen, *Viking Fortresses of the Trelleborg Type* (Copenhagen, 1965).

13. Blomquist, "Stadsbebyggelse," col. 612.

14. The archiepiscopal see of Uppsala was established in 1164; that of Nidaros in 1152.

nineteenth-century evolutionary theory.[15] Christensen claims not to be affected by contemporary influences upon the writing of history, and he insists that one single archeological discovery, the Viking fortress Trelleborg, which was built at an uncertain date by an unknown builder for an indeterminate purpose, proves that the kingship in Denmark was strong and that the Danish state was already formed as early as the ninth century. In view of the efforts of King Godfred to stimulate the commerce of Hedeby by transporting merchants to it, Christensen and the Danish scholarly community accept the view that Hedeby was a town flourishing under royal protection. They would not accept the argument that Godfred's power may have been limited to southern Jutland.

Similar arguments are proposed for Sweden. The view that the Svear had only one king goes back to Tacitus (*Germania*, chap. 44). The author of the *Vita Anscharii*, Rimbert, whose viewpoint may have been that of the imperial court but was not necessarily an educated one, says that Birka was also under royal protection. King Björn did have power in Birka, but did he have power over the populi or negociatores? How dependent on Björn was the praefectus regi? Did the placitum make laws for Birka, or for the surrounding territory? These questions cannot be answered, but they do show that one cannot accept the unity of the Swedish kingdom as an article of faith or without reservation.

If, then, we allow that the influence of an entrepreneur on town origins is problematical before the twelfth century, when *locators* became active in colonialization, we must ask if the town owed more to the local inhabitants or to its visitors. The answer is made difficult to determine by the nature of the written as well as the archeological sources. When Scandinavians began to keep historical records in earnest in the twelfth century, they tended to suggest that the institutions flourishing in their own day had existed much earlier. For example, the military code, or Vederlov (Law of Protection), which belongs to the age of the Valdemars (1157–1241), an era of strong kingship, is ascribed by Svend Aagesen, a twelfth-century Danish historian, to the time of Canute the Great.

The twelfth century is also the period when the towns of today—provincial markets (*landsbyer*), seats of bishops, and harbor towns (for example, Copenhagen)—began to develop. These towns frequently had large numbers of foreign visitors who had extraterritorial privileges. Within their own quarters, the German merchants of Visby (by an agreement of 1143, which gave privileges to the Gotlanders at Lübeck and to

15. Christensen, "Denmark between the Viking Age and the Time of the Valdemars," p. 29.

the Germans on Gotland) were responsible for policing their own members and were virtually independent of Swedish royal authority. The basic problem is determining whether such privileges would have existed by the right of hospitality, or were a new phenomenon. One can avoid the issue of extraterritoriality by arguing that the earliest towns, and later Visby in particular, were developed by foreigners. This implies that the Scandinavians were too backward in the Middle Ages to build towns on their own. The argument also provides a facile explanation for the ability of the Hansa to dominate so much of Scandinavian commerce in the late Middle Ages. The argument, however, avoids dealing with the contention that all of this was due to a weak kingship which was not able to assert authority over the towns or the merchants because it lacked that authority in the first place.

We must return to the most surprising feature of the archeological record of the earliest towns: they are unwalled. Does this prove that the towns flourished in an era of political stability or that the districts in which they lay were at peace? Unfortunately we do not know what legal or religious sentiments the Scandinavians might have had with regard to the peace of the town, such as Christians are supposed to have had about the sanctity of a church or monastery. The ninth century was certainly not a stable period politically and the Vikings were no respecters of towns elsewhere in Europe. In view of the torments of the age, it is most unlikely that foreign visitors to Scandinavia would have lived in unwalled enclosures in what they could only have regarded as a hostile environment. Walls and fortifications were added later, perhaps by the foreign population, or when the town became large enough to attract local or foreign pirates. Thus it is reasonably certain that the towns had an indigenous origin, and attracted foreign visitors later. Because of the weakness of the native kings and the better organization of the outlanders, the visitors eventually came to dominate Scandinavian urban culture.

Contributors

Carlo M. Cipolla, University of Turin and University of California, Berkeley
Sidney Cohen, Louisiana State University
S. D. Goitein, Institute for Advanced Study, Princeton University
David Herlihy, Harvard University
Richard C. Hoffmann, York University
Diane Owen Hughes, Victoria College, University of Toronto
Benjamin Z. Kedar, The Hebrew University of Jerusalem
Bariša Krekić, University of California, Los Angeles
Frederic C. Lane, Johns Hopkins University, Emeritus
Harry A. Miskimin, Yale University
John Munro, University of Toronto
Edward Peters, University of Pennsylvania
Joshua Prawer, The Hebrew University of Jerusalem
Joseph R. Strayer, Princeton University, Emeritus
John Teall, Mount Holyoke College
A. L. Udovitch, Princeton University

Publications (1933–1976) of Robert S. Lopez

Books

Genova marinara nel Duecento: Benedetto Zaccaria ammiraglio e mercante. Messina-Milan: Principato, 1933.

Studi sull'economia genovese nel medio evo. Turin: Lattes, 1936.

Storia delle colonie genovesi nel mediterraneo. Bologna: Zanichelli, 1938.

[Editor with J. Buchler and K. W. Kapp]. *Introduction to Contemporary Civilization in the West,* II, New York: Columbia University Press, 1946.

Il ritorno all'oro nell'Occidente duecentesco. Naples: Edizioni Scientifiche Italiane, 1955.

[With Irving W. Raymond]. *Medieval Trade in the Mediterranean World.* New York: Columbia University Press, 1955. Paperback ed. New York: Norton, 1969.

La Prima crisi della banca in Genova, secolo XIII. Milan: University of Bocconi, 1956.

The Tenth Century: How Dark the Dark Ages? New York: Rinehart, 1959.

La Naissance de l'Europe. Paris: Armand Colin, 1962; Portuguese trans. Lisbon: Cosmos, 1965, rev. English ed. London: Dent, 1966; New York: Evans-Lippincott, 1967, rev. Italian ed., Turin: Einaudi, 1966. Spanish trans. Barcellona: Labor, 1966. Slovakian trans. Lubiana: Drzavna Založba Slovenije, 1969.

The Three Ages of the Italian Renaissance. Charlottesville: University of Virginia Press, 1970. Paperback ed. Boston: Little, Brown, 1972.

The Commercial Revolution of the Middle Ages. Englewood Cliffs, N.J.: Prentice-Hall, 1971. Italian trans. Turin: Einaudi, 1974, rev. French ed. Paris: Aubier-Montaigne, 1974.

Su e giù per la storia di Genova. Genoa: University of Genoa, 1975.

[With T. G. Barnes, J. Blum, and R. Cameron]. *Civilizations, Western and World.* Boston: Little, Brown & Company, 1975.

Articles

"Il principio della guerra Veneto-Turca nel 1463." *Archivio Veneto*, ser. 3, *15* (1934), 45–131.

"L'attività economica di Genova nel marzo 1253 secondo i Cartulari Notarili." *Atti della Società Ligure di Storia Patria, 64* (1934), 166–270.

"Risse tra Pisani e Genovesi nella Napoli di Federico II." *Rassegna Storica Napoletana, 3* (1935), 91–106.

"Un 'Consilium' di giuristi torinesi nel dugento." *Bollettino Storico-Bibliografico Subalpino, 38* (1936), 143–50.

"Contributo alla storia delle miniere argentifere di Sardegna." *Studi economico-giuridici della R. Università di Cagliari, 24* (1936), 3–18.

"Il predominio economico dei genovesi nella monarchia spagnola." *Giornale Storico e Letterario della Liguria, 12* (1936), 65–74.

"Le relazioni commerciali tra Genova e la Francia nel medio evo." *Cooperazione Intellettuale, 6* (1937), 75–86.

"La colonizzazione genovese nella storiografia più recente." *Atti del Terzo Congresso di Studi Coloniali, 3* (1937), 247–61.

"Aux origines du capitalisme génois." *Annales d'histoire économique et sociale, 9* (1937), 429–54; Italian trans. in C. M. Cipolla, *Storia dell'economia italiana.* Turin: Boringhieri, 1959, I, 285–312.

"Stato e individuo nella storia della colonizzazione genovese." *Nuova Rivista Storica, 21* (1937), 305–17.

"Dieci documenti sulla storia della guerra di Corsa." Casale Monferrato, Miglietta and Milan, p. 16.

"Sensali nel medio evo." *Nuova Rivista Storica, 22* (1938), 108–12.

"The English and the Manufacture of Writing Materials in Genoa." *Economic History Review, 10* (1940), 132–37.

"Byzantine Law in the Seventh Century and its Reception by the Germans and the Arabs." *Byzantion, 16* (1942–43), 445–61.

"Mohammed and Charlemagne: A Revision." *Speculum, 18* (1943), 14–38; reprinted in *Bedeutung und Rolle des Islam.* Darmstadt, 1967. pp. 65–104.

"European Merchants in the Medieval Indies: The Evidence of Commercial Documents." *Journal of Economic History, 3* (1943), 164–84.

"Silk Industry in the Byzantine Empire." *Speculum, 20* (1945), 1–42.

[With R. L. Reynolds]. "Odoacer: German or Hun?" *American Historical Review, 52* (1946), 36–53, 841–45.

"Le Facteur économique dans la politique Africaine des Papes." *Revue Historique, 198* (1947), 178–88.

"Le Problème des relations Anglo-Byzantines du septième au dixième siècle." *Byzantion, 18* (1946–48), 139–62.

"Italian Leadership in the Medieval Business World." *Journal of Economic History, 8* (1948), 63–68.

"Stati Uniti, Storia, 1938–48" and "Franklin D. Roosevelt" (with S. H. Brockunier), *Enciclopedia Italiana*, app. II, pp. 749–50, 897–900.

"Du Marché temporaire à la colonie permanente: la politique commerciale au Moyen Age." *Annales: économies, sociétés, civilisations, 4* (1949), 389–405.

"Continuità e adattamento nel medioevo: un millennio di storia delle associazioni di monetieri." *Studi in Onore di Gino Luzzatto.* Milan, 1949. pp. 74–117.

"I primi passi della colonia genovese in Inghilterra." *Bollettino Ligustico per la Storia e la Cultura Regionale, 2* (1950), 66–70.

"Alfonso el Sabio y el primer Almirante de Castilla Genovés." *Cuadernos de Historia de España, 14* (1950), 5–16.

"La Crise du Besant au dixième siècle et la date du livre du préfet." *Mélanges Henri Gregoire, 2* (1950), 403–18.

"The Unexplored Wealth of the Notarial Archives in Pisa and Lucca." *Mélanges d'Histoire du Moyen Age dédiés a Louis Halphen* (Paris, 1951), pp. 417–32.

"Harmenopoulos and the Downfall of the Bezant." *Tomos Konstantinou Armenopoulou.* Salonika: University of Thessalonike, 1951. pp. 111–25.

"The Dollar of the Middle Ages." *Journal of Economic History, 11* (1951), 209–34.

X"Still Another Renaissance?" *American Historical Review, 17* (1951–52), 1–21.

"Majorcans and Genoese on the North Sea Route in the Thirteenth Century." *Revue Belge de Philologie et d'Histoire, 29* (1951), 1163–79.

"Ugo Vento primo ammiraglio genovese di Castiglia." *Bollettino Ligustico per la Storia e la Cultura Regionale, 3* (1951), 65–71.

"The Trade of Medieval Europe: The South." *The Cambridge Economic History of Europe.* Cambridge: Cambridge University Press, 1952. II, 257–354, 537–56.

"China Silk in Europe in the Yuan Period." *Journal of the American Oriental Society, 72* (1952), 72–76.

"Economie et architecture médiévales: Cela aurait-il tué ceci?" *Annales: économies, sociétés, civilisations, 8* (1952), 433–38.

"Hard Times and Investment in Culture." *Symposium on The Renaissance.* New York: Metropolitan Museum of Art, 1953, pp. 19–34.

"Nuove luci sugli italiani in Estremo Oriente prima di Colombo." *Studi Columbiani nel V Centenario della Nascita, 3* (1952), 337–98.

"An Aristocracy of Money in the Early Middle Ages." *Speculum, 28* (1953), 1–43.

"The Origin of the Merino Sheep." *The Joshua Starr Memorial Volume.* New York, 1953, pp. 161–68.

"Metodi di guerra nel Trecento." *Bollettino Ligustico per la Storia e la Cultura Regionale, 5* (1953), 57–59.

"L'evoluzione die trasporti terrestri nel medio evo." *Bollettino Civico Istituto Columbiano, 1,* fasc. 3 (1953), 24–33.

"Concerning Surnames and Places of Origin." *Medievalia et Humanistica, 8* (1954), 6–16.

"Les Influences orientales et l'éveil économique de l'occident." *Journal of World History/Cahiers d'Histoire Mondiale, 1* (1954), 594–622.

"Venezia e le grandi linee dell'espansione commerciale del secolo XIII." *La Civiltà Veneziana nel secolo di Marco Polo. Conferenze per il centenario.* Florence: Sansoni, 1955. pp. 37–82.

"The Norman Conquest of Sicily." *History of the Crusades.* Philadelphia, 1955. 1, 54–67.

"Some Tenth Century Towns." *Medievalia et Humanistica, 9* (1955), 4–6.

"El origen de la Oveja Merina." *Estudios de Historica Moderna, 4* (1954). Barcelona, 1955. pp. 3–11.

"La città dell'Europa post-carolingia: il commercio dell'Europa post-carolingia." *Settimane di studio del centro italiano di studi sull'alto medioevo II: I problemi comuni dell'Europa post-carolingia.* Spoleto, 1955. pp. 547–99.

"East and West in the Early Middle Ages: Economic Relations." *Relazioni del*

X Congresso Internazionale di Scienze Storiche, Roma, 1955. Florence: Sansoni, 1955. III, 113–63.

"L'Opera storica di Vito Vitale." *Bollettino Ligustico per la Storia e la Cultura regionale*, *8* (1956), 101–105.

"The Evolution of Land Transport in the Middle Ages." *Past and Present*, *9* (1956), 17–29.

"Back to Gold, 1252." *Economic History Review*, 2nd ser., *9* (1956), 219–40.

"Un Borgne au Royaume des Aveugles: La position de Byzance dans l'économie Européene du Haut Moyen Age." *Bulletin de l'Association Marc Bloch de Toulouse*, *5–6* (1953–55), 25–30.

"Une lettre du professeur R. S. Lopez." *Journal of the Economic and Social History of the Orient*, *1* (1957), 3–8.

"Il dollaro dell'alto medio evo." *Miscellanea in Onore di Roberto Cessi*. Rome: Edizioni di Storia e Letteratura, 1958. I, 111–19.

"Le Marchand Génois: un profil collectif." *Annales: économies, sociétés, civilisations*, *8* (1958), 501–15.

"Epilogo." *Settimane di studio del Centro Italiano di studi sull'alto medioevo, VI; La città nell'alto medioevo*. Spoleto, 1959. pp. 731–48.

"The Role of Trade in the Economic Readjustment of Byzantium in the Seventh Century." *Dumbarton Oaks Papers* (1959), 69–85.

"Moneta e monetieri nell'Italia barbarica." *Settimane di studio del Centro Italiano di studi sull'alto medioevo, VIII: Moneta e scambi nell'alto medioevo*. Spoleto, 1961. pp. 57–88.

"Epilogo." Ibid., pp. 725–44.

"L'Artisanat et la vie urbaine en Pologne médiévale: discussion générale." *Ergon*, *3* (1962), 524–27.

"Familiari, procuratori e dipendenti di Benedetto Zaccaria." *Miscellanea di storia Ligure in onore di Giorgio Falco*. Milan: Feltrinelli, 1962. pp. 209–49.

"Il medioevo negli Stati Uniti." *Studi medievali*, *3* (1962), 677–82.

[With H. A. Miskimin]. "The Economic Depression of the Renaissance." *The Economic History Review*, 2d. ser., *14* (1962), 408–26.

"The Crossroads within the Wall." *The Historian and the City*. Cambridge, Mass.: Harvard University and M.I.T. Press, 1963. pp. 26–43.

"L'Extrême frontière du commerce de l'Europe médiévale." *Moyen Age*, *69* (1963), 479–90.

"Quattrocento Genovese." *Rivista storica Italiana*, *75* (1963), 710–27.

"Discorso inaugurale." *Settimane di studio del Centro Italiano di studi sull'alto medioevo, XI: Centri e vie di irradiazione della civiltà nell'alto medioevo*. Spoleto, 1964. pp. 15–47.

[With C. M. Cipolla and H. A. Miskimin]. "The Economic Depression of the Renaissance?" *The Economic History Review*, 2d. ser., *16* (1964), 519–29.

"Market Expansion: The Case of Genoa." *Journal of Economic History*, *24* (1964), 445–64.

"Genoa: History." *Encyclopaedia Britannica*, 1964.

"Uno Scienziato e un'alta coscienza (Gino Luzzatto)." *Nuova Rivista Storica*, *49* (1965), 149–52.

"The Middle Ages, A Success Story." *Ventures*, *2* (1965), 6–10.

"L'Importanza del mondo islamico nella vita economica europea." *Settimane di studio del Centro Italiano di studi sull'alto medioevo, XII: L'Occidente e l'Islam nell'alto medioevo*. Spoleto, 1965. pp. 433–60.

"Da Mercanti a agricoltori: aspetti della colonizzazione genovese in Corsica." *Homenaje a Jaime Vicens Vives*, I, Barcelona, 1965, 525–32.

"Marquis et Monostrateges." *Mélanges offert a René Crozet*, I, Poitiers, 1966, 77–80.

"Prima del ritorno all'oro nell'occidente duecentesco: i primi denari grossi d'argento." *Rivista Storica Italiana*, *79* (1967), 174–81.

"Of Towns and Trade." *Life and thought in the Early Middle Ages*. Minneapolis: University of Minnesota Press, 1967. pp. 60–84.

"Stars and Spices: The Earliest Italian Manual of Commercial Practice." In *Economy, Society, and Government in Medieval Italy*, edited by D. Herlihy, R. S. Lopez, and V. Slessarev. Kent, Ohio: Kent State University Press, 1969. pp. 35–42.

"Guglielmo Boccanegra." *Dizionario Biografico degli Italiani*, *10* (1969), 31–35.

"Renaissance Recipes for Raising Remarkable Man." *History and Education: Reports of the Yale Conferences on the Teaching of Social Studies*. New Haven, 1969. pp. 1–10.

[With H. A. Miskimin and A. Udovitch]. "England to Egypt, 1350–1500: Long-Term Trends and Long-Distance Trade." In *Studies in the Economic History of the Middle East*, edited by M. A. Cook. London-New York: Oxford University Press, 1970. pp. 93–128.

"Un Texte inédit: Le plus ancien manuel italien de technique commerciale." *Revue Historique*, 493 (1970), 67–76.

"La Sicilia al tempo della conquista normanna." In *Richerche storiche ed economiche in memoria di Corrado Barbagallo*. Naples: Edizioni Scientifiche Italiane, II, 1970, pp. 107–21.

"Venise et Gênes: deux styles, une réussite." *Diogène* (1970), 43–51; English trans. *Diogenes* (1970), 39–47.

"Ricordo di Hajo Holborn." In H. Holborn, *Storia dell'Europa contemporanea*. Bologna: Il Mulino, 1970. pp. vii–xi.

"Les Méthodes commerciales des marchands occidentaux en Asie du XIe au XIVe siècle." In *Actes du Huitième Colloque International d'Histoire Maritime*. Paris: Sevepen, 1970. pp. 343–48.

"Genoa." *Encyclopaedia Americana*, XII, 421–23.

"Pirandello Old and New." *Yale Review*, *60* (1971), 228–40.

"Medieval and Renaissance Economy and Society." In *Perspectives on the European Past: Conversations with Historians*, edited by N. Cantor. New York: Macmillan, 1971. pp. 207–27.

"The Case is not Settled." In *Proceedings of the Vinland Map Conference*, edited by W. E. Washburn. Chicago: Chicago University Press, 1971. pp. 31–34.

"Agenda for Medieval Studies." *Journal of Economic History*, *31* (1971), 165–71.

"L'Architecture civile des villes médiévales: exemples et plans de recherche." In *Les Constructions civiles d'intérêt public dans les villes d'Europe au Moyen Age et sous l'Ancien Régime*. Brussels: Pro Civitate, 1971. pp. 15–31, 201–07.

"Discorso inaugurale." *Settimane di studio del Centro Italiano di studi sull'alto medioevo, XVIII: Artigianato e tecnica nella società dell'alto medioevo occidentale*, Spoleto, 1971. pp. 15–39

"L'Espansione economica dei comuni europei." In *Atti del Congresso Storico Internazionale per l'VIII Centenario della prima Lega Lombarda*. Milan, 1972, pp. 111–23.

"Une Histoire à trois niveaux: la circulation monétaire." *Mélanges en l'honneur de Fernand Braudel*, II, Paris: Privat, 1973. pp. 335–41.

"Il problema della bilancia dei pagamenti nel commercio di Levante." *Venezia e il Levante fino al secolo XV*. Florence: Olschki, 1973. pp. 431–52.

"I caratteri originali della citta medievale." *Concetto, storia, miti e immagini del medio evo*. Florence: Sansoni, 1973. pp. 19–24.

"Constantine VII Porphyrogenitus." *Encyclopaedia Britannica*. 15th ed., 1974. pp. 74–75.

"On Chapiteau des monnayeurs à Notre-Dame de Saintes?" *Mélanges E.-R. Labande*, Poitiers. 1974, pp. 501–03.

"Foreigners in Byzantium." *Miscellanea Charles Verlinden*. Brussels-Rome, 1975. pp. 341–52.

"Epilogue", in F. Chiappelli, ed., *Images of the New World in the Old World*, Berkeley: University of California Press, 1976.

"Il più antico manuale italiano di Practica della Mercatura." *Atti del III Congresso di Storia Economica*. Prato: Istituto Datini, 1976.

"Proxy in Medieval Trade." In W. C. Jordan, B. McNab, and T. F. Ruiz, eds., *Order and Innovation in the Middle Ages: Essays in Honor of Joseph R. Strayer*. Princeton: Princeton University Press, 1976. pp. 187–94.

"The Byzantine Economy in the Early Middle Ages." Gieysztor Festschrift. Warsaw: University of Warsaw Press, 1976.

"Italien: die Stadtwirtschaft, 1000–1400." In H. Kellenbenz and J. Van Houtte, eds., *Handbuch der europäische Sozial und Wirtschaftsgeschichte*. Stuttgart: Kleist, 1976.

Index